MOORISH LITERATURE

MOORISH LITERATURE

COMPRISING

ROMANTIC BALLADS,
TALES OF THE BERBERS,
STORIES OF THE KABYLIE, FOLK-LORE
AND
NATIONAL TRADITIONS

TRANSLATED INTO ENGLISH FOR THE FIRST TIME

WITH A SPECIAL INTRODUCTION

By

EPIPHANIUS WILSON, A.M.

REVISED EDITION

GYAN

Published by

GYAN

Gyan Publishing House
5, Ansari Road
Daryaganj, New Delhi-110002
Phone: 011-47034999, 9811692060
E-mail: books@gyanbooks.com

Distribution Network
gyanbooks.com
India, USA, Canada, UK, Australia, France

ISBN : 978-81-212-6216-3 (PB)
First Published, 1901

2nd Impression 2022

Printed at: Gyan Press, Delhi.

MOORISH LITERATURE
Author: EPIPHANIUS WILSON, A.M.

MOORISH LITERATURE

COMPRISING

ROMANTIC BALLADS,
TALES OF THE BERBERS,
STORIES OF THE KABYLIE, FOLK-LORE
AND
NATIONAL TRADITIONS

TRANSLATED INTO ENGLISH FOR THE FIRST TIME

WITH A SPECIAL INTRODUCTION BY
EPIPHANIUS WILSON, A.M.

REVISED EDITION

SPECIAL INTRODUCTION

THE Moorish ballads which appear in this volume are selected from a unique department of European literature. They are found in the Spanish language, but their character is oriental; their inspiration comes from the Mahometan conquerors of northern Africa, and while they exhibit a blending of Spanish earnestness and chivalry with the wild and dashing spirit of the Arab, they present a type of literature which is quite unparalleled in the Latin and Teutonic countries of the Mediterranean basin.

Spain is especially rich in ballad literature, infinitely richer than any other civilized nation. These ballads take various forms. By Cervantes and his countrymen they are styled romances, and the romance generally consists in a poem which describes the character, sufferings, or exploits of a single individual. The language is simple; the versification, often artless though melodious, is seldom elaborated into complexity of rhyme. But the heroic Moor is set before us in the most vivid colors. The hues and material of his cloak, his housings, his caftan, and his plumes are given, and quite a vocabulary is exhausted in depicting the color, sex, and breed of his war-horse. His weapons, lance, scimitar, and corslet of steel are dwelt upon with enthusiasm. He is as brave as Mars, and as comely as Adonis. Sometimes he dashes into a bull-ring and slays wild creatures in the sight of fair ladies and envious men. He throws his lance of cane, which is filled with sand, so high that it vanishes in the clouds. He is ready to strike down, in his own house, the Christian who has taken from him and wedded the lady of his choice. He is almost always in love with some lady who is unkind and cold, and for her he wanders at times in dark array, expressing his sombre mood in the device and motto which he paints upon his shield. Some of the ballads picture love more fortunate in the most charming manner, and the dark tortures of jealousy are powerfully described in others. The devotion of the Moor to his lady is scarcely caricatured in the mocking language of Cervantes, and is not exceeded by anything to be found in the history of French chivalry. But the god of these ballads is Allah, and they sometimes reveal a trace of ferocity which seems to be derived from religious fanaticism. Nor can the reader fail to be struck by the profound pathos which many of them express so well. The dirges are supremely beautiful, their language simple and direct, but perfect in descriptive touches and in the cadence of the reiterated burden.

Beside the ballads of warlike and amorous adventures, there are sea-songs, songs of captivity, and songs of the galley slave. The Spanish Moor is seized by some African pirate and carried away to toil in the mill of his master on some foreign shore, or he is chained to the rowing-bench of the Berber galley, thence to be taken and sold when the voyage is over to some master who leaves him to weep in solitary toil in the farm or garden. Sometimes he wins the love of his mistress, who releases him and flies in his company.

All these ballads have vivid descriptions of scenery. The towers of Baeza, the walls of Granada, the green *vegas* that spread outside every city, the valley of the Guadalquivir, and the rushing waters of the Tagus, the high cliffs of Cadiz, the Pillars of Hercules, and the blue waves of the Mediterranean make a life-like background to every incident. In the cities the ladies throng the balconies of curling iron-work or crowd the plaza where the joust or bull-fight is to be witnessed, or steal at nightfall to the edge of the *vega* to meet a lover, and sometimes to die in his arms at the hands of bandits.

There is a dramatic power in these ballads which is one of their most remarkable features. They are sometimes mere sketches, but oftener the story is told with consummate art, with strict economy of word and phrase, and the *dénouement* comes with a point and power which show that the Moorish minstrel was an artist of no mean skill and address.

The authors of the Moorish romances, songs, and ballads are unknown. They have probably assumed their present literary form after being part of the *répertoire* of successive minstrels, and some of the incidents appear in more than one version.

The most ancient of them are often the shortest, but they belong to the period when southern Spain under Mahometan rule was at the height of its prosperity, and Arabian learning, art, and literature made her rank among the first countries in Europe. The peninsula was conquered by the Moors in the caliphate of Walid I, 705–715 A.D., and the independent dynasty of the Ommiades was founded by Abderrhaman at Granada in 755 A.D. It was from this latter date that the Spanish Moors began to assume that special character in language, manners, and chivalric enthusiasm which is represented in the present ballads; the spirit of Christian knighthood is here seen blended with Arabian passion, impetuosity, and impulsiveness, and the Spanish language has supplanted, even among Mahometan poets, the oriental idiom. We may roughly estimate the period in which the Moorish romance flourished as comprised in the years between 1100 and 1600 A.D.

The term Moorish is somewhat indefinite, and is used in Spanish history as a synonym of Saracen or Mahometan. It cannot be called a national appellation, though originally in the Augustan age it was applied to the dwellers in Mauretania, with whom the Romans had first come in contact when the war with Hannibal was transferred from Italy and Spain to Africa. In the present day, it may be applied to all the races of northwestern Africa who have accepted Mahometanism; in which case it would include the aborigines of that region, who live not on the coast and in towns, but in the Atlas Mountain and the Sahara Desert. While these races, all Berbers under different local names, are Mussulmans in profession, they are not so highly civilized as their co-religionists who people the coast of the Mediterranean. They live a tribal life, and are blood-thirsty and predatory. They are of course mixed in race with the Arabians, but they are separate in their life and institutions, and they possess no written literature. Their oral literature is, however, abundant, though it is only within quite recent years that it has become known to America and Europe. The present collection of tales and fables is the first which has hitherto been made in the English language. The learned men who collected the tales of the Berbers and Kabyles (who are identical in ethnical origin) underwent many hardships in gathering from half-savage lips the material for their volume. They were forced to live among the wild tribesmen, join their nomad life, sit at their feasts, and watch with them round their camp-fire, while it was with difficulty they transferred to writing the syllables of a barbarous tongue. The memory of the Berber story-teller seems to be incredibly capacious and retentive, and the tales were recited over and over again without a variation. As is to be expected these tales are very varied, and many of them are of a didactic, if not ethical, cast. They are instructive as revealing the social life and character of these mountain and desert tribes.

We find the spirit of the vendetta pervading these tales with more than Corsican bitterness and unreasoning cruelty, every man being allowed to revenge himself by taking the life or property of another. This private and personal warfare has done more than anything else to check the advance in civilization of these tribesmen. The Berbers and Kabyles are fanatical Mahometans and look upon Christians and Jews as dogs and outcasts. It is considered honorable to cheat, rob, or deceive by lies one who does not worship Allah. The tales illustrate, moreover, the degraded position of women. A wife is literally a chattel, not only to be bought, but to be sold also, and to be treated in every respect as man's inferior—a mere slave or beast of burden. Yet the tribesmen are profoundly superstitious, and hold in great dread the evil spirits who they think surround them and to whom they attribute bodily and mental ills. An idiot is one who is possessed by a wicked demon, and is to be feared accordingly.

There are found current among them a vast number of fairy tales, such as equal in wildness and horror the strangest inventions of oriental imagination. Their tales of ogres and ogresses are unsoftened by any of that playfulness and bonhomie which give such undying charm to the "Thousand and One Nights." The element of the miraculous takes many original forms in their popular tales, and they have more than their share of the folk-lore legends and traditions such as Herodotus loved to collect. It was said of old that something new was always coming out of Africa, and certainly the contribution which the Berbers and Kabyles have made to the fund of wonder-stories in the world may be looked upon as new, in more than one sense. It is new, not only because it is novel and unexpected, but because it is fresh, original and highly interesting.

The fables of these tribes are very abundant and very curious. The great hero of the animal fable in Europe has always been the fox, whose cunning, greed, and duplicity are immortalized in the finest fable the world's literature possesses. The fables of northwest Africa employ the jackal instead of Reynard, whose place the sycophant of the lion not inaptly fills.

There are a number of men among the Kabyles and other Berber tribes who make a profession of reciting poems, tales, and proverbs, and travel from one village or encampment to another in search of an audience. They know the national traditions, the heroic legends, and warlike adventures that pertain to each community, and are honored and welcomed wherever they go. It was from these men that the various narratives contained in this collection were obtained, and the translation of them has engaged the talents and labors of some of the world's foremost oriental scholars.

CONTENTS

MOORISH BALLADS

ROMANCEROS MORISCOS

[*Metrical Translation by Epiphanius Wilson, A.M.*]

MOORISH BALLADS

FATIMA'S LOVE

ON the morn of John the Baptist, just at the break of day,
The Moors upon Granada's fields streamed out in bright array.
Their horses galloped o'er the sod, their lances flashed in air,
And the banners that their dames had wrought spread out their colors fair.
Their quivers bright flashed in the light with gold and silk brocade,
And the Moor who saw his love was there looked best in the parade,
And the Moor who had no lady love strove hard some love to gain.
'Mong those who from Alhambra's towers gazed on that warrior train.
There were two Moorish ladies there whom love had smitten sore;
Zarifa one, and Fatima the name the other bore.
Knit by warm friendship were their hearts till, filled with jealous pain,
Their glances met, as one fair knight came prancing o'er the plain.
Zarifa spoke to Fatima, "How has love marred thy face!
Once roses bloomed on either cheek, now lilies take their place;
And you, who once would talk of love, now still and silent stay.
Come, come unto the window and watch the pageant gay!
Abindarraez is riding by; his train is full in view;
In all Granada none can boast a choicer retinue."
"It is not love, Zarifa, that robs my cheek of rose;
No fond and anxious passion this mournful bosom knows;
My cheeks are pale and I am still and silent, it is true,—
For, ah! I miss my father's face, whom fierce Alabey slew.

And did I crave the boon of love, a thousand knights were fain
To fight for me in service true on yonder flowery plain.
And all the love I give to each to give me back again.
And for Abindarraez, whose heart and valiant might,
You praise and from the window watch, with rapturous delight ——"
The lady stopped, for at their feet knelt down the well-loved knight.

THE BRAGGART REBUKED

"If thou art brave in battle's hour
As thou art bold in pleasure's rout;
If thou canst make the lances fly
As thou canst fling thy words about;

"If thou canst in the vega fight
As thou the ladies' eyes canst praise;
And show on horseback half the skill
That marks thee in the dance's maze;

"Meet with the briskness of the joust
The challenge of the deadly lance,
And in the play of scimitars
Be sprightly as in festive dance;

"If thou art ready in the field
As thou art nimble on the square;
And canst the front of battle face
As though thou flirtest with the fair;

"If thou dost don thy shining mail
As lightly as thy festive suit,
And listenest to the trumpet call
As though it were thy lady's lute;

"And if, as in the gamesome hour
Thou flingest round the rattling reed
Against the foeman's moated camp,
Thou spurrest on thy thundering steed;

"If, when the foe is face to face,
Thou boastest as thou oft hast done
When far away his ranks were ranged,
And the fierce fight had not begun;—

"Go, Zaide, to the Alhambra go,
And there defend thy soldier fame;
For every tongue is wagging there,
And all, derisive, speak thy name.

"And if thou fear to go alone,
Take others with thee to thine aid;
Thy friends are ready at thy beck,
And Zaide need not be afraid!

"It is not in the palace court,
Amid the throng of ladies bright,
That the good soldier, by his tongue,
Proves himself valorous in the fight.

"It is not there his hands can show
What in the battle he can do;
But where the shock of onset tests
The fearless heart, the iron thew.

"Betake thee to the bloody field
And let thy sword thy praises sing;
But silence is most eloquent
Amid the courtiers of the King."

Thus Tarfe wrote, the Moorish knight,
His heart so filled with furious rage
That where his fiery pen had passed
It pierced and rent the flimsy page.

He called his varlet to his side,
"Now seek the Alhambra's hall," said he,
"And privately to Zaide say
That this epistle comes from me;

"And whisper, that none else may hear,
And say that I his coming wait,
Where Genil's crystal torrent laves
The pillars of yon palace gate."

THE ADMIRAL'S FAREWELL

The royal fleet with fluttering sail is waiting in the bay;
And brave Mustapha, the Admiral, must start at break of day.
His hood and cloak of many hues he swiftly dons, and sets
Upon his brow his turban gay with pearls and amulets;
Of many tints above his head his plumes are waving wide;
Like a crescent moon his scimitar is dangling at his side;
And standing at the window, he gazes forth, and, hark!
Across the rippling waters floats the summons to embark.

Blow, trumpets; clarions, sound your strain!
Strike, kettle-drum, the alarum in refrain.
Let the shrill fife, the flute, the sackbut ring
A summons to our Admiral, a salvo to our King!

The haughty Turk his scarlet shoe upon the stirrup placed,
Right easily he vaulted to his saddle-tree in haste.
His courser was Arabian, in whose crest and pastern show
A glossy coat as soft as silk, as white as driven snow.
One mark alone was on his flank! 'twas branded deep and dark;
The letter F in Arab script, stood out the sacred mark.
By the color of his courser he wished it to be seen
That the soul of the King's Admiral was white and true and clean.
Oh, swift and full of mettle was the steed which that day bore
Mustapha, the High Admiral, down to the wave-beat shore!
The haughty Turk sails forth at morn, that Malta he may take,
But many the greater conquest his gallant men shall make;
For his heart is high and his soul is bent on death or victory,
And he pauses, as the clashing sound comes from the distant sea;

Blow, trumpets; clarions, sound your strain!
Strike, kettle-drum, the alarum in refrain.
Let fife and flute, and sackbut in accord
Proclaim, Aboard! Aboard!
Thy pinnace waits thee at the slip, lord Admiral, aboard!

And as he hears the summons Love makes for him reply,
"O whither, cruel fortune, wilt thou bid the warrior fly?
Must I seek thee in the ocean, where the winds and billows roar?
Must I seek thee there, because in vain I sought thee on the shore?
And dost thou think the ocean, crossed by my flashing sail,
With all its myriad waters and its rivers, can avail
To quench the ardent fire of love that rages in my breast,
And soothe the fever of my soul into one hour of rest?
And as he mused, in bitter thought, Mustapha reached in haste
A balçony; till dawn of day before that house he paced,
And all his heart's anxieties he counted o'er and o'er,
And, when the darkness of the night toward opening twilight wore,
Upon the balcony there came the cause of all his sighs,
But a smile was on her rosy lips and a light was in her eyes.
"O lovely Zaida," he began, and gazed into her face,
"If my presence at thy window is a burden to thy peace,
One pledge bestow upon me, one pledge of love, I pray,
And let me kiss thy lily hand before I sail away."
"I grieve for thy departure," the lady made reply,
"And it needs no pledge to tell thee I am faithful till I die,
But if one token thou must have, take this ere thou depart;
('Twas fashioned by these hands of mine) and keep it on thy heart!"
The Moor rose in his stirrups, he took it from her hand,
'Twas a piece of lace of gold and silk shaped for a helmet band.
There was the wheel of fortune with subtile needle drawn,
(Ah, Fortune that had left him there dejected and forlorn!)
And as he paused, he heard the sound tumultuous come again,
'Twas from the fleet, down in the bay, and well he knew the strain.

Blow, trumpets; clarions, sound your strain;
Strike, kettle-drum, the alarum in refrain.
Let fife and flute, and sackbut in accord
Proclaim, Aboard! Aboard!
Thy pinnace waits thee at the slip, lord Admiral, aboard!

Oh, stay my foes, nor in such haste invite me to the field!
Here let me take the triumphs that softer conquests yield!
This is the goal of my desire, the aim of my design,
That Zaida's hand in mine be placed and her heart beat close to mine!
Then spake the fair Sultana, and she dropped a tender tear,
"Nay mourn not for the present pain, for future bliss is near.
The wings of Time are swift, and they bear a brighter day;
And when once the longed-for gift is here 'twill never pass away!"
Then the Moor's heart beat high with joy; to smiles were changed his sighs,
In silent ecstasy he gazed into the lady's eyes.
He rode to meet his waiting fleet, for favoring was the wind,
But while his body went on board, he left his heart behind!

Blow, trumpets; clarions, sound your strain!
Strike, kettle-drum, the alarum in refrain.
Let the shrill fife, the flute, the sackbut ring
A summons to our Admiral, a salvo to our King.

MORIANA AND GALVAN

'Twas Princess Moriana,
Upon a castle's height,
That played with Moorish Galvan
At cards for her delight;
And oft he lost the stakes he set,
Full many a coin I wis;
When Moriana lost, she gave
Her hand for him to kiss.
And after hours of pleasure
Moor Galvan sank to sleep;
And soon the lady saw a knight
Descend the mountain steep;
His voice was raised in sorrow,
His eyes with tears were wet,
For lovely Moriana
His heart could ne'er forget.

For her, upon St. John's Day,
While she was gathering flowers,
The Moors had made a captive,
Beneath her father's towers.
And Moriana raised her eyes
And saw her lover ride,
And on her cheeks her Moorish lord
The sparkling tears descried.
With anger raged his spirit,
And thus to her he cried:
"What ails thee, gentle lady?
Why flows with tears thine eye?
If Moors of mine have done thee wrong,
I swear that they shall die;
If any of thy maidens
Have caused thee this distress,
The whip across their shoulders
Shall avenge their wickedness.
Or, if the Christian countrymen
Have sorrow for thee made,
I will, with conquering armies,
Their provinces invade.
The warlike weapons that I don
Are festal robes to me;
To me the din of battle
Is sweet tranquillity;
The direst toils the warrior bears
With steadfast joy I meet;
To me the watch that nightlong las
Is like a slumber sweet."
"No Moors of thine within these halls
Have caused to me this pain;
No maidens waiting in my bower
Have showed to me disdain;
Nor have my Christian kinsmen
To mourn my spirit made,
Provoking thee in vengeance
Their province to invade.
Vain the deep cause of my distress
From Galvan's eye to hide—

'Tis that I see down yonder mount
  A knight in armor ride.
'Tis such a sight that does my tears
  From very heart-springs move;
For yonder knight is all to me,
  My husband and my love."
Straight the Moor's cheek with anger flushed,
  Till red eclipsed the brown,
And his clenched fist he lifted
  As if to strike her down.
He gnashed his teeth with passion,
  The fangs with blood were red,
He called his slaves and bade them
  Strike off the lady's head.
He bade them bind and take her
  First to the mountain's height,
That she the doom might suffer
  Within her husband's sight;
But all the lady answered,
  When she was brought to death,
Were words of faith and loyalty
  Borne on her parting breath:
"Behold, I die a Christian,
  And here repeat my vows
Of faithfulness to yonder knight,
  My loved and lawful spouse."

THE BEREAVED FATHER

"Rise up, rise up, thou hoary head,
  What madness causes thy delay?
Thou killest swine on Thursday morn,
  And eatest flesh on fasting day.

"'Tis now seven years since first I trod
  The valley and the wandering wood;
My feet were bare, my flesh was torn,
  And all my pathway stained in blood.

"Ah, mournfully I seek in vain
The Emperor's daughter, who had gone
A prisoner made by caitiff Moors,
Upon the morning of St. John.

"She gathered flowers upon the plain,
She plucked the roses from the spray,
And in the orchard of her sire
They found and bore the maid away."

These words has Moriana heard,
Close nestled in the Moor's embrace;
The tears that welled from out her eyes
Have wet her captor's swarthy face.

THE WARDEN OF MOLINA

The warden of Molina, ah! furious was his speed,
As he dashed his glittering rowels in the flank of his good steed,
And his reins left dangling from the bit, along the white highway,
For his mind was set to speed his horse, to speed and not to stay.
He rode upon a grizzled roan, and with the wind he raced,
And the breezes rustled round him like a tempest in the waste.
In the Plaza of Molina at last he made his stand,
And in a voice of thunder he uttered his command:
To arms, to arms, my captains!
Sound, clarions; trumpets, blow;
And let the thundering kettle-drum
Give challenge to the foe.

"Now leave your feasts and banquetings and gird you in your steel!
And leave the couches of delight, where slumber's charm you feel;
Your country calls for succor, all must the word obey,
For the freedom of your fathers is in your hands to-day.
Ah, sore may be the struggle, and vast may be the cost;
But yet no tie of love must keep you now, or all is lost.

In breasts where honor dwells there is no room in times like these
To dally at a lady's side, kneel at a lady's knees.
To arms, to arms, my captains!
Sound, clarions; trumpets, blow;
And let the thundering kettle-drum
Give challenge to the foe.

"Yes, in the hour of peril away with pleasure's thrall!
Let honor take the lance and steed to meet our country's call.
For those who craven in the fight refuse to meet the foe
Shall sink beneath the feet of all struck by a bitterer blow;
In moments when fair honor's crown is offered to the brave
And dangers yawn around our State, deep as the deadly grave,
'Tis right strong arms and sturdy hearts should take the sword of might,
And eagerly for Fatherland descend into the fight.
To arms, to arms, my captains!
Sound, clarions; trumpets, blow;
And let the thundering kettle-drum
Give challenge to the foe.

"Then lay aside the silken robes, the glittering brocade;
Be all in vest of leather and twisted steel arrayed;
On each left arm be hung the shield, safe guardian of the breast,
And take the crooked scimitar and put the lance in rest,
And face the fortune of the day, for it is vain to fly,
And the coward and the braggart now alone are doomed to die.
And let each manly bosom show, in the impending fray,
A valor such as Mars himself in fury might display.
To arms, to arms, my captains!
Sound, clarions; trumpets, blow;
And let the thundering kettle-drum
Give challenge to the foe.

He spoke, and at his valiant words, that rang through all the square,
The veriest cowards of the town resolved to do and dare;
And stirred by honor's eager fire forth from the gate they stream,

And plumes are waving in the air, and spears and falchions
gleam;
And turbaned heads and faces fierce, and smiles in anger
quenched,
And sweating steeds and flashing spurs and hands in fury
clenched,
Follow the fluttering banners that toward the vega swarm,
And many a voice re-echoes the words of wild alarm.
To arms, to arms, my captains!
Sound, clarions; trumpets, blow;
And let the thundering kettle-drum
Give challenge to the foe.

And, like the timid lambs that crowd with bleatings in the fold,
When they advancing to their throats the furious wolf behold,
The lovely Moorish maidens, with wet but flashing eyes,
Are crowded in a public square and fill the air with cries;
And tho', like tender women, 'tis vain for them to arm,
Yet loudly they re-echo the words of the alarm.
To heaven they cry for succor, and, while to heaven they pray,
They call the knights they love so well to arm them for the
fray.
To arms, to arms, my captains!
Sound, clarions; trumpets, blow;
And let the thundering kettle-drum
Give challenge to the foe.

The foremost Moorish nobles, Molina's chosen band,
Rush forward from the city the invaders to withstand.
There marshalled in a squadron with shining arms they speed,
Like knights and noble gentlemen, to meet their country's
need.
Twelve thousand Christians crowd the plain, twelve thousand
warriors tried,
They fire the homes, they reap the corn, upon the vega wide;
And the warriors of Molina their furious lances ply,
And in their own Arabian tongue they raise the rallying cry.
To arms, to arms, my captains!
Sound, clarions; trumpets, blow;
And let the thundering kettle-drum
Give challenge to the foe.

THE LOVES OF BOABDIL AND VINDARAJA

Where Antequera's city stands, upon the southern plain,
The captive Vindaraja sits and mourns her lot in vain.
While Chico, proud Granada's King, nor night nor day can rest,
For of all the Moorish ladies Vindaraja he loves best;
And while naught can give her solace and naught can dry her tear,
'Tis not the task of slavery nor the cell that brings her fear;
For while in Antequera her body lingers still,
Her heart is in Granada upon Alhambra's hill.
There, while the Moorish monarch longs to have her at his side,
More keen is Vindaraja's wish to be a monarch's bride.
Ah! long delays the moment that shall bring her liberty,
A thousand thousand years in every second seem to fly!
For she thinks of royal Chico, and her face with tears is wet,
For she knows that absence oft will make the fondest heart forget.
And the lover who is truest may yet suspicion feel,
For the loved one in some distant land whose heart is firm as steel.
And now to solve her anxious doubts, she takes the pen one day
And writes to royal Chico, in Granada far away.
Ah! long the letter that she wrote to tell him of her state,
In lonely prison cell confined, a captive desolate!
She sent it by a Moorish knight, and sealed it with her ring;
He was warden of Alhambra and stood beside the King,
And he had come sent by the King to Antequera's tower,
To learn how Vindaraja fared within that prison bower.
The Moor was faithful to his charge, a warrior stout and leal,
And Chico took the note of love and trembling broke the seal;
And when the open page he saw and read what it contained,
These were the words in which the maid of her hard lot complained:

The Letter of Vindaraja

"Ah, hapless is the love-lorn maid like me in captive plight,
For freedom once was mine, and I was happy day and night.
Yes, happy, for I knew that thou hadst given me thy love,
Precious the gift to lonely hearts all other gifts above.
Well mightest thou forget me, though 'twere treachery to say
The flame that filled thy royal heart as yet had passed away.
Still, though too oft do lovers' hearts in absent hours repine.
I know if there are faithful vows, then faithful will be thine!
'Tis hard, indeed, for lovers to crush the doubting thought
Which to the brooding bosom some lonely hour has brought.
There is no safety for the love, when languish out of sight
The form, the smile, the flashing eyes that once were love's delight;
Nor can I, I confess it, feel certain of thy vow!
How many Moorish ladies are gathered round thee now!
How many fairer, brighter forms are clustered at thy throne,
Whose power might change to very wax the heart of steel or stone!
And if, indeed, there be a cause why I should blame thy heart,
'Tis the delay that thou hast shown in taking here my part.
Why are not armies sent to break these prison bars, and bring
Back to her home the Moorish maid, the favorite of the King?
A maid whose eyes are changed to springs whence flow the flood of tears,
For she thinks of thee and weeps for thee through all these absent years.
Believe me, if 'twere thou, who lay a captive in his chain,
My life of joy, to rescue thee, my heart of blood I'd drain!
O King and master, if, indeed, I am thy loved one still,
As in those days when I was first upon Alhambra's hill,
Send rescue for thy darling, or fear her love may fade,
For love that needs the sunlight must wither in the shade.
And yet I cannot doubt thee; if e'er suspicion's breath
Should chill my heart, that moment would be Vindaraja's death.
Nor think should you forget me or spurn me from your arms,
That life for Vindaraja could have no other charms.
It was thy boast thou once did love a princess, now a slave,
I boasted that to thy behest I full obedience gave!

And from this prison should I come, in freedom once again,
To sit and hear thy words of love on Andalusia's plain,
The brightest thought would be to me that thou, the King, has seen
'Twas right to free a wretched slave that she might be thy Queen.
Hard is the lot of bondage here, and heavy is my chain,
And from my prison bars I gaze with lamentation vain;
But these are slight and idle things—my one, my sole distress
Is that I cannot see thy face and welcome thy caress!
This only is the passion that can my bosom rend;
'Tis this alone that makes me long for death, my sufferings end.
The plagues of life are naught to me; life's only joy is this—
To see thee and to hear thee and to blush beneath thy kiss!
Alas! perchance this evening or to-morrow morn, may be,
The lords who hold me here a slave in sad captivity,
May, since they think me wanton, their treacherous measures take
That I should be a Christian and my former faith forsake.
But I tell them, and I weep to tell, that I will ne'er forego
The creed my fathers fought for in centuries long ago!
And yet I might forswear it, but that that creed divine
'Tis vain I struggle to deny, for, ah, that creed is thine!"
King Chico read his lady's note and silent laid it down;
Then to the window he drew nigh, and gazed upon the town;
And lost in thought he pondered upon each tender line,
And sudden tears and a sigh of grief were his inward sorrow's sign.
And he called for ink and paper, that Vindaraja's heart
Might know that he remembered her and sought to heal its smart.
He would tell her that the absence which caused to her those fears
Had only made her dearer still, through all those mournful years.
He would tell her that his heart was sad, because she was not near—
Yes, far more sad than Moorish slave chained on the south frontier.

And then he wrote the letter to the darling Moorish slave,
And this is the tender message that royal Chico gave:

THE LETTER OF THE KING

"Thy words have done me grievous wrong, for, lovely Mooress, couldst thou think
That he who loves thee more than life could e'er to such a treachery sink?
His life is naught without the thought that thou art happy in thy lot;
And while the red blood at his heart is beating thou art ne'er forgot!
Thou woundest me because thy heart mistrusts me as a fickle fool;
Thou dost not know when passion true has one apt pupil taken to school.
Oblivion could not, could not cloud the image on his soul impressed,
Unless dark treachery from the first had been the monarch of his breast;
And if perhaps some weary hours I thought that Vindaraja's mind
Might in some happier cavalier the solace of her slavery find,
I checked the thought; I drove away the vision that with death was rife,
For e'er my trust in thee I lost, in battle I'd forego my life!
Yet even the doubt that thou hast breathed gives me no franchise to forget,
And were I willing that thy face should cease to fill my vision, yet
'Tis separation's self that binds us closer though the centuries roll,
And forges that eternal chain that binds together soul and soul!
And even were this thought no more than the wild vision of my mind,
Yet in a thousand worlds no face to change for thine this heart could find.
Thro' life, thro' death 'twere all the same, and when to heaven our glance we raise,

Full in the very heart of bliss thine eyes shall meet my ardent gaze.
For eyes that have beheld thy face, full readily the truth will own
That God exhausted, when he made thee, all the treasures of his throne!
And my trusting heart will answer while it fills my veins with fire
That to hear of, is to see thee; and to see, is to desire!
Yet unless my Vindaraja I could look upon awhile,
As some traveller in a desert I should perish for her smile;
For 'tis longing for her presence makes the spring of life to me,
And allays the secret suffering none except her eye can see.
In this thought alone my spirit finds refreshment and delight;
This is sweeter than the struggle, than the glory of the fight;
And if e'er I could forget her heaving breast and laughing eye,
Tender word, and soft caresses—Vindaraja, I should die!
If the King should bid me hasten to release thee from thy chain,
Oh, believe me, dearest lady, he would never bid in vain;
Naught he could demand were greater than the price that I would pay,
If in high Alhambra's halls I once again could see thee gay!
None can say I am remiss, and heedless of thy dismal fate;
Love comes to prompt me every hour, he will not let my zeal abate.
If occasion call, I yield myself, my soul to set thee free;
Take this offering if thou wilt, I wait thy word on bended knee.
Dost thou suffer, noble lady, by these fancies overwrought?
Ah, my soul is filled with sorrow at the agonizing thought;
For to know that Vindaraja languishes, oppressed with care,
Is enough to make death welcome, if I could but rescue her.
Yes, the world shall know that I would die not only for the bliss
Of clasping thee in love's embrace and kindling at thy tender kiss.

This, indeed, would be a prize, for which the coward death would dare—
I would die to make thee happy, tho' thy lot I might not share!
Then, though I should fail to lift the burden on my darling laid,
Though I could not prove my love by rescuing my Moorish maid,
Yet my love would have this witness, first, thy confidence sublime,
Then my death for thee, recorded on the scroll of future time!
Yes, my death, for should I perish, it were comfort but to think
Thou couldst have henceforth on earth no blacker, bitterer cup to drink!
Sorrow's shafts would be exhausted, thou couldst laugh at fortune's power.
Tho' I lost thee, yet this thought would cheer me in my parting hour.
Yet I believe that fate intends (oh, bear this forecast in thy mind!)
That all the love my passions crave will soon a full fruition find;
Fast my passion stronger grows, and if of love there measure be,
Believe it, dearest, that the whole can find its summary in me!
Deem that thou art foully wronged, whose graces have such power to bless,
If any of thy subject slaves to thee, their queen, should offer less.
And accept this pledged assurance, that oblivion cannot roll
O'er the image of thy beauty stamped on this enamored soul.
Then dismiss thy anxious musings, let them with the wind away,
As the gloomy clouds are scattered at the rising of the day.
Think that he is now thy slave, who, when he wooed thee, was thy King;
Think that not the brightest morning can to him contentment bring,
Till the light of other moments in thy melting eyes he trace,

And the gates of Paradise are opened in thy warm embrace.
Since thou knowest that death to me and thee will strike an equal blow,
It is just that, while we live, our hearts with equal hopes should glow.
Then no longer vex thy lover with complaints that he may change;
Darling, oft these bitter questions can the fondest love estrange;
No, I dream not of estrangement, for thy Chico evermore
Thinks upon his Vindaraja's image only to adore."

THE INFANTA SEVILLA AND PERANZUELOS

Upon Toledo's loftiest towers
  Sevilla kept the height;
So wondrous fair was she that love
  Was blinded at the sight.

She stood amid the battlements,
  And gazed upon the scene
Where Tagus runs through woodland
  And flowers and glades of green.

And she saw upon the wide highway
  The figure of a knight;
He rode upon a dappled steed,
  And all his arms were bright.

Seven Moors in chains he led with him,
  And one arm's length aloof
Came a dog of a Moor from Morocco's shore
  In arms of double proof.

His steed was swift, his countenance
  In a warlike scowl was set,
And in his furious rage he cursed
  The beard of Mahomet!

He shouted, as he galloped up:
  "Now halt thee, Christian hound;

I see at the head of thy captive band
  My sire, in fetters bound.

"And the rest are brothers of my blood,
  And friends I long to free;
And if thou wilt surrender all,
  I'll pay thee gold and fee."

When Peranzuelos heard him,
  He wheeled his courser round.
With lance in rest, he hotly pressed
  To strike him to the ground;
His sudden rage and onset came
  Swift as the thunder's sound.

The Moor at the first encounter reeled
  To earth, from his saddle bow;
And the Christian knight, dismounting,
  Set heel on the neck of his foe.

He cleft his head from his shoulders,
  And, marshalling his train,
Made haste once more on his journey
  Across Toledo's plain.

CELIN'S FAREWELL

He sadly gazes back again upon those bastions high,
The towers and fretted battlements that soar into the sky;
And Celin, whom the King in wrath has from Granada banned
Weeps as he turns to leave for aye his own dear native land;
No hope has he his footsteps from exile to retrace;
No hope again to look upon his lady's lovely face.
Then sighing deep he went his way, and as he went he said:
  "I see thee shining from afar,
  As in heaven's arch some radiant star.
  Granada, queen and crown of loveliness,
  Listen to my lament, and mourn for my distress.

"I see outstretched before my eyes thy green and beauteous shore,
Those meadow-lands and gardens that with flowers are dappled o'er.
The wind that lingers o'er those glades received the tribute given
By many a trembling calyx, wet with the dews of heaven.
From Genil's banks full many a bough down to the water bends,
Yon vega's green and fertile line from flood to wall extends;
There laughing ladies seek the shade that yields to them delight,
And the velvet turf is printed deep by many a mounted knight.
I see thee shining from afar,
As in heaven's arch some radiant star.
Granada, queen and town of loveliness,
Listen to my lament, and mourn for my distress.

"Ye springs and founts that sparkling well from yonder mountain-side,
And flow with dimpling torrent o'er mead and garden wide,
If e'er the tears that from my breast to these sad eyes ascend
Should with your happy waters their floods of sadness blend,
Oh, take them to your bosom with love, for love has bidden
These drops to tell the wasting woe that in my heart is hidden.
I see thee shining from afar,
As in heaven's arch some radiant star.
Granada, queen and crown of loveliness,
Listen to my lament, and mourn for my distress.

"Ye balmy winds of heaven, whose sound is in the rippling trees,
Whose scented breath brings back to me a thousand memories,
Ye sweep beneath the arch of heaven like to the ocean surge
That beats from Guadalquivir's bay to earth's extremest verge.
Oh, when ye to Granada come (and may great Allah send
His guardian host to guide you to that sweet journey's end!),
Carry my sighs along with you, and breathe them in the ear
Of foes who do me deadly wrong, of her who holds me dear.

Oh, tell them all the agony I bear in banishment,
That she may share my sorrow, and my foe the King relent.
I see thee shining from afar,
As in heaven's arch some radiant star.
Granada, queen and crown of loveliness,
Listen to my lament, and mourn for my distress."

CELIN'S RETURN

Now Celin would be merry, and appoints a festal day,
When he the pang of absence from his lady would allay:
The brave Abencerrages and Gulanes straight he calls,
His bosom friends, to join him as he decks his stately halls.
And secretly he bids them come, and in secret bids them go;
For the day of merriment must come unnoticed by his foe;
For peering eyes and curious ears are watching high and low,
But he only seeks one happy day may reparation bring
For the foul and causeless punishment inflicted by the King.
" For in the widest prison-house is misery for me,
And the stoutest heart is broken unless the hand is free."

His followers all he bade them dress in Christian array,
With rude and rustic mantles of color bright and gay;
With silken streamers in their caps, their caps of pointed crown,
With flowing blouse, and mantle and gaberdine of brown.
But he himself wore sober robes of white and lion gray,
The emblems of the hopeless grief in which the warrior lay.
And the thoughts of Adalifa, of her words and glancing eyes,
Gave colors of befitting gloom to tint his dark disguise.
And he came with purpose to perform some great and glorious deed,
To drive away the saddening thoughts that made the bosom bleed.
" For in the widest prison-house is misery to me,
And the stoutest heart is broken unless the arm be free."

There streams into Granada's gate a stately cavalcade
Of prancing steeds caparisoned, and knights in steel arrayed;
And all their acclamations raise, when Celin comes in sight—
"The foremost in the tournament, the bravest in the fight"—
And Moorish maiden Cegri straight to the window flies,
To see the glittering pageant and to hear the joyous cries.
She calls her maidens all to mark how, from misfortune free,
The gallant Celin comes again, the ladies' knight is he!
They know the story of his fate and undeserved disgrace,
And eagerly they gaze upon the splendor of his face.
Needs not his exploit in the fields, his valorous deeds to tell—
The ladies of Granada have heard and know them well!

> "For in the widest prison-house is misery to me,
> And the stoutest heart must break unless the warrior's arm be free."

The beauty of Granada crowds Elvira's gate this night;
There are straining necks and flushing cheeks when Celin comes in sight;
And whispered tales go round the groups, and hearts indignant swell,
As they think what in Granada that hero knight befell.
Now a thousand Moorish warriors to Celin's fame aspire,
And a thousand ladies gaze on him with passionate desire.
And they talk of Adalifa, to whom he made his vow,
Though neither speech nor written page unites them longer now.

> "For in the widest prison-house is misery to me,
> And the stoutest heart must break unless the warrior's arms be free."

The city waits his coming, for the feast has been prepared,
By rich and poor, by high and low the revel shall be shared;
And there are warriors high in hope to win the jousting prize,
And there are ladies longing for a smile from Celin's eyes.
But when the news of gladness reached Adalifa's ear,
Her loving heart was touched with grief and filled with jealous fear;
And she wrote to Celin, bidding him to hold no revel high,
For the thought of such rejoicing brought the tear-drop to her eye;

The Moor received the letter as Granada came in sight,
And straight he turned his courser's head toward Jaen's towering height,
And exchanged for hues of mourning his robe of festal white.
" For in the widest prison-house is misery to me,
And the stoutest heart is broke unless the warrior's arm be free."

BAZA REVISITED

Brave Celin came, the valiant son of him the *castelain*
Of the fortress of Alora and Alhama's windy plain.
He came to see great Baza, where he in former days
Had won from Zara's father that aged warrior's praise.
The Moor gazed on that fortress strong, the towers all desolate,
The castle high that touched the sky, the rampart and the gate.
The ruined hold he greeted, it seemed its native land,
For there his bliss had been complete while Zara held his hand.
And Fortune's cruel fickleness he furiously reviled,
For his heart sent madness to his brain and all his words were wild.
" O goddess who controllest on earth our human fate,
How is it I offend thee, that my life is desolate?
Ah! many were the triumphs that from Zara's hands I bore,
When in the joust or in the dance she smiled on me of yore.
And now, while equal fortune incessantly I chase,
Naught can I gather from thy hand but disaster and disgrace.
Since King Fernando brought his host fair Baza to blockade,
My lot has been a wretched lot of anguish unalloyed.
Yet was Fernando kind to me with all his kingly art,
He won my body to his arms, he could not win my heart."
While thus he spoke the mantle that he wore he cast away;
'Twas green, 'twas striped with red and white, 'twas lined with dismal gray.
" Best suits my fate, best suits the hue, in this misfortune's day;

Not green, not white nor purple, but the palmer's garb of gray.
I ask no plumes for helm or cap of nature's living green,
For hope has vanished from my life of that which might have been!
And from my target will I blot the blazon that is vain—
The lynx whose eyes are fixed upon the prey that it would gain.
For the glances that I cast around meet fortune's foul disdain;
And I will blot the legend, as an accursed screed.
'Twas writ in Christian letters plain that all the world might read:
'My good right arm can gain me more altho' its range be short,
Then all I know by eye-sight or the boundless range of thought.'
The blue tahala fluttering bright upon my armored brow
In brilliant hue assorts but ill with the lot I meet with now.
I cast away this gaudy cap, it bears the purple dye;
Not that my love is faithless, for I own her constancy;
But for the fear that there may be, within the maiden's sight,
A lover worthier of her love than this unhappy knight."
With that he took his lance in hand, and placed it in its rest,
And o'er the plain with bloody spur the mournful Celin pressed.
On his steed's neck he threw the reins, the reins hung dangling low,
That the courser might have liberty to choose where he would go;
And he said: "My steed, oh, journey well, and make thy way to find
The bliss which still eludes me, tho' 'tis ever in my mind.
Nor bit nor rein shall now restrain thy course across the lea,
For the curb and the bridle I only use from infamy to flee."

CAPTIVE ZARA

In Palma there was little joy, so lovely Zara found;
She felt herself a slave, although by captive chain unbound.
In Palma's towers she wandered from all the guests apart;
For while Palma had her body, 'twas Baza held her heart.
And while her heart was fixed on one, her charms no less enthralled
The heart of this brave cavalier, Celin Andalla called.
Ah, hapless, hapless maiden, for in her deep despair
She did not know what grief her face had caused that knight to bear;
And though the Countess Palma strove with many a service kind
To show her love, to soothe the pang that wrung the maiden's mind,
Yet borne upon the tempest of the captive's bitter grief,
She never lowered the sail to give her suffering heart relief.
And, in search of consolation to another captive maid,
She told the bitter sorrow to no one else displayed.
She told it, while the tears ran fast, and yet no balm did gain,
For it made more keen her grief, I ween, to give another pain.
And she said to her companion, as she clasped her tender hand:
"I was born in high Granada, my loved, my native land;
For years within Alhambra's courts my life ran on serene;
I was a princess of the realm and handmaid to a queen.
Within her private chamber I served both night and day,
And the costliest jewels of her crown in my protection lay.
To her I was the favorite of all the maids she knew;
And, ah! my royal mistress I loved, I loved her true!
No closer tie I owned on earth than bound me to her side;
No closer tie; I loved her more than all the world beside.
But more I loved than aught on earth, the gallant Moorish knight,
Brave Celin, who is solely mine, and I his sole delight.
Yes, he was brave, and all men own the valor of his brand;
Yes, and for this I loved him more than monarchs of the land.
For me he lived, for me he fought, for me he mourned and wept,

When he saw me in this captive home like a ship to the breakers swept.
He called on heaven, and heaven was deaf to all his bitter cry,
For the victim of the strife of kings, of the bloody war, was I;
It was my father bade him first to seek our strong retreat.
Would God that he had never come to Baza's castle seat!
Would God that he had never come, an armored knight, to stand
Amid the soldiers that were ranked beneath my sire's command.
He came, he came, that valiant Moor, beneath our roof to rest.
His body served my father; his heart, my sole behest;
What perils did he face upon that castle's frowning height!
Winning my father's praise, he gained more favor in my sight.
And when the city by the bands of Christians was assailed,
My soul 'neath terrors fiercer still in lonely terror quailed.
For I have lost my sire, and I have lost my lover brave,
For here I languish all alone, a subject and a slave.
And yet the Moor, altho' he left with me his loving heart,
I fear may have forgotten that I own his better part.
And now the needle that I ply is witness to the state
Of bondage, which I feel to-day with heart disconsolate.
And here upon the web be writ, in the Arabian tongue,
The legend that shall tell the tale of how my heart is wrung.
Here read: 'If thou hast ta'en my heart when thou didst ride away,
Remember that myself, my living soul, behind thee stay.'
And on the other side these words embroidered would I place:
'The word shall never fail that once I spake before thy face.'
And on the border underneath this posy, written plain:
'The promise that I made to thee still constant shall remain.'
And last of all, this line I add, the last and yet the best:
'Thou ne'er shalt find inconstancy in this unchanging breast.'
Thus runs the embroidery of love, and in the midst appears
A phœnix, painted clear, the bird that lives eternal years.
For she from the cold ashes of life at its last wane,
Takes hope, and spreads her wings and soars through skyey tracks again.
And there a hunter draws his bow outlined with skilful thread,

And underneath a word which says, 'Nay, shoot not at the dead.'
Thus spake the Moorish maiden, and in her eyes were tears of grief,
Tho' in her busy needle she seemed to find relief.
And the kindly countess called from far: "Zara, what aileth thee?
Where art thou? For I called, and yet thou didst not answer me."

THE JEALOUS KING

'Twas eight stout warriors matched with eight, and ten with valiant ten,
As Aliatare formed a band allied with Moslem men,
To joust, with loaded canes, that day in proud Toledo's ring,
Against proud Adelifa's host before their lord the King.
The King by proclamation had announced the knightly play,
For the cheerful trumpets sang a truce upon that very day;
And Zaide, high Belchite's the King, had sworn that war should cease,
And with Tarfe of Valentia had ratified the peace.
But others spread the news, that flew like fire from tongue to tongue,
That the King was doting-mad with love, for then the King was young;
And had given to Celindaja the ordering of the day.
And there were knights beside the King she loved to see at play.
And now the lists are opened and, lo! a dazzling band,
The Saracens, on sorrel steeds leap forth upon the sand;
Their trailing cloaks are flashing like the golden orange rind,
The hoods of green from their shoulders hang and flutter in the wind.
They carry targets blazoned bright with scimitars arow,
But each deadly blade is deftly made into a Cupid's bow.
A shining legend can be seen in letters ranged above;
And "Fire and Blood" the motto runs. It speaks of war and love.

In double file a company of warriors succeed;
The bold Aliatares come mounted on Arab steeds.
The livery that they wear is dyed in tint of crimson red;
And flower and leaf in white relief its surface overspread.
The globe of heaven, which many a star and constellation strow,
Borne upon Atlas' shoulders, is the blazon that they show.
And a Moor of Aliatar this motto does express,
Written upon a streamer, "I Endure through Weariness."
The Adelifas follow; a mighty race are they.
Their armor is more costly, their mantles are more gay.
Of bright carnation is the web, enriched with saffron streaks,
And for favors there are fluttering veils upon their helmet peaks.
A globe they blazon on their shields, but it is bruised and broke
By a savage with a bludgeon, who deals it many a stroke;
And a rod, and underneath it this motto tells the tale,
All written in Arabian scrip. It says, "The Strong Prevail."
The eight Azarques following these into the plaza spring,
With air of haughty arrogance they gallop round the ring.
Of blue and purple and pale gold are the mantles that they wear,
And for plumes they carry amulets that dangle high in air.
On their left arm are their targets, painted a dazzling green.
The orb of heaven is outlined there on which two hands are seen,
The motto, "Green is paramount," is lettered full in view;
Its arrogance explains to all those targets' vivid hue.
Then foams the King in rage to see his doting love was fleered,
And his heart is filled with bitter thought as that proud shield appeared.
And he called the warden of his keep, Celin his henchman tried,
And he pointed to Azarque, and, flushed with anger, cried—
"The sun upon that haughty shield myself will bid it set;
It works some mischief upon me, like an evil amulet.
Azarque drew his ready lance, his strong arm hurled it high,
The light shaft soared amid the clouds, and vanished in the sky.
And those whose vision followed it grew dizzy at the sight,
They knew not whither it had flown, nor where it would alight.

The ladies of the burgesses at many a window press
To see the javelin from his hand rise with such readiness,
And those who on the platform were seated with the King
Bent back to see how well the cane that gallant Moor could fling.
And as Azarque forward rides, as in retreat he flies,
" Now, Allah guard thee, gallant knight," with shouts the people cries.
" My curse upon him; he shall die," the jealous King replies.
But Celindaja paid no heed to all that cavalcade;
Her lips were parched, her throat was dry, her heart was sore dismayed.
She asked that they would bring her fruit, but yet she strove in vain
With juice of any earthly tree to slake her fevered pain.
" Now let the sport be ended," the angry King decreed.
The joust was late, and every judge in weariness agreed.
And as they closed the empty lists, they heard the King's command,
" Now seize, now seize Azarque, a traitor to this land."
The double lines of cavaliers who led the jousting train
Threw down upon the open square the spear of idle cane;
Then swiftly seized the lance of steel and couching it for fight,
According to the royal wish rode down upon the knight.
For arms and plea must ever bootless prove
To curb the passions of a king in love.

The other band came forth to save Azarque from his foes,
But the stout Moor waves his hand to them ere they in battle close,
Then calmly cries: " Tho' love, it seems, has no respect for law,
'Tis right that ye keep peace to-day and from the lists withdraw!
Nay, gentlemen, your lances lower before it be too late;
And let our foes their lances raise, in sign of passion's hate;
Thus without blood accorded be a victory and defeat.
'Tis only bloodshed makes the one more bitter or more sweet,
For arms or reason unavailing prove
To curb the passions of a king in love."

At last they seize the struggling Moor, the chains are on his
hands;
And the populace, with anger filled, arrange themselves in
bands.
They place a guard at every point, in haste to set him free,
But where the brave commander who shall lead to victory?
And where the leader who shall shout and stir their hearts to
fight?
These are but empty braggarts, but prowlers of the night,
Cut-throats and needy idlers—and so the tumult ends—
Azarque lies in prison, forsaken by his friends.
For, ah, both arms and reason powerless prove
To turn the purpose of a king in love.

Alone does Celindaja the coward crowd implore,
"Oh, save him, save him, generous friends, give back to me
my Moor."
She stands upon the balcony and from that lofty place
Would fling herself upon the stones to save him from disgrace.
Her mother round the weeping girl has flung her withered arm.
"O fool," she whispers in her ear, "in Mary's name be calm!"
Thou madly rushest to thy death by this distracted show.
Surely thou knowest well this truth, if anyone can know,
How arms and reason powerless prove
To turn the purpose of a king in love.

Then came a message of the King, in which the monarch said
That a house wherein his kindred dwelt must be a prison made.
Then Celindaja, white with rage: "Go to the King and say
I choose to be my prison-house for many and many a day,
The memory of Azarque, in which henceforth I live:
But the treachery of a monarch my heart will not forgive.
For the will of one weak woman shall never powerless prove
To turn the foolish purpose of a king who is in love.

"Alas for thee, Toledo! in former times they said
That they called thee for vengeance upon a traitor's head.
But now 'tis not on traitors, but on loyal men and true
That they call to thee for vengeance, which to caitiff hearts
are due.

And Tagus gently murmurs in his billows fresh and free
And hastens from Toledo to reach the mighty sea."
E'er she said more, they seized the dame, and led her to the gate,
Where the warden of the castle in solemn judgment sate.

THE LOVERS OF ANTEQUERA

The brave Hamete reined his steed and from the crupper bent,
To greet fair Tartagona, who saw him with content,
The daughter of Zulema, who had many a foe repelled
From the castle on the hill, which he in Archidora held;
For six-and-thirty years he kept the Christian host at bay,
A watchful warden, fearless of the stoutest foes' array.
And now adown the well-known path, a secret path and sure,
Led by the noble lady, hurried the gallant Moor.
The sentinels beneath the wall were careless, or they slept;
They heeded not Hamete as down the slope he crept.
And when he reached the level plain, full twenty feet away,
He hobbled fast his courser, lest he should farther stray.
Then to the Moorish lady he turned, as if to speak,
Around her waist he flung his arms and kissed her on the cheek.
"O goddess of my heart," he said, "by actions I will prove,
If thou wilt name some high emprise, how faithful is my love!
And in Granada I am great, and have much honored been,
Both by the King Fernando and Isabel his Queen.
My name is high, my lineage long, yet none of all my line
Have reached the pitch of glory which men allow is mine.
Narvarez is a knight of name, in love and arms adept,
In Antequera's castle he well the marches kept.
Jarifa was a captive maid, he loved Jarifa well,
And oft the maiden visited within her prison cell.
And, if the thing with honor and virtuous heart may be,
What he did with Jarifa, that would I do with thee."
A star was shining overhead upon the breast of night,
The warrior turned his course, and led the lady by its light.
They reached the foot of one tall rock, and stood within the shade,

Where thousand thousand ivy leaves a bower of beauty made.
They heard the genet browsing and stamping as he fed,
And smiling Love his pinions over the lovers spread.
But ere they reached the pleasant bower, they saw before them stand,
Armed to the teeth, with frowning face, a strange and savage band.
Yes, seventy men with sword in hand surrounded dame and knight,
The robbers of the mountain, and they trembled at the sight!
With one accord these freebooters upon Hamete fell,
Like hounds that on the stag at bay rush at the hunter's call,
Burned the Moor's heart at once with wrath, at once with passion's flame,
To save the life and, more than life, the honor of his dame.
Straight to his feet he sprung and straight he drew his mighty sword,
And plunged into the robber crowd and uttered not a word.
No jousting game was e'er so brisk as that which then he waged;
On arm and thigh with deadly blow the slashing weapon raged;
Though certain was his death, yet still, with failing heart, he prayed
That till his lady could escape, that death might be delayed.
But, in the dark, a deadly stone, flung with no warning sound,
Was buried in his forehead and stretched him on the ground.
The breath his heaving bosom left and, from his nerveless hand,
The sword fell clattering to the ground, before that bloody band.
And when the damsel saw herself within those caitiffs' power,
And saw the city mantled in the darkness of the hour,
No grief that ever woman felt was equal to her pain,
And no despair like that of hers shall e'er be known again.
Those villains did not see those locks, that shone like threads of gold;
Only the summer sunlight their wondrous beauty told.
They did not mark the glittering chain of gold and jewels fine,
That in the daylight would appear her ivory throat to twine.
But straight she took the scimitar, that once her lover wore,

It lay amid the dewy grass, drenched to the hilt in gore.
And, falling on the bloody point, she pierced her bosom through,
And Tartagona breathed her last, mourned by that robber crew.
And there she lay, clasping in death her lover's lifeless face,
Her valor's paragon, and she the glass of woman's grace.
And since that hour the tale is told, while many a tear-drop falls,
Of the lovers of the vega by Antequera's walls.
And they praise the noble lady and they curse the robber band,
And they name her the Lucretia of fair Andalusia's land.
And if the hearer of the tale should doubt that it be true,
Let him pass along the mountain road, till Ronda comes in view,
There must he halt and searching he may the story trace
In letters that are deeply cut on the rocky mountain's face.

TARFE'S TRUCE

"Oho, ye Catholic cavaliers
Who eye Granada day and night,
On whose left shoulder is the cross,
The crimson cross, your blazon bright.

"If e'er your youthful hearts have felt
The flame of love that brings delight,
As angry Mars, in coat of steel,
Feels the fierce ardor of the fight;

"If 'tis your will, within our walls,
To join the joust, with loaded reed,
As ye were wont, beneath these towers
The bloody lance of war to speed;

"If bloodless tumult in the square
May serve instead of battle's fray,
And, donning now the silken cloak,
Ye put the coat of steel away;

"Six troops of Saracens are here;
Six Christian troops, with targe and steed
Be ready, when the day is fixed,
To join the jousting of the reed.

"For 'tis not right that furious war,
Which sets the city's roofs in flames,
Should kindle with a fruitless fire
The tender bosom of our dames.

"In spite of all we suffer here
Our ladies are with you arrayed,
They pity you in this fierce war,
This labor of the long blockade.

"Amid the hardships of the siege
Let pleasure yield a respite brief;
(For war must ever have its truce)
And give our hardships some relief.

"What solace to the war-worn frame,
To every soul what blest release,
To fling aside the targe and mail,
And don one hour the plumes of peace!

"And he who shall the victor be
Among the jousters of the game,
I pledge my knightly word to him,
In token of his valorous fame,

"On his right arm myself to bind
The favor of my lady bright;
'Twas given me by her own white hand,
The hand as fair as it is white."

'Twas thus that Tarfe, valiant Moor,
His proclamation wrote at large;
He, King Darraja's favored squire,
Has nailed the cartel to his targe.

'Twas on the day the truce was made,
By Calatrava's master bold,

To change the quarters of his camp,
  And with his foes a conference hold.

Six Moorish striplings Tarfe sent
  In bold Abencerraje's train—
His kindred both in race and house—
  To meet the leaguers on the plain.

In every tent was welcome warm;
  And when their challenge they display,
The master granted their request
  To join the joust on Easter day.

In courteous words that cartel bold
  He answered; and a cavalcade
Of Christians, with the Moorish guards,
  Their journey to Granada made.

The guise of war at once was dropped;
  The armory closed its iron door;
And all put on the damask robes
  That at high festival they wore.

The Moorish youths and maidens crowd,
  With joyful face, the city square;
These mount their steeds, those sit and braid
  Bright favors for their knights to wear.

Those stern antagonists in war,
  Like friends, within the town are met;
And peacefully they grasp the hand,
  And for one day the past forget.

And gallant Almarada comes
  (Not Tarfe's self more brave, I ween),
Lord of a lovely Moorish dame,
  Who rules her lover like a queen.

A hundred thousand favors she
  In public or in private gives,
To show her lover that her life
  Is Almarada's while she lives!

And once upon a cloudy night,
  Fit curtain for his amorous mood,
The gallant Moor the high hills scaled
  And on Alhambra's terrace stood.

Arrived, he saw a Moorish maid
  Stand at a window opened wide;
He gave her many a precious gem;
  He gave her many a gift beside.

He spoke and said: "My lady fair,
  Though I have never wronged him, still
Darraja stands upon the watch,
  By fair or foul, to do me ill.

"Those eyes of thine, which hold more hearts
  Than are the stars that heaven displays;
That slay more Moors with shafts of love
  Than with his sword the master slays;

"When will they soften at my smile?
  And when wilt thou, my love, relent?
Let Tarfe go, whose words are big,
  While his sword-arm is impotent!

"Thou seest I am not such as he;
  His haughty words, so seldom true,
Are filled with boasting; what he boasts
  This sturdy arm of mine can do.

"My arm, my lance, ah! well 'tis known
  How oft in battle's darkest hour
They saved Granada's city proud
  From yielding to the Christian's power."

Thus amorous Almarada spoke
  When Tarfe came and caught the word;
And as his ear the message seized,
  His right hand seized upon his sword.

Yet did he deem some Christian troop
  Was in the darkness hovering by;

And at the thought, with terror struck,
He turned in eager haste to fly!

Darraja roused him at the din;
And with loud voice to Tarfe spoke;
He knew him from his cloak of blue,
For he had given the Moor that cloak!

THE TWO MOORISH KNIGHTS

Upon two mares both strong and fleet,
White as the cygnet's snowy wing,
Beneath Granada's arching gate
Passed Tarfe and Belchite's King.

Like beauty marks the dames they serve;
Like colors at their spear-heads wave;
While Tarfe kneels at Celia's feet,
The King is Dorelice's slave.

With belts of green and azure blue
The gallant knights are girded fair;
Their cloaks with golden orange glow,
And verdant are the vests they wear.

And gold and silver, side by side,
Are glittering on their garment's hem;
And, mingled with the metals, shine
The lights of many a costly gem.

Their veils are woven iron-gray,
The melancholy tint of woe—
And o'er their heads the dusky plumes
Their grief and desolation show.

And each upon his target bears
Emblazoned badges, telling true
Their passion and their torturing pangs,
In many a dark and dismal hue.

The King's device shines on his shield—
  A seated lady, passing fair;
A monarch, with a downcast eye,
  Before the dame is kneeling there.

His crown is lying at her feet
  That she may spurn it in disdain;
A heart in flames above is set;
  And this the story of his pain.

"In frost is born this flame of love"—
  Such legend circles the device—
"And the fierce fire in which I burn
  Is nourished by the breath of ice."

Upon her brow the lady wears
  A crown; her dexter hand sustains
A royal sceptre, gilded bright,
  To show that o'er all hearts she reigns.

An orb in her left hand she bears,
  For all the world her power must feel;
There Fortune prostrate lies; the dame
  Halts with her foot the whirling wheel.

But Tarfe's shield is blank and bare,
  Lest Adelifa should be moved
With jealous rage, to learn that he
  Her Moorish rival, Celia, loved.

He merely blazons on his targe
  A peaceful olive-branch, and eyes
That sparkle in a beauteous face,
  Like starlets in the autumn skies.

And on the branch of olive shines
  This legend: "If thy burning ray
Consume me with the fire of love,
  See that I wither not away."

They spurred their horses as they saw
  The ladies their approach surveyed;

And when they reached their journey's end
  The King to Dorelice said:

"The goddesses who reign above
  With envy of thy beauty tell;
When heaven and glory are thy gifts,
  Why should I feel the pangs of hell?

"Oh, tell me what is thy desire?
  And does heaven's light more pleasure bring
Than to own monarchs as thy slaves,
  And be the heiress to a king?

"I ask from thee no favor sweet;
  Nor love nor honor at thy hand;
But only that thou choose me out
  The servant of thy least command.

"The choicest nobles of the realm
  The glory of this office crave;
The lowliest soldier, with delight,
  Would die to prove himself thy slave.

"Each life, each heart is at thy feet;
  Thou with a thousand hearts mayst live;
And if thou wouldst not grant my prayer,
  Oh, take the warning that I give.

"For there are ladies in the court
  To my desires would fain consent,
And lovely Bendarrafa once
  These jealous words but lately sent:

"'Those letters and those written lines,
  Why dost thou not their sense divine?
Are they not printed on thy heart
  As thy loved image is on mine?

"'Why art thou absent still so long?
  It cannot be that thou art dead?'"
Then ceased the King and silent stood,
  While Tarfe to his Celia said:

"Celestial Celia be thy name;
  Celestial calm is on thy brow;
Yet all the radiance of thy face
  Thy cruelty eclipses now.

"A witch like Circe dost thou seem;
  For Circe could o'ercloud the sky;
Oh, let the sun appear once more,
  And bid the clouds of darkness fly!

"Ah, would to God that on the feast,
  The Baptist's consecrated day,
I might my arms about thee fling
  And lead thee from thy home away.

"Yet say not that 'tis in thy power
  To yield or all my hopes to kill;
For thou shalt learn that all the world,
  In leaguer, cannot bend my will.

"And France can tell how many a time
  I fought upon the tented field,
And forced upon their bended knee
  Her loftiest paladins to yield.

"I vanquished many a valiant knight
  Who on his shield the lilies bore;
And on Vandalia's plain subdued
  Of Red Cross warriors many a score.

"The noblest I had brought to yield
  Upon Granada's gory plain,
Did I not shrink with such vile blood
  The honor of my sword to stain."

At this the trumpets called to arms;
  Without one farewell word each knight
Turned from the lady of his heart
  And spurred his steed in headlong flight.

THE KING'S DECISION

Amid a thousand sapient Moors
  From Andalusia came,
Was an ancient Moor, who ruled the land,
  Rey Bucar was his name.

And many a year this sage had dwelt
  With the lady he loved best;
And at last he summoned the Cortes,
  As his leman made request.

The day was set on which his lords
  And commoners should meet,
And they talked to the King of his wide realm's need,
  As the King sat in his seat.

And many the laws they passed that day;
  And among them a law that said
That the lover who took a maid for his love
  The maid of his choice must wed;
And he who broke this ordinance
  Should pay for it with his head.

And all agreed that the law was good;
  Save a cousin of the King,
Who came and stood before him,
  With complaint and questioning;

" This law, which now your Highness
  Has on your lieges laid,
I like it not, though many hearts
  It has exultant made.

" Me only does it grieve, and bring
  Disaster on my life;
For the lady that I love the best,
  Is already wedded wife;

" Wedded she is, wedded amiss;
  Ill husband has she got,

And oft does pity fill my heart
  For her distressful lot.

"And this one thing I tell thee, King,
  To none else has it been told:
If I think her love is silver,
  She thinks my love is gold."

Then spake Rey Bucar in reply,
  This sentence uttered he:
"If thy love be wedded wife, the law
  Hath no penalty for thee."

ALMANZOR AND BOBALIAS

The King Almanzor slept one night,
  And, oh! his sleep was blest;
Not all the seven Moorish kings
  Could dare to break his rest.

The infante Bobalias
  Bethought of him and cried:
"Now rouse thee, rouse thee, uncle dear!
  And hasten to my side.

"And bid them fetch the ladders
  Owned by my sire the King;
And the seven mules that carry them
  Into my presence bring.

"And give to me the seven stout Moors
  Who shall their harness set,
For the love, the love of the countess
  I never can forget."

"Ill-mannered art thou, nephew,
  And never wilt amend;
The sweetest sleep I ever slept,
  Thou bringest to an end."

Now they have brought the ladders
  Owned by his sire the King.
And, to bear the load along the road,
  Seven sturdy mules they bring;

And seven stout Moors, by whom the mules
  In housings are arrayed.
And to the walls of the countess
  Their journey have they made.
There, at the foot of yonder tower,
  They halt their cavalcade.

In the arms of the count Alminique
  The countess lay at rest;
The infante has ta'en her by the hand,
  And caught her to his breast.

THE MOORISH INFANTA AND ALFONZO RAMOS

Beneath the shade of an olive-tree
  Stood the infanta fair;
A golden comb was in her hands,
  And well she decked her hair.

To heaven she raised her eyes, and saw,
  That early morning-tide,
A clump of spears and an armored band
  From Guadalquivir ride.

Alfonzo Ramos with them came,
  The admiral of Castile.
"Now welcome, Alfonzo Ramos!
  Now welcome, steed and steel,
What tidings do you bring of my fleet,
  What tidings of woe or weal?"

"I'll tell thee tidings, lady,
  If my life thou wilt assure."
"Tell on, Alfonzo Ramos,
  Thy life shall be secure."

"Seville, Seville has fallen,
To the arms of the Berber Moor."

"But for my word thy head this day
To the vultures had been tost!"
"If head of mine were forfeited,
'Tis thine must pay the cost."

THE BULL-FIGHT OF ZULEMA

He was a valorous gentleman, a gay and gallant knight,
Like stars on heaven's fifth circle was the splendor of his might.
In peace, accomplished in the arts of great Apollo's choir,
In war, the brilliant swordsman that Mars might well admire.
His great exploits were written on history's brightest page,
And rightly was he reckoned as the mirror of his age;
Great deeds he did with point of lance and won bright honor's crown,
Before the year when each red cheek was clothed in manly down.
And such he was through all the world by minstrel harps extolled,
Both for the vigor of his arm and for his bearing bold.
His very foes, whom he had made surrender in the fight,
While trembling at his valor, asked blessings on the knight.
And Fame herself, whose pace is swift, whose voice like fire can run,
Grew weary with reciting the deeds that he had done.
To tell aright his jeopardies, escapes, and rescues wrought,
A swifter-flying pinion and a louder tongue she sought!
Such was Zulema, such was he, the warrior of renown,
The son of that Zulema who ruled Toledo's town.
Ah! bright the fame the father left, for it shall never die—
The glory of his greater son shall keep its memory.
Now once it happened that he reached a city's towering gate;
'Twas Avila, and there that day the games they celebrate.
The mighty square, when he arrived, was changed into a bower;
And every knight wore fluttering plumes and every dame a flower.

The scene was strange, because the Moor, in southern cities reared,
Had never seen how gay Castile on festal days appeared.
He marked the Adelifas in the King's pavilion stand,
And he asked, and his prayer was granted, to join the champion band.
Yet when they gave consent they feared that great Zulema's might
Would surely quite excel in joust the best Castilian knight.
But a thousand times they asked that heaven would give to him success,
And a thousand times they wondered at his glorious Moorish dress.
Full many a lady's beck and smile were on the warrior bent,
And they looked on his manly beauty and they sighed with deep content.
But now Zulema by the hand the wardens take and greet,
And 'mid the highest noblemen they yield the knight a seat.
His seat was placed in honor 'mid ladies gay and bright,
Mid warriors of Castile, the first in courage and in might.
Then suddenly, more swift than wind, more wild than comet's glare,
Jerama's bull, far famed was he, rushed on the crowded square.
Ah! brave was he in flashing eyes, and fierce was he in heart,
His brow was like a storm-cloud, each horn a giant's dart,
His wide-spread nostrils snorted fire, his neck was short and deep,
His skin was black as the thunder-cloud that crowns the mountain's steep.
Before his coming fled the crowd, until the sunny square
Was emptied of the multitude, and every stone was bare.
Those only who on horseback sat remained to face the foe.
Now trembling with alarm they stand, and now with hope they glow.
Good sport they looked to have with him, and lay him in the dust,
But the Andalusian hero evaded every thrust.
And sometimes, with a gallant charge he threw them from their seat,
He gored them with his savage horn, and trod them with his feet!

Ah! great the shame of the vanquished knights; they dared not raise their eyes
To the ladies who looked down and smiled from banks and balconies.
For those soft eyes were fixed no more upon each vanquished knight,
But on the monster proud and strong who conquered them in fight.
The dames upon the royal seat to Zulema turned their eyes,
And one, the loveliest of them all, who wore a strange disguise,
Yet through her veil such rays she shot that she seemed like the sun on high
When he rises, quenching all the stars that filled the midnight sky.
She made a sign to him and spoke directly from her heart,
Whose tongue is in a woman's eye. Ah! well it plays its part!
She bade him to redeem the day and avenge each gallant knight
Who had fallen in the dust before the foe in stubborn fight.
And the Moor with gracious mien assents, and from his seat descends;
But first with glance and waving scarf a tender message sends
To the lovely Moorish damsel who had called him to the fray,
And had filled his heart with sudden love upon the festal day.
And as he leapt into the sand it was as if he flew,
For love lent wings at his lady's nod, some glorious deed to do.
And when the bull beheld approach, upon the bloody sand,
His bold and tall antagonist, a dagger in his hand,
He roared like thunder, with his hoofs he pawed the dusty ground,
The plaza shook, the castle tower re-echoed to the sound!
Long subject to the hand of man, and in subjection born,
He thought to subject human foe to hoof and mighty horn.
Zulema started toward the beast, loud cries would hold him back,
But well he knew that victory would follow his attack.
The bull was on him with a bound, and, glaring face to face,
They stood one moment, while a hush fell on the crowded place.
With bold right hand Zulema drew his keen and mighty blade;
Blow after blow 'mid blood and dust upon his foe he laid;
The startled beast retired before such onslaught of his foe,

And the people shouted loud applause and the King himself bowed low.
The bull with tossing head roared forth a challenge to the knight,
As Zulema turned, and with a bound rushed to the desperate fight.
Ah! cruel were the strokes that rained upon that foaming flank!
Into the sand that life-blood like a shower of autumn sank.
He roars, he snorts, he spurns the ground, the bloody dust flies high,
Now here, now there, in angry pain they see the monster fly.
He turns to see what new-found foe has crossed his path to-day;
But when Zulema faces him he stops to turn away.
For the third time the fight begins; the bull with many a roar
Turns to his foe, while from his lips run mingled foam and gore.
The Moor enraged to see the beast again before him stand,
Deals him the deep, the fatal wound, with an unerring hand.
That wound, at last, has oped the gate through which may enter death,
And staggering to the dust the beast snorts forth his latest breath.
As the bull falls, the crowded square rings with a loud acclaim,
And envy burns in many a knight, and love in many a dame.
The highest nobles of the land the conqueror embrace;
He sees the blush of passion burn on many a damsel's face.
And Fame has blown her trumpet and flies from town to town,
And Apollo takes his pen and writes the hero's title down.

THE RENEGADE

Through the mountains of Moncayo,
  Lo! all in arms arrayed,
Rides pagan Bobalias,
  Bobalias the renegade.

Seven times he was a Moor, seven times
  To Christ he trembling turned;

At the eighth, the devil cozened him
And the Christian cross he spurned,
And took back the faith of Mahomet,
In childhood he had learned.

He was the mightiest of the Moors,
And letters from afar
Had told him how Sevila
Was marshalling for war.

He arms his ships and galleys,
His infantry and horse,
And straight to Guadalquivir's flood
His pennons take their course.

The flags that on Tablada's plain
Above his camp unfold,
Flutter above three hundred tents
Of silk brocade and gold.

In the middle, the pavilion
Of the pagan they prepare;
On the summit a ruby stone is set,
A jewel rich and rare.

It gleams at morn, and when the night
Mantles the world at length,
It pours a ray like the light of day,
When the sun is at its strength.

THE TOWER OF GOLD

Brave Arbolan a prisoner lay
Within the Tower of Gold;
By order of the King there stood
Four guards to keep the hold.
'Twas not because against his King
He played a treacherous part;
But only that Guhala's charms
Had won the captive's heart.

"Guhala, Guhala,
My longing heart must cry;
This mournful vow I utter now—
To see thee or to die."

No longer free those sturdy limbs!
Revenge had bid them bind
The iron chain on hands and feet;
They could not chain his mind!
How dolorous was the warrior's lot!
All hope at last had fled;
And, standing at the window,
With sighing voice he said:

"Guhala, Guhala,
My longing heart must cry;
This mournful vow I utter now—
To see thee or to die."

He turned his eyes to where the banks
Of Guadalquivir lay;
"Inhuman King!" in grief he cried,
"Thy mandates I obey;
Thou bidst them load my limbs with steel;
Thy cruel sentinel
Keeps watch beside my prison door;
Yet who my crime can tell?

"Guhala, Guhala,
My longing heart must cry;
This mournful vow I utter now—
To see thee or to die."

THE DIRGE FOR ALIATAR

No azure-hued tahalia now
Flutters about each warrior's brow;
No crooked scimitars display
Their gilded scabbards to the day.
The Afric turbans, that of yore
Were fashioned on Morocco's shore,
To-day their tufted crown is bare;
There are no fluttering feathers there.
In mourning garments all are clad,
Fit harness for the occasion sad;
But, four by four the mighty throng
In slow procession streams along.
Ah! Aliatar! well he knew
The soldiers of his army true,
The soldiers whose afflicted strain
Gives utterance to their bosom's pain.

Sadly we march along the crowded street,
While trumpets hoarsely blare and drums tempestuous beat.

The phœnix that would shine in gold
On the high banner's fluttering fold,
Scarce can the breeze in gladness bring
To spread aloft its waving wing.
It seemed as if the fire of death
For the first time had quenched her breath.
For tribulation o'er the world
The mantle of despair had furled;
There was no breeze the ground to bless,
The plain lay panting in distress;
Beneath the trailing silken shroud
Alfarez carried through the crowd.

Sadly we march along the crowded street,
While trumpets hoarsely blare and drums tempestuous beat.

For Aliatar, one sad morn,
Mounted his steed and blew his horn;

A hundred Moors behind him rode;
Fleeter than wind their coursers strode.
Toward Motril their course is made,
While foes the castle town blockade;
There Aliatar's brother lay,
Pent by the foes that fatal day.
Woe work the hour, the day, when he
Vaulted upon his saddle-tree!
Ne'er from that seat should he descend
To challenge foe or welcome friend,
Nor knew he that the hour was near,
His couch should be the funeral bier.

Sadly we march along the crowded street,
While trumpets hoarsely blare and drums tempestuous beat.

That day the master's knights were sent,
As if on sport and jousting bent;
And Aliatar, on his way,
By cruel ambush they betray;
With sword and hauberk they surround
And smite the warrior to the ground.
And wounded deep from every vein
He bleeding lies upon the plain.
The furious foes in deadly fight
His scanty followers put to flight,
In panic-stricken fear they fly,
And leave him unavenged to die.

Sadly we march along the crowded street,
While trumpets hoarsely blare and drums tempestuous beat.

Ah sadly swift the news has flown
To Zaida in the silent town;
Speechless she sat, while every thought
Fresh sorrow to her bosom brought;
Then flowed her tears in larger flood,
Than from his wounds the tide of blood.
Like dazzling pearls the tear-drops streak
The pallid beauty of her cheek.

Say, Love, and didst thou e'er behold
A maid more fair and knight more bold?
And if thou didst not see him die,
And Zaida's tears of agony,
The bandage of thine orbs draw tight—
That thou mayst never meet the sight!

Sadly we march along the crowded street,
While trumpets hoarsely blare and drums tempestuous beat.

Not only Zaida's eyes are wet,
For him her soul shall ne'er forget;
But many a heart in equal share
The sorrow of that lady bare.
Yes, all who drink the water sweet
Where Genil's stream and Darro meet,
All of bold Albaicins's line,
Who mid Alhambra's princes shine—
The ladies mourn the warrior high,
Mirror of love and courtesy;
The brave lament him, as their peer;
The princes, as their comrade dear;
The poor deplore, with hearts that bleed,
Their shelter in the time of need.

Sadly we march along the crowded street,
While trumpets hoarsely blare and drums tempestuous beat.

THE SHIP OF ZARA

It was the Moorish maiden, the fairest of the fair,
Whose name amid the Moorish knights was worshipped everywhere.
And she was wise and modest, as her race has ever been,
And in Alhambra's palace courts she waited on the Queen,
A daughter of Hamete—of royal line was he,
And held the mighty castle of Baja's town in fee.
Now sad and mournful all the day the maiden weeping sat,
And her captive heart was thinking still of the distant caliphat,
Which in the stubborn straits of war had passed from Moslem reign,

And now was the dominion of King Ferdinand of Spain.
She thought upon the dreary siege in Baja's desert vale
When the fight was long and the food of beasts and men began to fail,
And her wretched father, forced to yield, gave up his castle hold,
For falling were the towers, falling fast his warriors bold.
And Zara, lovely Zara, did he give into the care
Of the noble Countess Palma, who loved the maiden fair.
And the countess had to Baja come when Queen Isabella came,
The lovely vega of the town to waste with sword and flame.
And the countess asked of Zara if she were skilled in aught,
The needle, or the 'broidery frame, to Christian damsels taught.
And how she made the hours go by when, on Guadalquivir's strand,
She sat in the Alhambra, a princess of the land.
And, while her eyes were full of tears, the Moorish maid replied:
" 'Twas I the silver tinsel fixed on garments duly dyed;
'Twas I who with deft fingers with gold lace overlaid
The dazzling robes of flowery tint of velvet and brocade.
And sometimes would I take my lute and play for dancers there;
And sometimes trust my own weak voice in some romantic air;
But now, this moment, I retain but one, one mournful art—
To weep, to mourn the banishment that ever grieves my heart.
And since 'tis thou alone whose bread, whose roof my life didst save,
I weep the bitterest tears of all because I am a slave!
Yet wouldst thou deign, O lady dear, to make more light to me
The hours I pass beneath thy roof, in dark captivity,
I bid thee build for me, if thou approve of the design,
An ocean bark, well fitted to cross the surging brine;
Let it be swift, let it be strong, and leave all barks behind,
When on the surges of the main it feels the favoring wind.
We'll launch it from the sloping shore, and, when the wind is high,
And the fierce billows threatening mix their foam-tops with the sky,

We'll lower the mainsail, lest the storm should carry us away,
And sweep us on the reefs that lurk in some deep Afric bay.
And on the lofty topmast shall this inscription stand,
Written in letters which they use in every Christian land:
'This ship is tossed in many a storm, it lands on many a shore,
And the wide sea, beneath the wind, it swiftly travels o'er;
'Tis like the human heart which brings no treasure and no gain,
Till, tossed by hard misfortune, it has known the sea of pain.'
And let there be upon the fringe round this inscription hung
Another legend which shall say in the Arabian tongue:
'Oh, might it be that Allah, the merciful, would send
To all my captive miseries a swift and happy end.'"
The countess said: "To build this ship methinks would please me well,
Such tasks the sorrows of thy heart might lighten or dispel;
And, Zara, when the summer comes, and winds and floods are free,
We'll build our bark, we'll hoist our sail, and start across the sea."

HAMETE ALI

Hamete Ali on his way toward the city goes,
His tunic is a brilliant green with stripes of crimson rose,
In sign that no despondency this daring wanderer knows.
His arm, that wears the twisted steel, reflects the sunlight sheen,
And bound to it by many a knot is hung his hood of green.
And o'er his bonnet azure-blue, two feathery plumes there fly;
The one is green as the summer and one is blue as sky.
He does not wear these hues to show that he is passion's slave,
They are emblems of the life that beats within his bosom brave.
Yet dusky is his lance's hue and dusky is his shield,
On which are serpents scattered upon a golden field.
Their venomed tongues are quivering and ears before them stand,
To show how slanderous hearts can spread their poison o'er the land.
A lettered motto in the midst which everyone may read,
Is written in Arabian script, ah! good that all should heed!

" 'Tis naught but innocence of heart can save me from the blow
With which the slanderous serpents would lay their victim low."
Upon a piebald colt he rode along the valley's side,
The bravest of the valiant Moors and once Granada's pride.
In furious rage descending from bold Ubeda's steep,
He crossed the vale and mounted to Baza's castle keep.
Defiant still of Fortune's power, his thoughts at last found vent,
For Fortune had been cruel, and in words of discontent,
As if he blamed the serpent upon his shield displayed,
The torrent of his heart broke forth and in wrath the warrior said:
" O wasters of the brightest hope I knew in years long past!
O clouds by which the blazing sun of bliss is overcast!
O blight of love, O ruin of aspirations pure!
Vile worms, that gnaw and waste away the treasures most secure!
Attempt no more to banish me from my own native land,
That in my place of honor ye, envious slaves, may stand;
I, too, have friends, whose swords are keen, whose love is strong and leal.
To them I look for my defence by stratagem or steel.
And, Fortune, do thy worst; it is not meant,
By Allah, that his knight should die in banishment.

" Permit it not that in the generous breasts of those whose blood
Flows in my veins, who by my side as faithful champions stood,
Those cursed asps, whose effigies my shield's circumference fill,
Could plant the thoughts of villany by which they work me ill.
Just heaven forbids their words should blot the honor of my name,
For pure and faithful is my heart, howe'er my foes defame;
And Zaida, lovely Zaida, at a word that did me wrong,
Would close her ears in scornful ire and curse the slanderous tongue.
And, Fortune, do thy worst; it is not meant,
By Allah, that his knight should die in banishment.

"Nay, Fortune, turn no more thy wheel, I care not that it rest,
Nor bid thee draw the nail that makes it stand at man's behest.
Oh, may I never say to thee, when for thy aid I call,
Let me attain the height of bliss whate'er may be my fall!
And when I roam from those I love, may never cloud arise
To dim my hope of a return and hide me from their eyes.
Yet doubtless, 'tis the absent are oftenest forgot,
Till those who loved when they were near in absence love them not.
And, Fortune, do thy worst; it is not meant,
By Allah, that his knight should die in banishment.

"And since 'tis my unhappy lot, through slander's cruel wiles,
I should be robbed so many years of Zaida's cheering smiles,
Yet those who say that I am false, and name Celinda's name,
Oh, may they gain no end at length but obloquy and shame!
It is not just that to these words and to these anxious fears,
These wild complaints, the god of love should close his heedless ears!
Yes, I deserve a better fate, the fate that makes more sure;
The fame of those whose slanderous tongue in banishment endure.
And, Fortune, do thy worst; it is not meant,
By Allah, that his knight should die in banishment."

He spoke, and, lo! before him he saw the city stand,
With walls and towers that frowned in might upon that fertile land.
And he saw the glittering banners of Almanzor set on high,
And swaying in the gentle breeze that filled the summer sky.
And those who stood upon the walls, soon as he came in sight,
Streamed forth from the portcullis with welcome for the knight,
For they marvelled at the prancing steed that rushed across the plain,
They marvelled at his thundering voice and words of deep disdain.
And, Fortune, do thy worst; it is not meant,
By Allah, that his knight should die in banishment.

And as he rode into the town and galloped to the square,
Upon the balconies he saw bright dames with faces bare;

They stood, they gazed with eyes of love and gestures of delight,
For they joyed to see among them so stout, so fair a knight.
And all of Baza's people with cries his coming greet,
And follow at his horse's tail from street to crowded street.
His heart with gratitude was filled, his bosom filled with pride,
And with doffed bonnet, lo, he bowed and once again he cried:
"And, Fortune, do thy worst; it is not meant,
By Allah, that his knight should die in banishment."

They led him to the warden's house, and there was feasting high.
Brave men and beauteous women in crowds were standing by.
The trumpets blew in merry strain, the Moorish horns resound,
And the strain of joy was echoed from every castle round.
And from his colt dismounting he laid his lance aside,
And greeted all the multitude that filled the plaza wide.
Then to the strong tower of the place he hurried from the street,
And as he went a thousand times his lips would still repeat:
"And, Fortune, do thy worst; it is not meant,
By Allah, that his knight should die in banishment."

ZAIDE'S LOVE

Then Zaide stood enraptured and gazed with placid eye,
For the moment when his heart's desire should be fulfilled was nigh.
Propitious was the moment, and happy was the hour,
When all that he had longed for had come into his power.
And he said: "Thrice happy is the wall, and happy is the bar,
Tho' from my fond embraces, Zaida, it keeps thee far;
For long as thou shalt live on earth, my Zaida, thou art mine;
And the heart that in my bosom beats, long as it beats, is thine.
And happy is the green, green sod on which thy feet are set,
For the pressure of thy tender foot the grass shall ne'er forget,
Shall ne'er forget the white, white heel that o'er the pathway came,

Leaving behind it, everywhere, the print of snow and flame.
But far more happy is the knight, if e'er should Allah send
To this dark separation a bright and peaceful end.
For seems to me the hours that pass, without thy presence dear,
Wear the dark robe of sorrow, that orphaned children wear.
I seek to have thee with me, for it is only to the weak
That the happiness is wanting that they do not dare to seek.
And if the doom of death is ours, it will not haste the more
Because we scorn to think of it upon this happy shore.
But ere it come, that doom of death which fills us with alarms,
May Allah grant to me the boon of resting in thine arms!
And if, in that supremest bliss, fate favors my design,
And love is crowned, the lot of life contented I resign.
O darling Zaida, blest is he, 'mid thousands, who can say
That on that bosom, in those arms he for one moment lay!
Come, darling, to thy Zaide's side, and yield to him thy love;
Thou knowest him brave and good and kind, all other knights above;
In owning him thy lover true, thou wilt a partner count
Who above all in valor's list is champion paramount.
Thy beauty's sway should be unchecked as death's prevailing might,
But, ah, how many worlds would then sink into endless night!
But come, fair Zaida, quickly come to these expectant arms,
And let me win at last the prize of victory o'er thy charms.
It is a debt thou owest me, oh, let the debt be paid."
Then Zaida rose and showed herself in beauty's robe arrayed,
And the Moor cried: "May Allah grant thy sun may ever shine,
To light with its full splendor this lonely life of mine!
And tho' my stammering tongue be dumb, and like a broken lute,
And in its loudest efforts to speak thy praise be mute,
It can at least announce to thee, loud as the thunder's peal,
The service that I owe to thee, the passion that I feel."
The Moorish lady smiled at this, and spake in tender tone;
"If all this silent tongue of thine has said be loyal shown,
If all thy vows be from thy heart, and all thy heavy sighs
From out a breast unchanging, a constant spirit rise,

I swear that I would grant thy wish and follow thy behest;
But, ah, I fear lest thy fierce love should bring to me no rest,
I fear these honeyed words that from thy lips so lightly fly
At last should prove a serpent's fang to sting me till I die."
Then swore to her the Moor: "If this the end should ever be,
May the firm earth beneath my feet yawn wide and swallow me!
And may the blessed sunlight, the symbol of my hope,
Wither these orbs and leave me in eternal night to grope!"
At this the lovers joined their hands and hearts, and, with a kiss,
Sealed all their vows of friendship and promises of bliss—
Their love was strong and solid and constant should remain,
Till death should end their bondage and break the golden chain.

ZAIDA'S JEALOUSY.

Kind friend of Bencerraje's line, what judgment dost thou hold
Of all that Zaida's changeful moods before thine eyes unfold?
Now by my life I swear that she to all would yield her will;
Yet by my death I swear that she to all is recreant still.
Come near, my friend, and listen while I show to you this note,
Which to the lovely lady in bitter grief I wrote;
Repeat not what I read to thee, for 'twere a deadly shame,
Since thou her face admirest, should slander smirch her name:
"O Moorish maiden, who like time, forever on the wing,
Dost smiles and tears, with changing charm, to every bosom bring,
Thy love is but a masquerade, and thou with grudging hand
Scatterest the crumbs of hope on all the crowds that round thee stand.
With thee there is no other law of love and kindliness
But what alone may give thee joy and garland of success.
With each new plume thy maidens in thy dark locks arrange,
With each new tinted garment thy thoughts, thy fancies change.
I own that thou art fairer than even the fairest flower
That at the flush of early dawn bedecks the summer's bower.
But, ah, the flowers in summer hours change even till they fade,

And thou art changeful as the rose that withers in the shade.
And though thou art the mirror of beauty's glittering train,
Thy bosom has one blemish, thy mind one deadly stain;
For upon all alike thou shed'st the radiance of thy smile,
And this the treachery by which thou dost the world beguile.
I do not plead in my complaint thy loveliness is marred,
Because thy words are cruel, because thy heart is hard;
Would God that thou wert insensible as is the ocean wild
And not to all who meet thee so affable and mild;
Ah, sweetest is the lingering fruit that latest comes in time,
Ah, sweetest is the palm-tree's nut that those who reach must climb.
Alas! 'twas only yesterday a stranger reached the town—
Thou offeredst him thy heart and bade him keep it for his own!
O Zaida, tell me, how was this? for oft I heard thee say
That thou wert mine and 'twas to me thy heart was given away.
Hast thou more hearts than one, false girl, or is it changefulness
That makes thee give that stranger guest the heart that I possess?
One heart alone is mine, and that to thee did I resign.
If thou hast many, is my love inadequate to thine?
O Zaida, how I fear for thee, my veins with anger glow;
O Zaida, turn once more to me, and let the stranger go.
As soon as he hath left thy side his pledges, thou wilt find,
Were hollow and his promises all scattered to the wind.
And if thou sayst thou canst not feel the pains that absence brings,
'Tis that thy heart has never known love's gentle whisperings.
'Tis that thy fickle mind has me relinquished here to pine,
Like some old slave forgotten in this palace court of thine.
Ah, little dost thou reck of me, of all my pleasures flown,
But in thy pride dost only think, false lady, of thine own.
And is it weakness bids me still to all thy faults be blind
And bear thy lovely image thus stamped upon my mind?
For when I love, the slight offence, though fleeting may be the smart,
Is heinous as the treacherous stroke that stabs a faithful heart.
And woman by one look unkind, one frown, can bring despair

Upon the bosom of the man whose spirit worships her.
Take, then, this counsel, 'tis the last that I shall breathe to thee,
Though on the winds I know these words of mine will wasted be:
I was the first on whom thou didst bestow the fond caress,
And gave those pledges of thy soul, that hour of happiness;
Oh, keep the faith of those young days! Thy honor and renown
Thou must not blight by love unkind, by treachery's heartless frown.
For naught in life is safe and sure if faith thou shouldst discard,
And the sunlight of the fairest soul is oft the swiftest marred.
I will not sign this letter nor set to it my name;
For I am not that happy man to whom love's message came,
Who in thy bower thy accents sweet enraptured heard that day,
When on thy heaving bosom, thy chosen love, I lay.
Yet well thou'lt know the hand that wrote this letter for thine eye,
For conscience will remind thee of thy fickle treachery.
Dissemble as thou wilt, and play with woman's skill thy part,
Thou knowest there is but one who bears for thee a broken heart."
Thus read the valiant castellan of Baza's castle tower,
Then sealed the scrip and sent it to the Moorish maiden's bower.

ZAIDA OF TOLEDO

Upon a gilded balcony, which decked a mansion high,
A place where ladies kept their watch on every passer-by,
While Tagus with a murmur mild his gentle waters drew
To touch the mighty buttress with waves so bright and blue,
Stands Zaida, radiant in her charms, the flower of Moorish maids,
And with her arching hand of snow her anxious eyes she shades,
Searching the long and dusty road that to Ocaña leads,
For the flash of knightly armor and the tramp of hurrying steeds.

The glow of amorous hope has lit her cheek with rosy red,
Yet wrinkles of too anxious love her beauteous brow o'erspread;
For she looks to see if up the road there rides a warrior tall—
The haughty Bencerraje, whom she loves the best of all.
At every looming figure that blots the vega bright,
She starts and peers with changing face, and strains her eager sight;
For every burly form she sees upon the distant street
Is to her the Bencerraje whom her bosom longs to greet.
And many a distant object that rose upon her view
Filled her whole soul with rapture, as her eager eyes it drew;
But when it nearer came, she turned away, in half despair,
Her vision had deceived her, Bencerraje was not there.
" My own, my Bencerraje, if but lately you descried
That I was angry in my heart, and stubborn in my pride,
Oh, let my eyes win pardon, for they with tears were wet.
Why wilt thou not forgive me, why wilt thou not forget?
And I repented of that mood, and gave myself the blame,
And thought, perhaps it was my fault that, at the jousting game,
There was no face among the knights so filled with care as thine,
So sad and so dejected, yes, I thought the blame was mine!
And yet I was, if thou with thought impartial wilt reflect,
Not without cause incensed with thee, for all thy strange neglect.
Neglect that not from falseness or words of mine had sprung
But from the slanderous charges made by a lying tongue;
And now I ask thee pardon, if it be not too late,
Oh, take thy Zaida to thy heart, for she is desolate!
For if thou pardon her, and make her thine again, I swear
Thou never wilt repent, dear love, thou thus hast humored her!
It is the law of honor, which thou wilt never break,
That the secret of sweet hours of love thou mayst not common make.
That never shouldst thou fail in love, or into coldness fall,
Toward thy little Moorish maiden, who has given thee her all."

She spoke; and Bencerraje, upon his gallant bay,
Was calling to her from the street, where he loitered blithe and gay,
And quickly she came down to him, to give him, e'er they part,
Her rounded arms, her ivory neck, her bosom, and her heart!

ZAIDE REBUKED

See, Zaide, let me tell you not to pass along my street,
Nor gossip with my maidens nor with my servants treat;
Nor ask them whom I'm waiting for, nor who a visit pays,
What balls I seek, what robe I think my beauty most displays.
'Tis quite enough that for thy sake so many face to face
Aver that I, a witless Moor, a witless lover chase.
I know that thou art a valiant man, that thou hast slaughtered more,
Among thy Christian enemies, than thou hast drops of gore.
Thou art a gallant horseman, canst dance and sing and play
Better than can the best we meet upon a summer's day.
Thy brow is white, thy cheek is red, thy lineage is renowned,
And thou amid the reckless and the gay art foremost found.
I know how great would be my loss, in losing such as thee;
I know, if I e'er won thee, how great my gain would be:
And wert thou dumb even from thy birth, and silent as the grave,
Each woman might adore thee, and call herself thy slave.
But 'twere better for us both I turn away from thee,
Thy tongue is far too voluble, thy manners far too free;
Go find some other heart than mine that will thy ways endure,
Some woman who, thy constancy and silence to secure,
Can build within thy bosom her castle high and strong,
And put a jailer at thy lips, to lock thy recreant tongue.
Yet hast thou gifts that ladies love; thy bearing bold and bright
Can break through every obstacle that bars them from delight.
And with such gifts, friend Zaide, thou spreadest thy banquet board,
And bidst them eat the dish so sweet, and never say a word!

But that which thou hast done to me, Zaide, shall cost thee dear;
And happy would thy lot have been hadst thou no change to fear.
Happy if when thy snare availed to make the prize thine own,
Thou hadst secured the golden cage before the bird was flown.
For scarce thy hurrying footsteps from Tarfe's garden came,
Ere thou boastedst of thine hour of bliss, and of my lot of shame.
They tell me that the lock of hair I gave thee on that night,
Thou drewest from thy bosom, in all the people's sight,
And gav'st it to a base-born Moor, who took the tresses curled,
And tied them in thy turban, before the laughing world.
I ask not that thou wilt return nor yet the relic keep,
But I tell thee, while thou wearest it, my shame is dire and deep:
They say that thou hast challenged him, and swearest he shall rue
For all the truths he spake of thee—would God they were not true!
Who but can laugh to hear thee blame the whispers that reveal
Thy secret, though thy secret thyself couldst not conceal.
No words of thine can clear thy guilt nor pardon win from me,
For the last time my words, my glance, have been addressed to thee."
Thus to the lofty warrior of Abencerraje's race
The lady spoke in anger, and turned away her face:
"'Tis right," she said, "the Moor whose tongue has proved to me unkind
Should in the sentence of my tongue fit retribution find."

ZAIDA'S INCONSTANCY

O fairest Zaida, thou whose face brings rapture to mine eyes!
O fairest Zaida, in whose smile my soul's existence lies!
Fairest of Moorish maidens, yet in revengeful mood,
Above all Moorish maidens, stained by black ingratitude.
'Tis of thy golden locks that love has many a noose entwined,
And souls of free men at thy sight full oft are stricken blind;
Yet tell me, proud one, tell me, what pleasure canst thou gain
From showing to the world a heart so fickle and so vain?
And, since my adoration thou canst not fail to know,
How is it that thy tender heart can treat thy lover so?
And art thou not content my fondest hopes to take away,
But thou must all my hope, my life, destroy, in utter ruin lay?
My faithful love, sweet enemy! how ill dost thou requite!
And givest in exchange for it but coldness and despite;
Thy promises, thy pledge of love, thou to the gale wouldst fling;
Enough that they were thine, false girl, that they should all take wing.
Remember how upon that day thou gavest many a sign
Of love and lavished'st the kiss which told me thou wert mine.
Remember, lovely Zaida, though memory bring thee pain,
Thy bliss when 'neath thy window I sang my amorous strain.
By day, before the window, I saw my darling move,
At night, upon the balcony, I told thee of my love.
If I were late or absence detained me from thy sight,
Then jealous rage distraught thy heart, thine eyes with tears were bright.
But now that thou hast turned from me, I come thy face to greet,
And thou biddest me begone, and pass no longer through thy street.
Thou biddest me look on thee no more, nor even dare to write
The letter or the *billet-doux*, that caused thee once delight.
Yes, Zaida, all thy favors, thy love, thy vows, are shown
To be but false and faithless, since thou art faithless grown.

But why? thou art a woman, to fickle falseness born;
Thou prizest those who scorn thee—those who love thee thou dost scorn.
I change not, thou art changed, whose heart once fondly breathed my name;
But the more thy bosom turns to ice, the fiercer burns my flame;
For all thy coldness I with love and longing would repay,
For passion founded on good faith can never die away.

ZAIDE'S DESOLATION

It was the hour when Titan from Aurora's couch awoke,
And on the world her radiant face in wonted beauty broke,
When a Moor came by in sad array, and Zaide was his name.
Disguised, because his heart was sad with love's consuming flame;
No shield he bore, he couched no lance, he rode no warrior steed;
No plume nor mantle he assumed, motto or blazon screed;
Still on the flank of his mantle blank one word was written plain,
In the Moorish of the people, " I languish through disdain."
A flimsy cape his shoulders clad, for, when the garb is poor,
Nobility is honored most because 'tis most obscure.
If he in poverty appeared, 'twas love that made him so;
Till love might give the wealth he sought thus mourning would he go.
And still he journeys through the hills and shuns the haunts of men;
None look upon his misery in field or lonely fen.
Fair Zaida ne'er forgets that he is prince of all the land,
And ruler of the castles that at Granada stand;
But gold or silver or brocade can ne'er supply the lack
Of honor in a noble line whose crimes have stained it black;
For sunlight never clears the sky when night has spread her cloak,
But only when the glory of the morning has awoke.
He lives secure from jealous care, holding the priceless dower

Which seldom falls to loving hearts or sons of wealth and power.
Poor is his garb, yet at his side a costly blade appears,
'Tis through security of mind no other arms he bears.

'Tis love that from Granada's home has sent him thus to rove,
And for the lovely Zaida he languishes with love—
The loveliest face that by God's grace the sun e'er shone above.
From court and mart he lives apart, such is the King's desire;
Yet the King's friend Alfaqui is the fair maiden's sire.
Friend of the King, the throne's support, a monarch's son is he,
And he has sworn that never Moor his daughter's spouse shall be.
He has no ease till the monarch sees his daughter's loveliness.
But she has clasped brave Zaide's hand, and smiled to his caress,
And said that to be his alone is her sole happiness.
And after many journeys wide, wearied of banishment,
He sees the lofty tower in which his Moorish maid is pent.

ZAIDA'S LAMENT

Now the hoarse trumpets of the morn were driving sleep away;
They sounded as the fleeting night gave truce unto the day.
The hubbub of the busy crowd ceased at that dulcet sound,
In which one moment high and low peace and refreshment found.
The hoot of the nocturnal owl alone the silence broke,
While from the distance could be heard the din of waking folk;
And, in the midst of silence, came the sound as Zaida wept,
For all night long in fear of death she waked while others slept.

And as she sighed, she sang aloud a melancholy strain;
" And who would wish to die," she said, " though death be free from pain?"

For evil tongues, who thought to win her favor with a lie,
Had told her that the bold Gazul ordained that she should die;
And so she donned a Moor's attire, and put her own away,
And on the stroke of midnight from Xerez took her way.
And as she sighed, she sang aloud a melancholy strain;
" And who would wish to die," she said, " though death be free from pain? "

She rode a nimble palfrey and scarce could great Gazul
Excel the ardent spirit with which her heart was full.
Yet at every step her palfrey took, she turned her head for fear,
To see if following on her track some enemy were near.
And as she went, she sang aloud a melancholy strain;
" And who would wish to die," she said, " though death be free from pain? "

To shun suspicion's eye, at last she left the king's highway,
And took the journey toward Seville that thro' a bypath lay;
With loosened rein her gallant steed right swiftly did she ride,
Yet to her fear he did appear like a rock on the rough way-side.
And as she went, she sang aloud a melancholy strain;
" And who would wish to die," she said, " though death be free from pain? "

So secretly would she proceed, her very breath she held,
Tho' with a rising storm of sighs her snowy bosom swelled.
And here and there she made a halt, and bent her head to hear
If footsteps sounded; then, assured, renewed her swift career.
And as she went, she sang aloud a melancholy strain;
" And who would wish to die," she said, " though death be free from pain? "

Her fancy in the silent air could whispering voices hear;
" I'll make of thee a sacrifice, to Albenzaide dear; "
This fancy took her breath away, lifeless she sank at length,

And grasped the saddle-bow; for fear had sapped her spirit's strength.
And as she went, she sang aloud a melancholy strain;
"And who would wish to die," she said, "though death be free from pain?"

She came in sight of proud Seville; but the darkness bade her wait
Till dawn; when she alighted before a kinsman's gate.
Swift flew the days, and when at last the joyful truth she learned,
That she had been deceived; in joy to Xerez she returned.
And as she went, she sang aloud a melancholy strain;
"And who would wish to die," she said, "though death be free from pain?"

ZAIDA'S CURSE

And Zaida Cegri, desolate,
Whom by the cruel cast of fate,
Within one hour, the brandished blade
From wife had mourning widow made,
On Albenzaide's corse was bowed,
Shedding hot tears, with weeping loud.
Bright as the gold of Araby
Shone out her locks unbound;
And while, as if to staunch the blood,
Her hand lay on the wound,
She fixed her glances on Gazul,
Still by his foes attacked.
"'Twas cruel rage, not jealous love,
That urged this wicked act."
(Thus she began with trembling voice.)
"And I to God will pray
That for thy treacherous violence
Thy dastard life shall pay.
And midway, on thy journey down
To fair Sidonia's castled town,
Mayst thou alone, with no retreat,
The valiant Garci-Perez meet;
And mayst thou, startled at the sight,

Lose all the vigor of thy might;
Thy reins with palsied fingers yield;
And find no shelter in thy shield.
There sudden death or captive shame
Blot all thy valor but the name.
Thy warrior garb thou turnest
  To the livery of the slave;
Thy coat of steel is no cuirass,
  No harness of the brave;
When to Sidonia thou art come,
  To meet thy amorous mate,
May foul suspicion turn her heart
  From love to deadly hate.
Begone! no more the course pursue
Of faithless love and vows untrue.
To remain true to such as thee
Were naught but blackest perjury.
I fear not, hound, thy sword of might;
Turn, traitor, turn and leave my sight,
For thou wert born to change thy mind,
And fling all fealty to the wind.
Ignoble origin is thine,
For lovers of a noble line
Have no such rancorous hearts as thine.
And here I pray that God will bring
  His curse upon thy soul,
That thou in war, in peace, in love
  May meet with failure foul,
And that Sanlucar's lady,
  Whom thou wishest for a bride,
Thee from her castle entrance
  May spurn thee in her pride.
A widowed wife with bleeding heart,
Hear me one moment ere we part!
Thy knightly service I distrust,
I hear thy voice with deep disgust."
Cut to the heart by words so rude,
The Moor within the palace stood;
Say what he could, 'twas but to find
His vain word wasted on the wind.

THE TOURNAMENT OF ZAIDE

By Zaide has a feast been pledged to all Granada's dames,
For in his absence there had been dire lack of festive games,
And, to fulfil the promise the noble man had made,
He called his friends to join him in dance and serenade.
There should be sport of every kind; the youths in white arrayed
Were, to the ladies all unknown, to lead the camisade.
And ere the radiance of dawn could tint the valley-side,
The merry Moor had come abroad, his friends were at his side.
He gathered round a company, they formed a joyous train;
There were fifty gentlemen, the noblest names in Spain.
Before the dawn they sallied forth the ladies to surprise
And all that snowy gowns conceal to see with open eyes.
They bound their brows with garlands of flowerets sweet and bright,
In one hand each a cane-stalk bore, in one a taper white,
And the clarions began to blow, and trump and Moorish horn,
And whoop and shout and loud huzzas adown the street were borne.
From right to left the clamor spread along the esplanade.
And envious Abbaicin a thousand echoes made.
The startled horses galloped by, amid the people's yells;
The town to its foundation shook with the jingle of their bells.
Amid the crowd some run, some shout, "Stop, stop!" the elders say;
Then all take order and advance to Alcazaba's way;
Others from Vavataubin to Alpujarra fare,
Down the street of the Gomelas or to Vivarrambla Square.
Now the whole town is on its feet, from wall to towering wall
They surge with shouts or flock around the tower and castle tall.
The ladies who are tenderest and given most to sleep
Awaken at the hubbub and from their windows peep.
And there are seen dishevelled locks clasped by the lily hand;
And snowy throat and bosom bare, revealed in public, stand;
And in their drowsy disarray, and in their anxious fear,

Each Moorish lady is surprised with many a sudden tear;
And many a heart was filled that night with feverish unrest,
As one tall maid looked through the pane with white and heaving breast.
And many a Moorish girl was seen by revellers that night
Or running in confusion or halting from affright;
But no one saw fair Zaida, except by memory's sight;
And Zaide in the darkness, with Muza as his guide,
Hurried about the city; what a crowd was at their side!
What racket, and what riot, what shout and prank and play!
It would have had no end unless the sun had brought the day,
And now the leading revellers mustered their ranks once more;
To close the frolic with one word; "Go home; the game is o'er."

ZAIDE'S COMPLAINT

Brave Zaide paces up and down impatiently the street
Where his lady from the balcony is wont her knight to greet,
And he anxiously awaits the hour when she her face will show
Before the open lattice and speak to him below.
The Moor is filled with desperate rage, for he sees the hour is fled
When day by day the dazzling ray of sunlight gilds that head,
And he stops to brood in desperate mood, for her alone he yearns
Can aught soothe the fire of fierce desire with which his bosom burns.
At last he sees her moving with all her wonted grace,
He sees her and he hastens to their old trysting-place;
For as the moon when night is dark and clouds of tempest fly
Rises behind the dim-lit wood and lights the midnight sky,
Or like the sun when tempests with inky clouds prevail,
He merges for one moment and shows his visage pale;
So Zaida on her balcony in gleaming beauty stood,
And the knight for a moment gazed at her and checked his angry mood.
Zaide beneath the balcony with trembling heart drew near;
He halted and with upward glance spoke to his lady dear:

"Fair Moorish maiden, may thy life, by Allah guarded still,
Bring thee the full fruition of that that thou dost will;
And if the servants of thy house, the pages of my hall,
Have lied about thine honor, perdition seize them all;
For they come to me and murmur low and whisper in my ear
That thou wishest to disown me, thy faithful cavalier;
And they say that thou art pledged to one a Moor of wealth and pride,
Who will take thee to his father's house and claim thee as his bride,
For he has come to woo thee from the wide lands of his sire;
And they say that his scimitar is keen and his heart a flame of fire.
And if, fair Zaida, this is true, I kneel before thy feet
Imploring thou wilt tell me true, and fling away deceit;
For all the town is talking, still talking of our love,
And the tongues of slander, to thy blame, to my derision move."
The lady blushed, she bowed her head, then to the Moor replied:
"Dear heart of mine, of all my friends the most undoubted friend,
The time has come our friendship should have an early end;
If all, indeed, these tidings know, as you yourself declare,
Pray tell me who of all the town first laid this secret bare.
For if the life that now I lead continue, I shall die.
'Tis cheered by love, but tortured by hopeless agony.
God only knows why I the sport of cruel fate should be.
God only knows the man who says that I am false to thee.
Thou knowest well that Zaida has loved thee long and true,
Tho' her ancient lineage, Moorish knight, is more than is thy due,
And thou knowest well the loud expostulations of my sire.
Thou knowest how my mother curses me with curses dire
Because I wait for thee by day, for thee by night I wait.
Tho' far thou comest in the eve, yet dost thou tarry late.
They say to hush the common talk 'tis time that I be wed,
And to his home by some fond Moor in bridal veil be led.
Ah! many are the lovely dames, tall and of beauteous face,
Who are burning in Granada to take my envied place.

They look at thee with loving eyes and from the window call;
And, Zaide, thou deservest well the brightest of them all,
For thou thyself thine amorous eyes have turned and yet will turn
Upon the Moorish maidens who for thy embraces burn."
Then with dejected visage the Moor this answer made,
While a thousand thoughts of sorrow his valorous breast invade:
"Ah, little did I think," he said, "and little did I know
That thou, my lovely Zaida, would ever treat me so;
And little did I think thou wouldst have done this cruel deed
And by thy changeful heart would thus have made my heart to bleed.
And this for one unworthy, a man who could not claim
That thou should sacrifice to him thy love, thy life, thy name.
And art thou she who long ago, when evening veiled the sky,
Didst say to me with tender smile from the lofty balcony,
'Zaide, I am thine own, thine own, thine own I still shall be,
And thou the darling of my soul art life itself to me'?"

GUHALA'S LOVE

The bravest youth that e'er drew rein
Upon Granada's flowery plain,
A courteous knight, of gentle heart,
Accomplished in the jouster's art;
Well skilled to guide the flying steed,
And noted for each warlike deed;
And while his heart like steel was set
When foeman in the battle met,
'Twas wax before his lady's eyes
And melted at her amorous sighs;
And he was like a diamond bright
Amid the sword-thrusts of the fight,
And in the zambra's festive hour
Was gracious as the summer's flower.
In speech he showed the generous mind,
Where wit and wisdom were combined;

And, while his words no envy woke,
He weighed each sentence that he spoke.
And yet his mantle was of blue,
And tinged with sorrow's violet hue;
For fair Guhala, Moorish maid,
Her spell upon his heart had laid;
And thus his cape of saffron bare
The color emblem of despair;
On turban and on tassel lie
The tints that yield an August sky;
For anxious love was in his mind;
And anxious love is ever blind.
With scarce a word did he forsake
The lady pining for his sake;
For, when the festal robe he wore,
Her soul the pall of sorrow wore.
And now he journeyed on his way
To Jaen, for the jousting day,
And to Guhala, left alone,
All relic of delight was gone.
Tho' the proud maid of matchless face
A thousand hearts would fain embrace,
She loved but one, and swiftly ran
And spake her mind to Arbolan.
"O Arbolan, my Moor, my own,
Surely thy love is feeble grown!
The least excuse can bid thee part,
And tear with pain this anxious heart.
Oh, that it once were granted me
To mount my steed and follow thee;
How wouldst thou marvel then to see
That courage of true love in me,
Whose pulse so feebly throbs in thee."
Thus to see Arbolan depart
So fills with grief Guhala's heart.
The Moorish maid, while on he sped,
Lies sickening on her mournful bed.
Her Moorish damsels strive to know
The secret of this sudden blow;
They ask the cause that lays her low;

They seek the sad disease to heal,
Whose cause her feigning words conceal.
And less, indeed, the doubling folds
The Moor within his turban holds,
Than are the wiles Guhala's mind
In search of secrecy can find.
To Zara only, whom she knows,
Sole friend amid a ring of foes,
The sister of her lover leal,
She will the secret cause reveal.
And seeking an occasion meet
To tell with truth and tongue discreet,
While from her eyes the tear-drops start,
She opens thus her bleeding heart:
"O Zara, Zara, to the end,
Thou wilt remain my faithful friend.
How cruel is the lot I bear,
Thy brother's peril makes me fear!
'Tis for his absence that I mourn.
I sicken, waiting his return!"
Such were the words Guhala said.
The love-lorn and afflicted maid
Nor further power and utterance found,
But, fainting, sank upon the ground;
For strength of love had never art
To fill with life a pining heart.

AZARCO OF GRANADA

Azarco left his heart behind
  When he from Seville passed,
And winsome Celindaja
  As hostage held it fast.
The heart which followed with the Moor
  Was lent him by the maid,
And at their tearful parting,
  "Now guard it well," she said.
"O light of my distracted eyes,
  When thou hast reached the fight,

In coat of double-proof arrayed,
  As fits a gallant knight,
Let loyal love and constancy
  Be thy best suit of mail,
In lonely hours of absence,
  When faith is like to fail.
The Moorish girls whom thou shalt meet
  Are dazzling in their grace,
Of peerless wit and generous heart,
  And beautiful of face.
These in the dance may lure thy heart
  To think of me no more,
But none will e'er adore thee
  As I, thy slave, adore.
For to live lonely without thee
  Untouched by jealous fear,
Is more than my poor heart can brook,
  Thou art to me so dear.
If e'er in festal halls thou meet
  Some peril to my peace,
Azarco, turn thy look away,
  And check thine eyes' caprice.
For 'tis by wandering eyes the foes
  Of constancy increase.
May Allah and the prophet
  Make thy pathway safe and clear;
And may one thought be thine abroad
  And Celindaja's here."

AZARCO REBUKED

"Draw rein, draw rein one moment,
  And calm thy hurrying steed,
Who bounds beneath the furious spur
  That makes his flank to bleed.
Here would I, by my grief distraught,
  Upon the very spot,
Remind thee of the happy hours
  Thou, faithless, hast forgot.

When thou, upon thy prancing barb,
  Adown this street would pace,
And only at my window pause
  To gaze into my face.
At thought of all thy cruelty
  A stricken slave I pine;
My heart is burning since it touched
  That frozen breast of thine.
How many pledges didst thou give,
  To win me for thine own!
Our oaths were mutual; I am true,
  Whilst thou art recreant grown.
My eyes, they thrilled thee yesterday,
  To-day thou hast no fears;
For love is not alike two days
  Within a thousand years.
I thought thy name a pledge to me
  Of fondest hope; no less
That thou wouldst take as pledges true
  My kiss and soft caress.
What were thy glowing words but lures
  Thy victim's eyes to blind?
Now safe from treachery's hour I bear
  No rancor in my mind.
But better had I known the truth,
  When I desired to know,
And listened to thy pleading words,
  And read thy written vow.
Nay, give me no excuses vain,
  For none of them I ask,
Plead truth to her thou cozenest now—
  They'll serve thee in the task.
And if my counsel thou wilt take,
  Forget these eyes, this heart,
Forget my grief at thy neglect—
  Forget me—and depart."
Thus to the Moor, Azarco,
  The lovely Zaida cried,
And closed her lattice, overwhelmed
  With sorrow's rising tide.

He spurred his barb and rode away,
  Scattering the dust behind,
And cursed the star that made his heart
  Inconstant as the wind.

ADELIFA'S FAREWELL

Fair Adelifa tore her hair,
Her cheeks were furrowed o'er with care,
When brave Azarco she descried
Ascending the tall galley's side.
She flung the dust upon her head,
She wrung her lily hands and shed
Hot tears, and cursed the bitter day
That bore her heart's delight away.
"Thou, who my glory's captain art,
And general of my bleeding heart,
Guardian of every thought I know,
And sharer of my lot of woe;
Light that illumes my happy face,
The bliss of my soul's dwelling-place;
Why must thou disappear from me,
Thou glass wherein myself I see?
Azarco, bid me understand
What is it thou dost command—
Must I remain and wait for thee?
Ah, tedious will that waiting be.
To war thou farest, but I fear
Another war awaits thee here.
Thou thinkest in some rural nest
Thou'lt set me to be safe at rest.
Ah, if my absence cause thee pain,
My love attend thee on yon plain.
Thy valiant arms' unaided might
Shall win thee victory in the fight.
My faith, Azarco, is thy shield;
It will protect thee in the field.
Thou shalt return with victory,
For victory embarks with thee.

But thou wilt say, Azarco dear,
That women's lightness is to fear.
As with armed soldiers, so you find,
Each woman has a different mind.
And none shall ever, without thee,
Me in the dance or revel see;
Nor to the concert will I roam,
But stay in solitude at home.
The Moorish girls shall never say
I dress in robes of holiday;
'Twere vain to make the body fine
Whose soul is on the sea with thine."
With this Celinda came in sight,
Bahata's sister tall and bright;
This to an end her farewell brought,
But not her dark and anxious thought.

AZARCO'S FAREWELL

"Now saddle me the silver gray,
  The steed of noble race,
And give to me the shield of Fez,
  And my strong corslet lace;
Give me a double-headed lance,
  With points of temper fine;
And, with the casque of stubborn steel,
  That purple cap of mine.
Its plumes unite the saffron's tint
  With heron's crest of snow,
And one long spray of fluttering gray.
  Then give it e'er I go,
And I'll put on the hood of blue
  That Celin's daughter fair,
My Adelifa, best-beloved,
  Once gave to me to wear.
And the square boss of metal bring,
  That circling boughs entwine
With laurels, in whose leaves of gold
  The clustered emeralds shine.

Adonis, hastening to the hunt,
  His heavenly mistress shuns,
The mountain boars before him flee,
  And, 'Die,' the motto runs."
'Twas thus the Moor Azarco spoke,
  Just as the war begun,
To stout Almoralife
  Of Baza, Zelma's son.
Almoralife, brave and wise,
  Full many a minstrel sings,
A knight who in Granada
  Was counted with its kings.
And when they bring the boss of gold
  He heaves a thousand sighs
O'er brave Adonis and his doom,
  Who by the wild boar dies.
"O Adelifa, soul of mine,
  Rejoice, and murmur not,
Up to the end be merry,
  When worms shall be thy lot.
My day of life must needs be short,
  Thy firmness must be long;
Although thou art a woman,
  Unlike thy sex, be strong.
Be not like Venus, tho' in form
  Thou art indeed her peer,
For she forgot in absence,
  And did to death her dear.
And when alone, upon my face
  And likeness fix thine eyes,
And none admit to do me wrong,
  And thy soft heart surprise.
'Twixt sadness and repining
  Love runs his changing way,
The gay he oft makes sorrowful,
  The sorrowful makes gay.
Then, mark, love, in my portrait mark,
  The wide eyes' mute appeal,
For this enchanted painting
  Can speak and breathe and feel.

Think how those eyes shed many a tear,
When for thy face they yearn;
And let those tears thy patience win
To tarry my return."
At this Galvano came to say
That ship and favoring gale
Awaited him, and all his host
Were eager to set sail.
The Moor went forth to victory,
He was not pleasure's slave;
His gallant heart was ever prompt
To keep the pledge he gave.

CELINDA'S COURTESY

Azarco on his balcony
With humble Cegri stood.
He talked, and Cegri listened
In a sad and listless mood;
For of his own exploits he read,
Writ in an open scroll,
But envious Cegri heard the tale
With rage and bitter dole.
And thro' Elvira's gate, where spreads
A prospect wide and free,
He marked how Phœbus shot his rays
Upon the Spanish sea;
And bending to the land his eye
To notice how the scene
Of summer had its color changed
To black from radiant green,
He saw that, thro' the gate there passed
A light that was not day's,
Whose splendor, like a dazzling cloud,
Eclipsed the solar rays.
That presence changed the tint of earth,
Drew off the dusky veil,
And turned to living verdure
The leafage of the dale.

"Till now," Azarco said, "the scene
Has filled my heart with pain;
'Tis freshened by Celinda's face,
Or passion turns my brain.
Ah, well may men her beauty praise,
For its transcendent might
Elates the human spirit,
And fills it with delight."
And as he saw her coming in,
The Moor his bonnet doffed,
And bowed to do her honor,
And spoke in accents soft.
Celinda court'sied to the ground,
Such favor was not slight,
Her kindly greeting gratified
The fond hopes of the knight.
And glad and gloomy, each in turn,
For such a quick success,
He checked a thousand words of love,
That might his joy express.
And following her with eager eyes—
"I owe thee much," said he,
"Who dost reward with such a boon
My merest courtesy.
That favor, tho' unmerited,
Sweet lady, shall remain
Counted among those choicest gifts
Our reckoning cannot gain.
Its memory shall suffice to chase
The grinding pangs of care;
And softening turn the ills of life
To glory's guerdon rare."
On this Celinda took her leave,
And vanished from his view,
And, thinking proudly of her smile,
Azarco straight withdrew.

GAZUL'S DESPONDENCY

Scarce half a league from Gelva the knight dismounted stood,
Leaning upon his upright spear, and bitter was his mood.
He thought upon Celinda's curse, and Zaida's fickle mind,
" Ah, Fortune, thou to me," he cried, " hast ever proved unkind."
And from his valiant bosom burst a storm of angry sighs,
And acts and words of anguish before his memory rise.
" Celinda's loss I count as naught, nor fear her wicked will;
I were a fool, thus cursed by her, to love the lady still."
In rage from out the sod he drew his spear-head, as he spoke,
And in three pieces shivered it against a knotted oak.
He tore away the housings that 'neath his saddle hang,
He rent his lady's favor as with a lion's fang—
The silken ribbon, bright with gold, which in his crest he bore,
By loved Celinda knotted there, now loved by him no more.
He drew, as rage to madness turned, her portrait from his breast;
He spat on it, and to that face derisive jeers addressed.
" Why should I dress in robes of joy, whose heart is wounded sore,
By curses, that requite so ill the duteous love I bore?
Stripped as I am of every hope, 'tis better I go bare,
For the black mantle of my soul is but tormenting care;
I vengeance take on yonder oak, pierced by my lance's steel—
I dote, for, ah! the trees I wound, cannot, like women, feel."
He took the bridle off his steed, " Roam as thou wilt," said he.
" As I gave Zaida her release, I give release to thee."
The swift horse galloped out of sight; in melancholy mood,
The knight, unhorsed and helmetless, his lonely path pursued.

GAZUL IN LOVE

Not greater share did Mars acquire of trophies and renown,
Than great Gazul took with him from Gelva's castled town;
And when he to Sanlucar came his lady welcomed him,
His cup of happiness at last was beaded to the brim.

Alone the joyful lovers stood within a garden glade;
Amid the flowers, those happy hours fled to the evening shade.
With fingers deft Celinda wove a wreath, in which were set
The rose's rudy petals and the scented mignonette.
She plaited him a baldric, with violets circled round,
For violets are for lovers, and with this his waist she bound.
And then the flowery garland she tied upon his head,
"Thy face is delicate and fair as Ganymede's," she said;
"And if great Jove beheld thee now, he'd send his eagle down,
To take thee to the palace halls that high Olympus crown."
The brave Gazul his lady took and kissed her with a smile;
"She could not be so fair," said he, "the girl, who by her guile
Brought ruin on the Trojan realm, and set its towers afire,
As thou art, lady of my heart and queen of my desire."
"If I, indeed, seem fair to thee, then let the bridal rite
Me and the husband of my heart for evermore unite."
"Ah, mine will be the gain," he said, and kissed her with delight.

CELINDA'S INCONSTANCY

Gazul, like some brave bull that stands at bay to meet his fate,
Has fled from fair Celinda's frown and reached Sanlucar's gate.
The Moor bestrides a sorrel mare, her housings are of gray,
The desperate Moor is clad in weeds that shall his grief display.
The white and green that once he wore to sable folds give room,
Love's purple tints are now replaced by those of grief and gloom.
His Moorish cloak is white and blue, the blue was strewn with stars,
But now a covering like a cloud the starry radiance mars.
And from his head with stripes of black his silken streamers flow,
His bonnet blue he dyes anew in tints of grief and woe.
Alone are seen the tints of green upon his sword-belt spread,
For by that blade the blood of foes in vengeance shall be shed.
The color of the mantle which on his arm he bore
Is like the dark arena's dust when it is drenched in gore.

Black as the buskins that he wears, and black his stirrup's steel,
And red with rust of many a year the rowels at his heel.
He bears not lance or headed spear, for that which once he bore
Was shivered into splinters beside Celinda's door.
He bears a rounded target, whose quarterings display
The full moon darting through the clouds her ineffectual ray.
For though her orb be full the clouds eclipse her silver light;
The motto: "Fair but cruel, black-hearted though so bright."
And as Celinda stripped the wings which on adventure brave
Sustained his flight—no more shall plume above his helmet
    wave.
'Twas noon one Wednesday when Gazul to Gelva's portal
    came,
And straight he sought the market-place to join the jousting
    game;
The ruler of the city looked at him with surprise,
And never lady knew the knight, so dark was his disguise.
As they had been as soft as wax, he pierced the targets through
With javelins of the hollow cane that in the vega grew;
Not one could stand before the Moor; the tilters turned and
    fled,
For by his exploits was revealed the warrior's name of dread.
The lists were in confusion, but calm was on his brow,
As, lifting up his eyes to heaven, he breathed a desperate vow;
"Would God the malediction of Celinda had come true!
And the spears of my assailant had pierced my bosom through!
And that the dames who pitied me had cursed me where I
    stand!
And bravely falling I became a hero of the land!
That never succor came to me, for that were rapture high
To her the angry lioness who prays that I may die!"
He spoke, he spurred his courser fleet, and started for the
    plain,
And swore within Celinda's sight he'd ne'er return again.

THE BULL-FIGHT

The zambra was but ended, and now Granada's King
Abdeli called his court to sit on Vivarrambla's ring;
Of noble line the bride and groom whose nuptials bade prepare,
The struggle between valiant knights and bulls within the square.
And, when on the arena the mighty bull was freed,
Straight to the deadly conflict one warrior spurred his steed;
His mantle was of emerald of texture damascene,
And hope was in his folded hood as in his mantle green;
Six squires went with him to the ring beside their lord to stand;
Their livery was brilliant green, so did their lord command.
Hope was the augury of his love; hope's livery he wore;
Yet at his side each squire of his a trenchant rapier bore.
Each rapier true was black in hue and sheathed in silver ore;
At once the people knew the knight from his audacious mien—
Gazul the brave was recognized as soon as he was seen!
With graceful dignity he took his station on the sand,
And like a second Mars he seized his rapier in his hand;
With courage strong he eyed the bull, who pawed the ground till high
The dust of the arena was mingled with the sky.
All at the sight were terrified, and now with deadly speed,
His horns as keen as points of steel, he rushes at the steed.
The brave Gazul was on the watch, to ward the threatened blow,
And save his steed, and with one stroke to lay the assailant low.
The valiant bull, with lowered head advancing to the strife,
Felt from skilled hand the tempered brand pierce to his very life.
Deep wounded to the gory ground, where he had stoutly stood,
The hornèd warrior sank at last, bathed in his own heart's blood.
Still, on his ruddy couch he lay, his courage quenched at last.
At this exploit the plaudits of the assembly filled the blast;
They hailed the knight whose bravery and skill had done the deed,

And slain the hero of the ring, and saved his goodly steed,
And done such pleasure to the King, and to Celinda fair,
To the Queen of Spain and all her train who sat assembled there.

LOVERS RECONCILED

Soon as in rage Celinda had closed her lattice fast
And scorned the Moor ungrateful for his service in the past,
Her passion with reflection turns and in repentance ends;
She longs to see the Moor again and make to him amends;
For in the dance of woman's love through every mood they range
And those whose hearts are truest are given most to change.
And when she saw the gallant knight before the people all
Shiver his lance to splinters against her palace wall,
And when she saw his cloak of green was changed to mourning gray,
She straightway took her mantle with silver buttons gay,
She took her hood of purple pleached with the gold brocade,
Whose fringes and whose borders were all in pearls arrayed,
She brought a cap with sapphires and emeralds bespread;
The green was badge of hope, the blue of jealous rancor dead.
With waving plumes of green and white she decked a snowy hood,
And armed with double heads of steel a lance of orange-wood—
For colors of the outer man denote the inner mood.
A border too of brilliant green around a target set,
The motto this, " 'Tis folly a true lover to forget."
And first she learned where bold Gazul was entertained that day,
And they told her how his coming had put off the tilters' play,
And at her pleasure-house she bade him meet her face to face;
And they told him how Celinda longed for his loved embrace,
And thrice he asked the messenger if all were not a jest,
For oft 'tis dangerous to believe the news we love the best,
For lovers' hopes are often thorns of rancor and unrest.
They told him that the words were true; and without further speech

The glory of his lady's eyes he sallied forth to reach.
He met her in a garden where sweet marjoram combined
With azure violets a scent that ravished every wind.
The musk and jasmine mingled in leaf and branch and flower,
Building about the lovers a cool and scented bower.
The white leaf matched her lily skin, the red his bounding heart.
For she was beauty's spotless queen, he valor's counterpart.
For when the Moor approached her he scarcely raised his eye,
Dazed by the expectation that she had raised so high.
Celinda with a trembling blush came forth and grasped his hand;
They talked of love like travellers lost in a foreign land.
Then said the Moor, "Why give me now love's sweetest paths to trace,
Who in thy absence only live on memories of thy face?
If thou should speak of Xerez," he said with kindling eye,
"Now take my lance, like Zaida's spouse this moment let me die,
And may I some day find thee in a rival's arms at rest,
And he by all thy arts of love be tenderly caressed;
Unless the Moor whose slander made me odious in thy eyes
In caitiff fraud and treachery abuse thine ear with lies."
The lady smiled, her heart was light, she felt a rapture new;
And like each flower that filled their bower the love between them grew,
For little takes it to revive the love that is but true;
And aided by his lady's hand he hastes her gems to don,
And on his courser's back he flings a rich caparison,
A head-stall framed of purple web and studded o'er with gold;
And purple plumes and ribbons and gems of price untold;
He clasped the lady to his heart, he whispered words of cheer,
And then took horse to Gelva to join the tilting there.

CALL TO ARMS

What time the sun in ocean sank, with myriad colors fair,
And jewels of a thousand hues tinted the clouds of air,
Brave Gazul at Acala, with all his host, drew rein—
They were four hundred noblemen, the stoutest hearts in Spain—
And scarcely had he reached the town when the command was given:
"Now let your shots, your cross-bows, sound to the vault of heaven!
Let kettle-drums and trumpets and clarions blend their strain;
Zulema, Tunis' King, now lands upon the coast of Spain,
And with him ride, in arms allied, Marbello and his train."

And though at night he entered no torch or lamp he hath,
For glorious Celinda is the sun upon his path;
And as he enters in the town at once the word is given:
"Now let your shots, your cross-bows, sound to the vault of heaven!
Let kettle-drums and trumpets and clarions blend their strain;
Zulema, Tunis' King, now lands upon the coast of Spain,
And with him ride, in arms allied, Marbello and his train."

Gazul dismounted from his steed and hastened to his bride;
She sat there mournful and alone and at his sight she sighed;
He flung his arms about the girl; she shrank from his embrace,
And while he looked in wonder, she hid her blushing face;
He said, "And can it be that thou should'st shrink from my embrace?"
Before she answered with one voice the air around was riven—
"Now let your shots, your cross-bows, sound to the vault of heaven!
Let kettle-drums and trumpets and clarions blend their strain;
Zulema, Tunis' King, now lands upon the coast of Spain,
And with him ride, in arms allied, Marbello and his train."

" Ah, traitor," she replied to him, " four months wert thou
away,
And I in vain expected some tidings day by day."
And humbly did the Moor reply, " Do I deserve the blame?
Who drops the lance to take the pen, he does a deed of shame."
They sank into each other's arms just as the word was given:
" Now let your shots, your cross-bows, sound to the vault of
heaven!
Let kettle-drums and trumpets and clarions blend their
strain;
Zulema, Tunis' King, now lands upon the coast of Spain,
And with him ride, in arms allied, Marbello and his train."

GAZUL CALUMNIATED

Gazul, despairing, issues
From high Villalba's gate,
Cursing the evil fortune
That left him desolate.
Unmoved he in Granada saw
What feuds between the foes
The great Abencerrajes
And the Andallas rose.
He envied not the Moors who stood
In favor with the King!
He did not crave the honors
That rank and office bring.
He only cared that Zaida,
Her soft heart led astray
By lying words of slander,
Had flung his love away.
And thinking on her beauteous face,
Her bearing proud and high,
The bosom of the valiant Moor
Heaved with a mournful sigh.
" And who has brought me this disdain,
And who my hope betrayed,
And thee, the beauteous Zaida,
False to thy purpose made?

And who has caused my spoils of war,
  The palm and laurel leaf,
To wither on my forehead, bowed
  Beneath the load of grief?
'Tis that some hearts of treachery black
  With lies have crossed thy way,
And changed thee to a lioness,
  By hunters brought to bay.
O tongues of malediction!
  O slanderers of my fame!
Thieves of my knightly honor!
  Ye lay up naught but shame.
Ye are but citadels of fraud,
  And castles of deceit;
When ye your sentence pass, ye tread
  The law beneath your feet.
May Allah on your cruel plots
  Send down the wrath divine,
That ye my sufferings may feel,
  In the same plight as mine.
And may ye learn, ye pitiless,
  How heavy is the rod
That brings on human cruelty
  The chastisement of God.
Ye who profess in word and deed
  The path of truth to hold
Are viler than the nightly wolves
  That waste the quiet fold."
So forth he rode, that Moorish knight,
  Consumed by passion's flame,
Scorned and repulsed by Zaida,
  The lovely Moorish dame.
Then spake he to the dancing waves
  Of Tagus' holy tide,
"Oh, that thou hadst a tongue, to speak
  My story far and wide!
That all might learn, who gaze on thee
  At evening, night, or morn,
Westward to happy Portugal,
  The sufferings I have borne."

GAZUL'S DESPAIR

Upon Sanlucar's spacious square
  The brave Gazul was seen,
Bedecked in brilliant array
  Of purple, white, and green.
The Moor was starting for the joust,
  Which many a warrio brings
To Gelva, there to celebrate
  The truce between the kings.
A fair Moor maiden he adored,
  A daughter of the brave,
Who struggled at Granada's siege;
  Granada was their grave.
And eager to accost the maid,
  He wandered round the square;
With piercing eyes he peered upon
  The walls that held the fair.
And for an hour, which seemed like years,
  He watched impatient there;
But when he saw the lady mount
  Her balcony, he thought,
That the long hour of waiting
  That vision rendered short.
Dismounting from his patient steed,
  In presence of his flame,
He fell upon his knees and kissed
  The pavement in her name.
With trembling voice he spoke to her,
  "I cannot, cannot meet,
In any joust where you are near,
  Disaster and defeat.
Of yore I lived without a heart,
  Kinsmen, or pedigree;
But all of these are mine, if thou
  Hast any thought of me.
Give me some badge, if not that thou
  Mayst recognize thy knight,
At least to deck him, give him strength,

And succor in the fight."
Celinda heard in jealous doubt;
For some, with envious art,
Had told her that fair Zaida still
Ruled o'er the warrior's heart.
She answered him in stormy rage:
"If in the joust thou dost engage
With such success as I desire,
And all thy broken oaths require,
Thou wilt not reach Sanlucar's square
So proud as when thou last wert there.
But there shalt meet, disconsolate,
Eyes bright with love and dark with hate.
God grant that in the deadly joust
The enemies that thou hast roused,
May hurl at thee the unparried dart
And pierce thee, liar, to the heart.
Thy corpse within thy mantle bound
May horses trail along the ground.
Thou comest thy revenge to seek,
But small the vengeance thou shalt wreak.
Thy friends shall no assistance yield;
Thy foes shall tread thee in the field;
For thou the woman-slayer, then,
Shall meet thy final fate from men.
Those damsels whom thou hast deceived
Shall feel no pang of grief;
Their aid was malediction,
Thy death is their relief.
The Moor was true in heart and soul,
He thought she spake in jest.
He stood up in his stirrups,
Her hand he would have pressed.
"Lady," he said, "remember well
That Moor of purpose fierce and fell
On whom my vengeance I did wreak
Hast felt the curse that now you speak.
And as for Zaida, I repent
That love of mine on her was spent.
Disdain of her and love of thee

Now rule my soul in company.
The flame in which for her I burned
To frost her cruelty has turned.
Three cursed years, to win her smile,
  In knightly deeds I wrought,
And nothing but her treachery
  My faithful service brought,
She flung me off without a qualm,
  Because my lot was poor,
And gave, because the wretch was rich,
  Her favor to a Moor."
Celinda as these words she heard
Impatiently the lattice barred,
And to the lover's ardent sight
It seemed that heaven was quenched in night.
A page came riding up the street,
Bringing the knight his jennets fleet,
With plumes and harness all bedight
And saddled well with housings bright;
The lance which he on entering bore
Brandished the knight with spirit sore,
  And dashed it to the wall,
And head and butt, at that proud door,
  In myriad fragments fall.
He bade them change from green to gray
  The plumes and harness borne that day
By all the coursers of his train.
  In rage disconsolate,
He rode from Gelva, nor drew rein
  Up to Sanlucar's gate.

VENGEANCE OF GAZUL

Not Rodamont the African,
  The ruler of Argel,
And King of Zarza's southern coast,
  Was filled with rage so fell,
When for his darling Doralice
  He fought with Mandricard,

As filled the heart of bold Gazul
  When, past Sidonia's guard,
He sallied forth in arms arrayed,
  With courage high prepared
To do a deed that mortal man
  Never before had dared.
It was for this he bade them bring
  His barb and coat of mail;
A sword and dusky scabbard
  'Neath his left shoulder trail;
In Fez a Christian captive
  Had forged it, laboring
At arms of subtile temper
  As bondsman of the King.
More precious 'twas to bold Gazul
  Than all his realms could bring.
A tawny tinted *alquizel*
  Beneath his arms he wore;
And, to conceal his thoughts of blood,
  No towering spear he bore.
He started forth for Jerez,
  And hastening on his course,
Trampled the vega far and wide
  With hoof-prints of his horse.
And soon he crossed the splashing ford
  Of Guadelate's tide,
Hard by the ancient haven
  Upon the valley-side.
They gave the ford a famous name
  The waters still retain,
Santa Maria was it called,
  Since Christians conquered Spain.
The river crossed, he spurred his steed,
  Lest he might reach the gate
Of Jarez at an hour unfit,
  Too early or too late.
For Zaida, his own Zaida,
  Had scorned her lover leal,
Wedding a rich and potent Moor
  A native of Seville;

The nephew of a castellan,
  A Moorish prince of power,
Who in Seville was seneschal
  Of castle and of tower.
By this accursed bridal
  Life's treasure he had lost;
The Moor had gained the treasure,
  And now must pay the cost.
The second hour of night had rung
  When, on his gallant steed,
He passed thro' Jerez' gate resolved
  Upon a desperate deed.
And lo! to Zaida's dwelling
  With peaceful mien he came,
Pondering his bloody vengeance
  Upon that house of shame.
For he will pass the portal,
  And strike the bridegroom low;
But first must cross the wide, wide court,
  Ere he can reach his foe.
And he must pass the crowd of men,
  Who in the courtyard stand,
Lighting the palace of the Moor,
  With torches in their hand.
And Zaida in the midst comes forth,
  Her lover at her side;
He has come, amid his groomsmen,
  To take her for his bride.
And bold Gazul feels his heart bound
  With fury at the sight;
A lion's rage is in his soul,
  His brow is black as night.
But now he checks his anger,
  And gently on his steed
Draws near, with smile of greeting,
  That none may balk the deed.
And when he reached the bridal,
  Where all had taken their stand,
Upon his mighty sword-hilt
  He sudden laid his hand;

And in a voice that all could hear
  "Base craven Moor," said he,
"The sweet, the lovely Zaida
  Shall ne'er be bride to thee.
And count me not a traitor, I
  Defy thee face to face,
Lay hand upon thy scimitar
  If thou hast heart of grace."
And with these words he dealt one stroke,
  A cruel stroke and true,
It reached the Moor, it struck his heart
  And pierced it through and through.
Down fell the wretch, that single stroke
  Had laid him with the dead—
"Now let him die for all his deeds,"
  The assembled people said.
Gazul made bravely his defence,
  And none could check his flight;
He dashed his rowels in his steed,
  And vanished in the night.

GAZUL AND ALBENZAIDE

"Tho' thou the lance can hurl as well
  As one a reed might cast,
Talk not of courage for thy crimes
  Thy house's honor blast.
Seek not the revel or the dance,
  Loved by each Moorish dame.
The name of valor is not thine,
  Thou hast a coward's name;
And lay aside thy mantle fair
  Thy veil and gaberdine,
And boast no more of gold and gems—
  Thou hast disgraced thy line.
And see thine arms, for honor fit,
  Are cheap and fashioned plain;
Yet such that he whose name is lost
  May win it back again.

And Albenzaide keep thy tastes
  Proportioned to thy state;
For oft from unrestrained desires
  Spring hopes infatuate.
Flee from thy thoughts, for they have wings,
  Whose light ambition lifts
Thy soul to empty altitudes,
  Where purpose veers and drifts.
Fling not thyself into the sea,
  From which the breezes blow
Now with abrupt disdain, and now
  With flattering whispers low.
For liberty once forfeited
  Is hard to be regained,
And hardest, when the forfeit falls
  On heart and hand unstained."
Thus spake Gazul, the Moorish lord
  Of fame and honor bright;
Yet, as a craven beggar,
  Fair Zaida scorned the knight.

GAZUL'S ARMS

"Now scour for me my coat of mail,
  Without delay, my page,
For, so grief's fire consumes me,
  Thy haste will be an age;
And take from out my bonnet
  The verdant plumes of pride,
Which once Azarco gave me,
  When he took to him his bride.
And in their place put feathers black,
  And write this motto there:
'Heavy as lead is now his heart,
  Oppressed with a leaden care.'
And take away the diamonds,
  And in their place insert
Black gems, that shall to all proclaim
  The deed that does me hurt,

For if thou take away those gems
  It will announce to all
The black and dismal lot that does
  Unfortuned me befall.
And give to me the buskins plain,
  Decked by no jewels' glow,
For he to whom the world is false
  Had best in mourning go.
And give to me my lance of war,
  Whose point is doubly steeled,
And, by the blood of Christians,
  Was tempered in the field.
For well I wish my goodly blade
  Once more may burnished glow;
And if I can to cleave in twain
  The body of my foe.
And hang upon my baldric,
  The best of my ten swords.
Black as the midnight is the sheath,
  And with the rest accords.
Bring me the horse the Christian slave
  Gave to me for his sire,
At Jaen; and no ransom
  But that did I require.
And even though he be not shod,
  Make haste to bring him here;
Though treachery from men I dread,
  From beasts I have no fear.
The straps with rich enamel decked
  I bid you lay aside;
And bind the rowels to my heel
  With thongs of dusky hide."
Thus spake aloud the brave Gazul,
  One gloomy Tuesday night;
Gloomy the eve, as he prepared
  For victory in the fight.
For on that day the news had come
  That his fair Moorish maid
Had wedded with his bitterest foe,

The hated Albenzaide.
The Moor was rich and powerful,
But not of lineage high,
His wealth outweighed with one light maid
Three years of constancy.
Touched to the heart, on hearing this,
He stood in arms arrayed,
Nor strange that he, disarmed by love,
'Gainst love should draw his blade.
And Venus, on the horizon,
Had shown her earliest ray
When he Sidonia left, and straight
To Jerez took his way.

THE TOURNAMENT

His temples glittered with the spoils and garlands of his love,
When stout Gazul to Gelvas came, the jouster's skill to prove.
He rode a fiery dappled gray, like wind he scoured the plain;
Yet all her power and mettle could a slender bit restrain;
The livery of his pages was purple, green, and red—
Tints gay as was the vernal joy within his bosom shed.
And all had lances tawny gray, and all on jennets rode,
Plumes twixt their ears; adown their flanks the costly housings flowed.
Himself upon his gallant steed carries the circling shield,
And a new device is blazoned upon its ample field.
The phœnix there is figured, on flaming nest it dies,
And from its dust and ashes again it seems to rise.
And on the margin of the shield this motto is expressed:
" 'Tis hard to hide the flames of love once kindled in the breast."
And now the ladies take their seats; each jouster mounts his steed;
From footmen and from horsemen flies fast the loaded reed.
And there appears fair Zaida, whom in a luckless day
The Moor had loved, but since, that love in loathing passed away.

Her treachery had grieved his heart, and she who did the wrong
Mourned with repentant heart amid that gay and happy throng.
And with her was Zafira, to whom her husband brings
More bliss and happiness than reign amid Granada's kings.
And when she looked at brave Gazul his deeds her grief renew;
The more she sees, the more her heart is ravished at the view.
And now she blushes with desire, now grows with envy pale;
Her heart is like the changing beam that quivers in the scale.
Alminda sees the lovely dame with sudden anguish start,
And speaks with hope she may reveal the secret of her heart.
And troubled Zaida makes reply, "A sudden thought of ill
Has flashed across my mind and caused the anguish that I feel."
"'Twere better," said Alminda, "to check thy fancy's flight,
For thought can rob the happiest hours of all their deep delight."
Then said the maid of Xerez, "To me thou showest plain
Thou hast not felt black envy's tooth nor known what is disdain.
To know it, would thy spirit move to pity my despair,
Who writhe and die from agony, in which thou hast no share."
Zafira seized the lady's hand, and silence fell around,
As mixed in loud confusion brushed the jousters to the ground.
In came the Berber tribesmen, in varied cloaks arrayed;
They ranged themselves in companies against the palisade.
The sound of barbarous trumpets rang, the startled horses reared,
And snort and neigh and tramp of hoofs on every side was heard,
Then troop meets troop, and valiant hearts the mimic fight pursue;
They hurl their javelins o'er the sand and pierce the bucklers through.
Long time the battling hosts contend, until that festive day,
The shout, the clash, the applauding cry, in silence die away.

They fain had prayed that time himself would stop Apollo's car.
They hate to see the sunset gloom, the rise of evening's star.
And even when the sun is set, he who a foe discerns,
With no less vigor to his targe the loaded javelin turns,
The onset joined, each lance discharged, the judge's voice is heard;
He bids the heralds sound a truce, and the wide lists are cleared.

ABENUMEYA'S LAMENT

The young Abenumeya, Granada's royal heir,
Was brave in battle with his foe and gallant with the fair.
By lovely Felisarda his heart had been ensnared,
The daughter of brave Ferri, the captain of the guard.
He through the vega of Genil bestrode his sorrel steed,
Alone, on melancholy thoughts his anxious soul to feed,
The tints that clothed the landscape round were gloomy as the scene
Of his past life, wherein his lot had naught but suffering been.
His mantle hue was of iron gray bestrewn with purple flowers,
Which bloomed amid distress and pain, like hope of happier hours.
And on his cloak were columns worked, (his cloak was saffron hued,)
To show that dark suspicion's fears had tried his fortitude;
His shield was blazoned with the moon, a purple streak above,
To show that fears of fickleness are ever born with love.
He bore an azure pennant 'neath the iron of his spear,
To show that lovers oft go wrong deceived by jealous fear.
The hood he wore was wrought of gold and silk of crimson clear;
His bonnet crest was a heron plume with an emerald stone beneath;
And under all a motto ran, "Too long a hope is death."
He started forth in such array, but armed from head to heel
With tempered blade and dagger and coat of twisted steel.
And hangling low at his saddle-bow was the helmet for his head;

And as he journeyed on his way the warrior sighed and said:
"O Felisarda, dearest maid, him in thy memory keep
Who in his soul has writ thy name in letters dark and deep.
Think that for thee in coat of mail he ever rides afield,
In his right hand the spear must stand, his left must grasp the shield.
And he must skirmish in the plain and broil of battle brave,
And wounded be, for weapons ne'er from jealousy can save."
And as he spoke the lonely Moor from out his mantle's fold
With many a sigh, that scorched the air, a lettered page unrolled.
He tried in vain to read it but his eyes with tears were blind,
And mantling clouds of sorrow hid the letters from his mind.
The page was moistened by the tears that flowed in plenteous tide,
But by the breath of sighs and sobs the softened page was dried.
Fresh wounds he felt at sight of it, and when the cause he sought,
His spirit to Granada flew upon the wings of thought.
He thought of Albaicin, the palace of the dame,
With its gayly gilded capitals and its walls of ancient fame.
And the garden that behind it lay in which the palm was seen
Swaying beneath the load of fruit its coronet of green.
"O mistress of my soul," he said, "who callest me thine own,
How easily all bars to bliss thy love might trample down!
But time, that shall my constancy, thy fickleness will show,
The world shall then my steadfast heart, thy tongue of treachery know.
Woe worth the day when, for thy sake, I fair Granada sought,
These anxious doubts may cloud my brow, they cannot guard thy thought.
My foes increase, thy cruelty makes absence bitterer still,
But naught can shake my constancy, and none can do me ill.
On this from Alpujarra the tocsin sounded high.
He rushed as one whose life is staked to save the maid or die.

THE DESPONDENT LOVER

He leaned upon his sabre's hilt,
  He trod upon his shield,
Upon the ground he threw the lance
  That forced his foes to yield.
His bridle hung at saddle-bow,
  And, with the reins close bound,
His mare the garden entered free
  To feed and wander round.
Upon a flowering almond-tree
  He fixed an ardent gaze;
Its leaves were withered with the wind
  That flowers in ruin lays.
Thus in Toledo's garden park,
  Did Abenamar wait,
Who for fair Galliana
  Watched at the palace gate.
The birds that clustered on the towers
  Spread out their wings to fly,
And from afar his lady's veil
  He saw go floating by.
And at this vision of delight,
  Which healed his spirit's pain,
The exiled Moor took courage,
  And hope returned again.
"O Galliana, best beloved,
  Whom art thou waiting now?
And what has treacherous rendered
  My fortune and thy vow?
Thou sweearedst I should be thine own,
  Yet 'twas but yesterday
We met, and with no greeting
  Thou wentest on thy way.
Then, in my silence of distress,
  I wandered pondering—
If this is what to-day has brought,
  What will to-morrow bring?
Happy the Moor from passion free,

In peace or turmoil born,
Who without pang of hate or love,
Can slumber till the morn.
O almond-tree, thou provest
That the expected hours
Of bliss may often turn to bane,
As fade thy dazzling flowers.
A mournful image art thou
Of all that lays me low,
And on my shield I'll bear thee
As blazon of my woe.
For thou dost bloom in many a flower,
Till blasted by the wind,
And 'tis of thee this word is true—
"The season was not kind."
He spoke and on his courser's head
He slipped the bridle rein,
And while he curbed his gentle steed
He could not curb his pain,
And to Ocana took his course,
O'er Tagus' verdant plain.

LOVE AND JEALOUSY

"Unless thou wishest in one hour
Thine April hope shouldst blighted be,
Oh, tell me, Tarfe, tell me true,
How I may Zaida chance to see.
I mean the foreigner, the wife
New wedded, her with golden hair,
And for each lock a charm besides
She counts—for she is passing fair.
Her, whom the Moorish nobles all
To heaven in their laudation raise,
Till the fine ladies of the land
Are left to languish in dispraise.
The mosque I visit every day,
And wait to see her come in sight;
I wait to see her, where the rout
And revel lengthen out the night.

However, cost me what it may,
  I cannot meet the lovely dame.
Ah, now my eyes are veiled in tears,
  Sure witness of my jealous flame.
And tell me, Tarfe, that my rage
  Has cause enough, for since I've been
Granada's guest (and would to God
  Granada I had never seen!)
My lord forsakes me every night,
  Nor till the morning comes again;
He shuns as painful my caress,
  My very presence brings him pain;
Little indeed he recks of me,
  If only he may elsewhere reign.
For if we in the garden meet,
  Or if we in the chamber be,
His actions his estrangement prove,
  He has not even words for me.
And if I say to him, 'My life!'
  He answers me, 'My dearest dear,'
Yet with a coldness that congeals
  My very heart with sudden fear.
And all the while I strive to make
  His soul reveal a traitorous thought,
He turns his back on me, as if
  To him my trembling fear was naught.
And when about his neck I cling,
  He drops his eyes and bows his face,
As if, from thought of other arms
  He longed to slip from my embrace.
His bosom heaves with discontent,
  Deep as from hell the sigh is wrenched;
My heart with dark suspicion beats,
  And all my happiness is quenched.
And if I ask of him the cause,
  He says the cause in me is found;
That I am vain, the rover I,
  And to another's bosom bound.
As if, since I have known his love,
  I at the window show my face,

Or take another's hand in mine,
  Or seek the bull-ring, joust, or race;
Or if my footsteps have been found
  To wander a suspected place,
The prophet's curse upon me fall,
  Unless to keep the nuptial pact
And serve the pleasure of my lord.
  I kept the Koran's law exact!
But wherefore should I waste the time
  These tedious questions to recall?
Thou knowest the chase on which he hies,
  And yet in silence hidest all.
Nay, swear not—I will naught believe;
  Thine oaths are but a fowler's net,
And woe betide the dame who falls
  Into the snare that thou hast set.
For men are traitors one and all;
  And all their promises betray;
Like letters on the water writ,
  They vanish, when love's fires decay.
For to fulfil thy promise fair,
  What hours thou hast the whole day long,
What chances on the open road,
  Or in the house when bolts are strong.
O God! but what a thought is this?
  I strangle, in the sudden thrall
Of this sharp pang of agony,
  Oh, hold me, Tarfe, lest I fall."
Thus Adelifa weeping cried
  At thought of Abenamar's quest:
In Moorish Tarfe's arms she fell,
  And panting lay upon his breast.

THE CAPTIVE OF TOLEDO

Upon the loftiest mountain height
  That rises in its pride,
And sees its summits mirrored
  In Tagus' crystal tide,
The banished Abenamar,
  Bound by a captive chain,
Looks on the high-road to Madrid
  That seams the dusty plain.
He measures, with his pining eyes,
  The stretching hills that stand
Between his place of banishment
  And his sweet native land.
His sighs and tears of sorrow
  No longer bear restraint,
And thus in words of anguish
  He utters his complaint:
"Oh, dismal is the exile
  That wrings the heart with woes
And locks the lips in silence,
  Amid unfeeling foes.

O road of high adventure,
  That leadest many a band
To yon ungrateful country where
  My native turrets stand,
The country that my valor
  Did oft with glory crown,
The land that lets me languish here,
  Who won for her renown.
Thou who hast succored many a knight,
  Hast thou no help for me,
Who languish on Toledo's height
  In captive misery?
'Tis on thy world-wide chivalry
  I base my word of blame,
'Tis that I love thee most of all,
  Thy coldness brings me shame.

Oh, dismal is the exile,
  That wrings my heart with woes,
And locks my lips in silence
  Among unfeeling foes.

The warden of fierce Reduan
  With cruelty more deep
That that of a hidalgo,
  Has locked this prison keep;
And on this frontier set me,
  To pine without repose,
To watch, from dawn to sunset,
  Over his Christian foes.
Here like a watch-tower am I set
  For Santiago's lord,
And for a royal mistress
  Who breaks her plighted word.
And when I cry with anguish
  And seek in song relief,
With threats my life is threatened,
  Till silence cloak my grief.
Oh, dismal is the exile,
  That wrings my heart with woes,
And locks my lips in silence
  Among unfeeling foes.

And when I stand in silence,
  Me dumb my jailers deem,
And if I speak, in gentle words,
  They say that I blaspheme.
Thus grievously perverting
  The sense of all I say,
Upon my lips the raging crowd
  The gag of silence lay.
Thus heaping wrong on wrong my foes
  Their prisoner impeach,
Until the outrage of my heart
  Deprives my tongue of speech.
And while my word the passion
  Of my sad heart betrays,

My foes are all unconscious
  Of what my silence says.
Now God confound the evil judge
  Who caused my misery,
And had no heart of pity
  To soften his decree.
Oh, dismal is the exile,
  That wrings my heart with woes,
And locks my lips in silence
  Among unfeeling foes.

THE BLAZON OF ABENAMAR

By gloomy fortune overcast,
  Vassal of one he held in scorn,
Complaining of the wintry world,
  And by his lady left forlorn,
The wretched Abenamar mourned,
  Because his country was unkind,
Had brought him to a lot of woe,
  And to a foreign home resigned.
A stranger Moor had won the throne,
  And in Granada sat in state.
Many the darlings of his soul
  He claimed with love insatiate,
He, foul in face, of craven heart,
  Had won the mistress of the knight;
Her blooming years of beauteous youth
  Were Abenamar's own by right.
But royal favor had decreed
  A foreign tyrant there should reign,
For many a galley owned him lord
  And master, in the seas of Spain.
Oh, haply 'twas that Zaida's self,
  Ungrateful like her changing sex,
Had chosen this emir, thus in scorn
  Her Abenamer's soul to vex.
This was the thought that turned to tears
  The eyes of the desponding knight,

As on his sufferings past he thought,
  His labors and his present plight;
His hopes, to disappointment turned;
  His wealth, now held in alien hands,
His agony o'er love betrayed,
  Lost honor, confiscated lands.
And as his loyalty had met
  Such ill requital from the King,
He called his page and bade him straight
  A limner deft before him bring.
For he would have him paint at large,
  In color, many a new device
And write his sufferings on his shield.
  No single blazon would suffice.
And first a green field parched and seared;
  A coal, in myriad blazes burned,
And like his ardent hopes of yore,
  At length to dust and ashes turned.
And then a miser, rich in gold,
  Who locks away some jewel bright,
For fear the thief a gem may steal,
  Which yet can yield him no delight.
A fair Adonis done to death
  Beneath the wild boar's cruel tusk.
A wintry dawn on pallid skies,
  A summer's day that turns to dusk.
A lovely garden green and fair
  Ravaged and slashed by strokes of steel;
Or wasted in its trim parterres
  And trampled by the common heel.
So spake the brave heart-broken Moor;
  Until his tears and struggling sighs
Turned to fierce rage; the painting then
  He waited for with eager eyes.
He asks that one would fetch a steed,
  Of his good mare no more he recks,
For womankind have done him wrong,
  And she is woman in her sex.
The plumes of yellow, blue, and white
  From off his bonnet brim he tears,

He will no longer carry them;
  They are the colors Zaida wears.
He recks no more of woman's love,
  His city now he bids farewell,
And swears he will no more return
  Nor in Granada seek to dwell.

WOMAN'S FICKLENESS

A stout and valorous gentleman,
  Granada knew his worth,
And rich with many a spoil of love,
  Went Abenamar forth.
Upon his bonnet, richly dyed,
  He bore a lettered scroll,
It ran, " 'Tis only love that makes
  The solace of my soul."
His bonnet and his brow were hid
  Beneath a hood of green,
And plumes of violet and white
  Above his head were seen.
And 'twixt the tassel and the crown
  An emerald circlet shone.
The legend of the jewel said,
  "Thou art my hope alone."
He rode upon a dappled steed
  With housings richly dight,
And at his left side clanking hung
  A scimitar of might.
And his right arm was sleeved in cloth
  Of tawny lion's hue,
And at his lance-head, lifted high,
  A Turkish pennon flew.
And when he reached Daraja's camp
  He saw Daraja stand
Beside his own perfidious love,
  And clasp her by the hand.
He made to her the wonted sign,
  Then lingered for a while,

For jealous anguish filled his heart
  To see her tender smile.
He spurred his courser to the blood;
  One clattering bound he took,
The Moorish maiden turned to him.
  Ah, love was in her look!
Ah, well he saw his hopeless fate,
  And in his jealous mood
The heart that nothing feared in fight
  Was whelmed in sorrow's flood.
"O false and faithless one," he said,
  "What is it that I view?
Thus the foreboding of my soul
  I see at last come true;
Shame that a janizary vile,
  Of Christian creed and race,
A butt of bright Alhambra's feasts,
  Has taken now my place.
Where is the love thou didst avow,
  The pledge, the kiss, the tear,
And all the tender promises
  Thou whisperedst in my ear?
Thou, frailer than the withered reed,
  More changeful than the wind,
More thankless than the hardest heart
  In all of womankind;
I marvel not at what I see,
  Nor yet for vengeance call;
For thou art woman to the core,
  And in that name is all."
The gallant Moor his courser checked,
  His cheek with anger burned,
Men saw, that all his gallant mien
  To gloom and rage was turned.

KING JUAN

"Abenamar, Abenamar," said the monarch to the knight,
"A Moor art thou of the Moors, I trow, and the ladies' fond delight,
And on the day when first you lay upon your mother's breast,
On land and sea was a prodigy, to the Christians brought unrest;
The sea was still as a ruined mill and the winds were hushed to rest.
And the broad, broad moon sank down at noon, red in the stormy west.
If thus thou wert born thou well mayst scorn to ope those lips of thine,
That out should fly a treacherous lie, to meet a word of mine."
"I have not lied," the Moor replied, and he bowed his haughty head
Before the King whose wrath might fling his life among the dead.
"I would not deign with falsehood's stain my lineage to betray;
Tho' for the truth my life, in sooth, should be the price I pay.
I am son and squire of a Moorish sire, who with the Christians strove,
And the captive dame of Christian name was his fair wedded love;
And I a child from that mother mild, who taught me at her knee
Was ever told to be true and bold with a tongue that was frank and free,
That the liar's art and the caitiff heart would lead to the house of doom;
And still I must hear my mother dear, for she speaks to me from the tomb.
Then give me my task, O King, and ask what question thou mayst choose;
I will give to you the word that is true, for why should I refuse?"
"I give you grace for your open face, and the courteous words you use.

What castles are those on the hill where grows the palm-tree and the pine?
They are so high that they touch the sky, and with gold their pinnacles shine."
"In the sunset's fire there glisten, sire, Alhambra's tinted tiles;
And somewhat lower Alijire's tower upon the vega smiles,
And many a band of subtile hand has wrought its pillared aisles.
The Moor whose thought and genius wrought those works for many moons
Received each day a princely pay—five hundred gold doubloons—
Each day he left his labor deft, his guerdon was denied;
Nor less he lost than his labor cost when he his hand applied.
And yonder I see the Generalifé with its orchard green and wide;
There are growing there the apple and pear that are Granada's pride.
There shadows fall from the soaring wall of high Bermeja's tower;
It has flourished long as a castle strong, the seat of the Soldan's power."
The King had bent and his ear had lent to the words the warrior spoke,
And at last he said, as he raised his head before the crowd of folk:
"I would take thee now with a faithful vow, Granada for my bride,
King Juan's Queen would hold, I ween, a throne and crown of pride;
That very hour I would give thee dower that well would suit thy will;
Cordova's town should be thine own, and the mosque of proud Seville.
Nay, ask not, King, for I wear the ring of a faithful wife and true;
Some graceful maid or a widow arrayed in her weeds is the wife for you,
And close I cling to the Moorish King who holds me to his breast,
For well I ween it can be seen that of all he loves me best."

ABENAMAR'S JEALOUSY

Alhambra's bell had not yet pealed
Its morning note o'er tower and field;
Barmeja's bastions glittered bright,
O'ersilvered with the morning light;
When rising from a pallet blest
With no refreshing dews of rest,
For slumber had relinquished there
His place to solitary care,
Brave Abenamar pondered deep
How lovers must surrender sleep.
And when he saw the morning rise,
While sleep still sealed Daraja's eyes,
Amid his tears, to soothe his pain,
He sang this melancholy strain:
"The morn is up,
The heavens alight,
My jealous soul
Still owns the sway of night.
Thro' all the night I wept forlorn,
Awaiting anxiously the morn;
And tho' no sunlight strikes on me,
My bosom burns with jealousy.
The twinkling starlets disappear;
Their radiance made my sorrow clear;
The sun has vanished from my sight,
Turned into water is his light;
What boots it that the glorious sun
From India his course has run,
To bring to Spain the gleam of day,
If from my sight he hides away?
The morn is up,
The heavens are bright,
My jealous soul
Still owns the sway of night."

ADELIFA'S JEALOUSY

Fair Adelifa sees in wrath, kindled by jealous flames,
Her Abenamer gazed upon by the kind Moorish dames.
And if they chance to speak to him, or take him by the hand,
She swoons to see her own beloved with other ladies stand.
When with companions of his own, the bravest of his race,
He meets the bull within the ring, and braves him to his face,
Or if he mount his horse of war, and sallying from his tent
Engages with his comrades in tilt or tournament,
She sits apart from all the rest, and when he wins the prize
She smiles in answer to his smile and devours him with her eyes.
And in the joyous festival and in Alhambra's halls,
She follows as he treads the dance at merry Moorish balls.
And when the tide of battle is rising o'er the land,
And he leaves his home, obedient to his honored King's command,
With tears and lamentation she sees the warrior go
With arms heroic to subdue the proud presumptuous foe.
Though 'tis to save his country's towers he mounts his fiery steed
She has no cheerful word for him, no blessing and godspeed;

And were there some light pretext to keep him at her side,
In chains of love she'd bind him there, whate'er the land betide.
Or, if 'twere fair that dames should dare the terrors of the fight,
She'd mount her jennet in his train and follow with delight.
For soon as o'er the mountain ridge his bright plume disappears,
She feels that in her heart the jealous smart that fills her eyes with tears.
Yet when he stands beside her and smiles beneath her gaze,
Her cheek is pale with passion pure, though few the words she says.
Her thoughts are ever with him, and they fly the mountain o'er
When in the shaggy forest he hunts the bristly boar.

In vain she seeks the festal scene 'mid dance and merry song,
Her heart for Abenamar has left that giddy throng.
For jealous passion after all is no ignoble fire,
It is the child of glowing love, the shadow of desire.
Ah! he who loves with ardent breast and constant spirit must
Feel in his inmost bosom lodged the arrows of distrust.
And as the faithful lover by his loved one's empty seat
Knows that the wind of love may change e'er once again they meet,
So to this sad foreboding do fancied griefs appear
As he who has most cause to love has too most cause for fear.
And once, when placid evening was mellowing into night,
The lovely Adelifa sat with her darling knight;
And then the pent-up feeling from out her spirit's deeps
Rose with a storm of heavy sighs and trembled on her lips:
"My valiant knight, who art, indeed, the whole wide world to me,
Clear mirror of victorious arms and rose of chivalry,
Thou terror of thy valorous foe, to whom all champions yield,
The rampart and the castle of fair Granada's field,
In thee the armies of the land their bright example see,
And all their hopes of victory are founded upon thee;
And I, poor loving woman, have hope in thee no less,
For thou to me art life itself, a life of happiness.
Yet, in this anxious trembling heart strange pangs of fear arise,
Ah, wonder not if oft you see from out these faithful eyes
The tears in torrents o'er my cheek, e'en in thy presence flow.
Half prompted by my love for thee and half by fears of woe,
These eyes are like alembics, and when with tears they fill
It is the flame of passion that does that dew distil.
And what the source from which they flow, but the sorrow and the care
That gather in my heart like mist, and forever linger there.
And when the flame is fiercest and love is at its height,
The waters rise to these fond eyes, and rob me of my sight,
For love is but a lasting pain and ever goes with grief,
And only at the spring of tears the heart can drink relief.
Thus fire and love and fear combined bring to my heart distress,
With jealous rage and dark distrust alarm and fitfulness.

These rage within my bosom; they torment me till I'd weep.
By day and night without delight a lonely watch I keep.
By Allah, I beseech thee, if thou art true to me,
That when the Moorish ladies turn round and gaze on thee,
Thou wilt not glance again at them nor meet their smiling eye,
Or else, my Abenamar, I shall lay me down and die.
For thou art gallant, fair, and good; oh, soothe my heart's alarms,
And be as tender in thy love as thou art brave in arms.
And as they yield to thee the prize for valor in the field
Oh, show that thou wilt pity to thy loving lady yield."
Then Abenamar, with a smile, a kiss of passion gave.
"If it be needful," he replied, "to give the pledge you crave,
To tell thee, Adelifa, that thou art my soul's delight
And lay my inmost bosom bare before thy anxious sight,
The bosom on whose mirror shines thy face in lines of light,
Here let me ope the secret cell that thou thyself may see,
The altar and the blazing lamp that always burn for thee.
And if perchance thou art not thus released from torturing care,
Oh, see the faith, the blameless love that wait upon thee there.
And if thou dost imagine I am a perjured knight,
I pray that Allah on my head may call down bane and blight,
And when into the battle with the Christian I go
I pray that I may perish by the lances of the foe;
And when I don my armor for the toils of the campaign,
That I may never wear the palm of victory again,
But as a captive, on a shore far from Granada, pine,
While the freedom that I long to have may never more be mine.
Yes, may my foes torment me in that sad hour of need;
My very friends, for their own ends, prove worthless as a reed.
My kin deny, my fortune fly, and, on my dying day,
My very hopes of Paradise in darkness pass away.
Or if I live in freedom to see my love once more,
May I meet the fate which most I hate, and at my palace door
Find that some caitiff lover has won thee for his own,
And turn to die, of mad despair, distracted and alone.
Wherefore, my life, my darling wife, let all thy pain be cured;
Thy trust in my fidelity be from this hour assured.

No more those pearly tears of thine fall useless in the dust
No more the jealous fear distract thy bosom with mistrust.
Believe me by the oath I swear my heart I here resign,
And all I have of love and care are, Adelifa, thine.
Believe that Abenamar would his own life betray
If he had courage thus to throw life's choicest gem away."
Then Adelifa smiled on him and at the words he said,
Upon his heaving bosom her blushing cheek she laid.
And from that hour each jealous thought far from her mind
 she thrust
And confidence returned again in place of dark distrust.

FUNERAL OF ABENAMAR

The Moors of haughty Gelves have changed their gay attire.
The caftan and the braided cloak, the brooch of twisted wire,
The gaudy robes, the mantles of texture rich and rare,
The fluttering veils and tunic bright the Moors no longer wear.
And wearied is their valorous strength, their sinewy arms
 hang down;
No longer in their lady's sight they struggle for the crown.
Whether their loves are absent or glowing in their eyes,
They think no more of jealous feud nor smile nor favor prize;
For love himself seems dead to-day amid that gallant train
And the dirge beside the bier is heard and each one joins the
 strain,
And silently they stand in line arrayed in mourning black
For the dismal pall of Portugal is hung on every back.
And their faces turned toward the bier where Abenamar lies,
The men his kinsmen silent stand, amid the ladies' cries
And thousand thousands ask and look upon the Moorish
 knight,
By his coat of steel they weeping kneel, then turn them from
 the sight.
And some proclaim his deeds of fame, his spirit high and brave,
And the courage of adventure that had brought him to the
 grave.
Some say that his heroic soul pined with a jealous smart,
That disappointment and neglect had broke that mighty heart;
That all his ancient hopes gave way beneath the cloud of grief,

Until his green and youthful years were withered like a leaf;
And he is wept by those he loved, by every faithful friend,
And those who slandered him in life speak evil to the end.
They found within his chamber where his arms of battle hung
A parting message written all in the Moorish tongue:
" Dear friends of mine, if ever in Gelves I should die,
I would not that in foreign soil my buried ashes lie.
But carry me, and dig my grave upon mine own estate,
And raise no monument to me my life to celebrate,
For banishment is not more dire where evil men abound,
Than where home smiles upon you, but the good are never
found."

BALLAD OF ALBAYALDOS

Three mortal wounds, three currents red,
The Christian spear
Has oped in head and thigh and head—
Brave Albayaldos feels that death is near.

The master's hand had dealt the blow,
And long had been
And hard the fight; now in his heart's blood low
He wallows, and the pain, the pain is keen.

He raised to heaven his streaming face
And low he said:
" Sweet Jesus, grant me by thy grace,
Unharmed to make this passage to the dead.

" Oh, let me now my sins recount,
And grant at last
Into thy presence I may mount,
And thou, dear mother, think not of my past.

" Let not the fiend with fears affright
My trembling soul;
Though bitter, bitter is the night
Whose darkling clouds this moment round me roll.

"Had I but listened to your plea,
  I ne'er had met
Disaster; though this life be lost to me,
  Let not your ban upon my soul be set.

"In him, in him alone I trust,
  To him I pray,
Who formed this wretched body from the dust.
  He will redeem me in the Judgment Day.

"And Muza, one last service will I ask,
  Dear friend of mine:
Here, where I died, be it thy pious task
  To bury me beneath the tall green pine.

"And o'er my head a scroll indite, to tell
  How, on this sod,
Fighting amid my valiant Moors, I fell.
  And tell King Chico how I turned to God,

"And longed to be a Christian at the last,
  And sought the light,
So that the accursed Koran could not cast
  My soul to suffer in eternal night."

THE NIGHT RAID OF REDUAN

Two thousand are the Moorish knights that 'neath the banner stand
Of mighty Reduan, as he starts in ravage thro' the land.
With pillage and with fire he wastes the fields and fruitful farms,
And thro' the startled border-land is heard the call to arms;
By Jaen's towers his host advance and, like a lightning flash,
Ubeda and Andujar can see his horsemen dash,
    While in Baeza every bell
      Does the appalling tidings tell,
      "Arm! Arm!"
      Rings on the night the loud alarm.

So silently they gallop, that gallant cavalcade,
The very trumpet's muffled tone has no disturbance made.
It seems to blend with the whispering sound of breezes on their way,
The rattle of their harness and the charger's joyous neigh.
But now from hill and turret high the flaming cressets stream
And watch-fires blaze on every hill and helm and hauberk gleam.
From post to post the signal along the border flies
And the tocsin sounds its summons and the startled burghers rise,
While in Baeza every bell
Does the appalling tidings tell,
"Arm! Arm!"
Rings on the night the loud alarm.

Ah, suddenly that deadly foe has fallen upon the prey,
Yet stoutly rise the Christians and arm them for the foe,
And doughty knights their lances seize and scour their coats of mail,
The soldier with his cross-bow comes and the peasant with his flail.
And Jaen's proud hidalgos, Andujar's yeomen true,
And the lords of towered Ubeda the pagan foes pursue;
And valiantly they meet the foe nor turn their backs in flight,
And worthy do they show themselves of their fathers' deeds of might,
While in Baeza every bell
Does the appalling tidings tell,
"Arm! Arm!"
Rings on the night the loud alarm.

The gates of dawn are opened and sunlight fills the land,
The Christians issuing from the gates in martial order stand,
They close in fight, and paynim host and Christian knights of Spain,
Not half a league from the city gate, are struggling on the plain.
The din of battle rises like thunder to the sky,
From many a crag and forest the thundering echoes fly,

And there is sound of clashing arms, of sword and rattling steel,
Moorish horns, the fife and drum, as the scattering squadrons reel,
And the dying moan and the wounded shriek for the hurt that none can heal,
While in Baeza every bell
Does the appalling tidings tell,
"Arm! Arm!"
Rings on the night the loud alarm.

SIEGE OF JAEN

Now Reduan gazes from afar on Jaen's ramparts high,
And tho' he smiles in triumph yet fear is in his eye,
And vowed has he, whose courage none charged with a default,
That he would climb the ramparts and take it by assault,
Yet round the town the towers and walls the city's streets impale,
And who of all his squadrons that bastion can scale?
He pauses until one by one his hopes have died away,
And his soul is filled with anguish and his face with deep dismay.
He marks the tall escarpment, he measures with his eye
The soaring towers above them that seem to touch the sky.
Height upon height they mount to heaven, while glittering from afar
Each cresset on the watch-towers burns like to a baleful star.
His eyes and heart are fixed upon the rich and royal town,
And from his eye the tear of grief, a manly tear, flows down.
His bosom heaves with sighs of grief and heavy discontent,
As to the royal city he makes his sad lament:
"Ah, many a champion have I lost, fair Jaen, at thy gate,
Yet lightly did I speak of thee with victory elate,
The prowess of my tongue was more than all that I could do,
And my word outstripped the lance and sword of my squadron strong and true.
And yet I vowed with courage rash thy turrets I would bring
To ruin and thy subjects make the captives of my King.

That in one night my sword of might, before the morrow's sun,
Would do for thy great citadel what centuries have not done.
I pledged my life to that attempt, and vowed that thou shouldest fall,
Yet now I stand in impotence before thy castle tall.
For well I see, before my might shall win thee for my King,
That thou, impregnable, on me wilt rout and ruin bring,
Ah, fatal is the hasty tongue that gives such quick consent,
And he who makes the hasty vow in leisure must repent.
Ah! now too late I mourn the word that sent me on this quest,
For I see that death awaits me here whilst thou livest on at rest,
For I must enter Jaen's gates a conqueror or be sent
Far from Granada's happy hills in hopeless banishment;
But sorest is the thought that I to Lindaraja swore:
If Jaen should repulse me I'd return to her no more;
No more a happy lover would I linger at her side,
Until Granada's warrior host had humbled Jaen's pride."
Then turning to his warriors, the Moorish cavalier
Asks for their counsel and awaits their answer while with fear.
Five thousand warriors tried and true the Moors were standing near,
All armed with leathern buckler, all armed with sword and spear.
"The place," they answer, "is too strong, by walls too high 'tis bound,
Too many are the watch-towers that circle it around.
The knights and proud hidalgos who on the wall are seen,
Their hearts are bold, their arms are strong, their swords and spears are keen.
Disaster will be certain as the rising of the day,
And victory and booty are a slippery prize," they say,
"It would be wise in this emprise the conflict to forego;
Not all the Moors Granada boasts could lay proud Jaen low."

THE DEATH OF REDUAN

He shrank not from his promise, did Reduan the brave,
The promise to Granada's King with daring high he gave;
And when the morning rose and lit the hills with ruddy glow,
He marshalled forth his warriors to strike a final blow.
With shouts they hurry to the walls, ten thousand fighting men—
Resolved to plant the crescent on the bulwarks of Jaen.
The bugle blast upon the air with clarion tonè is heard,
The burghers on the city wall reply with scoffing word;
And like the noise of thunder the clattering squadrons haste,
And on his charger fleet he leads his army o'er the waste.
In front of his attendants his march the hero made,
He tarried not for retinue or clattering cavalcade,
And they who blamed the rash assault with weak and coward minds
Deserted him their leader bold or loitered far behind.
And now he stands beneath the wall and sees before him rise
The object of the great campaign, his valor's priceless prize;
He dreams one moment that he holds her subject to his arms,
He dreams that to Granada he flies from war's alarms,
Each battlement he fondly eyes, each bastion grim and tall,
And in fancy sees the crescents rise above the Christian wall.
But suddenly an archer has drawn his bow of might,
And suddenly the bolt descends in its unerring flight,
Straight to the heart of Reduan the fatal arrow flies,
The gallant hero struck to death upon the vega lies.
And as he lies, from his couch of blood, in melancholy tone,
Thus to the heavens the hero stout, though fainting, makes his moan,
And ere his lofty soul in death forth from its prison breaks,
Brave Reduan a last farewell of Lindaraja takes:
"Ah, greater were the glory had it been mine to die,
Not thus among the Christians and hear their joyful cry,
But in that happy city, reclining at thy feet,
Where thou with kind and tender hands hast wove my winding-sheet.
Ah! had it been my fate once more to gaze upon thy face,

And love and pity in those eyes with dying glance to trace,
Altho' a thousand times had death dissolved this mortal frame,
Soon as thy form before me in radiant beauty came,
A thousand times one look of thine had given me back my breath,
And called thy lover to thy side even from the gate of death.
What boots it, Lindaraja, that I, at Jaen's gate,
That unsurrendered city, have met my final fate?
What boots it, that this city proud will ne'er the Soldan own,
For thee and not for Jaen this hour I make my moan;
I weep for Lindaraja, I weep to think that she
May mourn a hostage and a slave in long captivity.
But worse than this that some proud Moor will take thee to his heart,
And all thy thoughts of Reduan new love may bid depart.
And dwelling on thy beauty he will deem it better far,
To win fair Lindaraja than all the spoils of war,
Yet would I pray if Mahomet, whose servant I have been,
Should ever from the throne of God look on this bloody scene,
And deem it right to all my vows requital fit to make,
And for my valor who attacked the town I could not take,
That he would make thy constancy as steadfast as the tower
Of Jaen's mighty fortress, that withstood the Moorish power;
Now as my life be ebbing fast, my spirit is oppressed,
And Reduan the warrior bold is sinking to his rest,
Oh, may my prayers be answered, if so kind heaven allow,
And may the King forgive me for the failure of my vow,
And, Lindaraja, may my soul, when it has taken its flight,
And for the sweet Elysian fields exchange these realms of night,
Contented in the joys and peace of that celestial seat,
Await the happy moment when we once more shall meet."

THE AGED LOVER

'Twas from a lofty balcony Arselia looked down
On golden Tagus' crystal stream that hemmed Toledo's town;
And now she watched the eddies that dimpled in the flood
And now she landward turned her eye to gaze on waste and wood,
But in all that lay around her she sought for rest in vain,
For her heart, her heart was aching, and she could not heal the pain.
'Tis of no courtly gallant the Moorish damsel dreams,
No lordly emir who commands the fort by Tagus' streams,
'Twas on the banks of Tornes stood the haughty towers of note
Where the young alcayde loved by the maid from cities dwelt remote.
And never at Almanzor's court had he for honor sought,
Though he dwelt in high Toledo in fair Arselia's thought;
And now she dreams of love's great gift, of passion's deep delight,
When far away from her palace walls a stranger came in sight.
It was no gallant lovelorn youth she saw approaching fast,
It was the hero Reduan whose vernal years were past.
He rode upon a sorrel horse and swiftly he came nigh,
And stood where the dazzling sun beat down upon her balcony;
And with a thoughtful air upon the maiden turned his eye,
For suddenly the aged knight feels all his heart on fire,
And all the frost of his broken frame is kindling with desire.
And while he fain would hide his pain he paces up and down
Before the palace turrets that Toledo's rampart crown.
With anger glows the maiden's mind, "Now get thee gone," she cries,
"For can it be that love of me in blood like thine can rise?
I sicken at the very thought; thy locks, old man, are gray,
Thy baldness and thy trembling hand a doting age betray.
Ah, little must thou count my years of beauty and of bloom,
If thou wouldst wed them with a life thus tottering to the tomb,
Decrepitude is now thy lot, and wherefore canst thou dare
To ask that youthful charms these vile infirmities should share?"

And Moorish Reduan heard her words, and saw the meaning plain.
Advancing to the balcony he answered her again:
"The sun is king of everything, o'er all he holds his sway,
And thou art like the sun—thy charms I own and I obey;
Thy beauty warms my veins again, and in its rays, forsooth,
I feel the blithe, courageous mood of long-forgotten youth;
Sure love of mine can harm thee not, as sunlight is not lost
When its kind radiance dissolves the fetters of the frost."
Then turning round, a parchment did Reduan unfold,
And on it was a writing in characters of gold;
The meaning of the posy at once the maiden caught:
"Since I can venture, I can have; as yet, I am not naught."
He shows upon his shield a sun, circled with burning rays;
And on the rim was written a little verse which says,
"Two suns, one on my shield, and one in beauty's eyes, I trace."
Then at the cold disdain he saw upon her lovely face,
He covered with a gauzy veil the blazon of his shield,
"The sun upon my targe," he cried, "before thy light must yield."
But as the maid still pouted and eyed him with disdain,
"The mimic sun," continued he, "which here is blazoned plain,
Is overcast and hides itself from the true orb of day,
And I by beauty's radiance eclipsed must ride away."
And as he spoke the Moor struck deep the rowels in his steed,
And rode away from Tagus' side across the grassy mead.
The Moorish maiden recked not if he were far or near,
Her thoughts returned to fancies sweet of her absent cavalier.

FICKLENESS REBUKED

While in the foeman's ruddy gore
  I waded to the breast,
And for mine own, my native shore
  Fought braver than the best,
While the light cloak I laid aside,
  And doffed the damask fold,
And donned my shirt of mail, the spoil
  Of foeman brave and bold,

Thou, fickle Mooress, puttest on
  Thine odorous brocade,
And hand in hand with thy false love
  Wert sitting in the shade.
Thus on the scutcheon of thy sires
  Thou plantest many a stain;
The pillars of thine ancient house
  Will ne'er be firm again.
But, oh, may Allah vengeance take
  For thine unkind deceit,
And sorely weeping mayst thou pay
  The vengeance that is meet.
Thus shalt thou pay—thy lover's bliss
  Thou shalt not, canst not share,
But feel the bitter mockery
  Thy day-long shame must bear.
And what revenge 'twill be to note
  When thou dost kiss his brow,
How thy gold tresses, soft and light,
  Blend with his locks of snow;
And what revenge to hear him
  To thee his loves recount,
Praising some Moorish lass, or mark
  His sons thy staircase mount.
Yes, thou shalt pay the penalty,
  When, from sweet Genil's side,
Thou passest to the stormy waves
  Of Tagus' rushing tide;
Abencerrajes are not there,
  And from thy balcony
Thou shalt not hear the horsemen
  With loud hoof rushing by.
Thoughts of lost days shall haunt thee then
  And lay thy spirit waste,
When thy past glories thou shalt see
  All faded and effaced;
All gone, those sweet, seductive wiles—
  The love note's scented scroll—
The words, and blushing vows, that brought
  Damnation to thy soul.

Thus the bright moments of the past
  Shall rise to memory's eye,
Like vengeance-bearing ministers
  To mock thy misery.
For time is father of distress;
  And he whose life is long
Experiences a thousand cares,
  A thousand shapes of wrong.
Thou shalt be hated in the court,
  And hated in the stall,
Hated in merry gathering,
  In dance and festival.
Thou shalt be hated far and wide;
  And, thinking on this hate,
Wilt lay it to the black offence
  That thou didst perpetrate.
Then thou wilt make some weak defence,
  And plead a father's will,
That forced thee shuddering to consent
  To do the act of ill.
Enjoy then him whom thus constrained
  Thou choosest for thine own;
But know, when love would have his way,
  He scorns a father's frown.

THE GALLEY-SLAVE OF DRAGUT

Ah, fortune's targe and butt was he,
  On whom were rained the strokes from hate
From love that had not found its goal,
  From strange vicissitudes of fate.
A galley-slave of Dragut he,
  Who once had pulled the laboring oar,
Now, 'mid a garden's leafy boughs,
  He worked and wept in anguish sore.
"O Mother Spain! for thy blest shore
  Mine eyes impatient yearn;
For thy choicest gem is bride of mine,
  And she longs for my return.

They took me from the galley bench;
  A gardener's slave they set me here,
That I might tend the fruit and flowers
  Through all the changes of the year;
Wise choice, indeed, they made of me!
  For when the drought has parched the field,
The clouds that overcast my heart
  Shall rain in every season yield.
O mother Spain! for thy blest shore
  Mine eyes impatient yearn;
For thy choicest gem is bride of mine,
  And she longs for my return.

They took me from the galley's hold;
  It was by heaven's all-pitying grace,
Yet, even in this garden glade,
  Has fortune turned away her face.
Though lighter now my lot of toil,
  Yet is it heavier, since no more
My tear-dimmed eyes, my heart discern,
  Across the sea, my native shore.
O mother Spain! for thy blest shore
  Mine eyes impatient yearn;
For thy choicest gem is bride of mine,
  And she longs for my return.

And you, ye exiles, who afar
  In many a foreign land have strayed;
And from strange cities o'er the sea
  A second fatherland have made—
Degenerate sons of glorious Spain!
  One thing ye lacked to keep you true,
The love no stranger land could share;
  The courage that could fate subdue.
O mother Spain! for thy blest shore
  Mine eyes impatient yearn;
For thy choicest gem is bride of mine,
  And she longs for my return."

THE CAPTIVE'S LAMENT

Where Andalusia's plains at length end in the rocky shore,
And the billows of the Spanish sea against her boundaries roar,
A thousand ruined castles, that were once the haughty pride
Of high Cadiz, in days long past, looked down upon the tide.
And on the loftiest of them all, in melancholy mood,
A solitary captive that stormy evening stood.
For he had left the battered skiff that near the land wash lay,
And here he sought to rest his soul, and while his grief away,
While now, like furies, from the east the gale began to blow,
And with the crash of thunder the billows broke below.

Ah, yes, beneath the fierce levant, the wild white horses pranced;
With rising rage the billows against those walls advanced;
But stormier were the thoughts that filled his heart with bitter pain,
As he turned his tearful eyes once more to gaze upon the main.
"O hostile sea," these words at last burst from his heaving breast;
"I know that I return to die, but death at least is rest.
Then let me on my native shore again in freedom roam,
For here alone is shelter, for here at last is home."
And now, like furies, from the east the gale began to blow,
And with the crash of thunder the billows broke below.

'Twas Tagus' banks to me a child my home and nurture gave;
Ungrateful land, that lets me pine unransomed as a slave.
For now to-day, a dying man, am I come back again,
And I must lay my bones on this, the farthest shore of Spain.
It is not only exile's sword that cuts me to the heart;
It is not only love for her from whom they bade me part;
Nor only that I suffer, forgot by every friend,
But, ah! it is the triple blow that brings me to my end."
And now, like furies, from the east the gale began to blow,
And with the crash of thunder the billows broke below.

"The fire with which my bosom burns, alas! thy coolest breeze
Can never slake, nor can its rage thy coolest wave appease;
The earth can bring no solace to the ardor of my pain,
And the whole ocean waters were poured on it in vain.
For it is like the blazing sun that sinks in ocean's bed,
And yet, with ardor all unquenched, next morning rears its head.
Thus from the sea my suffering's flame has driven me once more,
And here I land, without a hope, upon this arid shore."
And now, like furies, from the east the gale began to blow,
And with the crash of thunder the billows broke below.

Oh, call me not, oh, call me not, thou voice of other years,
The fire that flames within my heart has dried the spring of tears.
And, while my eyes might well pour forth those bitter drops of pain,
The drought of self-consuming grief has quenched the healing rain.
Here, let me cry aloud for her, whom once I called mine own,
For well I wot that loving maid for me has made her moan.
'Tis for her sake my flight I urge across the sea and land,
And now 'twixt shore and ocean's roar I take my final stand."
And now, like furies, from the east the gale began to blow,
And with the crash of thunder the billows broke below.

Then stooping to the earth he grasped the soil with eager hand,
He kissed it, and with water he mixed the thirsty sand.
"O thou," he said, "poor soil and stream, in the Creator's plan
Art the end and the beginning of all that makes us man!
From thee rise myriad passions, that stir the human breast,
To thee at last, when all is o'er, they sink to find their rest.
Thou, Earth, hast been my mother, and when these pangs are o'er,

Thou shalt become my prison-house whence I can pass no more."

And now, like furies, from the east the gale began to blow,
And with the crash of thunder the billows broke below.

And now he saw the warring winds that swept across the bay
Had struck the battered shallop and carried it away.
" O piteous heaven," he cried aloud, " my hopes are like yon bark:
Scattered upon the storm they lie and never reach their mark."
And suddenly from cloudy heavens came down the darkling night
And in his melancholy mood the captive left the height.
He gained his boat, with trembling hand he seized the laboring oar
And turning to the foaming wave he left his native shore.
" Ah, well I wot on ocean's breast when loud the tempest blows
Will rest be found when solid ground denies the heart repose.
Now let the hostile sea perceive no power of hers I dread,
But rather ask her vengeance may fall upon my head."
Into the night the shallop turned, while floated far behind
The captive's lamentation like a streamer on the wind.

And now, like furies, from the east the gale began to blow,
And with the crash of thunder the billows broke below.

STRIKE SAIL!

A Turkish bark was on the sea, the sunny sea of Spain,
In sight of cliffs that Hercules made boundaries of the main;
And one, Celimo's captive slave, as fierce the billows grew,
Was listening as the ship-master this order gave the crew:

" Strike sail! Strike sail! The furious gale
Is rising fast! Strike sail!"

Fierce fell on them the opposing winds, the ship was helpless driven;
And with the ocean's flood were blent the thunder-drops of heaven.

And as the inky clouds were rent, the fiery lightning flared,
And 'mid the terror-stricken crew one voice alone was heard:
"Strike sail! Strike sail! The furious gale
Is rising fast! Strike sail!"

And one there sat upon the deck, in captive misery,
Whose tears ran mingling with the flood, the flood of sky and sea.
Lost in the tempest of his thoughts, he fondly breathed a prayer,
Whose mournful words were echoed by the mount of his despair:
"Strike sail! Strike sail! The furious gale
Is rising fast! Strike sail!"

"If I am captive and a slave, the time shall come when God
Will bring me freed, to tread once more my own, my native sod!
Then all my ancient glory shall return to me for aye.
Till then, my soul, be patient and wait that happy day!"
"Strike sail! Strike sail! The furious gale
Is rising fast! Strike sail!"

THE CAPTIVE'S ESCAPE

The fair Florida sat at ease, upon a summer's day,
Within a garden green and fair that by the river lay,
And gayly asked that he her spouse would tell his darling wife
The cause of his captivity, the history of his life.
"Now tell me, dearest husband, I pray thee tell me true,
Who were thy parents, and what land thy birth and nurture knew?
And wherefore did they take thee a captive from that place,
And who has given thee liberty, thy homeward path to trace?"
"Yes, I will tell thee, gentle wife, and I will tell thee true,
For tender is the light I see within thine eyes of blue.
In Ronda did my father raise his castle on the height;
And 'twas in Antequera first my mother saw the light.
Me, to this dark captivity, the dastard Moors ensnared,
Just as the peace had ended and war was not declared.

They took me off in fetters, to barter me for gold,
Velez-de-la-Gomèra was the town where I was sold.
Seven weary days, and for each day a long and weary night,
They set me on the auction-block, before the people's sight.
Yet not a Moorish gentleman and not a Moorish wife
A maravedi offered for the mournful captive's life.
At last there came a Moorish dog, in rich attire, and gave
A thousand golden pieces to have me for his slave.
He led me to his lofty house, and bade me there remain,
Mocked by his lowest underlings, and loaded with a chain.
Ah! vile the life he led me, and deep revenge I swore;
Ah! black the life he gave me, and hard the toils I bore!
By day I beat the piled-up hemp cut from the vega plain;
By night, within the darkened mill, I ground for him the grain.
And though the very corn I ground, I longed to take for meat,
He placed a bridle on my mouth that I should nothing eat!
Therefore, it pleased the God who rules the heavens, the land, the sea,
That the mistress of that mighty house looked tenderly on me.
And when the Moor a-hunting went, one happy autumn day,
She came into my prison-house and took my chains away;
She bade me sit upon her lap, I answered with delight;
Ah, many a gallant present she made to me that night!
She bathed me and she washed my wounds, and garments fresh she gave,
Far brighter than were fit to deck the body of a slave;
And love's delight we shared that night, for I grew gay and bold!
And in the morn she gave to me a hundred crowns of gold.
She oped the gates, she bade me, with smiles, once more be free;
We fled, for fear that Moorish hound would slay both her and me.
And so it pleased the God who rules the earth and heavens above,
To prove his deep compassion and the greatness of his love;
And thus my sad captivity, my days of wandering, o'er,
Florida, in thy loving arms I nestle as of yore!

THE SPANIARD OF ORAN

Right gallant was that gentleman, the warlike knight of Spain,
Who served the King in Oran, with sword and lances twain;
But, with his heart's devotion and passion's ardent fire,
He served a gentle Afric maid of high and noble sire.
And she was fair as noble, and well could she requite
The devotion of a lover and the courage of a knight.
And when one summer evening they paid their vows again,
They heard the alarum ring to arms across the darkling plain;
For the foes' approach had roused the watch and caused the war-like sound.
The silver moon had shed its ray upon their targes round,
The targes shot the message to the silent watch-towers by,
And watch-towers sent their tidings by flames that lit the sky;
And the fires had called the bells on high to ring their clear alarms—
That tocsin roused the lover locked in the lady's arms.
Ah, sorely felt he in his heart the spur of honor prick,
But love's appeal that held him, it pierced him to the quick.
'Twas cowardice to dally and shrink that foe to face,
But, ah, it was ingratitude to leave her in that case.
And hanging round her lover's neck, she saw that he turned pale,
And seized his sword and cast one glance upon his coat of mail;
And, with a burst of sighs and tears she bowed her beauteous head;
"Oh, rise, my lord, gird on thy arms, and join the fray," she said;
Oh, let my tears this couch bedew; this couch of joy shall be
As dolorous as the dreary field of battle, without thee!
Arm, arm thyself and go to war! Hark, hark! the foes approach.
Thy general waits; oh, let him not thy knightliness reproach!
Oh, direly will he visit thee for cowardice to-day,
For dire the crime in any clime of soldiers who betray.
Well canst thou glide unnoticed to the camp, without thy sword;

Wilt thou not heed my tears, my sighs—begone without a word!
Thy bosom is not made of flesh, for, ah! thou canst not feel,
Thou hast no need of arms in fight, for it is hard as steel."
The Spaniard gazed upon her, his heart was full of pride;
She held him fast and even her words retained him at her side.
"Lady," he said, and kissed her, "spite of thy words unwise,
Thou art as sweet as ever in thy lover's faithful eyes.
And since to love and honor this night thou hast appealed,
I take my arms and go, for right it is to thee I yield;
I go into the battle and my body seeks the fight,
But my soul behind me lingers in thy bosom of delight;
Oh, grant me, Lord and Master, to seek the camp below,
Oh, let me take the name to-night and I will cheerful go,
Bearing the sword, the lance, and coat of mail against the foe!"

FAMOUS PAINTINGS FROM THE PARIS SALON.

THE ABDUCTION.

Photogravure from the original painting by U. Checa, exhibited in the Paris Salon of 1897.

MOORISH ROMANCES

—

[*Metrical Translation by J. Lockhart*]

MOORISH ROMANCES

THE BULL-FIGHT OF GAZUL

[Gazul is the name of one of the Moorish heroes who figure in the "*Historia de las Guerras Civiles de Granada.*" The following ballad is one of very many in which the dexterity of the Moorish cavaliers in the bull-fight is described. The reader will observe that the shape, activity, and resolution of the unhappy animal destined to furnish the amusement of the spectators, are enlarged upon, just as the qualities of a modern race-horse might be among ourselves: nor is the bull without his name. The day of the Baptist is a festival among the Mussulmans, as well as among Christians.]

KING ALMANZOR of Granada, he hath bid the trumpet sound,
He hath summonded all the Moorish lords, from the hills and plains around;
From vega and sierra, from Betis and Xenil,
They have come with helm and cuirass of gold and twisted steel.

'Tis the holy Baptist's feast they hold in royalty and state,
And they have closed the spacious lists beside the Alhambra's gate;
In gowns of black and silver laced, within the tented ring,
Eight Moors to fight the bull are placed in presence of the King.

Eight Moorish lords of valor tried, with stalwart arm and true,
The onset of the beasts abide, as they come rushing through;
The deeds they've done, the spoils they've won, fill all with hope and trust,
Yet ere high in heaven appears the sun they all have bit the dust.

Then sounds the trumpet clearly, then clangs the loud tambour,
Make room, make room for Gazul—throw wide, throw wide the door;
Blow, blow the trumpet clearer still, more loudly strike the drum,
The Alcaydé of Algava to fight the bull doth come.

And first before the King he passed, with reverence stooping low,
And next he bowed him to the Queen, and the Infantas all a-row;
Then to his lady's grace he turned, and she to him did throw
A scarf from out her balcony was whiter than the snow.

With the life-blood of the slaughtered lords all slippery is the sand,
Yet proudly in the centre hath Gazul ta'en his stand;
And ladies look with heaving breast, and lords with anxious eye,
But firmly he extends his arm—his look is calm and high.

Three bulls against the knight are loosed, and two come roaring on,
He rises high in stirrup, forth stretching his rejón;
Each furious beast upon the breast he deals him such a blow
He blindly totters and gives back, across the sand to go.

"Turn, Gazul, turn," the people cry—the third comes up behind,
Low to the sand his head holds he, his nostrils snuff the wind;
The mountaineers that lead the steers, without stand whispering low,
"Now thinks this proud alcaydé to stun Harpado so?"

From Guadiana comes he not, he comes not from Xenil,
From Gaudalarif of the plain, or Barves of the hill;
But where from out the forest burst Xarama's waters clear,
Beneath the oak-trees was he nursed, this proud and stately steer.

Dark is his hide on either side, but the blood within doth boil,
And the dun hide glows, as if on fire, as he paws to the turmoil.
His eyes are jet, and they are set in crystal rings of snow;
But now they stare with one red glare of brass upon the foe.

Upon the forehead of the bull the horns stand close and near,
From out the broad and wrinkled skull, like daggers they appear;
His neck is massy, like the trunk of some old knotted tree,
Whereon the monster's shaggy mane, like billows curled, ye see.

His legs are short, his hams are thick, his hoofs are black as night,
Like a strong flail he holds his tail in fierceness of his might;
Like something molten out of iron, or hewn from forth the rock,
Harpado of Xarama stands, to bide the alcaydé's shock.

Now stops the drum—close, close they come—thrice meet, and thrice give back;
The white foam of Harpado lies on the charger's breast of black—
The white foam of the charger on Harpado's front of dun—
Once more advance upon his lance—once more, thou fearless one!

Once more, once more;—in dust and gore to ruin must thou reel—
In vain, in vain thou tearest the sand with furious heel—
In vain, in vain, thou noble beast, I see, I see thee stagger,
Now keen and cold thy neck must hold the stern alcaydé's dagger!

They have slipped a noose around his feet, six horses are brought in,
And away they drag Harpado with a loud and joyful din.
Now stoop thee, lady, from thy stand, and the ring of price bestow
Upon Gazul of Algava, that hath laid Harpado low.

THE ZEGRI'S BRIDE

[The reader cannot need to be reminded of the fatal effects which were produced by the feuds subsisting between the two great families, or rather races, of the Zegris and the Abencerrages of Granada. The following ballad is also from the "*Guerras Civiles.*"]

Of all the blood of Zegri, the chief is Lisaro,
To wield rejón like him is none, or javelin to throw;
From the place of his dominion, he ere the dawn doth go,
From Alcala de Henares, he rides in weed of woe.

He rides not now as he was wont, when ye have seen him speed
To the field of gay Toledo, to fling his lusty reed;
No gambeson of silk is on, nor rich embroidery
Of gold-wrought robe or turban—nor jewelled tahali.

No amethyst nor garnet is shining on his brow,
No crimson sleeve, which damsels weave at Tunis, decks him now;
The belt is black, the hilt is dim, but the sheathed blade is bright;
They have housened his barb in a murky garb, but yet her hoofs are light.

Four horsemen good, of the Zegri blood, with Lisaro go out;
No flashing spear may tell them near, but yet their shafts are stout;
In darkness and in swiftness rides every armed knight—
The foam on the rein ye may see it plain, but nothing else is white.

Young Lisaro, as on they go, his bonnet doffeth he,
Between its folds a sprig it holds of a dark and glossy tree;
That sprig of bay, were it away, right heavy heart had he—
Fair Zayda to her Zegri gave that token privily.

And ever as they rode, he looked upon his lady's boon.
"God knows," quoth he, "what fate may be—I may be slaughtered soon;

Thou still art mine, though scarce the sign of hope that bloomed
whilere,
But in my grave I yet shall have my Zayda's token dear."

Young Lisaro was musing so, when onward on the path,
He well could see them riding slow; then pricked he in his
wrath.
The raging sire, the kinsmen of Zayda's hateful house,
Fought well that day, yet in the fray the Zegri won his spouse.

THE BRIDAL OF ANDALLA

[The Following ballad has been often imitated by modern poets, both in Spain and in Germany:

" Pon te a las rejas azules, dexa la manga que labras,
Melanckolica Xarifa, veras al galan Andalla," etc.]

" Rise up, rise up, Xarifa, lay the golden cushion down;
Rise up, come to the window, and gaze with all the town.
From gay guitar and violin the silver notes are flowing,
And the lovely lute doth speak between the trumpet's lordly
blowing,
And banners bright from lattice light are waving everywhere,
And the tall, tall plume of our cousin's bridegroom floats
proudly in the air:
Rise up, rise up, Xarifa, lay the golden cushion down;
Rise up, come to the window, and gaze with all the town.

" Arise, arise, Xarifa, I see Andalla's face,
He bends him to the people with a calm and princely grace,
Through all the land of Xeres and banks of Guadalquivir
Rode forth bridegroom so brave as he, so brave and lovely
never.
Yon tall plume waving o'er his brow of purple mixed with
white,
I guess 'twas wreathed by Zara, whom he will wed to-night;
Rise up, rise up, Xarifa, lay the golden cushion down;
Rise up, come to the window, and gaze with all the town.

" What aileth thee, Xarifa, what makes thine eyes look down?
Why stay ye from the window far, nor gaze with all the town?

I've heard you say on many a day, and sure you said the truth,
Andalla rides without a peer, among all Granada's youth.
Without a peer he rideth, and yon milk-white horse doth go
Beneath his stately master, with a stately step and slow;
  Then rise, oh, rise, Xarifa, lay the golden cushion down;
  Unseen here through the lattice, you may gaze with all the town."

The Zegri lady rose not, nor laid her cushion down,
Nor came she to the window to gaze with all the town;
But though her eyes dwelt on her knee, in vain her fingers strove,
And though her needle pressed the silk, no flower Xarifa wove;
One bonny rose-bud she had traced, before the noise drew nigh—
That bonny bud a tear effaced, slow drooping from her eye.
  "No—no," she sighs—"bid me not rise, nor lay my cushion down,
  To gaze upon Andalla with all the gazing town."

"Why rise ye not, Xarifa, nor lay your cushion down?
Why gaze ye not, Xarifa, with all the gazing town?
Hear, hear the trumpet how it swells, and how the people cry!
He stops at Zara's palace gate—why sit ye still—oh, why?"
"At Zara's gate stops Zara's mate; in him shall I discover
The dark-eyed youth pledged me his truth with tears, and was my lover?
  I will not rise, with dreary eyes, nor lay my cushion down,
  To gaze on false Andalla with all the gazing town!"

ZARA'S EAR-RINGS

"My ear-rings! my ear-rings! they've dropped into the well,
And what to say to Muça, I cannot, cannot tell."
'Twas thus, Granada's fountain by, spoke Albuharez' daughter,
"The well is deep, far down they lie, beneath the cold blue water—
To me did Muça give them, when he spake his sad farewell,
And what to say when he comes back, alas! I cannot tell.

"My ear-rings! my ear-rings! they were pearls in silver set,
That when my Moor was far away, I ne'er should him forget,
That I ne'er to other tongue should list, nor smile on other's
tale,
But remember he my lips had kissed, pure as those ear-rings
pale—
When he comes back, and hears that I have dropped them in
the well,
Oh, what will Muça think of me, I cannot, cannot tell.

"My ear-rings! my ear-rings! he'll say they should have been,
Not of pearl and of silver, but of gold and glittering sheen,
Of jasper and of onyx, and of diamond shining clear,
Changing to the changing light, with radiance insincere—
That changeful mind unchanging gems are not befitting well—
Thus will he think—and what to say, alas! I cannot tell.

"He'll think when I to market went, I loitered by the way;
He'll think a willing ear I lent to all the lads might say;
He'll think some other lover's hand, among my tresses noosed,
From the ears where he had placed them, my rings of pearl un-
loosed;
He'll think, when I was sporting so beside this marble well,
My pearls fell in,—and what to say, alas! I cannot tell.

"He'll say, I am a woman, and we are all the same;
He'll say I loved when he was here to whisper of his flame—
But when he went to Tunis my virgin troth had broken,
And thought no more of Muça, and cared not for his token.
My ear-rings! my ear-rings! O luckless, luckless well,
For what to say to Muça, alas! I cannot tell.

"I'll tell the truth to Muça, and I hope he will believe—
That I thought of him at morning, and thought of him at eve;
That, musing on my lover, when down the sun was gone,
His ear-rings in my hand I held, by the fountain all alone;
And that my mind was o'er the sea, when from my hand they
fell,
And that deep his love lies in my heart, as they lie in the well."

THE LAMENTATION FOR CELIN

At the gate of old Granada, when all its bolts are barred,
At twilight at the Vega gate there is a trampling heard;
There is a trampling heard, as of horses treading slow,
And a weeping voice of women, and a heavy sound of woe.
"What tower is fallen, what star is set, what chief come these bewailing?"
"A tower is fallen, a star is set. Alas! alas for Celin!"

Three times they knock, three times they cry, and wide the doors they throw;
Dejectedly they enter, and mournfully they go;
In gloomy lines they mustering stand beneath the hollow porch,
Each horseman grasping in his hand a black and flaming torch;
Wet is each eye as they go by, and all around is wailing,
For all have heard the misery. "Alas! alas for Celin!"—

Him yesterday a Moor did slay, of Bencerraje's blood,
'Twas at the solemn jousting, around the nobles stood;
The nobles of the land were by, and ladies bright and fair
Looked from their latticed windows, the haughty sight to share;
But now the nobles all lament, the ladies are bewailing,
For he was Granada's darling knight. "Alas! alas for Celin!"

Before him ride his vassals, in order two by two,
With ashes on their turbans spread, most pitiful to view;
Behind him his four sisters, each wrapped in sable veil,
Between the tambour's dismal strokes take up their doleful tale;
When stops the muffled drum, ye hear their brotherless bewailing,
And all the people, far and near, cry—"Alas! alas for Celin!"

Oh! lovely lies he on the bier, above the purple pall,
The flower of all Granada's youth, the loveliest of them all;
His dark, dark eyes are closed, his rosy lip is pale,
The crust of blood lies black and dim upon his burnished mail,
And evermore the hoarse tambour breaks in upon their wailing,
Its sound is like no earthly sound—"Alas! alas for Celin!"

The Moorish maid at the lattice stands, the Moor stands at his door,
One maid is wringing of her hands, and one is weeping sore—
Down to the dust men bow their heads, and ashes black they strew
Upon their broidered garments of crimson, green, and blue—
Before each gate the bier stands still, then bursts the loud bewailing,
From door and lattice, high and low—"Alas! alas for Celin!"

An old, old woman cometh forth, when she hears the people cry;
Her hair is white as silver, like horn her glazèd eye.
'Twas she that nursed him at her breast, that nursed him long ago;
She knows not whom they all lament, but soon she well shall know.
With one deep shriek she thro' doth break, when her ears receive their wailing—
"Let me kiss my Celin ere I die—Alas! alas for Celin!"

THE STORY OF SIDI BRAHIM OF MASSAT

[*Translated by René Busset and Chauncey C. Starkweather*]

THE STORY OF SIDI BRAHIM OF MASSAT

I

THE Taleb Sidi Brahim, son of Amhammed of Massat, in the province of Sous, tells the following story about himself: When he was still a child at his father's house he went to the mosque to read with a taleb. He studied with him for twelve and a half years. His father gave him bread and kouskous, and he ate eight deniers' worth a day. I will make known the country of Massat. It contains seventeen towns. In the middle of these is a market. The Jews have a refuge in the village of the chief named Mobarek-ben-Mahomet. He lives with a sheik called Brahim-Mahomet-Abon-Djemaa. These two chiefs levy a tax on the Jews. They receive from them four ounces per family at the beginning of each month. If the festival of the Mussulmans coincides with the Sabbath of the Jews, the latter pay to each of the chiefs one ounce for a Jew or a Jewess, boy or girl, little or big. The following are the details of the population of Massat. It includes 1,700 men. As to the women, little boys or girls, only the Lord knows their number. There are 1,250 houses. The horses amount to 180. They ride them and make them work like oxen and mules. They also fight on horseback. The country has trees, vines, figs, cacti, dates, oranges, lemons, apples, apricots, melons, and olives. There is a river which flows from there to the sea. The commerce is considerable. There are Jews and Mussulmans. The number of books in the mosque is unknown, unless it be by God. The teachers are numerous as well as the pilgrims, the descendants of Mahomet, and the saints. May God aid us with his blessing!

We will now speak of the tribute which the people of Massat pay yearly to Prince Mouley-Abd-Er-Rahman. Up to our days they had, for fifty-one years, given him 5,000 livres of silver. The prince said to them, "You must pay 1,000 livres more." They answered, "By the Lord, we will only give you as before, 5,000 livres, a slave, a servant, and a horse." The kaid Abd-el-Cadik, who was caliph of the King of Taroundant, hastened to send against them forty-five horsemen, and said to them: "You must give me six thousand livres of silver, and a slave, a servant, and a horse in addition." They refused and drove away the cavalry, saying, "Return to the kaid who sent you against us, and say to him that we will not increase our tribute as he demands." The horsemen returned and arrived at Taroundant. The kaid asked him, "Tell me what happened to you with the people of Massat." They answered him, "They read in their assembly the letter that you sent them, and told us to go back, and that they would pay no larger sum." The kaid called a council and asked what had better be done with the people of Massat. The sheiks of the Achtouks answered, "Make complaints to the Sultan at Morocco." He wrote to the Sultan, asking him to send an army to destroy the rebels of Massat. The Sultan sent a force of 3,500 horsemen, to whom he gave for chief, Ettaib Eddin, who rejoined them near the khalifah of the King at Taroundant. When the royal troops arrived, the fourth night, he started and led them to the taleb Mahomet of the Aggars, in the midst of the country of the Achtouks. The taleb said to him: "Return to Taroundant. Let your lieutenant go with them and we will talk about it." The kaid answered, "Very well." The chiefs of the Achtouks mounted their horses and led the army toward the country of Hama, in the mountain which is between the Achtouks and Ida-Oultit. The troops hastened toward the foot of the mountain, near the river Alras, in the country of Takourt. The mountaineers marched against them and fought for three days until the holy men and the sherifs arrived and quieted them. The mountaineers came down toward the army. The kaid betrayed them. He seized fourteen of their leaders and sent them to the kaid at Taroundant. He cut off their heads and hung them up at the gate. As to the army that was above the river Alras, it attacked the people of Massat on account of the tribute demanded by the kaid. It made the onset with cavalry, and destroyed the country. The natives received them with powder, and they fought half a day. The natives gained the advantage in the fight. The enemy abandoned their cannons. The natives slew them until the Sultan's troops retreated. They captured 700 horses. The troops of the Sultan abandoned their baggage except six chests of silver. Many guns were broken on that day, until the flying invaders reached the country of the Achtouks. The people of Massat had for allies the tribes of Aglou and Tizpit, who equalled them in number. As for the cannons abandoned the day of the battle, the conquerors took two of them to their country. They kept them until they were repaid the 6,500 livres of silver, which had been taken from them. Then they gave back the cannons. Such is the complete story of that which happened between the tribe of Massat, the Khalifah of the King, and the neighboring tribes.

II

Information about the country of Tazroualt. The Taleb Sidi Brahim, son of Mahomet, of Massat in Sous, tells the following: He started for the zaouiah of Tazroualt, to study there during seven months with the taleb Sidi Mahomet Adjeli, one of the greatest lights. The number of students was seventy-four. Forty-two of these studied the law. The others read the Koran. None of the students paid for his living. It was furnished by the chief of the country, Hecham. He gave to the zaouiah mentioned, six servants and six slaves to cook the food of the students. The number of the villages of this country is nine. The Kashlah of Hecham is situated in the middle of the country. The Jewish quarter is at the left. The market is held every day at the entrance to the fort. This latter is built of stone, lime, and pine planks and beams. Riches abound. Caravans go from there to Timbuctoo, the Soudan, Sahara, and Agadir-Ndouma. They go to these countries to buy ivory, ostrich feathers, slaves, gold and silver. If it hurries, a caravan consumes a whole year in visiting these places. The people of the different countries buy from them and give in exchange other merchandise, such as linen, cotton, silks, iron, steel, incense, corals, cloves, spikenard, haberdashery, pottery, glass, and everything that comes, as they say, from the country of Christians. When these goods enumerated above have arrived, the merchants, both Jews and Mussulmans, come forward and buy them according to the needs of their business. I will add here, with more details, some words about Hecham. He has twelve sons, all horsemen, who have thirty-six horses. As for oxen, sheep, and camels, God alone could tell the figure. The number of the wives that Hecham has married is four white and six slaves—the latter black. His only son has as many white wives as his father, but more black ones. The men of Tizeroualt are of the number of 1,400. But for the women, boys, and girls, God alone knows the figure. They possess 200 horses, beside those of Hecham. There are 750 houses; the number of books in the mosque is 130—in the Chelha language.

III

The sheik Sidi Hammad, son of Mahomet Mouley Ben-Nacer, has written his book in Amazir. It is entitled the "Kitab-amazir." This work treats of obligations and traditions of things permitted and forbidden.

IV

There are 3,500 men in the Aglou country. They have 2,200 houses and 960 horses. This district is on the sea-coast and possesses a stone-harbor. There are barks which are used in fishing. The inhabitants were living in tranquillity when one day, as they were starting out to fish, a ship arrived off shore. They fled in fear and left it in the sea. The ship waited till midnight. Then it entered the port and ran up a red flag. It remained at anchor for fifteen days. The people of Aglou assembled day and night, big and little, even the horsemen before it. No one was missing. The chiefs of the town wrote letters which they sent to all the villages. They sent one to Sidi Hecham couched in these words: "Come at once. The Christians have made an expedition against us, and have taken this port." Sidi Hecham sent messengers to all the provinces over which he ruled and said in his letters: "You must accompany me to the country of Aglou, for the Christians have made an expedition against us." All the neighboring tribes assembled to march against the Christians. When Sidi

Hecham had joined them he said, "You must raise a red flag like theirs."

They raised it. When it was seen by those on the ship, a sailor came ashore in a small boat and approached the Mussulmans there assembled.

"Let no one insult the Christian," said Sidi Hecham, "until we learn his purpose in landing here."

They asked him, "What do you want?"

The Christian replied, "We wish to receive, in the name of God, pledges of security."

All who were present said, "God grants to you security with us."

The Christian then continued, "My object is to trade with you."

"That is quite agreeable to us," answered Hecham. Then Hecham asked the Christian what he wanted to purchase."

"Oil, butter, wheat, oxen, sheep, and chickens," said he.

When the Mussulmans heard this they gathered together wheat, oil, oxen, and everything he had mentioned. He made his purchases, and was well supplied. The master of the ship then said:

"Our business is finished. We must go back home. But we shall return to you." Hecham answered:

"That which I have done for you is not pleasing to the people of Aglou. It is only on account of the pledge of security that I have been able to restrain them. I have given you all you asked. Next time you come, bring us fifty cannons and ten howitzers."

"Very well," answered the Christian, "I shall return this time next year."

"Do as you promise," replied Hecham, "and I will give you whatever you want in the country of the Mussulmans."

V

A Story about the Country of Ait-Bamouran

There arrived in this country at the beginning of the year another ship which stopped at a place called Ifni, in the tribe of Ait-Bamouran, and stayed there three days. Then one of the sailors got into a small boat, came ashore, and said to the inhabitants, "I will buy bread, meat, and water from you."

The Mussulmans brought him bread, figs, and water, saying: "You must send two of your men ashore while we go on board the ship with you."

"It is well," replied the Christian. Then he went to get two of his men whom he brought ashore and said to the Mussulmans: "You must give me one of your men."

They gave him a hostage to remain on board the Christian ship. Then they filled a boat, and boarded the ship themselves to deliver what they had sold. They ran all over the ship looking at everything. Then they said, "Come with us to the spring and we will draw water." The Christians accompanied them to the fountain to fill their water-casks. The other natives, to the number of fifteen, got into a boat and went to the ship. With the water-party and the hostages ashore there were only four Christians on the ship when the Mussulmans boarded it.

"Don't come aboard till our men have come back," said the Christians.

"We will come aboard by force," he was answered, and the attack began. One of the Christians killed a native with a gun. Then they fought until the Christians were overcome. Two Christians were killed and the rest captured and taken ashore and imprisoned with the others of the water-party. The ship was sold for 180 mithkals. The Christians were all sold and dispersed among the tribes. The news of this spread to Taccourt. The merchants there sent to Ait-Bamouran and bought all the Christians at any price. They secured seven. Three were missing, of whom two were in the country of Ait-bou-Bekr with the chief of that tribe named Abd-Allah, son of Bou-Bekr. The third, who was a boy, was with the sheik of Aglou, who said:

"I will not sell this one, for he has become as dear to me as a son." Then addressing the young boy he said, "I wish to convert you; be a Mussulman." The boy acquiesced and embraced Islamism. The day of his abjuration the sheik killed in his honor an ox for a festival, and gave to the convert the name of Mahomet. Then he sent to say to all his tribe:

"Come to my house. I have prepared a repast." The Mussulmans came and diverted themselves with their horses and gunpowder. The chief told them, "I have given a fourth of my possessions, a slave, and a servant to this young man." He added, "He shall live with my son." They both occupied the same room, and the master taught the young convert the whole Koran. The Mussulmans called him Sidi Mahomet, son of Ali. Seven Christians were ransomed and sent back to their own country.

VI

Information about the country Tiznit: This place is a kind of a city surrounded on all sides by a wall, and having only two gates. The water is in the centre, in a fountain. The fortress is built above the fountain, in the middle of the city. It is entirely constructed of mortar, cut stone, marble, and beams, all from Christian countries. It was the residence of the khalifah of the King in the time of Mouley-Soliman. When this prince died, the people of Tiznit revolted, drove away the lieutenant, and made a concerted attack upon the citadel, which they completely destroyed. They took the stones and beams and built a mosque on the spot, near the fountain of which we have spoken. But when Mouley-Abd-Er-Rahman came to the throne he sent a caliph to Tiznit. He gave him 300 horsemen. When the caliph arrived near the town he waited three days and they gave him food and barley. At the end of this time he made a proclamation summoning all the people to him. When they came he read them the royal edict and said:

"I must enter your city to occupy the fortress of the King!"

They said: "No; go back whence you came and say to your master: 'You shall not rule over us. Your fortress is totally destroyed, and with the material we have built a big mosque in the middle of our city.'"

Prince Mouley-Abd-Er-Rahman sent at once against them his son Sidi-Mahomet with the khalifah and 6,000 horsemen. The people of Tiznit were informed of the approach of the army under the Sultan's son, and that the advancing guard was near. The soldiers arrived in the middle of the country of the Achtouks and camped in the city of Tebouhonaikt near the river Alras. There was a day's march between them and Tiznit. The inhabitants, frightened, sent deputies to the other districts, saying:

"Come and help us, for the Sultan's son has come and ordered us to build him a fort in the space of one month or he will fall upon us, cut a passage, and destroy our city." The tribes around Tiznit assembled and marched against the royal army. The Sultan's son stayed twenty-two days at Tebouhonaikt, then he crossed the river Alras and marched against the rebels. He surrounded Tiznit on all sides. The inhabitants made a sortie, engaged in battle, and fought till the morning star. At the fall of day the battle recommenced. The royal army was defeated and driven across the river Alras. The son of the Sultan killed eight rebels and thirty-five horses, but many of his soldiers fell. He retreated to Morocco.

VII

Information about the country of Taragoust: This is a unique district situated near the source of the Ourd-Sous. It is distant from Taroundant about a day and a half's march. When a young man becomes of age his father buys him a gun and a sabre. The market is in the middle of the country. But no man goes there without his weapons. The sheiks judge each one in the market for four months in the year in turn and during their period of office. They decided who was guilty and demanded price of blood for those killed in the market. One of them said:

"I will give nothing. Find the murderer. He will give you the price of blood."

The sheik replied: "Pay attention. Give us part of your goods."

"I will give you nothing," he answered.

In this way they quarrelled, until they began fighting with

guns. Each tried to steal the other's horses and oxen in the night and kill the owner. They kept acting this way toward each other until Ben-Nacer came to examine the villages where so many crimes were committed, and he reëstablished peace and order.

VIII

Concerning guns and sabres: They were all brought into the city of Adjadir in the government of Sidi Mahomet-ben-Abd-Alla. They introduced guns, poniards, sabres, English powder, and everything one can mention from the country of the Christians. Sidi Mahomet-ben-Abd-Allah sent there his khalifah, called Ettaleb Calih. He busied himself during his administration in amassing a great fortune. The guns imported into the provinces were called merchandise of the taleb Calih. This officer revolted against the Sultan, sent him no more money, and consulted him no longer in the administration of affairs. When the prince ordered him to do such and such a thing with the Christians, Mussulmans, or others, he replied:

"I shall do as I please, for all the people of Sous are under my hand. I leave the rest to you." The Sultan sent much money to Sidi Mahomet-ben-Abd-Allah, and ordered him with troops against the rebel. The latter fought against the divan until he was captured and put in fetters and chains. The partisans of the Emperor said to him:

"We have captured your khalifah Ettaleb Calih and his accomplices."

The prince responded: "Make him a bonnet of iron and a shirt of iron, and give him but a loaf of bread a day." In a letter that he sent he said also:

"Collect all the goods you can find and let the Christian ships take them all to Taccourt, leaving nothing whatever." Guns, sabres, powder, sulphur, linens, cottons, everything was transported.

During the reign of Sidi Mouley Soliman he built the city as it is at present. He increased it, and said to the Christians:

"You must bring me cannons, mortars, and powder, and I

will give you in exchange wheat, oil, wool, and whatever you desire."

The Christians answered: "Most willingly, we shall return with our products." They brought him cannons, mortars, and powder. In return he supplied them with woollens, wheat, oil, and whatever they desired.

The Ulmas reproached him, saying: "You are not fulfilling the law in giving to the Christians wheat, oil, and woollens. You are weakening the Mussulmans."

He answered them: "We must make sacrifices of these goods for two or three years, until the Christians have stocked us with cannons, powder, and so forth. These I will place in the coast towns to drive off the infidels when they arrive."

IX

More words about guns: They only make them in three cities in the interior of Sous. The workmen are very numerous. They make also gun-barrels, pistols, gun-locks, and all such things. As for sabres and poniards, they are made by Arab armorers. They make powder in every province, but only in small quantities.

FIVE BERBER STORIES

—

[*Translated by G. Mercier and Chauncey C. Starkweather*]

FIVE BERBER STORIES

DJOKHRANE AND THE JAYS

THE ancestor of the grandfather of Mahomet Amokrane was named Djokhrane. He was a Roman of old times, who lived at T'kout at the period of the Romans. One of his countrymen rose against them, and they fought. This Roman had the advantage, until a bird of the kind called jays came to the assistance of Djokhrane, and pecked the Roman in the eyes until he saved his adversary. From that time forth he remained a friend to Djokhrane. The latter said to his children:

"As long as you live, never eat this bird. If you meet anyone who brings one of these birds to eat, buy it and set it free." To this day when anyone brings a jay to one of his descendants, he buys it for silver and gives it liberty. This story is true, and is not a lie.

THE OGRE AND THE BEAUTIFUL WOMAN

Some hunters set out with their camels. When they came to the hunting-ground they loosed their camels to let them graze, and hunted until the setting of the sun, and then came back to their camp. One day while one of them was going along he saw the marks of an ogre, each one three feet wide, and began to follow them. He proceeded and found the place where the ogre had lately made his lair. He returned and said to his companions:

"I've found the traces of an ogre. Come, let us seek him."

"No," they answered, "we will not go to seek him, because we are not stronger than he is."

"Grant me fourteen days," said the huntsman. "If I return, you shall see. If not, take back my camel with the game."

The next day he set out and began to follow the traces of the ogre. He walked for four days, when he discovered a cave, into which he entered. Within he found a beautiful woman, who said to him:

"What brings thee here, where thou wilt be devoured by this ogre?"

"But thou," answered the hunter, "what is thy story and how did the ogre bring thee here?"

"Three days ago he stole me," she replied. "I was betrothed to the son of my uncle, then the ogre took me. I have stayed in the cavern. He often brings me food. I stay here, and he does not kill me."

"Where does he enter," asked the hunter, "when he comes back here?"

"This is the way," she answered. The hunter went in to the middle of the cave, loaded his gun, and waited. At sunset the ogre arrived. The hunter took aim and fired, hitting the ogre between the eyes as he was sitting down. Approaching him he saw that he had brought with him two men to cook and eat them. In the morning he employed the day in collecting the hidden silver, took what he could, and set out on the return. On the fourteenth day he arrived at the place where he had left his comrades, and found them there.

"Leave the game you have secured and return with me to the cave," he said to them. When they arrived they took all the arms and clothing, loaded it upon their camels, and set out to return to their village. Half way home they fought to see which one should marry the woman. The powder spoke between them. Our man killed four, and took the woman home and married her.

THE FALSE VEZIR

A king had a wife who said to him: "I would like to go and visit my father."

"Very well," said he; "wait to-day, and to-morrow thou shalt go with my vezir." The next day they set out, taking the children with them, and an escort lest they should be attacked on the way. They stopped at sunset, and passed the night on the road. The vezir said to the guards, "Watch that we be not taken, if the robbers should come to seize us." They guarded the tent. The vezir asked the King's wife to marry him, and killed one of her sons because she refused. The next day they set out again. The next night he again asked the King's wife to marry him, threatening to kill a second child should she refuse. She did refuse, so he killed the second son. The next morning they set out, and when they stopped at night again he asked the King's wife to marry him.

"I'll kill you if you refuse."

She asked for delay, time to say her prayers. She prayed to God, the Master of all worlds, and said: "O God, save me from the vezir." The Master of the worlds heard her prayer. He gave her the wings of a bird, and she flew up in the sky.

At dawn she alighted in a great city, and met a man upon the roadside. She said: "By the face of God, give me your raiment and I'll give thee mine."

"Take it, and may God honor you," he said. Then she was handsome. This city had no king. The members of the council said:

"This creature is handsome; we'll make him our king." The cannon spoke in his honor and the drums beat.

When she flew up into the sky, the vezir said to the guards: "You will be my witnesses that she has gone to the sky, so that when I shall see the King he cannot say, 'Where is she?'" But when the vezir told this story, the King said:

"I shall go to seek my wife. Thou hast lied. Thou shalt accompany me." They set out, and went from village to village. They inquired, and said: "Has a woman been found here recently? We have lost her." And the village people said, "We have not found her." They went then to another village and inquired. At this village the Sultan's wife recognized them, called her servant, and said to him, "Go, bring to me this man." She said to the King, "From what motive hast thou come hither?"

He said, "I have lost my wife."

She answered: "Stay here, and pass the night. We will give thee a dinner and will question thee."

When the sun had set she said to the servant, "Go, bring the dinner, that the guests may eat." When they had eaten she said to the King, "Tell me your story."

He answered: "My story is long. My wife went away in the company of a trusted vezir. He returned and said: 'By God, your wife has gone to heaven.'

"I replied: 'No, you have lied. I'll go and look for her.'"

She said to him, "I am your wife."

"How came you here?" he asked.

She replied: "After having started, your vezir came to me and asked me to marry him or he would kill my son. 'Kill him,' I said, and he killed them both."

Addressing the vezir, she said: "And your story? Let us hear it."

"I will return in a moment," said the vezir, for he feared her. But the King cut off his head.

The next day he assembled the council of the village, and his wife said, "Forgive me and let me go, for I am a woman."

THE SOUFI AND THE TARGUI

Two Souafa were brothers. Separating one day one said to the other: "O my brother, let us marry thy son with my daughter." So the young cousins were married, and the young man's father gave them a separate house. It happened that a man among the Tonareg heard tell of her as a remarkable woman. He mounted his swiftest camel, ten years old, and went to her house. Arrived near her residence, he found some shepherds.

"Who are you?" he said.

"We are Souafa."

He confided in one of them, and said to him: "By the face of the Master of the worlds, O favorite of fair women, man of remarkable appearance, tell me if the lady so and so, daughter of so and so, is here."

"She is here."

"Well, if you have the sentiments of most men, I desire you to bring her here, I want to see her."

"I will do what you ask. If she'll come, I'll bring her. If not, I will return and tell you."

He set out, and, arriving at the house of the lady, he saw some people, and said "Good-evening" to them.

"Come dine with us," they said to him.

"I have but just now eaten and am not hungry." He pretended to amuse himself with them to shorten the night, in reality to put to sleep their vigilance. These people went away to amuse themselves while he met the lady.

"A man sends me to you," he said, "a Targui, who wants to marry you. He is as handsome as you are, his eyes are fine, his nose is fine, his mouth is fine."

"Well, I will marry him." She went to him and married him, and they set out on a camel together. When the first husband returned, he found that she had gone. He said to himself: "She is at my father's or perhaps my uncle's." When day dawned he said to his sister, "Go see if she is in thy father's house or thy uncle's." She went, and did not find her there. He went out to look for her, and perceived the camel's traces. Then he saddled his own camel.

The women came out and said: "Stay! Do not go; we will give thee our own daughters to marry."

"No," he replied, "I want to find my wife." He goes out, he follows the tracks of the camel, here, here, here, until the sun goes down. He spends the night upon the trail. His camel is a runner of five years. When the sun rises he starts and follows the trail again.

About four o'clock he arrives at an encampment of the Touareg, and finds some shepherds with their flocks. He confides in one of these men, and says to him: "A word, brave man, brother of beautiful women, I would say a word to thee which thou wilt not repeat."

"Speak."

"Did a woman arrive at this place night before last?"

"She did."

"Hast thou the sentiments of a man of heart?"

"Truly."

"I desire to talk to her."

"I will take thee to her. Go, hide thy camel; tie him up. Change thy clothing. Thou wilt not then be recognized among the sheep. Bring thy sabre and come. Thou shalt walk as the sheep walk."

"I will walk toward you, taking the appearance of a sheep, so as not to be perceived."

"The wedding-festival is set for to-night, and everybody will be out of their houses. When I arrive at the tent of this lady I will strike a stake with my stick. Where I shall strike, that is where she lives."

He waits and conceals himself among the flocks, and the women come out to milk. He looks among the groups of tents. He finds his wife and bids her come with him.

"I will not go with thee, but if thou art hungry, I will give thee food."

"Thou'lt come with me or I will kill thee!"

She goes with him. He finds his camel, unfastens him, dons his ordinary clothing, takes his wife upon the camel's back with him, and departs. The day dawns. She says:

"O thou who art the son of my paternal uncle, I am thirsty." Now she planned a treachery.

He said to her: "Is there any water here?"

"The day the Targui took me off we found some in that pass." They arrived at the well.

"Go down into the well," said the Soufi.

"I'm only a woman. I'm afraid. Go down thyself." He goes down. He draws the water. She drinks. He draws more water for the camel, which is drinking, when she pours the water on the ground.

"Why dost thou turn out the water?"

"I did not turn it out; thy camel drank it." And nevertheless she casts her glances and sees a dust in the distance. The Targui is coming. The woman says:

"Now I have trapped him for thee."

"Brava!" he cries, and addressing the Soufi: "Draw me some water that I may drink." He draws the water, and the Targui drinks. The woman says to him: "Kill him in the well. He is a good shot. Thou art not stronger than he is."

"No," he answered, "I do not want to soil a well of the tribes. I'll make him come up." The Soufi comes up till his shoulders appear. They seize him, hoist and bind him, and tie his feet together. Then they seize and kill his camel.

"Bring wood," says the Targui to the woman; "we'll roast some meat." She brings him some wood. He cooked the meat and ate it, while she roasted pieces of fat till they dripped upon her cousin.

"Don't do that," says the Targui.

She says, "He drew his sword on me, crying, 'Come with me or I will kill thee.'"

"In that case do as you like." She dropped the grease upon his breast, face, and neck until his skin was burnt. While she was doing this, the Targui felt sleep coming upon him, and said to the woman, "Watch over him, lest he should slip out of our hands."

While he slept the Soufi speaks: "Word of goodness, O excellent woman, bend over me that I may kiss thy mouth or else thy cheek. She says: "God make thy tent empty. Thou'lt die soon, and thou thinkest of kisses?"

"Truly I am going to die, and I die for thee. I love thee more than the whole world. Let me kiss thee once. I'll have a moment of joy, and then I'll die." She bends over him, and he kisses her.

She says, "What dost thou want?"

"That thou shalt untie me." She unties him. He says to her: "Keep silent. Do not speak a word." Then he unfastens the shackles that bind his feet, puts on his cloak, takes his gun, draws out the old charge and loads it anew, examines the flint-lock and sees that it works well. Then he says to the woman, "Lift up the Targui." The latter awakes.

"Why," says he, "didst thou not kill me in my sleep?"

"Because thou didst not kill me when I was in the well. Get up. Stand down there, while I stand here."

The Targui obeys, and says to the Soufi: "Fire first."

"No, I'll let thee fire first."

The woman speaks: "Strike, strike, O Targui, thou art not as strong as the Soufi."

The Targui rises, fires, and now the woman gives voice to a long "you—you." It strikes the *chechias* that fly above his head. At his turn the Soufi prepares himself and says:

"Stand up straight now, as I did for thee." He fires, and hits him on the forehead. His enemy dead, he flies at him and cuts his throat.

He then goes to the camel, cuts some meat, and says to the woman: "Go, find me some wood. I want to cook and eat."

"I will not go," she says. He approaches, threatening her, and strikes her. She gets up then and brings him some wood. He cooks the meat and eats his fill. He thinks then of killing the woman, but he fears that the people of his tribe will say, "Thou didst not bring her back." So he takes her on the camel and starts homeward. His cousins are pasturing their flocks on a hill. When he had nearly arrived a dust arose. He draws near, and they see that it is he. His brother speaks, "What have they done to thee?"

He answers, "The daughter of my uncle did all this."

Then they killed the woman and cut her flesh in strips and threw it on a jujube-tree. And the jackals and birds of prey came and passed the whole day eating it, until there was none left.

AHMED EL HILALIEU AND EL REDAH

Ahmed el Hilalieu was not loved by people in general. His enemies went and found an old sorceress, and spoke to her as follows: "O sorceress, we want you to drive this man out of our country. Ask what you will, we will give it to you!"

She said to them: "May God gladden your faces. Call aloud. Our man will come out and I will see him." They obeyed her, crying out that a camel had escaped. Straightway Ahmed goes to find his father, and tells him his intention of going to join in the search. He starts forth mounted on his courser, and on the way meets some people, who tell him, "It is nothing." He makes a half turn, not forgetting to water his horse, and meets at the fountain the sorceress, who was drawing water.

"Let me pass," he said to her, "and take your buckskin out of my way."

"You may pass," she answered. He started his horse, which stepped on the buckskin and tore it.

"You who are so brave with a poor woman," she said, "would you be able to bring back Redah Oum Zaid?"

"By the religion of Him whom I adore, you shall show me where this Redah lives or I'll cut off your head."

"Know, then, that she lives far from here, and that there is between her and you no less than forty days' journey."

Ahmed went home, and took as provisions for the journey forty dates of the deglet-nour variety, putting them into his pocket. He mounted his steed and departed.

He goes and goes without stopping, until he comes to the country of the sand. The charger throws his feet forward and buries himself in the sand up to his breast, but soon stops, conquered and worn out by fatigue. Ahmed el Hilalieu then addresses him:

> " My good gray horse, of noble mien, the sand,
> The cruel sand would eat your very eyes.
> The air no longer thy loud whinnies bears,
> No strength is left thee in thy head or heart.
> The prairies of Khafour I'll give to thee,
> With Nouna's eyes I'll quench thy thirst, by God.
> A mule's whole pack of barley shalt thou have
> That Ben Haddjouna shall bring here for thee."

In his turn the steed spoke and said: " Dismount, unfasten the breast-strap, tighten the girth, for some women are coming to show themselves to us in this country." Ahmed unfastened the breast-strap, then remounts and departs. While he proceeds he sees before him the encampment of a tribe, and perceives a horseman coming, mounted on a white mare, engaged in herding camels.

" Blessings upon you!" cried Ahmed; " you behind the camels!" The horseman kept silence, and would not return his salutations.

" Greetings to you," cried Ahmed again, " you who are in the middle of the camels." The same obstinate silence.

" Greetings to you, you who are before the camels." The horseman still was silent. Ahmed then said: " Greetings to you, you who own the white mare."

" Greetings to you!" replied the horseman.

" How comes it that you would not answer my greetings for so long?"

The horseman answered: " You cried to me, ' Greetings to you, you who are behind the camels.' Now, behind them are their tails. Then you said, ' Greetings to you, you who are in the middle of the camels.' In the middle of them are their bellies. You said, again, ' Greetings to you, you who are before the camels.' Before them are their heads. You said, 'Greetings to you, O master of the white mare.' And then I answered to you, 'Greetings to you also.'"

Ahmed el Hilalieu asked of the shepherd, "What is your name?"

"I am called Chira."

"Well, Chira, tell me where Redah lives. Is it at the city of the stones or in the garden of the palms?"

"Redah dwells in the city. Her father is the Sultan. Seven kings have fought for her, and one of them has refreshed his heart. He is named Chalau. Go, seek the large house. You will be with Redah when I see you again."

Ahmed sets out, and soon meets the wife of the shepherd, who comes before him and says, "Enter, be welcome, and may good luck attend you!" She ties his horse, gives him to drink, and goes to find dates for Ahmed. She takes care to count them before serving him with them. He takes out a pit, closes the date again, puts them all together, and puts down the pit. He ate nothing, and he said to the woman: "Take away these dates, for I have eaten my fill." She looks, takes up the tray, counts the dates again, and perceives that none of them has been eaten. Nevertheless, there is a pit, and not a date missing. She cries out:

"Alas! my heart for love of this young man
Is void of life as is this date of pit."

Then she heaved a sigh and her soul flew away.

Ahmed remained there as if in a dream until the shepherd came back. "Your wife is dead," he said to him, "and if you wish, I'll give you her weight in gold and silver."

But the shepherd answers: "I, too, am the son of a sultan. I have come to pay this woman a visit and desire to see her. Calm yourself. I will take neither your gold nor silver. This is the road to follow; go, till you arrive at the castle where she is."

Ahmed starts, and when he arrives at the castle, he stands up in his stirrups and throws the shadow of his spear upon the window.

Redah, addressing her negress, said to her: "See now what casts that shadow. Is it a cloud, or an Arab's spear?"

The negress goes to see, comes back to her mistress, and says to her, "It is a horseman, such as I have never seen the like of before in all my life."

"Return," said Redah, "and ask him who he is." Redah goes to see, and says:

> "O horseman, who dost come before our eyes,
> Why seekest thou thy death? Tell me upon
> Thine honor true, what is thine origin?

He answers:

> "Oh, I am Ahmed el Hilalieu called. Well known
> 'Mongst all the tribes of daughters of Hilal.
> I bear in hand a spear that loves to kill,
> Who'er attacks me counts on flight and dies."

She says to him:

> "Thou'rt Ahmed el Hilalieu? Never prowls
> A noble bird about the Zeriba;
> The generous falcon turns not near the nests,
> O madman! Why take so much care
> About a tree that bears not any dates?"

He answers:

> "I will demand of our great Lord of all
> To give us rain to cover all the land
> With pasturage and flowers. And we shall eat
> Of every sort of fruit that grows on earth."

Redah:

> "We women are like silk. And only those
> Who are true merchants know to handle us."

Ahmed el Hilalieu then says:

> "I've those worth more than thou amid the girls
> Of Hilal, clad in daintiest of silk
> Of richest dye, O Redah, O fifth rite."

And, turning his horse's head, he goes away. But she recalls him:

> "I am an orange, thou the gardener;
> I am a palm and thou dost cut my fruit;
> I am a beast and thou dost slaughter me.
> I am—upon thine honor—O gray steed,
> Turn back thy head. For we are friends henceforth."

She says to the negress, "Go open wide the door that he may come."

The negress admits him, and ties up his horse. On the third day he sees the negress laughing.

"Why do you laugh, negress?"

"You have not said your prayers for three days."

ܒܗ ܢܥܠ ܕܥܠܡܐ
ܡܠܟܟܬܐ ܟܗܘܬܐ ܒܒ
ܡܥܒܪ ܢܒܘܗܝ
ܘܠܡܢ ܀
ܗܒ ܡܡܠܐ ܣܠܝܐ
ܟܠ ܒܢܝ ܠܡܫܬܘܕܝܘ
ܡܫܡܫ ܒܟܠ ܠܫܡܝܐ
ܒܗܘܢ ܘܦܠܓ ܠܥܡܐ
ܢܫܡܥܘܢ ܠܗ ܀ ܐܢܐ
ܒܒ ܗܝܟ ܗܘܕܝܐ
ܒܠ ܠܝܘ

ܗܒ ܐܢܐ ܢܥܡ
ܗܢܘܢ ܕܗܘܢܐ
ܠܡܫܝܚܐ ܘܠܫܠܝܚܐ
ܒܠܘܢ ܐܘܦܣܩܝܐ
ܥܡ ܕܝܠܗ ܀ ܐܢܐ
ܒܠ ܒܫܠܝܐ
ܫܘܒܚܐ ܡܪܝܐ
ܘܒܟܠ ܠܗ ܒܡܢܐ
ܕܒܥܒܕܘܗܝ ܕܒܥܡܪܐ
ܡܫܝܚܐ ܐܢ ܒܥܕܢܐ

POEMS OF THE MAGHREB

—

[*Translated by M. C. Sonneck and Chauncey C. Starkweather*]

POEMS OF THE MAGHREB

ALI'S ANSWER

[ARGUMENT.—It is related that a young man named Aly ben Bou Fayd, falling in love with a young woman, begged his father to ask her in marriage for him. His father refused. Angered, Aly procured a gun, engraved his name upon it, and betook himself to the chase. His father having claimed this gun he answered :]

YOU ask the gun I have that bears my name.
I will not give it, save against my will.

How comes it, father, that you treat me thus?
You say, "Bring back the gun to put in pledge."
Now, may God pardon you for acting thus!
I leave you in your land, and, all for you,
I swear by God I never shall return.

Your conduct is unwise. Our enemies
Insult me, O my father. And I think
That you will give up your ancestral home
And garden too. And can I after that
Recover my good gun?

I shall not be
Enfeebled that I am no more with you.
No longer are you father unto me,
And I shall be no more your cherished son.
I think, my sire, that you are growing old.
Your teeth are falling out from day to day.
They whom you visit will not serve you more.

Your friends won't serve you longer, and your sire,
He who begot you, will not help you now.
In your adversity no help will come

From all your kindred's high nobility.
May God make easy all the paths you tread!

His uncle having threatened him with death, he answered:

Keep far away from him who has not come
To thee in his misfortune. Leave him free.
My uncle writes to me this very day
That if he held in his own hands the leaf
Of my life's destiny he'd blot it out.
If he had in his hands this leaf, O say to him:

Let him efface it openly, nor hide
You'll not be able, save with God's own help
To bear the separation. As for those
Who are so evil, we will spare them now.
The barrel of this gun is rusted red.
The lock is forceless, 'twill no longer act.
Misfortune overtake the man who leaves
His child to perish! For the least of things
He says to me, "Come, give me up this gun."

I go to seek the desert. I will go
Among the tribe they call Oulad Azyz,
And live by force. But, pray you say to her,
The fair one with the deftly braided hair,
I leave the tribe, but shall return for her.

I disappear, but shall come back for her.
And while I live, I never shall forget.
I swear it by the head of that sweet one
Who for the sake of Ali was accused.
The cup of passion which I offered her
O'ercame her lovely spirit's tenderness.

The cup of love intoxicated her.
O God, Creator of us all, give her
The strength to bear my absence! Sad for me
The hour I dream of her I love so well.
Her love is in my heart and burns it up.

My heart is sad. 'Tis love that crushes it.
It leaves my heart reduced to naught but dust.
So that I am consumed by vigils long,
And never taste refreshing sleep at all.
So that I'm like a bird with broken wings,

Just like a bird who tries to lift its wings!
And so my spirit is not healed. There comes
To me no comfort nor relief. The eyes
Of my beloved are as bright as day.
One word from her would send the friends to death.

IN HONOR OF LALLA AYCHA-EL-MANNOUBYYA

A fire burns at the bottom of my heart,
For love has conquered me, and I am now
His hostage and his prisoner. My soul
Is torn out from my body, and sweet sleep
Keeps far aloof from my tired eyelids' need.
'Tis Aycha causes this, the pretty one.
With blackest eyes, Aycha the pure, from whom
I'm parted now, whose name is finest gold.
Why? why? Oh, tell me, El Mannoubyya.

Why all this coldness, O my best beloved?
For thy dear love I have drunk deep of scorn.
For thy love, maiden with the darksome looks,
I wither while thou bear'st a port of oak.
The fire that burns me eats my very soul.
My spirit is distracted by these proofs.
O thou, rebellious to my warm desires,
My black-eyed beauty, if thou'rt vexed with me
I'll make apology before the world,
I'll bring an offering to thee at once,
The symbol of my homage. May it please!

Instruct me, sympathetic with my pain
Have you not said: "I'll bring thee soon good news"?
O come! That in my sleep my eyes may see
Thee coming toward me, my black-pupilled one!

Awaiting thy fair image I'm consumed,
I am exhausted. Why, El Mannoubyya?

I long have hoped to see thee, O my sweet.
And ever farther off appears the end
Of my awaiting. All my nights are passed
In cries for thee, as some poor mariner
Cries to the angry floods that dash aloft.
For thee I'm mad with love, my pretty one,
Struck with thy mien so full of nobleness.
And I alone must wither, 'mongst my friends.
O unpersuadable, with teasing eyes,
I am in a most pitiable state.
Since thou repell'st me and declin'st to keep
Thy promise to me, I'll not hesitate
To call thee before God.

Unless thou deign'st
To cast thy looks on me the coming day,
I shall, all clad in vestments rich, make plaint
Unto the envoy of our God, the last
Of all the prophets. For thou said'st to me,
"I'll draw thee from the sea of thy despair."
I worship at thy sanctuary, sweet,
My beauty, with large eyes of darkest night.
Why? why? El Mannoubyya, tell me why.

Let thyself bend and call thy servitor,
Inhabitant of Tunis—city green.
I will apologize and come to thee,
O cruel one, with heavy frontlets dark.
We've heard the story of thy deeds so fine.
From common brass whene'er thou walk'st abroad,
Thou drawest silver pure, queen of thy time,
'Mongst men illumined by thy piety.
The wretch, led on by love, accosted thee.
Receiving grace, despite his base design
He was, nathless, forgiven and saved from sin;
So was it from eternity decreed.
They all consulted thee, queen of thy day,

And thou didst answer: "This man truly loved.
Pour him a cup of wine." By thee he came
Unto perfection's acme, step by step.
Our Lord, all-powerful, gave to thee this power.

These are thy merits, fairest citizen!
To whom God gave strength irresistible.
O beauty with enchanting eyes, Aycha,
Our queen.

Si Alimed Khoudja, greatest bard
Of all that time, has said: "I wrote these words
The year one thousand one hundred just,
But thou who read'st these lines, where'er it be,
Add to these numbers, after ninety-eight."
Now I salute all those united here
And him who hates me here I steep in scorn.
Why? why? El Mannoubyya! Why?

SAYD AND HYZYYA

Give me your consolation, noble friends;
The queen of beauties sleeps within the tomb.
A burning fire consumes my aching breast;
I am undone. Alas! O cruel fate!
My heart's with slim Hyzyya in the grave.

Alas! we were so happy a short while
Ago, just like the prairie flow'rs in spring;
How sweet to us was life in those dear days!
Now like a phantom's shadow she has gone,
That young gazelle, of utter loveliness.
Removed by stern, inevitable fate.

When she walked forth, not looking right or left,
My beauteous loved one rendered fools the wise.
Impressed thus was the great bey of the camp.
A gleaming poniard rested in his belt.
He went hemmed in by soldiers and a horde
Of horsemen, glad to follow where he led.

All haste to bring him costly gifts. He bore
A sabre of the Ind, and with one stroke
He cleaved a bar of iron, split a rock.
How many rebels fell beneath his blow!
Haughty and proud, he challenged all who came.
Enough now we have glorified the bey.
Speak, singer, in a song that's sweet and new,
The praises of the dainty girl I loved,
The daughter of good Ahmed ben el Bey.

Give me your consolation, noble friends;
The queen of beauties sleeps within the tomb.
A burning fire consumes my aching breast;
I am undone! Alas! O cruel fate!

She lets her tresses flow in all the breeze,
Exhaling sweet perfume. Thy brows are arched
In beauty's curve. Thy glance is like a ball
Shot from a Christian's gun, which hits the mark.
Thy cheek is lovely as the morning rose
Or bright carnation, and thy ruby blood
Gives it the shining brightness of the sun.
Thy teeth are ivory-white, and thy warm kiss
Is sweet as milk or honey loved by all.
Oh, see that neck, more white than palm-tree's heart,
That sheath of crystal, bound with bands of gold.
Thy chest is marble, and thy tender breasts
Are apples whose sweet scent makes well the ill.
Thy body is, like paper, shining, white,
Or cotton or fine linen, or, again,
Just like the snow that falls in a dark night.
Hyzyya lets her sash hang gracefully,
Down-falling to the earth, in fold on fold.
Her fine limbs jingle with gems she wears.
Her slippers clink with coupled rings of gold.

We were encamped at Bazer. Every day
At dawn I saw the beauty, and we were
So glad together! Every dawn I brought
My wishes to my love and followed fate
More happy than if I alone possessed

All riches and all treasures of the earth.
Wealth equals not the tinkle of her gems.
When I had crossed the mountain there I met
Hyzyya, and she walked amid the fields
With every grace, and made her bracelets ring.
My reason wandered, heart and head were vexed.

After a happy summer passed at Tell,
We came, my dearest one and I, Sahara-ward.

The litters now are closed, the powder sounds.
My gray horse to Hyzyya bears me swift.
The palanquin of my coquette's on route.
At Azal when night comes we pitch our tents.
Sydy-l-Ahsen is before us now;
Ez-Zerga, too. Then faring on we go
To Sydy Sayd, and Elmetkeouk,
And Medoukal-of-palms, where we arrive
At eventide. We saddle up at dawn,
Just when the breeze begins. Our halting-place,
Sydy Mehammed, decks this peaceful earth.
From there the litters seek El Mekheraf.
My charger gray straight as an eagle goes.
I wend to Ben Serÿer with my love,
Of tattooed arms. When we had crossed Djedy
We passed the wide plain, and we spent the night
At Rous-et-toual, near the gleaming sands.
Ben Djellal was our next day's resting-place;
And, leaving there, I camped at El Besbas,
And last at El-Herymek, with my love.

How many festivals beheld us then!
In the arena my good steed of gray
Fled like a ghost. And sweet Hyzyya there,
Tall as a flagstaff, bent her gaze on me,
Her smile disclosing teeth of purest pearl.
She spoke but in allusions, causing thus
That I should understand whate'er she meant.
Hamyda's daughter then might be compared
Unto the morning-star or a tall palm,
Alone, erect among the other trees.

The wind uprooted it, and dashed it down.
I did not look to see it fall, this tree
I hoped forever to protect. I thought
That God, divinely good, would let it live.
But God, the Master, dashed it to the earth.

I take up now my song. We made but one
Encampment, at Oned Itel. 'Twas there
My friend, the queen of damsels, said farewell.
'Twas in the night she paid the debt of death.
'Twas there my dark-eyed beauty passed away.
She pressed her heart to mine and, sighing, died.
My cheeks were flooded with a sea of tears.
I thought to lose my reason. I went forth
And wandered through the fields, ravines, and hills.
She bore my soul away, my black-eyed love.
The daughter of a noble race. Alas!
She still increased the burnings of my heart.

They wrapped her in a shroud, my noble love.
The fever took me, burning up my brain.
They placed her on a bier, all decked with gems.
And I was in a stupor, dull to see
All that was passing on that dreadful day.
They bore my beauty in a palanquin—
Her pretty palanquin—this lovely girl,
Cause of my sorrows, tall as a straight staff.
Her litter is adorned with odd designs,
Shining as brilliant as the morning-star,
And like the rainbow glowing 'midst the clouds,
All hung with silk and figured damask-cloth.
And I, like any child, was in despair,
Mourning Hyzyya. Oh, what pangs I felt
For her whose profile was so pure! She nevermore
Will reappear upon this earth again.
She died the death of martyrs, my sweet love,
My fair'st one, with Koheul-tinted lids!

They took her to a country that is called
Sydy Kaled, and buried her at night,
My tattooed beauty. And her lovely eyes,

Like a gazelle's, have never left my sight.
O sexton, care now for my sweet gazelle,
And let no stones fall on Hyzyya's grave.
I do adjure thee by the Holy Book
And by the letters which make up the name
Of God, the Giver of all good, let no
Earth fall upon the dame with mirror decked.

Were it to claim her from a rival's arms
I would attack three troops of warriors.
I'd take her from a hostile tribe by force.
Could I but swear by her dear head, my love,
My black-eyed beauty—I would never count
My enemies, 'though they a hundred were.
Were she unto the strongest to belong
I swear she never would be swept from me.

In the sweet name Hyzyya I'd attack
And fight with cavaliers innumerable.
Were she to be the spoil of conqueror,
You'd hear abroad the tale of my exploits.
I'd take her by main strength from all who vied.
Were she the meed of furious encounters
I'd fight for years for her, and win at last!
For I am brave. But since it is the will
Of God, the mighty and compassionate,
I cannot ward away from me this blow.
I'll wait in patience for the happy day
When I shall join thee. For I only think
Of thee, my dearest love, of thee alone!

My gray steed fell dead as he leaped. O friends,
After my love, he's gone and left me, too.
My charger, 'mid these hills, was of all steeds
The fleetest, and in fiercest war's attack
All saw him at the head of the platoon.
What prodigies he wrought in war's red field!
He showed himself ahead of all his peers.
A blood-mare was his mother. He excelled
In all the contests 'twixt the wandering camps;
I tourneyed with him careless of my fate.

When just a month had passed I lost the steed.
Hyzyya first, and then this noble horse.
He did not long survive my well-beloved.
They both are gone, leaving their last farewells.
O grief! my charger's reins have fallen down.
God made my life a death, in leaving me
Behind. For them I die. Oh, cruel hurt!
I weep for this just as a lover weeps.
Each day my heart burns fiercer, and my joy
Has fled away. Now tell me, O my eyes,
Why shed so many tears? Beyond a doubt
The pleasures of the world will capture you.
And will you grant no mercy? My sad soul
But sees its torments grow. My pretty one,
With lashes black, who was my heart's delight,
Now sleeps beneath the sod. I do but weep
And my head whitens for the beauteous one,
With pearly teeth. My eyes no longer can
Endure the separation from their friend.

The sun that lights us to the zenith climbs,
Then gains the west. It disappears from sight
When it has gained the summit of the vault
Celestial. And the moon, which comes and shines
At Ramadan, beholds the hour approach
Of sleep, and says farewell to all the world.
To these would I compare the lovely queen
Of all this age, the daughter of Ahmed,
Descendant of a race illustrious,
The daughter of Donaonda.

Such is
The will of God, all-powerful Lord of men.
The Lord hath shown his will and borne away
Hyzyya. Grant me patience, O my Lord!
My heart dies of its hurt. Hyzyya's love
Did tear it from me when she left the earth.

She's worth a hundred steeds of noble race,
A thousand camels, and a grove of palms

In Zyban. Yes, all Djryd is she worth,
From near to far. The country of the blacks,
Haoussa and its people is she worth,
Arabians of Tell and dry Sahara,
And the encampments of the tribes, as far
As caravans can reach by all the ways,
All nomads and all travellers, she's worth,
And those who settle down as citizens.
The treasurer of all riches is she worth,
My black-eyed beauty. And if thou dost think
This all too small, add all the cities' folk.
She's worth all flocks and nicely chisel'd gold,
She's worth the palms of Dra and Chaouyya;
All that the sea contains, my love is worth,
The fields and cities from beyond Djebel
Amour, as far as Ghardaya. She is worth
All Mzab, the plains of Zab. She pleases, too,
The people of the Goubba, holy folk,
And friends of God. She's worth all noble steeds
However richly housed—or evening's star
When twilight comes. Too small—'tis all too small
For my sweet love, sole cure of all my woes.
O God majestic, pardon this poor wretch!
Pardon, O Lord and Master, him who grieves!

Just three-and-twenty years! That was the age
Of her who wore the silken sash. My love
Has followed her, ne'er to revive within
My widowed heart. Console me, Mussulmans,
My brothers, for the loss of my sweet one,
Gazelle of all gazelles, who dwelleth now
In her cold, dark, eternal home.
Console me, O young friends, for having lost
Her whom you'd call a falcon on its nest.
Naught but a name she left behind which I
Gave to the camp wherein she passed away.
Console me, men, for I have lost my fair,
Dear one, that silver *khelkals* wore.
Now is she covered with a veil of stone,
On strong foundation laid. Console me, friends,

For all this loss, for she loved none but me.
With my own hands my love's chest I tattooed,
Likewise her wrists, with checkered patterns odd,
Blue as the collar of the gentle dove.
Their outlines did not clash, so deftly drawn,
Although without *galam*—my handiwork.
I drew them 'twixt her breasts, and on her wrists
I marked my name. Such is the sport of fate!

Now Sa'yd, always deep in love with thee,
Shall never see thee more! The memory
Of thy dear name fills all his heart, my sweet.

Oh, pardon, God compassionate, forgive
Us all. Sa'yd is sad, he weeps for one
Dear as his soul. Forgive this love, Lord!
Hyzyya—join them in his sleep, O God most high.
Forgive the author of these verses here!
It is Mahomet that recites this tale.

O Thou who hast the future in thy hand,
Give resignation to one mad with love!
Like one exiled from home, I weep and mourn.
My enemies might give me pity now.
All food is tasteless, and I cannot sleep.
I write this with my love but three days dead.
She left me, said farewell, and came not back.

This song, O ye who listen, was composed
Within the year twelve hundred finished now,
The date by adding ninety-five years more. [1295.]

This song of Ould-es-Serge we have sung
In Ayd-el-Rebye, in the singing month,
At Sydy-Khaled-ben Sinan. A man,
Mahomet ben Guytoun, this song has sung
Of her you'll never see again alive.
My heart lies there in slim Hyzyya's tomb.

THE AÏSSAOUA IN PARIS*

Come, see what's happened in this evil year.
The earthquake tumbled all the houses down,
Locusts and crickets have left naught behind.

Hear what has happened to those negro scamps,
Musicians—rogues, and Aïssaoua.
They spoke of nothing but their project great.
Bad luck to him who lacks sincerity!

On learning of the tour of Rayyato
They all began to cry and run about,
Half with bare feet, although the rest were shod.
The Lord afflicts them much in this our world.
'Twas only negroes, poor house-colorers,
Who did not follow them about in crowds.

The Christian Salvador put them on ship.
One felt his breast turn and exclaimed, "I'm sick."
A wench poured aromatics on the fire,
And thus perfumed the air. For Paris now
They're off, to see the great Abd-el-Azyz.

The Christians packed them like a cricket-swarm,
Between the sea and church, upon the wharf
He drew them, wonders promising, and led
Them but to beggary.

He takes them to
His land to show them to the chief of all
His masters, to the Emperor. He hopes
To get a present and thus pay them back,
Retaining all the money he advanced.

* Former student of the Medersa of Algiers, bookbinder, lutemaker, and copier of manuscripts, Qaddour ben Omar ben Beuyna, best known among his coreligionists as Qaddour el Hadby (the hunchback), who died during the winter of 1897–1898, has sung for thirty years about all the notables of his city. This lively poem was composed by him on the occasion of the departure for Paris of a band of musicians, singers, and Aissaoua, who figured at the Exposition of 1867, under the direction of a professor of music named Salvador Daniel. The original is in couplets of six hemistichs.

Perhaps they'll show themselves upon some stage
Or elsewhere as his fancy leads. The blacks
Begin to dance to sound of castanets.
The Christians bet on what will happen next.

They say a letter has arrived which says
That they've suppressed ablutions and their prayers.
One has been very ill—" I do not know
What is the matter with me "—but the cause
Of all his illness was because he fell
On the perfuming-pans that they had brought.

For Imam they have ta'en the dancing-girl
Who leads the dances. With her boxes small
In basket made of grass, a picture fine!
Come, see it now; you'd think it was a ghost.

The Christian works them all, and most are seized
With folly. Would you know the first of all?
Well, sirs, 'tis Et-Try, and he is the son
Of one Et-Germezlyya. Never has
He thought of doing well, he lives for crime.

The shrewd " Merkanty " made a profit on them.
Et-Try served them as an interpreter.
The Christian ought to make them this year gain
A thousand d'oros. But I pray to God
To send those two men to the fires of hell.

Now Aly Et-Try is their manager;
He runs about all day, with naught achieved.
The Christian kept them in a stable shut,
And like a squad of soldiers took them out.
He herded them like oxen there, and naught
Was lacking but the drover's lusty cries.

Consider now the plight of Ould Sayyd,
The big-jawed one. He gained ten thousand francs,
And lost them all at gambling. Naught remains
Except the benches and some coffee-grounds.

The leader of musicians, wholly daft,
Whose beard is whiter than the whitest wool,
Has gone to Paris gay to see the sights.
(I hope he'll bring up in the fires of hell!)
If he comes back deceived, at least he'll say
He's been abroad, and dazzle all his friends.

The oboe-player, Sydy Ali, was
Barber and cafékeeper, eager for
A change, and crazy to get gold. "This trip,"
He told his friends, "is but a pilgrimage."
There's nothing lacking but the telbyya.

"I've taken trips before and with good luck.
I was the master, with my art acclaimed.
I was director of the Nouba, at
The court, when Turkey held the reins of power.
I was a court buffoon and broke my heart.
O Lord, why send'st thou not thy servant death?

"I left a workman in my shop so that
I might not lose my trade. I went to show
My oboe, for someone might ask for it.
I used to travel with musicians once."

God bless him!—what a workman. He conversed
With all the customers who passed that way.
He took them in the shop and told his case—
"I'm here for a short while." Then he began
To praise his patron, who, he said, would have
A gift for him.

And his lieutenant, named
Oulyd-el-Hadj Oualy, is a fool
Who thinks his word superior to all,
And that there's no one like him in this world.
When he has gone there and come back again,
He will be perfect. All he contradicts
Who speak to him, and will not let them lift
A finger. Little love he hath for those

Who speak with candor, but he's very fond
Of liars, and always bids them come to him.

"My childhood was so pampered!" he remarks,
And flies into a passion if one doubts.
He only lives on semolina coarse,
And empty is his paunch, all slack and limp.
Yet every day he tells you how he's dined.

"I have discovered," he is wont to say
"A certain semolina lately brought
By a Maltese, who lives some distance off.
You never saw the like. I'm going to have
Some fine cakes made of it, and some *meqrout.*"

And El-Hadj Mostefa was dragged along
By all these lies and by the love of gain.
If God had not abandoned him, he'd be
Still making lasts. But 'twas the crowd that led
Him on, and that is how it came to pass.

With them is donkey-faced Hamŷda, who
Sold flowers in the market-place. He left
His family no coins to live upon,
But told them only: "Moderate your pace.
I'll buy a house for you when I get back,
And we shall live in plenty evermore."

Sydy Ahmed et Tsoqba timbals had
As big as goat-skin bottles. He desired
To play in unison, but the musicians all
Abhorred him, for he could not keep in time.

The heart of Sydy Ahmed glows with love
For Ayn-bou-Sellouf, who is very fair.
I hope that cares and fainting-fits may swell
Him out, and yellow he will straight become
As yellow as a carrot in a field.

I love Sydy-t-Tayyeb when he sings
And plays the tambourine. Such ugliness

My eyes have never seen. You'd think he was
A clown. He says: "No one could vanquish me
Were I not just a trifle ill to-day."

Qaddour, the little cock, the drummer-boy,
Who hangs on walls and colors houses here
Or tars roofs with his mates, exclaims: "I took
This voyage just to get a bit of air."

Koutchouk stayed here, he did not go away.
Fresh apricots he sells down in the square.
"Repose," he murmurs, "is the best of foods,
And here my little heart shall stay in peace."

When Abd-el-Quader, undertaker's son,
Falls in his fits of folly, he binds round
His figure with a cord and does not lie
Inert and stiff. But still they scorpions see
In Allal's hand, Chaouch of Aïssaoua.

Faradjy—fop—eats fire and fig-leaves now;
The while Hasan the Rat excites him on
To doughty deeds with his loud tambourine,
Playing with all his might and all his soul.
They dragged the hedge-rows green of El Qettár
To pay this tribute to the Emperor.

That fop, Ben Zerfa, who chopped hashish seeds
Among us here, said: "We have had good luck
This summer, and I'm going to pay my debts.
I'll execute my drill with stick and sword
And serve my sheik the very best I can."

If you had seen Ben Zerfa as he ran,
So lightly, bearing on his sturdy back
A basket filled with, heaven alone knows what!
It looked like cactus-pears, the basket closed.

El Hadj Batâta—see his silly trance!
With shirt unbuttoned and with collar off,
And cap on eyes, at beating of the drums,
He shows his tuft denuded all of hair.

Even Móstafa ben el Meddâh desired
To go to Paris and his fortune make.
"On my return," he said, "I'll buy a lamp,
A coffee-tray, and goodly sugar-bowl;
A big and little mattress, too, I'll buy,
A carpet and a rug so soft and fine."
Es Snybla, bellows-faced, who used to work
For our good mayor, off to Paris went
To make the soldiers' coffee. When he comes
Back home again, so much he will have earned.
He will be richer than a merchant great.

Oh, welcome, Sydy Omar! All of Paris
Is charmed to see you, O my Snybla dear!
If he would only go to Mexico,
And stay there it would be a riddance good.

He is a cafékeeper, and his son
A baker. For associate he has
Sydy Aly Mehraz, who does his work
Astride a thorn; he surely doth deserve
Our compliments. All three you see are dressed
In duck, in fashion of the Christian men.
There's de Merzong; the people say he's good,
But still they fear him, he is so uncouth.
Good God! When he begins aloud to cry
In Soudanese, it is enough to make
You fly to the antipodes away.

Oulyd ben Zamoum saw his cares increase—
Since he is a musician, as he thinks,
The world is rid of him. And when he starts
To play the first string of the violin,
The while the Jewess doth begin to sing!

With him two Jews departed, and the like
You never saw on earth. A porcupine
The first resembled, and the other one
Was one-eyed. You should hear them play the lute!

Some persons heard my story from afar,
Oulyd Sydy Sáŷd, among them, and

Brymat, who laughed abundantly. And with
Them was the chief of Miliana. All
Were seated on an iron bench, within
The right-hand shop. They called me to their booth
Where I had coffee and some sweets. But when
They said, "Come take a smoke," I was confused.
"Impossible," I answered, "for I have
With Sydy Hasan Sydy Khelyl studied,
And the Senousyya. So I cannot."

Ben Aysa came to me, with angry air,
"The Antichrist," he said, "shall spring from thee.
I saw within that book you have at home
His story truly told." "You're right," said I,
"Much thanks!" And then I laughed to see
Him turn his eyes in wrath.

He said to me
'Tis not an action worthy of a man;
He glared at me with eyes as big as cups
And face an egg-plant blue. He wanted to
Get at me, in his rage, and do me harm.

With him my uncle was, Mahomet-ben-
El-Haffaf, who remains at prayer all day.
He heard this prelude and he said to them,
"It is not an affair." "Fear not," they said,
"For they will put you also in the song."

He's tickled by the urchins' eulogies,
Who praise him as the master of chicane.
"'Tis finished now for thee to climb up masts."
They add: "You're but a laughing-stock for all.
You've stayed here long enough. You'd better go
And teach Sahary oxen how to read!"

When I recited all these lines to Sy
Mahomet Oulyd el-Isnam, who has
To the supreme degree the gift of being
A bore he said to me, "Now this is song
Most flat." The mice in droves within his shop
Have eaten an ounce of wool.

He is installed
Within the chamber of El Boukhary.
In posture of a student, in his hands
Some sky-blue wool. "It is," he says, "to make
Some socks for little children, for I have
But little wool."

When I had finished quite
This dittyramb, and El-Hadj-ben-er-Rebha
Became acquainted with it, he began
To laugh, telling his beads the while, and then
His decoration from his wallet took,
Which had been there enclosed.

My song spread wide.
They found it savory. Respected sirs,
It is the latest Friday in the month
Of El Mouloud and in the year we call
Twelve hundred ninety-four, that I complete
This tale fantastic.

Would you know my name?
I am Qaddour, well known to all the world,
Binder to Sydy Boû Gdour, and attired
In gechchabyya-blouse. And if my back
Were not deformed, none could compete with me.

They told me, "When those folk come back again
Thou'd better hide thyself for fear of harm.
They'll break thy hump and send thee home to heaven."
"Oh, I'll protect myself," I said, "or else complain
To the police."

If I were not so busy
I'd still have many other things to say.
Those who have heard my prattle say it's good;
So say the singers and musicians, too,
Ez Zohra ben-el-Foul among them, who
Pays compliments to me, from window-seat.

He who hath nothing found that's useful here
Will find in this my song what suits him best.

But if he wants to see here something more,
Then stretch him 'neath the stick and give him straight
A thousand blows upon the belly; then
Take him away to the physician, who
Will bleed him well.

And now may hearts not be
Made sad by what I have so lightly said.
I've placed myself among you, so that I
May not incur your blame, O brothers mine.
I've told you my deformity, and all
My miseries unveiled before your gaze.

SONG OF FATIMA *

My spirit is in pain, for it cannot
Forget my sweet gazelle, with eyes so black.
A fire burns in my heart, and all my frame
But wastes and withers. Where's thy cure, O Taleb?

I find no medicine that cureth love,
In vain I search. Sweet Fatima's the cause
Of all my woes, with *khelkal* tinted blue.
My heart endureth passion's pangs, my grief
Continues. Where's thy remedy, O Taleb?
Thy remedy is lost, my good Lord Taleb.

Pray God for me, O Taleb, I implore.
But how to cure the malady of love?
There is no remedy, and all is lost.
I die for lack of strength to bear my trials.
It is to thee that I intrust myself,
The healer who must bring rest to my heart;
For now a living brand burns in my breast.
If thou art skilful, find a cure for me.

* This elegy is the work of a celebrated cheik of Tlemcen, Mahomet-Ben-Sahla, whose period was the first half of the eighteenth century. He left a son, Ben Medien, a poet, too, and his descendants still live, near Tlemcen, in a village called Feddan-es-Seba.

Look in thy book and calculate for me
If thou canst quench the burning brand within.
I will become thy slave, and thou may'st keep
Me or at auction sell. Where is thy cure!
Thy remedy is lost, my good Lord Taleb.

The Taleb looked at me and said: " Take heart,
O lover, courage! Thou hast sipped, I see,
The cup of death already, and thou hast
Not long to live. But hear my counsel now.
Have patience! 'Tis the only thing that will
Sustain thee. Thou shalt thus obtain the gifts
Of Him who only knows thy future days.
Thy fate shall be unrolled according to
The will of God, the sovereign Lord most high.

" Turn to thy God. Beseech him constantly.
He hears with mercy and he knows all souls.
He turns away no one who comes to him.
He sees the bottom of their hearts, and lists.
Bear his decrees with patience camels show.
They walk from land to land and hope to lose
At last their burdens." Where's thy cure, O Taleb?
Thy remedy is lost, my good Lord Taleb.

O Taleb, search within thy book and find
The letters that give birth to friendship sweet.
Write them for me, and skilful be, I pray,
So God may give me happiness by them,
And cause my dear gazelle to pardon me,
And drive my bitter sorrows all away.
My punishment too long has lasted. I
Am tired of waiting. Never was adventure
More strange than mine.

My cares continue, and
I am fatigued with efforts obstinate.
The trouble that I've taken to deserve
That pretty one, has been for me like that
Of daring merchant who doth undertake
A venture and gets nothing back but loss

And weariness. Where is thy cure, O Taleb?
Thy remedy is lost, my good Lord Taleb.

The Taleb answered unto me and said:
" Support her rigors. Listen now to me,
And I will give thee counsel sound and good.
Turn thy true heart aside from memory.
Forget thy love as she's forgotten thee.
Courage! Her loss now wastes and makes thee pale.
For her thou hast neglected everything,
And sacrificed a good part of thy days.

" My counsels heed and turn me not aside.
Hear what sages in their proverbs say:
'That which is bitter never can turn sweet.'
'Leave him whose intercourse is troublesome,
And cleave to one who hath an easy way.'
'Endure the pangs of love until they pass,'"
Where is thy cure, O Taleb? Tell me where.
Thy remedy is lost, O good Lord Taleb.

If thou art powerful, Taleb, my excuse
Accept, and give assistance to my cause.
Thy words are all in vain, they but increase
My woes. For ne'er can I forget my love,
My dear accomplished beauty. While I live,
I love her, queen of beauties, and she is
Soul of my soul, light of my eyes, my sweet.

And, oh, how grows my love! A slave I'd be,
Obedient to a man despised. Perhaps
That which is far removed, the nearest comes.
And if the moment comes, thou know'st it well
Who knoweth all the proverbs! He that's well
Shall perish, and the invalid be cured.
Where is thy cure, O Taleb? Tell me where.
Thy remedy is lost, my good Lord Taleb.

And then the Taleb answered him and said:
" Thou'rt taken in the snares of Qeys—thou know'st.
He laid strong siege to Leyla's heart and then

Awaited trembling at the trysting-place.
Thou now hast wooed thy love for two long years
And she will not relent, nor speak to thee.
God bless us both!"

The Lord is generous.
He sees. If trouble comes, he'll make it pass.
My lot is sad and I am full of fear.
The mountains tall would melt and turn to sand
If I to them my sorrows should relate.
Where is thy cure, O Taleb? Tell me where.
Thy remedy is lost, O good Lord Taleb.

O Taleb, should I tell my tale of grief
Unto a sabre of the Ind, 'twould melt
On hearing my laments. My heart cannot
Endure these tortures, and my breast's on fire.

My tale is finished, here I end my song,
And publish forth my name along with it;
It is Ben Sahla. I do not conceal
How I am called, and in my black despair
I do not cease my lamentations loud.

O ye who have experienced the stings
Of love, excuse me now and blame me not
In this affair. I know that I shall die,
O'ercome by woe. The doctor of my heart
Protracts my suffering. He cures me not,
Nor yet cuts short the thread of my sad life.
Where is thy cure, O Taleb? Tell me where.
Thy remedy is lost, O good Lord Taleb.

THE CITY GIRL AND THE COUNTRY GIRL

O thou who hearest me, I will recite
One of these stories I am master of—
A tale that's true. By these I move the hearts
Of lovers like to thee, and I divert
Their minds with pleasant stories. As I hear,
So I relate them, and they please my friends,
By flow of wit and eloquence of thought.
I tell of beauties' battle. And my song
Is written in perfection, straight and clear.

Thinking of naught I walked along one day
When I had gone to see some beauties fair
Whose like I ne'er have seen in city nor
In country yet. I should have said
That they were sun and moon, and that the girls
Of that time were bright stars surpassing far
The Pleiades. The stars are envious
In their far firmaments, each of
The other. That's the reason why we see
Eclipses of the sun and moon.

My tale
Is true. The women, like unto the stars,
Are jealous also. Two young virgins met
The day I saw them, a sad day for them,
For one was jealous of the other one.

The citizeness said to the Bedouine:
"Look at thy similars and thou shalt see
In them but rustics, true dogs of the camp.
Now what art thou beside a city girl?
Thou art a Bedouine. Dost thou not dream
Of goat-skin bottles to be filled at dawn?
And loads of wood that thou must daily cut?
And how thou'rt doomed to turn the mill all night,
Fatigued, harassed? Thy feet, unshod, are chapped
And full of cracks. Thy head can never feel
The solace of uncovering, and thou,

All broken with fatigue, must go to sleep
Upon the ground, in soot and dust to lie,
Just like a serpent coiled upon himself.
Thy covering is the tatters of old tents,
Thy pillow is the stones upon the hearth.
All clad in rags thou hast a heavy sleep
Awaking to another stupid day.
Such is the life of all you country folk.
What art thou then compared to those who live
In shade of walls, who have their mosques for prayer
Where questions are discussed and deeds are drawn?"

The Arab woman to the city girl
Replied: "Get out! Thou'rt like a caverned owl.
And who art thou beside the Arab girls,
The daughters of those tribes whose standards wave
Above brave bands of horsemen as they speed?
Look at thy similars. The doctor ne'er
Can leave their side. Without an illness known
They're faded, pale, and sallow. The harsh lime
Hath filled thy blood with poison. Thou art dead,
Although thou seem'st alive. Thou ne'er hast seen
Our noble Arabs and their feats of strength,
Who to the deserts bring prosperity
By their sharp swords! If thou could'st see our tribe
When all the horsemen charge a hostile band,
Armed with bright lances and with shields to break
The enemy's strong blow! Those who are like
To them are famed afar and glorified.
They're generous hosts and men of nature free.
Within the mosques they've built and lodgings made
For *tolba* and for guests. All those who come
To visit them, bear gifts away, and give
Them praises. Why should they reside in town
Where everything's with price of silver bought?

The city girl replied: "Oh, Bedouine,
Thou dost forget all that thou hast to do.
Thou go'st from house to house, with artichokes
And mallows, oyster-plants, and such,

Thy garments soaked all through and through with grease.
This is thy daily life. I do not speak
Of what is hid from view. Thy slanders cease!
What canst thou say of me? Better than thee
I follow all the precepts of the Sonna
And note more faithfully the sacred hours.
Hid by my veil no eye hath seen my face:
I'm not like thee, forever in the field.
I've streets to go on when I walk abroad.
What art thou, then, beside me? I heard not
The cows and follow them about all day.
Thou eatest sorrel wild and heart of dwarf
Palm-tree. Thy feet are tired with walking far,
And thy rough hands with digging in the earth."

"Now what impels you, and what leads you on,"
The country girl of city girl inquired,
"To outrage us like this and say such words
Against us, you who are the very worst
Of creatures, in whom all the vices are
Assembled? You are wicked sinners all,
And Satan would not dare to tell your deeds.
You are all witches. And you would betray
Your brother, not to speak of husbands. You
Walk all unguarded in the street alone,
Against your husband's will. And you deny
Your holy faith. The curse of heav'n will weigh
Upon you when you go to meet your God.
Not one of you is honest. O ye blind
Who do not wish to see, whence comes your blindness?
You violate the law divine, and few
Among you fear the Lord. 'Tis in the country,
Amid the fields, that women worship God.
Why say'st thou that the city women sole
Are pious? Canst thou say my prayers for me?"

"What pleasure have the country girls?" replied
The city girl. "They've no amusements there.
There's nothing to divert the eyes. Their hands
They do not stain with henna, setting off

A rounded arm. Rich costumes they wear not,
Which cost some hundred silver pieces each,
Nor numerous garments decked with precious stones.
They are not coifed with kerchiefs of foulard
With flowers brocaded. Neither have they veils
Nor handkerchiefs of silk and broidered gold.
They never have a negress nurse to bring
Their children up and run on services
Throughout the house. And yet they boast as loud
As any braggart. Why bring'st thou the charge
That I a blameful life do lead, whilst thine
Deserves reproof? Dirt in the country holds
Supreme control. The water's scarce enough
To drink, with none left for the bath. The ground
Serves you as bed, and millet is your food,
Or rotten wheat and barley."

Then took up
The word, and spoke the Arab woman dark:
"Who are thy ancestors? Which is thy tribe
Among all those that fill the mighty world?
You're only Beny Leqyt, and the scum
Of people of all sorts. Thou call'st thyself
A city woman. What are city men?
Thy lords don't slander folk. 'Tis only those
Who come whence no one knows who have so rude
A tongue. Thou wouldst insult me, thou, of stock
Like thine, with such a name abroad! And thou
Wouldst taunt a Qorechyte, a Hachemite
Of glorious ancestors who earned their fame.
'Tis proper for a woman born of such
A stock illustrious to vaunt herself
Upon her origin. But thou, a vile
Descendant of a conquered race!

"Thou call'st
Thyself a Sunnite, yet thou knowest not
The three great things their Author gave to us:
(He knows all secrets.) First is Paradise,
Then the Koran, and then our Prophet great,

Destroyer of false faiths and for all men
The interceder. Whosoe'er loves him
Doth love the Arabs, too, and cleaves to them.
And whosoe'er hates them hates, too, in truth,
The chosen one of God. Thou hatest him,
For thou revil'st my ancestors, and seek'st
To lower their rank and vilify their fame.
Think on thine evil deeds, against the day
When in thy grave thou'lt lie, and that one, too,
When thou shalt rise again, insulter of
The Arabs, king of peoples on the earth."

" The Arabs I do not at all despise,"
The city woman said, " nor yet decry
Their honor, and 'tis only on account
Of thee I spoke against them. But 'tis thou
Who hast insulted all my family, and placed
Thy race above. He who begins is e'er
At fault, and not the one who follows. Thou
The quarrel didst commence. Pray God, our Lord,
To pardon me, as I will pray him, too,
And I the Arabs will no more attack.
If they offend me I will pardon them
And like them for our holy prophet's sake.
I shall awake in Paradise some day.
From them 'tis given, far beyond all price.
Frankly, I love them more than I do love
Myself. I love them from my very heart.
He who a people loveth shall arise
With them. And here's an end to all our words
Of bickering and mutual abuse."

I told them that it was my duty plain
To reconcile them. I accorded both
Of them most pure intentions. Then I sent
Them home, and made agreeable the way.
Their cares I drove away with honeyed words.
I have composed the verses of this piece,
With sense more delicate than rare perfume
Of orange-flower or than sugar sweet,

For those kind hearts who know how to forgive.
As for the evil-minded, they should feel
The *zeqqoum*. With the flowers of rhetoric
My song is ornamented: like the breast
Of some fair virgin all bedeckéd with stones
Which shine like bright stars in the firmament.
Some of its words will seem severe to those
Who criticise. I culled them like unto
A nosegay in the garden of allusions.
May men of lion hearts and spirit keen—
Beloved by God and objects of his care—
Receive my salutations while they live,
My countless salutations.

I should let
My name be known to him who's subject to
The Cherfa and obeys their mighty power.
The *mym* precedes, then comes the written *ha*.
The *mym* and *dal* complete the round and make
It comprehensible to him who reads
Mahomet. May God pardon me this work
So frivolous, and also all my faults
And errors. I place confidence in him,
Creator of all men, with pardon free
For all our sins, and in his mercy trust,
Because he giveth it to him who seeks.

The country girl and city girl appeared
Before the judge, demanding sentence just.
In fierce invectives for a while they joined,
But after all I left them reconciled.

POPULAR TALES OF THE BERBERS

—

[*Translated by René Basset and Chauncey C. Starkweather*]

POPULAR TALES OF THE BERBERS

STORIES OF ANIMALS

The Turtle, the Frog, and the Serpent

ONCE upon a time the turtle married a frog. One day they quarrelled. The frog escaped and withdrew into a hole. The turtle was troubled and stood in front of his door very much worried. In those days the animals spoke. The griffin came by that way and said: "What is the matter with you? You look worried this morning."

"Nothing ails me," answered the turtle, "except that the frog has left me."

The griffin replied, "I'll bring him back."

"You will do me a great favor."

The griffin took up his journey and arrived at the hole of the frog. He scratched at the door.

The frog heard him and asked, "Who dares to rap at the door of a king's daughter?"

"It is I, the griffin, son of a griffin, who lets no carrion escape him."

"Get out of here, among your corpses. I, a daughter of the King, will not go with you."

He departed immediately.

The next day the vulture came along by the turtle and found it worrying before its door, and asked what was the trouble. It answered: "The frog has gone away."

"I'll bring her back," said the vulture.

"You will do me a great favor."

The vulture started, and reaching the frog's house began to beat its wings.

The frog said: "Who comes to the east to make a noise at the house of the daughter of kings, and will not let her sleep at her ease?"

"It is I, the vulture, son of a vulture, who steals chicks from under her mother."

The frog replied: "Get away from here, father of the dunghill. You are not the one to conduct the daughter of a king."

The vulture was angry and went away much disturbed. He returned to the turtle and said: "The frog refuses to come back with me. Seek someone else who can enter her hole and make her come out. Then I will bring her back even if she won't walk."

The turtle went to seek the serpent, and when he had found him he began to weep. "I'm the one to make her come out," said the serpent. He quickly went before the hole of the frog and scratched at the door.

"What is the name of this other one?" asked the frog.

"It is I, the serpent, son of the serpent. Come out or I'll enter."

"Wait awhile until I put on my best clothes, gird my girdle, rub my lips with nut-shells, put some *koheul* in my eyes; then I will go with you."

"Hurry up," said the serpent. Then he waited a little while. Finally he got angry, entered her house, and swallowed her. Ever since that time the serpent has been at war with the frog. Whenever he sees one he chases her and eats her.

The Hedgehog, the Jackal, and the Lion

Once upon a time the jackal went in search of the hedgehog and said to it: "Come along. I know a garden of onions. We will fill our bellies."

"How many tricks have you?" asked the hedgehog.

"I have a hundred and one."

"And I," said the other, "have one and a half."

They entered the garden and ate a good deal. The hedgehog ate a little and then went to see if he could get out of the entrance or not. When he had eaten enough so that he could just barely slip out, he stopped eating. As for the jackal, he never stopped eating until he was swollen very much.

As these things were going on, the owner of the garden arrived. The hedgehog saw him and said to his companion:

"Escape! the master is coming." He himself took flight. But in spite of his exhortations the jackal couldn't get through the opening. "It is impossible," he said.

"Where are those one hundred and one tricks? They don't serve you now."

"May God have mercy on your parents, my uncle, lend me your half a trick." "Lie down on the ground," answered the hedgehog. "Play dead, shut your mouth, stretch out your paws as if you were dead, until the master of the garden shall see it and cast you into the street, and then you can run away."

On that the hedgehog departed. The jackal lay down as he had told him until the owner of the garden came with his son and saw him lying as if dead. The child said to his father:

"Here is a dead jackal. He filled his belly with onions until he died."

Said the man, "Go, drag him outside."

"Yes," said the child, and he took him and stuck a thorn into him.

"Hold on, enough!" said the jackal. "They play with reeds, but this is not sport."

The child ran to his father and said, "The jackal cried out, 'A reed! a reed!'"

The father went and looked at the animal, which feigned death. "Why do you tell me that it still lives?"

"It surely does."

"Come away and leave that carrion." The child stuck another thorn into the jackal, which cried, "What, again?" The child went to his father. "He has just said, 'What, again?'"

"Come now," said the man, and he sent away his son. The latter took the jackal by the motionless tail and cast him into the street. Immediately the animal jumped up and started to run away. The child threw after him his slippers. The jackal took them, put them on, and departed.

On the way he met the lion, who said, "What is that footwear, my dear?"

"You don't know, my uncle? I am a shoemaker. My father, my uncle, my mother, my brother, my sister, and the little girl who was born at our house last night are all shoemakers."

"Won't you make me a pair of shoes?" replied the lion.

"I will make you a pair. Bring me two fat camels. I will skin them and make you some good shoes."

The lion went away and brought the two fat camels. "They are thin," said the jackal. "Go change them for others."

He brought two thin ones.

"They are fat," said the jackal. He skinned them, cut some thorns from a palm-tree, rolled the leather around the lion's paws and fastened it there with the thorns.

"Ouch!" screamed the lion.

"He who wants to look finely ought not to say, 'Ouch.'"

"Enough, my dear."

"My uncle, I will give you the rest of the slippers and boots." He covered the lion's skin with the leather and stuck in the thorns. When he reached the knees, "Enough, my dear," said the lion. "What kind of shoes are those?"

"Keep still, my uncle, these are slippers, boots, breeches, and clothes."

When he came to the girdle the lion said, "What kind of shoes are those?"

"My uncle, they are slippers, boots, breeches, and clothing." In this way he reached the lion's neck. "Stay here," he said, "until the leather dries. When the sun rises look it in the face. When the moon rises, too, look it in the face."

"It is good," said the lion, and the jackal went away.

The lion remained and did as his companion had told him. But his feet began to swell, the leather became hard, and he could not get up. When the jackal came back he asked him, "How are you, my uncle?"

"How am I? Wretch, son of a wretch, you have deceived me. Go, go; I will recommend you to my children."

The jackal came near and the lion seized him by the tail. The jackal fled, leaving his tail in the lion's mouth.

"Now," said the lion, "you have no tail. When my feet get well I will catch you and eat you up."

The jackal called his cousins and said to them, "Let us go and fill our bellies with onions in a garden that I know." They went with him. Arriving he tied their tails to the branches of a young palm-tree, and twisted them well. "Who has tied our tails like this?" they asked. "No one will come before you have filled your bellies. If you see the master of the garden approach, struggle and fly. You see that I, too, am bound as you are." But he had tied an onion-stalk on himself. When the owner of the garden arrived, the jackal saw him coming. They struggled, their tails were all torn out, and stayed behind with the branches to which they were fastened. When the jackal saw the man, he cut the onion stem and escaped the first of all.

As for the lion, when his feet were cured, he went to take a walk and met his friend the jackal. He seized him and said, "Now I've got you, son of a wretch."

The other answered, "What have I done, my uncle?"

"You stuck thorns in my flesh. You said to me, 'I will make you some shoes.' Now what shall I do to you?"

"It was not I," said the jackal.

"It was you, and the proof is that you have your tail cut off."

"But all my cousins are without tails, like me."

"You lie, joker."

"Let me call them and you will see."

"Call them."

At his call the jackals ran up, all without tails.

"Which of you is a shoemaker?" asked the lion.

"All of us," they answered.

He said to them: "I am going to bring you some red pepper. You shall eat of it, and the one who says, 'Ouch!' that will be the one I'm looking for."

"Go and get it."

He brought them some red pepper, and they were going to eat it when the first jackal made a noise with his shoes, but he said to the lion, "My uncle, I did not say, 'Ouch!'" The lion sent them away, and they went about their business.

THE STOLEN WOMAN

It is related that a man of the Onlad Draabad married his cousin, whom he loved greatly. He possessed a single slave and some camels. Fearing lest someone should carry off his wife on account of her beauty, he resolved to take her to a place where no one should see her. He started, therefore, with his slave, his camels, and his wife, and proceeded night and day until he arrived at the shore of the great salt sea, knowing that nobody would come there.

One day when he had gone out to see his camels and his slave, leaving his wife alone in the tent, she saw a ship that had just then arrived. It had been sent by a sultan of a far country, to seek in the islands of the salt sea a more beautiful wife for him than the women of his land. The woman in the tent, seeing that the ship would not come first to her, went out first in front. The people said to her, "Come on board in order to see the whole ship." She went aboard. Finding her to be just the one for whom they were seeking, they seized her and took her to their Sultan. On his return, the husband, not finding his wife, realized that she had been stolen. He started to find the son of Keij, the Christian. Between them there existed a friendship. The son of Keij said to him: "Bring a ship and seven men, whose guide I will be on the sea. They need not go astray nor be frightened. The city is three or four months' journey from here." They set sail in a ship to find the city, and were on the way the time that he had said.

Arriving they cast their anchor near the city, which was at the top of a high mountain. Their chief went ashore and saw a fire lighted by someone. He went in that direction. It was an old woman, to whom he told his story. She gave him news of his wife. They agreed to keep silence between themselves. Then the old woman added: "In this place there are two birds that devour people. At their side are two lions like to them, and two men. All of these keep guard over your wife."

He bought a sheep, which he killed; then he went to the two birds and threw them a part of it. While they were quarrelling over it he passed by them and came near to the two lions, to which he did the same. Approaching the two men, he found them asleep. He went as far as the place where his wife was in prison, and attracted her attention by scratching her foot. He was disguised and said to her, "I have sought you to tell you something." He took her by the hand. They both went out, and he swore that if she made the slightest noise he would kill her. He also asked her which was the swiftest boat for the journey. She pointed out the best boat there, and they embarked in it. There were some stones on board, and when he threw one at a ship it was crushed from stem to stern, and all on board perished.

He started to find the son of Keij. While they were at sea a marine monster swallowed them and the ship on which they were sailing. The chief took some pitch and had it boiled in a kettle. The monster cast up the ship on the shore of the sea. They continued their journey, proceeding by the sea-side.

Behold one day they came to a deserted city. They desired to take what it contained of riches, silver, and gold. All of a sudden the image of an armed man appeared to them. They could not resist or kill him at first, but finally they destroyed him and took all the riches of the houses. When they arrived near the son of Keij he said to them: "I want only the ship." So the other man took the treasures and returned home with his wife.

The King, the Arab, and the Monster

In former times there was a king of the At Taberchant (the son of a negress), whose city was situated at the foot of a mountain. An enormous beast came against them, entered the city, and devoured all the people. The beast established itself in the city and stayed there a century. One day it was hungry. It came out into the plain, found some Arabs with their tents, their sheep, their oxen, their mares, and their camels. The beast fell upon them in the night and ate them all up, leaving the earth all white with their bones; then it went back to the city.

A single man escaped, thanks to his good mare. He arrived at a city of the At Taberchant and, starving, began to beg. The King of the Jews said to him: "Whence do you come into our country—you who invoke the lord of men [Mahomet]? You don't know where you are. We are Jews. If you will embrace our religion, we will give you food."

"Give me some food," said the Arab, "and I will give you some good advice."

The King took him to his house and gave him some supper, and then asked him what he had to say.

"An enormous monster has fallen upon us," said the Arab. "It ate up everybody. I will show you its city. It has two gates, one at the north and the other at the south."

"To-morrow," said the King.

When he awoke the next day, they mounted horses and followed the way to the gate of the monster's city. They looked at it and went away.

"What shall we do?" said the King.

"Let us make a great trap of the size of the entrance to the city, at the southern gate. At the northern gate we will place a forty-mule load of yellow sulphur. We will set it on fire, and then escape and see what will happen."

"Your advice is good," said the King.

They returned to the city of the Jews, ordered the smiths to make a big trap and commanded the citizens to furnish the sulphur. When all was ready, they loaded the mules, went to the monster's city, set the trap at the southern gate, and at the northern they placed the sulphur, which they set on fire, and then fled. The monster came out by the southern gate. Half of his body was caught in the trap that the two men had set. He was cut in two, filling the river with blood. The King and the Arab entered the city and found a considerable treasure, which they removed in eighty loads to the city of the Jews. When they had got back to the palace the King said to his companion: "Be my caliph. My fortune and thine shall be the same."

They sat down and had supper. The prince put in the stew some poison and turned it to the Arab. The latter observed what he had done and said, "Where did that bird come from?" When the King of the Jews raised his head to look, the Arab turned the dish around, placing the poison side of it in front of the King. He did not perceive the trick, and died on the spot. The Arab went to the gate of the city and said to the inhabitants: "I am your King. You are in my power. He who will not accept my religion, I will cut off his head." They all embraced Islamism and practised fasting and prayer.

The Lion, the Jackal, and the Man

In times past, when the animals spoke, there existed, they say, a laborer who owned a pair of oxen, with which he worked. It was his custom to start out with them early in the morning, and in the evening he returned with one ox. The next day he bought another and went to the fallow land, but the lion came and took one ox from him and left him only one. He was in despair, seeking someone to advise him, when he met the jackal and told him what had taken place between him and the lion. The jackal demanded:

"What will you give me if I deliver you from the lion?"

"Whatever you wish I will give it to you."

"Give me a fat lamb," answered the jackal. "You will follow my advice. To-morrow when the lion comes, I will be there. I will arrive on that hill on the other side. You will bring your axe very well sharpened and when I say to you, 'What is that which I see with you now?' you must answer, 'It is an ass which I have taken with me to carry barley.' I will say to you, 'I am looking for the lion, and not for an ass.' Then he will ask you, 'Who is speaking to you?' Answer him, 'It is the nems!' He will say to you, 'Hide me, for I am afraid of him.' When I ask you, 'Who is that stretched there before you?' answer, 'It is a beaver.' I will say, 'Take your axe and strike, to know if it be not the lion.' You will take your axe and you will strike the lion hard between the eyes. Then I will continue: 'I have not heard very well. Strike him again once more until he shall really be dead.'" The next day he came to him as before to eat an ox. When the jackal saw him he called his friend and said, "Who is that with you?"

"It is a beaver which is before me."

The jackal answered: "Where is the lion? I am looking for him."

"Who is talking to you?" asked the lion, of the laborer.

"The 'nems.'"

"Hide me," cried the lion, "for I fear him."

The laborer said to him, "Stretch yourself out before me, shut your eyes, and don't move." The lion stretched out before him, shut his eyes, and held his breath.

The peasant said to the jackal, "I have not seen the lion pass to-day."

"What is that stretched before you?"

"It is a beaver."

"Take your axe," said the jackal, "and strike that beaver." The laborer obeyed and struck the lion violently between the eyes.

"Strike hard," said the jackal again; "I did not hear very well."

He struck him three or four times more, until he had killed him. Then he called the jackal: "See, I have killed him. Come, let me embrace you for your good advice. To-morrow you must come here to get the lamb which I will give you." They separated and each went his way. As for the peasant, the next day, as soon as dawn, he took a lamb, put it into a sack, tied it up, went into the court-yard and hung it up. Then while he went to get his oxen to till his fields, at that moment, his wife opened the sack, set the lamb free, and replaced it by a dog. The peasant took the sack and went to his work. He attached his oxen and set to work, till the arrival of the jackal. The jackal said to him, "Where is that promise you made me?"

"It is in the sack. Open it and you'll find the lamb which I give you."

He followed his advice, opened the sack, and saw two eyes which shone more brightly than those of a lamb, and said to the laborer, "My friend, you have deceived me."

"How have I deceived you?" asked the other. "As for the lamb, I put him in the sack. Open it well; I do not lie."

The jackal followed his advice, he opened the sack, a dog jumped fiercely out. When the jackal saw the dog he ran away, but the dog caught him and ate him up.

Salomon and the Griffin

Our Lord Salomon was talking one day with the genii. He said to them: "There is born a girl at Dabersa and a boy at Djaberka. This boy and this girl shall meet," he added. The griffin said to the genii: "In spite of the will of the divine power, I shall never let them meet each other." The son of the King of Djaberka came to Salomon's house, but hardly had he arrived when he fell ill; then the griffin carried away the daughter of the King of Djaberka and put her upon a big tree at the shore of the sea. The wind impelled the prince, who had embarked. He said to his companions, "Put me ashore." He went under the big tree and fell asleep. The young girl threw leaves at him. He opened his eyes, and she said to him: "Beside the griffin, I am alone here with my mother. Where do you come from?"

"From Djaberka."

"Why," she continued, "has God created any human beings except myself, my mother, and our Lord Salomon?"

He answered her, "God has created all kinds of human beings and countries."

"Go," she said, "bring a horse and kill it. Bring also some camphor to dry the skin, which you will hang on the top of the mast." The griffin came, and she began to cry, saying, "Why don't you conduct me to the house of our Lord Salomon?"

"To-morrow I will take you."

She said to the son of the King, "Go hide inside the horse." He hid there.

The next day the griffin took away the carcass of the horse, and the young girl departed also. When they arrived at the house of our Lord Salomon, the latter said to the griffin, "I told you that the young girl and the young man should be united."

Full of shame the griffin immediately fled and took refuge in an island.

Adventure of Sidi Mahomet

One day Mouley Mahomet summoned Sidi Adjille to come to Morocco, or he would put him in prison. The saint refused to go to the city until the prince had sent him his chaplit and his "dalil" as pledges of safety. Then he started on the way and arrived at Morocco, where he neither ate nor drank until three days had passed. The Sultan said to him:

"What do you want at my palace? I will give it to you, whatever it may be."

Sidi Adjille answered, "I ask of you only one thing, that is, to fill with wheat the feed-bag of my mule."

The prince called the guardian, and said to him, "Fill the feed-bag of his mule." The guardian went and opened the door of the first granary and put wheat in the feed-bag until the first granary was entirely empty. He opened another granary, which was soon equally exhausted, then a third, and so on in this fashion until all the granaries of the King were emptied. Then he wanted to open the silos, but their guardian went and spoke to the Sultan, together with the guardian of the granaries.

"Lord," they said, "the royal granaries are all empty, and yet we have not been able to fill the feed-bag of the saint's mule."

The donkey-drivers came from Fas and from all countries, bringing wheat on mules and camels. The people asked them,

"Why do you bring this wheat?"

"It is the wheat of Sidi Mahomet Adjille that we are taking." The news came to the King, who said to the saint, "Why do you act so, now that the royal granaries are empty?" Then he called together the members of his council and wanted to have Sidi Mahomet's head cut off. "Go out," he said to him.

"Wait till I make my ablutions" [for prayer], answered the saint.

The people of the makhzen who surrounded him watched him among them, waiting until he had finished his ablutions, to take him to the council of the King and cut off his head. When Sidi Mahomet had finished washing, he lifted his eyes to heaven, got into the tub where was washing, and vanished completely from sight. When the guardians saw that he was no longer there, they went vainly to continue the search at his house at Tagountaft.

The Haunted Garden

A man who possessed much money had two daughters. The son of the caliph of the King asked for one of them, and the son of the cadi asked for the other, but their father would not let them marry, although they desired it. He had a garden near his house. When it was night, the young girls went there, the young men came to meet them, and they passed the night in conversation. One night their father saw them. The next morning he killed his daughters, buried them in his garden, and went on a pilgrimage.

That lasted so until one night the son of the cadi and the son of the caliph went to a young man who knew how to play on the flute and the rebab. "Come with us," they said to him, "into the garden of the man who will not give us his daughters in marriage. You shall play for us on your instruments." They agreed to meet there that night. The musician went to the garden, but the two young men did not go. The musician remained and played his music alone. In the middle of the night two lamps appeared, and the two young girls came out of the ground under the lamps. They said to the musician: "We are two sisters, daughters of the owner of the garden. Our father killed us and buried us here. You, you are our brother for this night. We will give you the money which our father has hidden in three pots. Dig here," they added. He obeyed, found the three pots, took them away, and became rich, while the two girls returned to their graves.

The Woman and the Fairy

A woman who was named Omm Halima went one day to the stream to wash at the old spring. Alone, in the middle of the day, she began her work, when a woman appeared to her and said: "Let us be friends, you and I, and let us make a promise. When you come to this spring, bring me some herma and perfumes. Cast them into the fountain which faces the qsar. I will come forth and I will give you money." And so the wife of Ben Sernghown returned every day and found the other woman, who gave her pieces of money. Omm Khalifah was poor. When she "became friends" with the fairy she grew rich all of a sudden. The people were curious to know how she had so quickly acquired a fortune. There was a rich man, the possessor of much property. He was called Mouley Ismail. They said to Omm Khalifah:

"You are the mistress of Mouley Ismail, and he gives you pieces of money."

She answered, "Never have I been his mistress." One day, when she went to the spring to bathe, the people followed her until she arrived. The fairy came to meet her as usual, and gave her money. The people surprised them together. But the fairy never came out of the fountain again.

Hamed-ben-Ceggad

There was in a city a man named Hamed-ben-Ceggad. He lived alone with his mother. He lived upon nothing but the chase. One day the inhabitants of the city said to the King:

"Hamed-ben-Ceggad is getting the better of you."

He said to them, "Tell me why you talk thus to me, or I will cut off your heads."

"As he only eats the flesh of birds, he takes advantage of you for his food."

The King summoned Hamed and said to him, "You shall hunt for me, and I will supply your food and your mother's, too." Every day Hamed brought game to the prince, and the prince grew very proud of him.

The inhabitants of the city were jealous of him, and went to the Sultan and said: "Hamed-ben-Ceggad is brave. He could bring you the tree of coral-wood and the palm-tree of the wild beasts."

The King said to him, "If you are not afraid, bring me the tree of coral-wood and the palm-tree of the wild beasts."

"It is well," said Hamed. And the next day he took away all the people of the city. When he came to the tree, he killed all the wild beasts, cut down the palm-tree, loaded it upon the shoulders of the people, and the Sultan built a house of coral-wood.

Seeing how he succeeded in everything, they said to the King, "Since he achieves all that he attempts, tell him to bring you the woman with the set of silver ornaments."

The prince repeated these words to Hamed, who said:

"The task you give me is harsh, nevertheless I will bring her to you." He set out on the way, and came to a place where he found a man pasturing a flock of sheep, carrying a mill-stone hanging to his neck and playing the flute. Hamed said to him: "By the Lord, I cannot lift a small rock, and this man hangs a millstone to his neck." The shepherd said: "You are Hamed-ben-Ceggad, who built the house of coral-wood?"

"Who told you?"

"A bird that flew into the sky." He added, "I will go with you."

"Come," said Hamed. The shepherd took the millstone from his neck, and the sheep were changed into stones.

On the way they met a naked man, who was rolling in the snow. They said [to themselves], "The cold stings us, and yet that man rolls in the snow without the cold killing him."

The man said to them, "You are Hamed-ben-Ceggad, who built the house of coral-wood?"

"Who told you that?"

"A bird that passed flying in the sky told me. I will accompany you."

"Come," said Hamed. After they had pursued their way some time, they met a man with long ears.

"By the Lord," they said, "we have only small ears, and this man has immense ones."

"It is the Lord who created them thus, but if it pleases God I will accompany you, for you are Hamed-ben-Ceggad."

They arrived at the house of the woman with the silver ornaments, and Hamed said to the inhabitants, "Give us this woman, that we may take her away."

"Very well," said her brother, the ogre. They killed an ox, placed it upon a hurdle, which they lifted up and put down with the aid of ninety-nine men.

"Give us one of your men who can lift this hurdle."

He who wore millstones hanging from his neck said, "I can lift it." When he had placed it on the ground, they served a *couscous* with this ox. The ogre said, "Eat all that we give you." They ate a little, and the man with the long ears hid the rest of the food. The brother continued: "You give us one of you who will go to gather a branch of a tree that stands all alone on the top of a mountain two days' march in the snow." The one who had rolled in the snow departed, and brought back the branch.

"There remains one more proof," said the ogre. "A partridge is flying in the sky; let one of you strike it." Hamed-ben-Ceggad killed it.

They gave him the woman, but before her departure her brother gave her a feather and said to her, "When anyone shall try to do anything to you against your will, cast this feather on the hearth and we will come to you."

People told the woman, "The old Sultan is going to marry you."

She replied, "An old man shall never marry me," and cast the feather into the fire. Her brother appeared, and killed all the inhabitants of the city, as well as the King, and gave the woman to Hamed-ben-Ceggad.

The Magic Napkin

A taleb made a proclamation in these terms: "Is there anyone who will sell himself for 100 mitquals?" A man agreed to sell himself. The stranger took him to the cadi, who wrote out the bill of sale. He took the 100 mitquals and gave them to his mother and departed with the taleb. They went to a place where the latter began to repeat certain formulas. The earth opened and the man entered it. The other said to him, "Bring me the candlestick of reed and the box." He took this and came out keeping it in his pocket.

"Where is the box?" asked the taleb.

"I did not find it."

"By the Lord, let us go." He took him to the mountains, cast a stone at him, and went away. He lay on the ground for three days. Then he came to himself, went back to his own country, and rented a house. He opened the box, found inside a silk napkin, which he opened, and in which he found seven folds. He unfolded one. Genii came around the chamber, and a young girl danced until the day dawned. The man stayed there all that day until night. The King came out that night, and, hearing the noise of the dance, he knocked at the door, with his vezir. They received him with a red *h'aik*. He amused himself until the day dawned. Then he went home with his vezir. The latter sent for the man and said, "Give me the box which you have at home." He brought it to the King, who said to him: "Give me the box which you have so that I may amuse myself with it, and I will marry you to my daughter." The man obeyed and married the Sultan's daughter. The Sultan amused himself with the box, and after his death his son-in-law succeeded him.

The Child and the King of the Genii

There was a sheik who gave instruction to two talebs. One day they brought to one of them a dish of *couscous* with meat. The genius stole him and bore him away. When they had arrived down there he taught him. One day the child was crying. The King of the genii asked him, "Why do you cry?"

"I am crying for my father and my mother. I don't want to stay here any longer."

The King asked his sons, "Who will take him back?"

"I," said one of them; "but how shall I take him back?"

"Carry him back after you have stuffed his ears with wool so that he shall not hear the angels worshipping the Lord."

They had arrived at a certain place, the child heard the angels worshipping the Lord, and did as they did. His guide released him and he remained three days without awaking. When he came to himself, he took up his journey and found a mother-dog which slept while her little ones barked, although yet unborn. He proceeded and met next an ass attacked by a swarm of flies. Further on he saw two trees, on one perched a blue bird. Afterward it flew upon the other tree and began to sing. He found next a fountain of which the bottom was of silver, the vault of gold, and the waters white. He went on and met a man who had been standing for three days without saying a word. Finally he arrived at a village protected by God, but which no one entered. He met a wise man and said to him:

"I want to ask you some questions."

"What do you wish to ask me?"

"I found a mother-dog which was asleep while her little ones were barking, although yet unborn."

The sage answered, "It is the good of the world that the old man should keep silence because he is ashamed to speak."

"I saw an ass attacked by a swarm of flies."

"It is Pjoudj and Madjoudj of God (Gog and Magog) and the Antichrist."

"I met two trees, a blue bird perched on one, then flew upon the other and began to sing."

"It is the picture of the man who has two wives. When he speaks to one the other gets angry."

"I saw a fountain of which the bottom was of silver, the vault of gold, and the waters white."

"It is the fountain of life; he who drinks of it shall not die."

"I found a man who was praying. I stayed three days and he did not speak."

"It is he who never prayed upon the earth and is now making amends."

"Send me to my parents," concluded the child.

The old man saw a light cloud and said to it, "Take this human creature to Egypt." And the cloud bore him to his parents.

The Seven Brothers

Here is a story that happened once upon a time. A man had seven sons who owned seven horses, seven guns, and seven pistols for hunting. Their mother was about to increase the family. They said to their father: "If we have a little sister we shall remain. If we have a little brother we shall go." The woman had a little boy. They asked, "Which is it?"

"A boy."

They mounted their horses and departed, taking provisions with them. They arrived at a tree, divided their bread, and ate it. The next day they started and travelled as far as a place where they found a well, from which they drew water. The older one said, "Come, let us put the young one in the well." They united against him, put him in, and departed, leaving him there. They came to a city.

The young man remained some time in the well where they had put him, until one day a caravan passing that way stopped to draw water. While the people were drinking they heard something moving at the bottom of the well. "Wait a moment," they said; they let down a rope, the young man caught it and climbed up. He was as black as a negro. The people took him away and sold him to a man who conducted him to his house. He stayed there a month and became white as snow. The wife of the man said:

"Come, let us go away together."

"Never!" he answered.

At evening the man returned and asked, "What is the negro doing?"

"Sell him," said the woman.

He said, "You are free. Go where you please."

The young man went away and came to a city where there was a fountain inhabited by a serpent. They couldn't draw water from this fountain without his eating a woman. This day it was the turn of the King's daughter to be eaten. The young man asked her:

"Why do you weep?"

"Because it is my turn to be devoured to-day."

The stranger answered, "Courage, I will kill the serpent, if it please God."

The young girl entered the fountain. The serpent darted toward her, but as soon as he showed his head the young man struck it with his stick and made it fly away. He did the same to the next head until the serpent was dead. All the people of the city came to draw water. The King said:

"Who has done this?"

"It is he," they cried, "the stranger who arrived yesterday." The King gave him his daughter and named him his lieutenant. The wedding-feast lasted seven days. My story is finished before my resources are exhausted.

Half-a-Cock

In times past there was a man who had two wives, and one was wise and one was foolish. They owned a cock in common. One day they quarrelled about the cock, cut it in two, and each took half. The foolish wife cooked her part. The wise one let her part live, and it walked on one foot and had only one wing. Some days passed thus. Then the half-a-cock got up early, and started on his pilgrimage. At the middle of the day he was tired and went toward a brook to rest. A jackal came there to drink. Half-a-Cock jumped on his back, stole one of his hairs, which it put under its wing and resumed its journey. It proceeded until evening and stopped under a tree to pass the night there. It had not rested long when it saw a lion pass near the tree where it was lying. As soon as it perceived the lion it jumped on its back and stole one of its hairs, which it put with that of the jackal. The next morning it got up early and took up its journey again. Arrived at the middle of a forest, it met a boar and said:

"Give me a hair from your back, as the king of the animals and the trickiest of them have done—the jackal and the lion."

The boar answered, "As these two personages so important among the animals have done this, I will also give you what you request." He plucked a hair from his back and gave it to Half-a-Cock. The latter went on his way and arrived at the palace of a king. It began to crow and to say:

"To-morrow the King will die, and I will take his wife."

Hearing these words the King gave to his negroes the command to seize Half-a-Cock, and cast him into the middle of the sheep and goat-pen to be trampled upon and killed by them, so that the King might get rid of his crowing. The negroes seized him and cast him into the pen to perish. When he got there Half-a-Cock took from under his wing the jackal's hair and burnt it in the fire. As soon as it was near the fire the jackal came and said:

"Why are you burning my hair? As soon as I smelled it, I came running."

Half-a-Cock replied, "You see what situation I am in. Get me out of it."

"That is an easy thing," said the jackal, and immediately

blowed in order to summon his brothers. They gathered around him, and he gave them this command: "My brothers, save me from Half-a-Cock, for it has a hair from my back which it has put in the fire. I don't want to burn. Take Half-a-Cock out of the sheep-pen, and you will be able to take my hair from its hands." At once the jackals rushed to the pen, strangled everything that was there, and rescued Half-a-Cock. The next day the King found his stables deserted and his animals killed. He sought for Half-a-Cock, but in vain. The latter, the next day at the supper hour, began to crow as it did the first time. The prince called his negroes and said to them:

"Seize Half-a-Cock and cast him into the cattle-yard so that it may be crushed under their feet."

The negroes caught Half-a-Cock and threw him into the middle of the cow-pen. As soon as it reached there, it took the lion's hair and put it into the fire. The lion came, roaring, and said:

"Why do you burn my hair? I smelled from my cave the odor of burning hair, and came running to learn the motive of your action."

Half-a-Cock answered: "You see my situation. Help me out of it."

The lion went out and roared to call his brothers. They came in great haste and said to him, "Why do you call us now?"

"Take the Half-a-Cock from the ox-yard, for it has one of my hairs, which it can put into the fire. If you don't rescue Half-a-Cock, it will burn the hair, and I don't want to smell the odor of burning hair while I am alive."

His brothers obeyed. They at once killed all the cattle in the pen. The King saw that his animals were all dead, and he fell into such a rage that he nearly strangled. He looked for Half-a-Cock to kill it with his own hands. He searched a long time without finding it, and finally went home to rest. At sunset Half-a-Cock came to his usual place and crowed as on the former occasions. The King called his negroes and said to them:

"This time when you have caught Half-a-Cock, put it in a house and shut all the doors till morning. I will kill it myself."

The negroes seized him immediately and put him in the treasure-room. When it got there, it saw money under its feet. It waited till it had nothing to fear from the masters of the house, who were all sound asleep, took from under its wing the hair of the boar, started a fire, and placed the hair in it. At once the boar came running and shaking the earth. It thrust its head against the wall. The wall shook and half of it fell down, and going to Half-a-Cock the boar said:

"Why are you burning my hair at this moment?"

"Pardon me, you see the situation in which I am, without counting what awaits me in the morning, for the King is going to kill me with his own hands if you don't get me out of this prison."

The boar replied: "The thing is easy; fear not, I will open the door so that you may go out. In fact, you have stayed here long enough. Get up, go and take money enough for you and your children."

Half-a-Cock obeyed. It rolled in the gold, took all that stuck to its wing and its foot, and swallowed as much as it could hold. It took the road it had followed the first day and when it had arrived near the house it called the mistress and said: "Strike now, be not afraid to kill me." His mistress began to strike until Half-a-Cock called from beneath the mat:

"Enough now. Roll the mat."

She obeyed and saw the earth all shining with gold.

At the time when Half-a-Cock returned from his pilgrimage the two women owned a dog in common. The foolish one seeing that her companion had received much money said to her:

"We will divide the dog between us."

The wise woman answered: "We can't do anything with it. Let it live, I will give you my half. Keep it for yourself. I have no need of it."

The foolish one said to the dog, "Go on a pilgrimage as Half-a-Cock did and bring me some gold."

The dog started to carry out the commands of his mistress. She began her journey in the morning and came to a fountain. As she was thirsty she started to drink. As she stopped she saw in the middle of the fountain a yellow stone. She took it in her mouth and ran back home. When she reached the house she called her mistress and said to her:

" Get ready the mats and the rods, you see that I have come back from the pilgrimage."

The foolish one prepared the mats under which the dog ran as soon as she heard the voice of her mistress and said, " Strike gently." The woman seized the rods and struck with all the force possible. The dog cried out to her a long while for her to stop the blows. Her mistress refused to stop until the animal was cold. She lighted up the mats and found the dog dead with the yellow stone in its mouth.

Strange Meetings

Once upon a time a man was on a journey and he met a mare who grazed in the meadow. She was thin, lean, and had only skin and bone. He went on until he came to a place where he found a mare which was fat, although she did not eat. He went on further until he met a sheep which kicked against a rock till evening to pass the night there. Advancing he met a serpent which hung in a hole from which it could not get out. Farther on, he saw a man who played with a ball, and his children were old men. He came to an old man who said to him:

" I will explain all that to you. The lean mare which you saw represents the rich man whose brothers are poor. The fat mare represents the poor man whose brothers are rich. The serpent which swings unable to enter nor to leave the hole is the picture of the word which once spoken and heard can never go back. The sheep which kicks against the rock to pass the night there, is the man who has an evil house. The one whose children you saw aged while he was playing ball, what does he represent? That is the man who has taken a pretty wife and does not grow old. His children have taken bad ones.

The King and His Family

In times gone by a king reigned over Maghreb. He had four sons. He started, he, his wife, and his children, for the Orient. They set sail, but their ship sank with them. The waves bore them all in separated directions. One wave took the wife; another bore the father alone to the middle of the sea on an island where he found a mine of silver. He dug out enough silver until he had a great quantity and he established himself in the country. His people after heard tell of him and learned that he dwelt in the midst of the sea. They built houses until there was a great city. He was king of that country. Whoever came poor to him he gave him pieces of money. A poor man married his wife. As for his sons, they applied themselves to a study, each in a different country. They all became learned men and feared God. The King had a search made for *tolbas* who should worship God. The first of the brothers was recommended to him. He sent for him. He sought also a *khodja.* The second brother was designated. He summoned him to the court. The prince also especially wanted an *adel.* Another brother was pointed to him. He made him come to him as, indeed, he also did the *imam,* who was none other than the fourth brother. They arrived at their father's without knowing him or being known by him. The wife and the man who had espoused her also came to the King to make complaint. When they arrived the wife went alone that night to the palace. The prince sent for the four *tolba* to pass the night with him until morning. During the night he spied upon them to see who they were. One of them said to the others, "Since sleep comes not upon us, let each one make known who he is."

One said: "My father was a king. He had much money and four sons whose names were like yours."

Another said: "My father was a king. My case is like yours."

Another said: "My father was a king. My case is like yours."

The fourth said in his turn: "My father, too, was a king. My case is like that of your three. You are my brothers."

Their mother overheard them and took to weeping until day.

They took her to the prince, who said, "Why do you weep?"

She answered: "I was formerly the wife of a king and we had four sons. We set sail, he, our children, and I. The ship which bore us was wrecked. Each one was borne away alone, until yesterday when they spoke before me during the night and showed me what had happened to them, to their father, and to their mother."

The King said, "Let me know your adventure."

They told him all that had happened. Then the prince arose, weeping, and said, "You are my children," and to the woman, "You are my wife." God reunited them.

BEDDOU

Two men, one of whom was named Beddou and the other Amkammel, went to market bearing a basket of figs. They met a man who was working, and said to him:

"God assist you!"

"Amen!" he answered. One of them wanted to wash himself, but there was no water. The laborer, him who was with him (*sic*), said, "What is your name?"

"Beddou."

"By the Lord, Beddou, watch my oxen while I go to drink."

"Go!"

When he had gone, he took away one of the oxen. On his return the laborer saw that one was missing. He went to the other traveller and asked him:

"By my father, what is your name?"

"Amkammel Ouennidhui" ("The Finisher"), he answered.

"By the Lord, Amkammel Ouennidhui, watch this ox for me while I go look for the one that is gone."

"Go!"

He stole the other one. When the laborer returned he didn't even find the second.

The two thieves went away, taking the oxen. They killed them to roast them. One drank all the water of the sea, the other all the fresh water, to wash it down. When they had finished, one stayed there to sleep, the other covered him with ashes. The former got up to get a drink and the ashes fell on the road. When he came back, the second covered himself with the ox-head. His brother, who had gone to get a drink, was afraid, and ran away. They divided the other ox to eat it. The one who had drunk the sea-water now drank fresh water, and the one who had drunk fresh water now drank sea-water. When they had finished their repast they took up their journey. They found an old woman who had some money, upon which she was sitting. When they arrived they fought. She arose to separate them. One of them took her place to pass the night, and pretended that he was dead. The old woman said to him:

"Get up, my son."

He refused. In the evening one of them stole the money, and said to his brother:

"Arise! Let us go!"

They went away to a place where was sleeping the one who had taken the money. The other took away the *dirkhems* and departed, leaving the first asleep. When he awaked he found nothing. He started in pursuit of the other, and when he arrived he found him dying of illness. The latter had said to his wife, "Bury me." She buried him. He who had first stolen the money went away. He said, "It is an ox."

"It is I, my friend," he cried. "Praise be to God, my friend! May your days pass in happiness!" Beddou said to him: "Let us go for a hunt."

They went away alone. Beddou added: "I will shave you."

He shaved him, and when he came to the throat he killed him and buried his head. A pomegranate-tree sprang up at this place. One day Beddou found a fruit, which he took to the King. When he arrived he felt that it was heavy. It was a head. The King asked him:

"What is that?"

"A pomegranate."

"We know what you have been doing," said the King, and had his head cut off. My story is finished.

The Language of the Beasts

Once upon a time there was a man who had much goods. One day he went to market. There came a greyhound, which ate some meat. The butcher gave it a blow, which made it yelp. Seeing this, the heart of the man was touched with compassion. He bought of the butcher half a piece of meat and flung it to the greyhound. The dog took it and went away. It was the son of a king of the nether world.

Fortune changed with the man. He lost all his possessions, and began to wash for people. One day, he had gone to wash something, he stretched it on the sand to dry. A jerboa appeared with a ring in its ear. The man ran after it, killed it, hid the ring, made a fire, cooked the jerboa and ate it. A woman came out of the earth, seized him, and demanded, "Haven't you seen my son, with an ear-ring?"

"I haven't seen anybody," he answered; "but I saw a jerboa which had a ring in its ear."

"It is my son." She drew him under the earth and told him: "You have eaten my son, you have separated me from him. Now I will separate you from your children, and you shall work in the place of my son." He who was changed into a greyhound saw this man that day, and said to him: "It is you who bought some meat for a greyhound and threw it to him?"

"It is I."

"I am that greyhound. Who brought you here?"

"A woman," answered the man, and he recounted all his adventure.

"Go and make a complaint to the King," answered the other. "I am his son. I'll tell him: 'This man did me a good service.' When he asks you to go to the treasure and take as much money as you wish, answer him: 'I don't want any. I only want you to spit a benediction into my mouth.' If he asks you, 'Who told you that?' answer, 'Nobody.'"

The man went and found the King and complained of the woman. The King called her and asked her: "Why have you taken this man captive?"

"He ate my son."

"Why was your son metamorphosed into a jerboa? When

men see one of those they kill him and eat him." Then addressing the man: "Give her back the ear-ring." He gave it to her.

"Go," said the King, "take this man to the place from which you brought him."

The son of the King then said to his father: "This man did me a favor; you ought to reward him."

The King said to him: "Go to the treasure, take as much money as you can."

"I don't want money," he answered; "I want you to spit into my mouth a benediction."

"Who told you that?"

"Nobody."

"You will not be able to bear it."

"I will be able."

"When I have spat into your mouth, you will understand the language of beasts and birds; you will know what they say when they speak; but if you reveal it to the people you will die."

"I will not reveal it." So the King spat into his mouth and sent him away, saying to the woman, "Go and take him back where you found him." She departed, and took him back there.

He mounted his ass and came back to his house. He arranged the load and took back to the people the linen he had washed. Then he remounted the beast to go and seek some earth. He was going to dig when he heard a crow say in the air:

"Dig beneath; you will sing when God has made you rich."

He understood what the crow said, dug beneath, and found a treasure. He filled a basket with it. On the top he put a little earth and went home, but often returned to the spot. On one of these occasions his ass met a mule, which said:

"Are you working still?"

The ass replied: "My master has found a treasure and he is taking it away."

The mule answered: "When you are in a crowd balk and throw the basket to the ground. People will see it, all will be discovered, and your master will leave you in peace."

The man had heard every word of this. He filled his basket

with earth only. When they arrived at a crowd of people the ass kicked and threw the load to the ground. Her master beat her till she had enough. He applied himself to gathering the treasure, and became a rich merchant.

He had at home some chickens and a dog. One day he went into the granary, and a hen followed him and ate the grain. A cock said to her:

"Bring me a little."

She answered, "Eat for yourself."

The master began to laugh. His wife asked him:

"What are you laughing at?"

"Nothing."

"You are laughing at me."

"Not at all."

"You must tell me what you are laughing at."

"If I tell you I shall die."

"You shall tell me, and you shall die."

"To-night." He brought out some grain and said to his wife, "Give alms." He invited the people, bade them to eat, and when they had gone he brought food to the dog, but he would not eat. The neighbor's dog came, as it did every day, to eat with his dog. To-day it found the food intact.

"Come and eat," it said.

"No," the dog answered.

"Why not?"

Then the dog told the other: "My master, hearing the chickens talk, began to laugh. His wife asked him: 'Why are you laughing?' 'If I tell you, I shall die.' 'Tell me and die.' That is why," continued the dog, "he has given alms, for when he reveals his secret he will die, and I shall never find anyone to act as he has."

The other dog replied: "As he knows our language, let him take a stick and give it to his wife until she has had enough. As he beats her let him say: 'This is what I was laughing at. This is what I was laughing at. This is what I was laughing at,' until she says to him, 'Reveal to me nothing.'"

The man heard the conversation of the dogs, and went and got a stick. When his wife and he went to bed she said to him, "Tell me that now."

Then he took the stick and beat her, saying: "This is what I was laughing at. This is what I was laughing at. This is what I was laughing at," until she cried out:

"Don't tell it to me. Don't tell it to me. Don't tell it to me."

He left her alone. When the dogs heard that, they rejoiced, ran out on the terrace, played, and ate their food. From that day the wife never again said to her husband, "Tell me that!" They lived happy ever after. If I have omitted anything, may God forgive me for it.

The Apple of Youth

There once lived a king who had five daughters and no sons. They grew up. He wanted them to marry, but they would not have any of the young men of the city. A youth came from a far country and stood under the castle, beneath the window of the youngest daughter. She saw him, and told her father she would marry him.

"Bring him in," said the King.

"He will come to-morrow."

"God be praised," said the King, "that you are pleased with us."

The young man answered, "Give me your daughter for a wife."

"Advise me," said the King.

The stranger said, "Go and wait till to-morrow."

The next day the young man said to the King: "Make all the inhabitants of the city come out. You will stand with the clerks at the entrance to the gate. Dress your daughters and let them choose their husbands themselves."

The people began to come out. The eldest daughter struck one of them on the chest with an apple, and they said: "That daughter has chosen a husband. Bravo!" Each one of the daughters thus selected a husband, and the youngest kept hers. A little while afterward, the King received a visit from one of his sons-in-law, who said to him, "What do you want us to give you?"

"I'll see what my daughters want," he answered. "Come back in six days."

When they went to see their wives the King said to them, "I will ask of you a thing about which they have spoken to me."

"What is it? We are anxious to know."

"It is an apple, the odor of which gives to the one who breathes it youth, no matter what his age may be."

"It is difficult," they answered. "We know not where it can be found."

"If you do not bring it to me, you cannot marry my daughter."

They kept silent, and then consulted with each other. The youngest said to them, "Seek the means to satisfy the King."

"Give us your advice——"

"Father-in-law, to-morrow we shall bring you the apple." His brothers-in-law added: "Go out. To-morrow we will meet you outside the city."

The next day they all five met together. Four of them said to the other, "Advise us or we will kill you."

"Cut off your fingers," he said.

The first one began, and the three others did the same. The youngest one took them and put them into his game-bag, and then he added, "Wait near the city till I come back."

He went out into the desert and came to the city of the ogress. He entered, and found her ready to grind some wheat. He said to the ogress, "Show me the apple whose color gives eternal youth to the old man who smells it."

"You are in the family of ogres," she said. "Cut a hair from the horse of their King. When you go into the garden cast this hair into the fire. You will find a tree, from which you must pick five fruits. When plucking them do not speak a word, and keep silence on your return. It is the smallest fruit that possesses the magic power."

He took the apple and went back to the city, where he found his companions. He concealed in his breast the wonderful fruit, and gave the others to his brothers-in-law, one to each. They entered the palace of the King, who was overjoyed to see them, gave them seats, and asked them, "Have you brought it or not?"

"We have brought it," they answered.

He said to the eldest, "Give me your apple first."

He took a mirror in his left hand, and the fruit in the right hand, bent down, and inhaled the odor of the apple, but without results. He threw it down upon the ground. The others gave him their apples, with no more success.

"You have deceived me," he said to them. "The apples do not produce the effect that I sought."

Addressing, then, the stranger, he said, "Give me your apple."

The other son-in-law replied: "I am not of this country. I will not give you my fruit."

"Give it to me to look at," said the King. The young man gave it to him, saying, "Take a mirror in your right hand and the apple in your left hand."

The King put the apple to his nose, and, looking at his beard, saw that it became black. His teeth became white. He grew young again. "You are my son," he said to the young man. And he made a proclamation to his subjects, "When I am dead he shall succeed me on the throne." His son-in-law stayed some time with him, and after the death of the King he reigned in his place and did not marry the other daughters of the King to his companions.

POPULAR TALES OF THE KABYLES

—

[*Translated by J. Rivière and Chauncey C. Starkweather*]

POPULAR TALES OF THE KABYLES

ALI AND OU ALI

ALI and Ou Ali were two friends. One day they met at the market. One of them bore ashes and the other carried dust. The first one had covered his goods with a little flour. The other had concealed his merchandise under some black figs. "Come, I will sell you some flour," said Ali.

"Come, I will sell you some black figs," answered Ou Ali.

Each regained his own horse. Ali, who thought he was carrying flour, found, on opening his sack, that it was only ashes. Ou Ali, who thought he was bearing black figs, found on opening his sack that it was nothing but dust. Another day they again greeted each other in the market. Ali smiled. Ou Ali smiled, and said to his friend:

"For the love of God, what is your name?"

"Ali; and yours?"

"Ou Ali."

Another time they were walking together, and said to each other:

"Let us go and steal."

One of them stole a mule and the other stole a rug. They passed the night in the forest. Now, as the snow was falling, Ali said to Ou Ali:

"Give me a little of your rug to cover me."

Ou Ali refused. "You remember," he added, "that I asked you to put my rug on your mule, and you would not do it." An instant afterward Ali cut off a piece of the rug, for he was dying of cold. Ou Ali got up and cut the lips of the mule. The next morning, when they awaked, Ou Ali said to Ali:

"O my dear friend, your mule is grinning."

"O my dear friend," replied Ali, "the rats have gnawed your rug."

And they separated. Some time afterward they met anew. Ali said to Ou Ali:

"Let us go and steal."

They saw a peasant, who was working. One of them went to the brook to wash his cloak there, and found it dry. He laid the blade of his sabre so that it would reflect the rays of the sun, and began to beat his cloak with his hands as if to wash it. The laborer came to the brook also, and found the man who was washing his cloak without water.

"May God exterminate you," said he, "who wash without water."

"May God exterminate you," answered the washer, "who work without a single ox."

The other robber watched the laborer, and had already stolen one of his oxen. The laborer went back to his plough, and said to the washer, "Keep this ox for me while I go and hunt for the other." As soon as he was out of sight the robber took away the ox left in his charge. The laborer returned, and seizing the goad by one end he gave a great blow on the plough-handle, crying:

"Break, now. It matters little."

The robbers met in a wood and killed the oxen. As they lacked salt, they went to purchase it. They salted the meat, roasted it, and ate it. Ali discovered a spring. Ou Ali not being able to find water, was dying of thirst.

"Show me your spring," he said to Ali, "and I will drink."

"Eat some salt, my dear friend," answered Ali. What could he do? Some days afterward Ou Ali put ashes on the shoes of Ali. The next day he followed the traces of the ashes, found the spring, and discovered thus the water that his friend was drinking. He took the skin of one of the oxen and carried it to the fountain. He planted two sticks above the water, hung the skin on the sticks, and placed the horns of the ox opposite the road. During the night his friend went to the spring. At the sight of the skin thus stretched out, fear seized him, and he fled.

"I am thirsty," said Ou Ali.

"Eat some salt, my dear friend," answered Ali, "for salt removes thirst."

Ali retired, and, after having eaten, ran to examine the skin that he had stretched out. Ou Ali ate the salt, and was dying of thirst.

"For the love of God," he said finally, "show me where you drink."

Ali was avenged. "Come, Jew-face, and I will show you the water." He made him drink at the spring, and said to him: "See what you were afraid of." The meat being finished, they started away. Ou Ali went to the house of Ali, and said to him:

"Come, we will marry you to the daughter of an old woman."

Now, the old woman had a herd of oxen. She said to Ali: "Take this drove to the fields and mount one of the animals." Ali mounted one of the oxen. He fell to the ground; the oxen began to run and trample on him. Ou Ali, who was at the house, said to the old woman:

"O my old woman, give me your daughter in marriage."

She called her daughter. "Take a club," she said to her, "and we will give it to him until he cries for mercy."

The daughter brought a club and gave Ou Ali a good beating. Ali, who was watching the herd, came at nightfall and met his friend.

"Did the old woman accept you?" he asked him.

"She accepted me," answered Ali. "And is the herd easy to watch?"

"From morning till night I have nothing to do but to repose. Take my place to-morrow, and mount one of the oxen."

The next day Ou Ali said to the old woman, "To-day I will take care of the herd." And, on starting, he recommended Ali to ask the old woman for her daughter's hand.

"It is well," answered Ali. Ou Ali arrived in the fields; one of the oxen seized him with his horns and tossed him into the air. All the others did the same thing. He regained the horse half dead. Ali, who had remained at the house, asked the old woman for her daughter's hand. "You ask me again?" said she. She took a club and gave it to him till he had had enough. Ou Ali said to Ali: "You have played me a trick." Ali answered him: "Without doubt they gave me the stick so hard that I did not hear the last blow."

"It is well, my dear friend. Ali owes nothing to Ou Ali."

They went away. The old woman possessed a treasure. Ou Ali therefore said to Ali: "I will put you in a basket, for you know that we saw that treasure in a hole." They returned to the old woman's house. Ali goes down into the hole, takes the treasure, and puts it into the basket. Ou Ali draws up the basket, takes it, abandons his friend, now a prisoner, and runs to hide the treasure in the forest. Ali was in trouble, for he knew not how to get out. What could he do? He climbed up the sides of the hole. When he found himself in the house, he opened the door and fled. Arriving at the edge of the forest he began to bleat. Ou Ali, thinking it was a ewe, ran up. It was his friend.

"O my dear," cried Ali, "I have found you at last."

"God be praised. Now, let us carry our treasure."

They started on the way. Ou Ali, who had a sister, said to Ali: "Let us go to my sister's house." They arrived at nightfall. She received them with joy. Her brother said to her:

"Prepare some pancakes and some eggs for us."

She prepared the pancakes and the eggs and served them with the food."

"O my sister," cried Ou Ali, "my friend does not like eggs; bring us some water." She went to get the water. As soon as she had gone, Ali took an egg and put it into his mouth. When the woman returned, he made such efforts to give it up that he was all out of breath. The repast was finished, and Ali had not eaten anything. Ou Ali said to his sister: "O my sister, my friend is ill; bring me a skewer." She brought him a skewer, which he put into the fire. When the skewer was red with the heat, Ou Ali seized it and applied it to the cheek of Ali. The latter uttered a cry, and rejected the egg. "Truly," said the woman, "you do not like eggs."

The two friends started and arrived at a village.

"Let us go to my sister's house," said Ali to his friend. She received them with open arms.

Ali said to her: "O my sister, prepare a good stew for us."

They placed themselves at the table at nightfall, and she served them with food.

"O my sister," cried Ali, "my friend does not like stew."

Ali ate alone. When he was satisfied, the two friends

started, without forgetting the treasure. On the way Ali said to Ou Ali: "Give it to me to-day and I will deposit it in my house." He took it and gave it to his wife. "Bury me," he said to her. "And if Ou Ali comes tell him that his old friend is dead, and receive him with tears." Ou Ali arrived, and asked the woman in tears to see the tomb of his dead friend. He took an ox-horn and began to dig in the earth that covered the body.

"Behind! behind!" cried the pretended dead man.

"Get up, there, you liar," answered Ali.

They went away together. "Give me the treasure," asked Ou Ali; "to-day I will take it to my house." He took it to his house, and said to his wife: "Take this treasure. I am going to stretch myself out as if I were dead. When Ali comes receive him weeping, and say to him: 'Your friend is dead. He is stretched out in the bedroom.'"

Ali went and said to the woman: "Get me some boiling water, for your husband told me to wash him when he should die." When the water was ready the woman brought it. Ali seized the kettle and poured it on the stomach of Ou Ali, who sprang up with a bound. Thus he got even for the trick of his friend. The two friends divided the treasure then, and Ali went home.

THE INFIDEL JEW

A man went on a journey. At the moment of departure he placed with a Jew, his friend, a jar filled with gold. He covered the gold with butter and said to the Jew: "I trust to your care this jar of butter, as I am going on a journey." On his return he hastened to the house of his friend. "Give me the jar of butter that I left with you," he said. The Jew gave it to him. But the poor traveller found nothing but butter, for the Jew had taken the gold. Nevertheless, he did not tell anybody of the misfortune that had happened to him. But his countenance bore traces of a secret sorrow. His brother perceived it, and said to him:

"What is the matter with you?"

"I intrusted a jar filled with gold to a Jew," he answered,

"and he only returned a jar of butter to me. I don't know what to do to recover my property."

His brother replied: "The thing is easy. Prepare a feast and invite your friend the Jew."

The next day the traveller prepared a feast and invited the Jew. During this time the brother of the traveller ran to a neighboring mountain, where he captured a monkey. During the night he entered the house of the Jew and found a child in the cradle. He took the child away and put the monkey in its place. When day had come the mother perceived the monkey tied in the cradle. She called her husband with loud cries, and said to him:

"See how God has punished us for having stolen your friend's gold. Our child is changed into a monkey. Give back the stolen property."

They immediately had the traveller summoned, and returned his gold to him. The next night the child was taken back to the cradle and the monkey was set free. As I can go no further, may God exterminate the jackal and pardon all our sins!

THE SHEIK'S HEAD

A man died, leaving a son. The child spent day and night with his mother. The sheik chanted a prayer every morning and waked him up. The child went to find the sheik, and said:

"Ali Sheik, do not sing so loudly, you wake us up every morning—my mother and me."

But the sheik kept on singing. The child went to the mosque armed with a club. At the moment when the sheik bowed to pray he struck him a blow and killed him. He ran to his mother, and said to her:

"I have killed that sheik; come, let us bury him."

They cut off his head and buried his body. The child went to the Thadjeinath, where the men of the village were assembled. In his absence his mother killed a sheep. She took the head and buried it in place of the sheik's head. The child arrived at the Thadjeinath and said to those present:

"I have killed the sheik who waked us up every morning."

"It is a lie," said they.

"Come to my mother's house and we will show you where we buried his head." They went to the house, and the mother said to them:

"Ali Sidi, this child is mad. It is a sheep that we have killed. Come and see where we buried its head." They went to the spot, dug, and found a sheep's head.

THE WAGTAIL AND THE JACKAL

At the time when all the animals spoke, a wagtail laid her eggs on the ground. The little ones grew up. A jackal and a fox came to them. The jackal said to the fox:

"Swear to me that the wagtail owes me a pound of butter."

The fox swore to it. The bird began to weep. A greyhound came to her and asked her what was the matter. She answered him:

"The fox has calumniated me."

"Well," said the hound, "put me in this sack of skin."

She put him in the sack. "Tie up the top well," said the hound. When the jackal returned she said to him:

"Come and measure out the butter."

The jackal advanced and unfastened the sack. He saw the hound, who stretched out his paws and said to the fox:

"I am ill; come and measure, fox."

The fox approached. The hound seized him. The jackal said, "Remember your false testimony."

THE FLUTE-PLAYER

A servant tended the sheep of his master. Arrived in the meadow, he played the flute. The sheep heard him, and would not browse. One day the master perceived that his sheep did not graze. He followed the servant to the fields and hid himself in the bush. The shepherd took his flute and began to play. His master began to dance so that the bushes brought blood upon him. He returned home.

"Who scratched you so?" asked his wife.

"The servant played on the flute, and I began to dance."

"That is a lie," said she; "people don't dance against their will."

"Well," answered the husband, "tie me to this post and make the servant play."

She tied him to the post and the servant took the flute. Our man began to dance. He struck his head against a nail in the post and died. The son of the dead man said to the servant:

"Pay me for the loss of my father."

They went before the cadi. On the way they met a laborer, who asked them where they were going.

"Before the cadi."

"Could you tell me why?"

"This man killed my father," answered the son of the dead man.

"It was not I that killed him," answered the shepherd; "I played on the flute, he danced and died."

"That is a lie!" cried the laborer. "I will not dance against my will. Take your flute and we shall see if I dance."

The shepherd took his flute. He began to play, and the laborer started dancing with such activity that his oxen left to themselves fell into the ravine.

"Pay me for my oxen," he cried to the shepherd.

"Come before the cadi," he answered. They presented themselves before the cadi, who received them on the second floor of the house. They all sat down. Then the cadi said to the servant:

"Take your flute and play before me. I will see how you play." The servant took his flute and all began to dance. The cadi danced with the others, and they all fell down to the ground floor and were killed. The servant stayed in the house of the cadi and inherited the property of all.

THE CHILD

A child had a thorn in his foot. He went to an old woman and said to her:

" Take out this thorn for me."

The old woman took out the thorn and threw it away.

" Give me my thorn," and he began to cry.

" Take an egg."

He went to another old woman, " Hide me this egg."

" Put it in the hen's nest."

In the night he took his egg and ate it. The next day he said to the old woman: " Give me my egg."

" Take the hen," she answered.

He went to another old woman, " Hide my hen for me."

" Put her on the stake to which I tie my he-goat."

At night he took away the hen. The next morning he demanded his hen.

" Look for her where you hid her."

" Give me my hen."

" Take the he-goat."

He went to another old woman, " O old woman, hide this goat for me."

" Tie him to the sheep's crib."

During the night he took away the buck. The next day he claimed the buck.

" Take the sheep."

He went to another old woman, " O old woman, keep my sheep for me."

" Tie him to the foot of the calf."

During the night he took away the sheep. Next morning he demanded his sheep.

" Take the calf."

He went to another old woman, " Keep my calf for me."

" Tie him to the cow's manger."

In the night he took away the calf. The next morning he asked for his calf.

" Take the cow."

He went to another old woman, " Keep my cow for me."

" Tie her to the foot of the old woman's bed."

In the night he took away the cow. The next morning he demanded his cow.

"Take the old woman."

He went to another old woman and left the old dame, whom he killed during the night. The next morning he demanded his old woman.

"There she is by the young girl."

He found her dead.

"Give me my old woman."

"Take the young girl."

He said to her: "From the thorn to the egg, from the egg to the hen, from the hen to the buck, from the buck to the sheep, from the sheep to the calf, from the calf to the cow, from the cow to the old woman, from the old woman to the young girl, and now come and marry me."

THE MONKEY AND THE FISHERMAN

A fisherman went one day to the sea to catch some fish. In the evening he sold his catch, and bought a little loaf of bread, on which he made his supper. The next day he returned to his fishing and found a chest. He took it to his house and opened it. Out jumped a monkey and said to him: "Bad luck to you. I am not the only one to conquer. You may bewail your sad lot."

"My lot is unbearable," he answered. The next day he returned to his fishing. The monkey climbed to the roof of the house and sat there. A moment afterward he cut all the roses of the garden. The daughter of the King saw him, and said to him:

"O Sidi Mahomet, what are you doing there? Come here, I need you."

He took a rose and approached.

"Where do you live?" asked the princess.

"With the son of the Sultan of India," answered the monkey.

"Tell him to buy me."

"I will tell him, provided he will accept."

The next day he stayed in the house and tore his face. The princess called him again. The monkey brought her a rose.

"Who put you in that condition?" she cried.

"It was the son of the Sultan of India," answered the monkey. "When I told him to buy you he gave me a blow."

The princess gave him 100 ecus, and he went away. The next day he scratched his face worse and climbed on the house. The daughter of the King called him:

"Sidi Mahomet!"

"Well?"

"Come here. What did you say to him?"

"I told him to buy you, and he gave me another blow."

"Since this is so, come and find me to-morrow."

The next day the monkey took the fisherman to a shop and bought him some clothes. He took him to the baths and made him bathe. Then he went along the road and cried:

"Flee, flee, here is the son of the Sultan of India!"

They went into a coffee-house, and Si Mahomet ordered two coffees. They drank their coffees, gave an ecu to the proprietor, and went out. While going toward the palace Si Mahomet said to the fisherman:

"Here we are at the house of your father-in-law. When he serves us to eat, eat little. When he offers us coffee, drink only a little of it. You will find silken rugs stretched on the floor; keep on your sandals."

When they arrived the fisherman took off his sandals. The King offered them something to eat; the fisherman ate a great deal. He offered them some coffee, and the fisherman did not leave a drop of it. They went out. When they were outside the palace Si Mahomet said to the fisherman:

"Jew of a fisherman, you are lucky that I do not scratch your face."

They returned to their house. Si Mahomet climbed upon the roof. The daughter of the King perceived him, and said:

"Come here."

The monkey approached.

"Truly you have lied. Why did you tell me that the son of the Sultan of India was a distinguished person?"

"Is he a worthless fellow?"

"We furnished the room with silken rugs, he took off his sandals. We gave him food, and he ate like a servant. We offered him some coffee, and he licked his fingers."

The monkey answered: "We had just come out of the coffee-house. He had taken too much wine and was drunken, and not master of himself. That is why he ate so much."

"Well," replied the princess, "come to the palace again to-morrow, but do not take him to the coffee-house first."

The next day they set out. On the way the monkey said to the fisherman: "Jew of a fisherman, if to-day you take off your sandals or eat too much or drink all your coffee, look out for yourself. Drink a little only, or I will scratch your eyes out."

They arrived at the palace. The fisherman walked on the silken rugs with his sandals. They gave him something to eat, and he ate little. They brought him some coffee, and he hardly tasted it. The King gave him his daughter. Si Mahomet said to the King:

"The son of the Sultan of India has quarrelled with his father, so he only brought one chest of silver."

In the evening the monkey and the fisherman went out for a walk. The fisherman said to Si Mahomet:

"Is it here that we are going to find the son of the Sultan of India?"

"I can show him to you easily," answered the monkey. "To-morrow I will find you seated. I will approach, weeping, with a paper in my hands; I will give you the paper, and you must read it and burst into tears. Your father-in-law will ask you why you weep so. Answer him: 'My father is dead. Here is the letter I have just received. If you have finally determined to give me your daughter, I will take her away and we will go to pay the last duties to my father.'"

"Take her," said the King. He gave him an escort of horsemen and soldiers. Arriving at the place, Si Mahomet said to the soldiers:

"You may return to the palace, for our country is far from here."

The escort went back to the palace, and the travellers continued on their journey. Soon Si Mahomet said to the fisherman: "Stay here till I go and look at the country of your father." He started, and arrived at the gates of a city he found closed he mounted upon the ramparts. An ogress perceived him, "I salute you, Si Mahomet."

"May God curse you, sorceress! Come, I am going to your house."

"What do you want of me, Si Mahomet?"

"They are seeking to kill you."

"Where can I hide?" He put her in the powder-house of the city, shut the door on her, and set the powder on fire. The ogress died. He came back to the fisherman.

"Forward," he said. They entered the city and established themselves there. One day Si Mahomet fell ill and died. The two spouses put him in a coffin lined with silk and buried him. My story is told.

THE TWO FRIENDS

Sidi El-Marouf and Sidi Abd-el-Tadu were travelling in company. Toward evening they separated to find a resting-place. Sidi Abd-el-Tadu said to his friend:

"Let us say a prayer, that God may preserve us from the evil which we have never committed."

Sidi El-Marouf answered, "Yes, may God preserve us from the evil that we have not done!"

They went toward the houses, each his own way. Sidi El-Marouf presented himself at a door. "Can you entertain a traveller?"

"You are welcome," said a woman to him. "Enter, you may remain for the night."

Night came. He took his supper. The woman spread a mat on the floor and he went to sleep. The woman and her husband slept also. When all was quiet, the woman got up, took a knife, and killed her husband. The next day at dawn she began to cry:

"He has killed my husband!"

The whole village ran up to the house and seized the stranger. They bound him, and everyone brought wood to burn the guilty man.

Sidi Abd-el-Tadu came also, and saw his friend in tears. "What have you done?" he asked.

"I have done no evil," answered Sidi El-Marouf.

"Did I not tell you yesterday," said Sidi Abd-el-Tadu,

"that we would say the prayer that God should preserve us from the evil we had never committed? And now you will be burned for a crime of which you are innocent!"

Sidi El-Marouf answered him, "Bring the woman here."

"Did he really kill your husband?" asked Sidi Abd-el-Tadu.

"He killed him," she replied.

There was a bird on a tree nearby. Sidi Abd-el-Tadu asked the bird. The bird answered:

"It was the woman who killed her husband. Feel in her hair and you will find the knife she used."

They searched her hair and found the knife still covered with blood, which gave evidence of the crime. The truth was known and innocence was defended. God avenged the injustice.

THE ROBBER AND THE TWO PILGRIMS

Two robbers spent their time in robbing. One of them got married, and the other continued his trade. They were a long time without seeing each other. Finally the one who was not married went to visit his friend, and said to him:

"If your wife has a daughter, you must give her to me."

"I will give her to you seven days after her birth."

The daughter was born, and the robber took her to bring up in the country. He built a house, bought flocks, and tended them himself. One day some pilgrims came to the house. He killed a cow for them and entertained them. The next day he accompanied them on their pilgrimage. The pilgrims said to him:

"If you come with us, two birds will remain with your wife."

The woman stayed in the country. One day the son of the Sultan came that way to hunt. One of the birds saw him and said to the woman, "Don't open the door." The prince heard the bird speak, and returned to the palace without saying a word. An old woman was called to cast spells over him, and said to the King:

"He could not see a woman he has never seen."

The prince spoke and said to her: "If you will come with me, I will bring her here." They arrived.

The old dame called the young woman, "Come out, that we may see you."

She said to the bird, "I am going to open the door."

The bird answered: "If you open the door you will meet the same fate as Si El-Ahcen. He was reading with many others in the mosque. One day he found an amulet. His betrothed went no longer to school, and as she was old enough he married her. Some days after he said to his father, 'Watch over my wife.' 'Fear nothing,' answered the father.

"He started, and came back. 'Watch over my wife,' he said to his father again. 'Fear nothing,' repeated his father. The latter went to the market. On his return he said to his daughter-in-law, 'There were very beautiful women in the market.' 'I surpass them all in beauty,' said the woman; 'take me to the market.'

"A man offered 1,000 francs for her. The father-in-law refused, and said to her: 'Sit down on the mat. The one that covers you with silver may have you.' A man advanced. 'If you want to marry her,' said her father-in-law, 'cover her with silver, and she will be your wife.'

"Soon Si El-Ahcen returned from his journey and asked if his wife were still living. 'Your wife is dead,' said his father; 'she fell from her mule.' Si El-Ahcen threw himself on the ground. They tried to lift him up. It was useless trouble. He remained stretched on the earth.

"One day a merchant came to the village and said to him, 'The Sultan married your wife.' She had said to the merchant, 'The day that you leave I will give you a message.' She wrote a letter to her husband, and promised the bearer a flock of sheep if he would deliver it.

"Si El Ahcen received the letter, read it, was cured, ran to the house, and said to his father: 'My wife has married again in my absence; she is not dead. I brought home much money. I will take it again.'

"He took his money and went to the city where his wife lived. He stopped at the gates. To the first passer-by he gave five francs, to the second five more.

"'What do you want, O stranger?' they asked. 'If you

want to see the Sultan we will take you to him.' They presented him to the Sultan.

"'Render justice to this man.' 'What does he want?' 'My lord,' answered Sidi El-Ahcen, 'the woman you married is my wife.' 'Kill him!' cried the Sultan. 'No,' said the witnesses, 'let him have justice.'

"'Let him tell me if she carries an object.' Si El-Ahcen answered: 'This woman was betrothed to me before her birth. An amulet is hidden in her hair.' He took away his wife, returned to the village, and gave a feast.

"If you open the door," continued the bird, "you will have the same fate as Fatima-ou-Lmelh. Hamed-ou-Lmelh married her. Fatima said to her father-in-law, 'Take me to my uncle's house.' Arriving there she married another husband. Hamed-ou-Lmelh was told of this, and ran to find her. At the moment he arrived he found the wedding over and the bride about to depart for the house of her new husband. Then Hamed burst into the room and cast himself out of the window. Fatima did the same, and they were both killed.

"The intended father-in-law and his family returned to their house, and were asked the cause of the misfortune. 'The woman was the cause,' they answered.

"Nevertheless, the father of Hamed-ou-Lmelh went to the parents of Fatima and said: 'Pay us for the loss of our son. Pay us for the loss of Fatima.'

"They could not agree, and went before the justice. Passing by the village where the two spouses had died they met an old man, and said, 'Settle our dispute.' 'I cannot,' answered the old man. Farther on they met a sheep, which was butting a rock. 'Settle our dispute,' they said to the sheep. 'I cannot,' answered the sheep. Farther on they met a serpent. 'Settle our dispute,' they said to him. 'I cannot,' answered the serpent. They met a river. 'Settle our dispute,' they said to it. 'I cannot,' answered the river. They met a jackal. 'Settle our dispute,' they said to him. 'Go to the village where your children died,' answered the jackal. They went back to the village, and applied to the Sultan, who had them all killed."

The bird stopped speaking, the pilgrims returned. The old woman saw them and fled. The robber prepared a feast for the pilgrims.

THE LITTLE CHILD

"Come, little child, eat your dinner."
"I won't eat it."
"Come, stick, beat the child."
"I won't beat him."
"Come, fire, burn the stick."
"I won't burn it."
"Come, water, quench the fire."
"I won't quench it."
"Come, ox, drink the water."
"I won't drink it."
"Come, knife, kill the ox."
"I won't kill him."
"Come, blacksmith, break the knife."
"I won't break it."
"Come, strap, bind the blacksmith."
"I won't bind him."
"Come, rat, gnaw the strap."
"I won't gnaw it."
"Come, cat, eat the rat."
"Bring it here."

"Why eat me?" said the rat; "bring the strap and I'll gnaw it."

"Why gnaw me?" said the strap; "bring the blacksmith and I'll bind him."

"Why bind me?" said the blacksmith; "bring the knife and I'll break it."

"Why break me?" said the knife; "bring the ox and I'll kill him."

"Why kill me?" said the ox; "bring the water and I'll drink it."

"Why drink me?" said the water; "bring the fire and I'll quench it."

"Why quench me?" said the fire; "bring the stick and I'll burn it."

"Why burn me?" said the stick; "bring the child and I'll strike him."

"Why strike me?" said the child; "bring me my dinner and I'll eat it."

THE WREN

A wren had built its nest on the side of a road. When the eggs were hatched, a camel passed that way. The little wrens saw it, and said to their father when he returned from the fields:

"O papa, a gigantic animal passed by."

The wren stretched out his foot. "As big as this, my children?"

"O papa, much bigger."

He stretched out his foot and his wing. "As big as this?"

"O papa, much bigger."

Finally he stretched out fully his feet and legs. "As big as this, then?"

"Much bigger."

"That is a lie; there is no animal bigger than I am."

"Well, wait," said the little ones, "and you will see." The camel came back while browsing the grass of the roadside. The wren stretched himself out near the nest. The camel seized the bird, which passed through its teeth safe and sound.

"Truly," he said to them, "the camel is a gigantic animal, but I am not ashamed of myself."

On the earth it generally happens that the vain are as if they did not exist. But sooner or later a rock falls and crushes them.

THE MULE, THE JACKAL, AND THE LION

The mule, the jackal, and the lion went in company. "We will eat the one whose race is bad," they said to each other.

"Lion, who is your father?"

"My father is a lion and my mother is a lioness."

"And you, jackal, what is your father?"

"My father is a jackal and my mother, too."

"And you, mule, what is your father?"

"My father is an ass, and my mother is a mare."

"Your race is bad; we will eat you."

He answered them: "I will consult an old man. If he says that my race is bad, you may devour me."

He went to a farrier, and said to him, "Shoe my hind feet, and make the nails stick out well."

He went back home. He called the camel and showed him his feet, saying: "See what is written on this tablet."

"The writing is difficult to decipher," answered the camel. "I do not understand it, for I only know three words—*outini, ouzatini, ouazakin*." He called a lion, and said to him: "I do not understand these letters; I only know three words—*outini, ouzatini, ouazakin*."

"Show it to me," said the lion. He approached. The mule struck him between the eyes and stretched him out stiff.

He who goes with a knave is betrayed by him.

THADHELLALA

A woman had seven daughters and no son. She went to the city, and there saw a rich shop. A little farther on she perceived at the door of a house a young girl of great beauty. She called her parents, and said:

"I have my son to marry; let me have your daughter for him."

They let her take the girl away. She came back to the shop and said to the man in charge of it:

"I will gladly give you my daughter; but go first and consult your father."

The young man left a servant in his place and departed. Thadhellala (that was her name) sent the servant to buy some bread in another part of the city. Along came a caravan of mules. Thadhellala packed all the contents of the shop on their backs and said to the muleteer:

"I will go on ahead; my son will come in a moment. Wait for him—he will pay you."

She went off with the mules and the treasures which she had packed upon them. The servant came back soon.

"Where is your mother?" cried the muleteer; "hurry and pay me."

"You tell me where she is and I will make her give me back what she has stolen." And they went before the justice.

Thadhellala pursued her way, and met seven young students. She said to one of them, "A hundred francs and I will marry you." The student gave them to her. She made the same offer to the others, and each one took her word.

Arriving at a fork in the road, the first one said, "I will take you," the second one said, "I will take you," and so on to the last.

Thadhellala answered: "You shall have a race as far as that ridge over there, and the one that gets there first shall marry me."

The young men started. Just then a horseman came passing by. "Lend me your horse," she said to him. The horseman jumped off. Thadhellala mounted the horse and said:

"You see that ridge? I will rejoin you there."

The scholars perceived the man. "Have you not seen a woman?" they asked him. "She has stolen 700 francs from us."

"Haven't you others seen her? She has stolen my horse?"

They went to complain to the Sultan, who gave the command to arrest Thadhellala. A man promised to seize her. He secured a comrade, and they both pursued Thadhellala, who had taken flight. Nearly overtaken by the man, she met a negro who pulled teeth, and said to him:

"You see my son coming down there; pull out his teeth." When the other passed the negro pulled out his teeth. The poor toothless one seized the negro and led him before the Sultan to have him punished. The negro said to the Sultan: "It was his mother that told me to pull them out for hm."

"Sidi," said the accuser, "I was pursuing Thadhellala."

The Sultan then sent soldiers in pursuit of the woman, who seized her and hung her up at the gates of the city. Seeing herself arrested, she sent a messenger to her relatives.

Then there came by a man who led a mule. Seeing her he said, "How has this woman deserved to be hanged in this way?"

"Take pity on me," said Thadhellala; "give me your mule and I will show you a treasure." She sent him to a certain place where the pretended treasure was supposed to be hidden. At this the brother-in-law of Thadhellala had arrived.

"Take away this mule," she said to him. The searcher for

treasures dug in the earth at many places and found nothing. He came back to Thadhellala and demanded his mule.

She began to weep and cry. The sentinel ran up, and Thadhellala brought complaint against this man. She was released, and he was hanged in her place.

She fled to a far city, of which the Sultan had just then died. Now, according to the custom of that country, they took as king the person who happened to be at the gates of the city when the King died. Fate took Thadhellala there at the right time. They conducted her to the palace, and she was proclaimed Queen.

THE GOOD MAN AND THE BAD ONE

Two men, one good and the other bad, started out together to do business, and took provisions with them. Soon the bad one said to the good one: "I am hungry; give me some of your food." He gave him some, and they both ate.

They went on again till they were hungry. "Give me some of your food," said the bad one. He gave him some of it, and they ate.

They went on until they were hungry. "Give me some of your food," said the bad one. He gave him some, and they ate.

They went on until they were hungry. The good man said to his companion: "Give me some of your food."

"Oh, no, my dear," said the bad one.

"I beg you to give me some of your food," said the good one.

"Let me pluck out one of your eyes," answered the bad one. He consented. The bad one took his pincers and took out one of his eyes.

They went on until they came to a certain place. Hunger pressed them. "Give me some of your food," said the good man.

"Let me pluck out your other eye," answered his companion.

"O my dear," replied the good man, "leave it to me, I beg of you."

"No!" responded the bad one; "no eye, no food."

But finally he said, "Pluck it out."

They proceeded until they came to a certain place. When hunger pressed them anew the bad one abandoned his companion.

A bird came passing by, and said to him: "Take a leaf of this tree and apply it to your eyes." He took a leaf of the tree, applied it to his eyes, and was healed. He arose, continued on his way, and arrived at a city where he found the one who had plucked out his eyes.

"Who cured you?"

"A bird passed near me," said the good man. "He said to me, 'Take a leaf of this tree.' I took it, applied it to my eyes, and was cured.

The good man found the King of the city blind.

"Give me back my sight and I will give you my daughter."

He restored his sight to him, and the King gave him his daughter. The good man took his wife to his house. Every morning he went to present his respects to the King, and kissed his head. One day he fell ill. He met the bad one, who said to him:

"Eat an onion and you will be cured; but when you kiss the King's head, turn your head aside or the King will notice your breath and will kill you."

After these words he ran to the King and said: "O King, your son-in-law disdains you."

"O my dear," answered the King, "my son-in-law does not disdain me."

"Watch him," answered the bad one; "when he comes to kiss your head he will turn away from you."

The King remarked that his son-in-law did turn away on kissing his head.

"Wait a moment," he said to him. Immediately he wrote a letter to the Sultan, and gave it to his son-in-law, commanding him to carry it to the Sultan. Going out of the house he met the bad one, who wanted to carry the letter himself. The good man gave it to him. The Sultan read the letter, and had the bad one's head cut off. The good man returned to the King.

"What did he say?" asked the King.

"Ah, Sidi, I met a man who wanted to carry the letter. I intrusted it to him and he took it to the Sultan, who condemned him to death in the city."

THE CROW AND THE CHILD

A man had two wives. He was a rich merchant. One of them had a son whose forehead was curved with a forelock. Her husband said to her:

"Don't work any more, but only take care of the child. The other wife will do all the work."

One day he went to market. The childless wife said to the other, "Go, get some water."

"No," she answered, "our husband does not want me to work."

"Go, get some water, I tell you." And the woman went to the fountain. On the way she met a crow half dead with fatigue. A merchant who was passing took it up and carried it away. He arrived before the house of the woman who had gone to the fountain, and there found the second woman.

"Give something to this crow," demanded the merchant.

"Give it to me," she answered, "and I will make you rich."

"What will you give me?" asked the merchant.

"A child," replied the woman.

The merchant refused, and said to her, "Where did you steal it?"

"From whom did I steal it?" she cried. "It is my own son."

"Bring him."

She brought the child to him, and the merchant left her the crow and took the boy to his home and soon became very rich. The mother came back from the fountain. The other woman said:

"Where is your son? Listen, he is crying, that son of yours."

"He is not crying," she answered.

"You don't know how to amuse him. I'll go and take him."

"Leave him alone," said the mother. "He is asleep."

They ground some wheat, and the child did not appear to wake up.

At this the husband returned from the market and said to the mother, "Why don't you busy yourself looking after your son?" Then she arose to take him, and found a crow in the cradle. The other woman cried:

"This is the mother of a crow! Take it into the other house; sprinkle it with hot water." She went to the other house and poured hot water on the crow.

Meanwhile, the child called the merchant his father and the merchant's wife his mother. One day the merchant set off on a journey. His mother brought some food to him in the room where he was confined.

"My son," she said, "will you promise not to betray me?"

"You are my mother," answered the child; "I will not betray you."

"Only promise me."

"I promise not to betray you."

"Well, know that I am not your mother and my husband is not your father."

The merchant came home from his journey and took the child some food, but he would not eat it.

"Why won't you eat?" asked the merchant. "Could your mother have been here?"

"No," answered the child, "she has not been here."

The merchant went to his wife and said to her, "Could you have gone up to the child's chamber?"

The woman answered, "I did not go up to the room."

The merchant carried food to the child, who said: "For the love of God, I adjure you to tell me if you are my father and if your wife is my mother."

The merchant answered: "My son, I am not your father and my wife is not your mother."

The child said to her, "Prepare us some food."

When she had prepared the food the child mounted a horse and the merchant a mule. They proceeded a long way, and arrived at the village of which the real father of the child was the chief. They entered his house. They gave food to the child, and said, "Eat."

"I will not eat until the other woman comes up here."

"Eat. She is a bad woman."

"No, let her come up." They called her. The merchant ran to the child.

"Why do you act thus toward her?"

"Oh!" cried those present, "she had a child that was changed into a crow."

"No doubt," said the merchant; "but the child had a mark."

"Yes, he had one."

"Well, if we find it, we shall recognize the child. Put out the lamp." They put it out. The child threw off its hood. They lighted the lamp again.

"Rejoice," cried the child, "I am your son!"

H'AB SLIMAN

A man had a boy and a girl. Their mother died and he took another wife. The little boy stayed at school until evening. The school-master asked them:

"What do your sisters do?"

One answered, "She makes bread."

A second, "She goes to fetch water."

A third, "She prepares the *couscous.*"

When he questioned H'ab Sliman, the child played deaf, the master struck him. One day his sister said to him: "What is the matter, O my brother? You seem to be sad."

"Our schoolmaster punishes us," answered the child.

"And why does he punish you?" inquired the young girl.

The child replied: "After we have studied until evening he asks each of us what our sisters do. They answer him: she kneads bread, she goes to get water. But when he questions me I have nothing to say, and he beats me."

"Is it nothing but for that?"

"That is all."

"Well," added the young girl, "the next time he asks you, answer him: 'This is what my sister does: When she laughs the sun shines; when she weeps it rains; when she combs her hair, legs of mutton fall; when she goes from one place to another, roses drop.'"

The child gave that answer.

"Truly," said the schoolmaster, "that is a rich match." A few days after he bought her, and they made preparations for her departure for the house of her husband. The stepmother of the young girl made her a little loaf of salt bread. She ate it and asked some drink from her sister, the daughter of her stepmother.

"Let me pluck out one of your eyes," said the sister.

"Pluck it out," said the promised bride, "for our people are already on the way."

The stepmother gave her to drink and plucked out one of her eyes.

"A little more," she said.

"Let me take out your other eye," answered the cruel woman.

The young girl drank and let her pluck out the other eye. Scarcely had she left the house than the stepmother thrust her out on the road. She dressed her own daughter and put her in the place of the blind one. They arrive.

"Comb yourself," they told her, and there fell dust.

"Walk," and nothing happened.

"Laugh," and her front teeth fell out.

All cried, "Hang H'ab Sliman!"

Meanwhile some crows came flying near the young blind girl, and one said to her: "Some merchants are on the point of passing this way. Ask them for a little wool, and I will restore your sight."

The merchants came up and the blind girl asked them for a little wool, and each one of them threw her a bit. The crow descended near her and restored her sight.

"Into what shall we change you?" they asked.

"Change me into a pigeon," she answered.

The crows stuck a needle into her head and she was changed into a pigeon. She took her flight to the house of the schoolmaster and perched upon a tree near by. The people went to sow wheat.

"O master of the field," she said, "is H'ab Sliman yet hanged?"

She began to weep, and the rain fell until the end of the day's work.

One day the people of the village went to find a venerable old man and said to him:

"O old man, a bird is perched on one of our trees. When we go to work the sky is covered with clouds and it rains. When the day's work is done the sun shines."

"Go," said the old man, "put glue on the branch where it perches."

They put glue on its branch and caught the bird. The daughter of the stepmother said to her mother:

"Let us kill it."

"No," said a slave, "we will amuse ourselves with it."

"No; kill it." And they killed it. Its blood spurted upon a rose-tree. The rose-tree became so large that it overspread all the village. The people worked to cut it down until evening, and yet it remained the size of a thread.

"To-morrow," they said, "we will finish it." The next morning they found it as big as it was the day before. They returned to the old man and said to him:

"O old man, we caught the bird and killed it. Its blood gushed upon a rose-tree, which became so large that it overspreads the whole village. Yesterday we worked all day to cut it down. We left it the size of a thread. This morning we find it as big as ever."

"O my children," said the old man, "you are not yet punished enough. Take H'ab Sliman, perhaps he will have an expedient. Make him sleep at your house." H'ab Sliman said to them, "Give me a sickle." Someone said to him: "We who are strong have cut all day without being able to accomplish it, and do you think you will be capable of it? Let us see if you will find a new way to do it."

At the moment when he gave the first blow a voice said to him:

"Take care of me, O my brother!"

The voice wept, the child began to weep, and it rained. H'ab Sliman recognized his sister.

"Laugh," he said. She laughed and the sun shone, and the people got dried.

"Comb yourself," and legs of mutton fell. All those who were present regaled themselves on them. "Walk," and roses fell. "But what is the matter with you, my sister?"

"What has happened to me."

"What revenge does your heart desire?"

"Attach the daughter of my stepmother to the tail of a horse that she may be dragged in the bushes."

When the young girl was dead, they took her to the house, cooked her, and sent her to her mother and sister.

"O my mother," cried the latter, "this eye is that of my sister Aftelis."

"Eat, unhappy one," said the mother, "your sister Aftelis has become the slave of slaves."

"But look at it," insisted the young girl. "You have not even looked at it. I will give this piece to the one who will weep a little."

"Well," said the cat, "if you give me that piece I will weep with one eye."

THE KING AND HIS SON

He had a son whom he brought up well. The child grew and said one day to the King, "I am going out for a walk."

"It is well," answered the King. At a certain place he found an olive-tree on fire.

"O God," he cried, "help me to put out this fire!"

Suddenly God sent the rain, the fire was extinguished, and the young man was able to pass. He came to the city and said to the governor:

"Give me a chance to speak in my turn."

"It is well," said he; "speak."

"I ask the hand of your daughter," replied the young man.

"I give her to you," answered the governor, "for if you had not put out that fire the city would have been devoured by the flames."

He departed with his wife. After a long march the wife made to God this prayer:

"O God, place this city here."

The city appeared at the very spot. Toward evening the Marabout of the city of which the father of the young bridegroom was King went to the mosque to say his prayers.

"O marvel!" he cried, "what do I see down there?"

The King called his wife and sent her to see what was this

new city. The woman departed, and, addressing the wife of the yoüng prince, asked alms of him. He gave her alms. The messenger returned and said to the King:

"It is your son who commands in that city."

The King, pricked by jealousy, said to the woman: "Go, tell him to come and find me. I must speak with him."

The woman went away and returned with the King's son. His father said to him:

"If you are the son of the King, go and see your mother in the other world."

He regained his palace in tears.

"What is the matter with you," asked his wife, "you whom destiny has given me?"

He answered her: "My father told me, 'Go and see your mother in the other world.'"

"Return to your father," she replied, "and ask him for the book of the grandmother of your grandmother."

He returned to his father, who gave him the book. He brought it to his wife, who said to him, "Lay it on the grave of your mother." He placed it there and the grave opened. He descended and found a man who was licking the earth. He saw another who was eating mildew. And he saw a third who was eating meat.

"Why do you eat meat?" he asked him.

"Because I did good on earth," responded the shade.

"Where shall I find my mother?" asked the prince.

The shade said, "She is down there."

He went to his mother, who asked him why he came to seek her.

He replied, "My father sent me."

"Return," said the mother, "and say to your father to lift up the beam which is on the hearth." The prince went to his father. "My mother bids you take up the beam which is above the hearth." The King raised it and found a treasure.

"If you are the son of the King," he added, "bring me someone a foot high whose beard measures two feet." The prince began to weep.

"Why do you weep," asked his wife, "you whom destiny has given me?"

The prince answered her, "My father said to me, 'Bring me someone a foot high whose beard measures two feet.'"

"Return to your father," she replied, "and ask him for the book of the grandfather of your grandfather."

His father gave him the book and the prince brought it to his wife.

"Take it to him again and let him put it in the assembly place, and call a public meeting." A man a foot high appeared, took up the book, went around the city, and ate up all the inhabitants.

MAHOMET-BEN-SOLTAN

A certain sultan had a son who rode his horse through the city where his father reigned, and killed everyone he met. The inhabitants united and promised a flock to him who should make him leave the city. An old woman took it upon herself to realize the wishes of her fellow-citizens. She procured some bladders and went to the fountain to fill them with the cup of an acorn. The old man came to water his horse and said to the old woman:

"Get out of my way."

She would not move. The young man rode his horse over the bladders and burst them.

"If you had married Thithbirth, a cavalier," cried the old woman, "you would not have done this damage. But I predict that you will never marry her, for already seventy cavaliers have met death on her account."

The young man, pricked to the quick, regained his horse, took provisions, and set out for the place where he should find the young girl. On the way he met a man. They journeyed together. Soon they perceived an ogress with a dead man at her side.

"Place him in the earth," said the ogress to them; "it is my son; the Sultan hanged him and cut off his foot with a sword."

They took one of the rings of the dead man and went on their way. Soon they entered a village and offered the ring to the governor, who asked them for another like it. They went away from there, returned through the country which they had traversed, and met a pilgrim who had made the tour of the world. They had visited every place except the sea. They turned toward the sea. At the moment of embarking, a whale barred their passage. They retraced their steps, and met the ogress, took a second ring from the dead man, and departed. At a place they found sixty corpses. A singing bird was guarding them. The travellers stopped and heard the bird say:

"He who shall speak here shall be changed into a rock and shall die. Mahomet-ben-Soltan, you shall never wed the young girl. Ninety-nine cavaliers have already met death on her account."

Mahomet stayed till morning without saying one word. Then he departed with his companion for the city where Thithbirth dwelt. When they arrived they were pressed with hunger. Mahomet's companion said to him:

"Sing that which you heard the bird sing." He began to sing. The young girl, whom they meant to buy, heard him and asked him from whom he had got that song.

"From my head," he answered.

Mahomet's companion said: "We learned it in the fields from a singing bird."

"Bring me that bird," she said, "or I'll have your head cut off."

Mahomet took a lantern and a cage which he placed upon the branch of the tree where the bird was perching.

"Do you think to catch me?" cried the bird. The next day it entered the cage and the young man took it away. When they were in the presence of the young girl the bird said to her:

"We have come to buy you."

The father of the young girl said to Mahomet: "If you find her you may have her. But if not, I will kill you. Ninety-nine cavaliers have already met death thus. You will be the hundredth."

The bird flew toward the woman.

"Where shall I find you?" it asked her.

She answered: "You see that door at which I am sitting; it is the usual place of my father. I shall be hidden underneath."

The next day Mahomet presented himself before the Sultan: "Arise," he said, "your daughter is hidden there."

The Sultan imposed this new condition: "My daughter resembles ninety-nine others of her age. She is the hundredth. If you recognize her in the group I will give her to you. But if not, I will kill you."

The young girl said to Mahomet, "I will ride a lame horse." Mahomet recognized her, and the Sultan gave her to him, with a serving-maid, a female slave, and another woman.

Mahomet and his companion departed. Arriving at a certain road they separated. Mahomet retained for himself his wife and the slave woman, and gave to his companion the two other women. He gained the desert and left for a moment his wife and the slave woman. In his absence an ogre took away his wife. He ran in search of her and met some shepherds.

"O shepherds," he said, "can you tell me where the ogre lives?"

They pointed out the place. Arriving, he saw his wife. Soon the ogre appeared, and Mahomet asked where he should find his destiny.

"My destiny is far from here," answered the ogre. "My destiny is in an egg, the egg in a pigeon, the pigeon in a camel, the camel in the sea."

Mahomet arose, ran to dig a hole at the shore of the sea, stretched a mat over the hole; a camel sprang from the water and fell into the hole. He killed it and took out an egg, crushed the egg in his hands, and the ogre died. Mahomet took his wife and came to his father's city, where he built himself a palace. The father promised a flock to him who should kill his son. As no one offered, he sent an army of soldiers to besiege him. He called one of them in particular and said to him:

"Kill Mahomet and I will enrich you."

The soldiers managed to get near the young prince, put out his eyes, and left him in the field. An eagle passed and said to Mahomet: "Don't do any good to your parents, but since your father has made you blind take the bark of this tree, apply it to your eyes, and you will be cured."

The young man was healed.

A short time after his father said to him, "I will wed your wife."

"You cannot," he answered. The Sultan convoked the Marabout, who refused him the dispensation he demanded. Soon Mahomet killed his father and celebrated his wedding-feast for seven days and seven nights.

THE WORLD'S GREAT CLASSICS

LIBRARY COMMITTEE

JUSTIN McCARTHY
RICHARD HENRY STODDARD
ARTHUR RICHMOND MARSH, A.B.
PAUL VAN DYKE, D.D.
ALBERT ELLERY BERGH

ILLUSTRATED WITH NEARLY THREE HUNDRED PHOTOGRAVURES ETCHINGS COLORED PLATES AND FULL PAGE PORTRAITS OF GREAT AUTHORS

CLARENCE COOK · ART EDITOR

THE COLONIAL PRESS
NEW YORK · LONDON

MELPOMENE

MELPOMENE: MUSE OF TRAGEDY.

Photogravure from the original painting by Paul Baudry in the foyer of the Grand Opera-House at Paris.

MALAYAN LITERATURE

COMPRISING

ROMANTIC TALES, EPIC POETRY

AND

ROYAL CHRONICLES

TRANSLATED INTO ENGLISH FOR THE FIRST TIME

WITH A SPECIAL INTRODUCTION BY

CHAUNCEY C. STARKWEATHER, A.B., LL.B

REVISED EDITION

THE COLONIAL PRESS

·FIFTH·AVE· ·NEW·YORK·

SPECIAL INTRODUCTION

EASILY the most charming poem of Malayan Literature is the Epic of Bidasari. It has all the absorbing fascination of a fairy tale. We are led into the dreamy atmosphere of haunted palace and beauteous plaisance: we glide in the picturesque imaginings of the oriental poet from the charm of all that is languorously seductive in nature into the shadowy realms of the supernatural. At one moment the sturdy bowman or lithe and agile lancer is before us in hurrying column, and at another we are told of mystic sentinels from another world, of Djinns and demons and spirit-princes. All seems shadowy, vague, mysterious, entrancing.

In this tale there is a wealth of imagery, a luxury of picturesqueness, together with that straightforward simplicity so alluring in the story-teller. Not only is our attention so captivated that we seem under a spell, but our sympathy is invoked and retained. We actually wince before the cruel blows of the wicked queen. And the hot tears of Bidasari move us to living pity. In the poetic justice that punishes the queen and rewards the heroine we take a childish delight. In other words, the oriental poet is simple, sensuous, passionate, thus achieving Milton's ideal of poetic excellence. We hope that no philosopher, philologist, or ethnologist will persist in demonstrating the sun-myth or any other allegory from this beautiful poem. It is a story, a charming tale, to while away an idle hour, and nothing more. All lovers of the simple, the beautiful, the picturesque should say to such learned peepers and botanizers, "Hands off!" Let no learned theories rule here. Leave this beautiful tale for artists and lovers of the story pure and simple. Seek no more moral here than you would in a rose or a lily or a graceful palm. Light, love, color, beauty, sympathy, engaging fascination—these may be found alike by philosopher and winsome youth. The story is no more immoral than a drop of dew or a lotus bloom; and, as to interest, in the land of the improviser and the story-teller one is obliged to be interesting. For there the audience is either spellbound, or quickly fades away and leaves the poet to realize that he must attempt better things.

We think that these folk-stories have, indeed, a common origin, but that it is in the human heart. We do not look for a Sigurd or Siegfried on every page. Imagine a nation springing from an ignorant couple on a sea-girt isle, in a few generations they would have evolved their Sleeping Beauty and their Prince Charming, their enchanted castles, and their Djinns and fairies. These are as indigenous to the human heart as the cradle-song or the battle-cry. We do not find ourselves siding with those who would trace everything to a first exemplar. Children have played, and men have loved, and poets have sung from the beginning, and we need not run to Asia for the source of everything. Universal human nature has a certain spontaneity.

The translator has tried to reproduce the faithfulness and, in some measure, to indicate the graceful phrases of the original poem. The author of Bidasari is unknown, and the date of the poem is a matter of the utmost uncertainty. Some have attributed to it a Javanese origin, but upon very slight evidence. The best authorities place its scene in the country of Palembang, and its time after the arrival of the Europeans in the Indian archipelago, but suggest that the legend must be much older than the poem.

The "Makota Radja Radja" is one of the most remarkable books of oriental literature. According to M. Aristide Marre, who translated it into French, its date is 1603. Its author was Bokhari, and he lived at Djohore. It contains extracts from more than fifty Arab and Persian authors. It treats of the duties of man to God, to himself and to society, and of the obligations of sovereigns, subjects, ministers, and officers. Examples are taken from the lives of kings in Asia. The author has not the worst opinion of his work, saying distinctly that it is a complete guide to happiness in this world and the next. He is particularly copious in his warnings to copyists and translators, cautioning them against the slightest negligence or inaccuracy, and promising them for faithfulness a passport to the glories of heaven. This shows that the author at least took the work seriously. That there is not a trace of humor in the book would doubtless recommend it to the dignified and lethargic orientals for whom it was written. Bokhari seemed to consider himself prophet, priest, and poet-laureate in one. The work has a high position in the Malayan Peninsula, where it is read by young and old. The "Crown of Kings" is written in the court language of Djohore. The author was a Mohammedan mendicant monk. He called the book the Crown of Kings because "every king who read and followed its precepts would be a perfect king, and thus only would his crown sit well on his head, and the book itself will be for him a true crown."

La Fontaine and Lamartine loved stories. The schoolmates of the latter called the latter "story-lover." They would have loved the story of the Princess Djouher Manikam, which is written in a simple and natural style and is celebrated in the East, or, as the Malays say, in the "country between windward and leeward."

From the "Sedjaret Malayou," worthless as it is as history, one may obtain side lights upon oriental life. Manners are portrayed in vivid colors, so that one may come to have a very accurate knowledge of them. Customs are depicted from which one may learn of the formality and regard for precedents which is a perspicuous trait of oriental character. The rigid etiquette of court and home may be remarked. From the view of morals here described, one may appreciate how far we have progressed in ethical culture from that prevailing in former times among the children of these winterless lands.

The readers of this series are to be congratulated in that they are here placed in possession of a unique and invaluable source of information concerning the life and literature of the far-away people of the Indian archipelago. To these pages an added interest accrues from the fact that the Philippines are now protected by our flag.

The name Malay signifies a wanderer. As a people they are passionate, vain, susceptible, and endowed with a reckless bravery and contempt of death. The Malays have considerable originality in versification. The pantoum is particularly theirs

—a form arising from their habits of improvisation and competitive versifying. They have also the epic or *sjair,* generally a pure romance, with much naïve simplicity and natural feeling. And finally, they have the popular song, enigma, and fable.

And so we leave the reader to his pleasant journey to the lands of Djinns and Mantris and spells and mystic talismans. He will be entertained by the chrestomathy of Bokhari; he will be entranced by the story of the winsome and dainty Bidasari.

Chauncey C. Starkweather

CONTENTS

ILLUSTRATIONS

THE EPIC OF BIDASARI

—

[*Metrical Translation by Chauncey C. Starkweather, A.B., LL.B.*]

BIDASARI

SONG I

HEAR now the song I sing about a king
Of Kembajat. A fakir has completed
The story, that a poem he may make.
There was a king, a sultan, and he was
Handsome and wise and perfect in all ways,
Proud scion of a race of mighty kings.
He filled the land with merchants bringing wealth
And travellers. And from that day's report,
He was a prince most valorous and strong,
Who never vexing obstacles had met.
But ever is the morrow all unknown.
After the Sultan, all accomplished man,
Had married been a year, or little more,
He saw that very soon he'd have an heir.
At this his heart rejoiced, and he was glad
As though a mine of diamonds were his.
Some days the joy continued without clouds.
But soon there came the moment when the prince
Knew sorrow's blighting force, and had to yield
His country's capital. A savage bird,
Garouda called, a very frightful bird,
Soared in the air, and ravaged all the land.
It flew with wings and talons wide outstretched,
With cries to terrify the stoutest heart.
All people, great and small, were seized with dread.
And all the country feared and was oppressed,
And people ran now this way and now that.
The folk approached the King. He heard the noise
As of a fray, and, angry, asked the guard,
"Whence comes this noise?" As soon as this he said

One of his body-guard replied with awe,
"Illustrious lord, most merciful of kings,
A fell garouda follows us about."
The King's face paled when these dread words he heard.
The officers arose and beat their breasts.
The sorrow of the King was greater still
Because the Queen was ill. He took her hand
And started without food or anything.
He trusted all to God, who watches o'er
The safety of the world. The suff'ring Queen
Spoke not a word and walked along in tears.
They went by far *campongs* and dreary fields
Beneath a burning sun which overwhelmed
Their strength. And so the lovely Queen's fair face
From palest yellow grew quite black. The prince
Approached the desert with his body torn
By thorns and brambles. All his care and grief
Were doubled when he saw his lovely wife
Who scarce could drag herself along and whom
He had to lead. Most desolate was he,
Turning his mind on the good Queen's sad lot.
Upon the way he gave up all to her.
Two months they journeyed and one day they came
Unto a *campong* of a merchant, where
They looked for rest because the Queen was weak.
The path was rugged and the way was hard.
The prince made halt before the palisades,
For God had made him stop and rest awhile.
The Sultan said: "What is this *campong* here?
I fain would enter, but I do not dare."
The good Queen wept and said: "O my beloved,
What shall I say? I am so tired and weak
I cannot journey more." The King was quite
Beside himself and fainted where he sat.
But on they journeyed to the riverside,
Stopping at every step.

And when the King
Had gained the bank he saw a little boat
With roof of bent bamboos and *kadjang* screen.
Then to the Queen, "Rest here, my precious one."

The silver moon was at the full, but veiled
With clouds, like to a maid who hides her face
And glances toward her lover timidly.
Then there was born a daughter, like a flower,
More beautiful than statue of pure gold,
Just like the tulips that the princess plucked.
The mother's heart was broken at the thought
That she must leave the babe, the child beloved
They both adored, such beauty it presaged.
The King with tears exclaimed, " How can we take
The infant with us o'er this stony road
Beset with thorns, and burned with dreadful heat?
Pearl of my palace, said he to the Queen,
" Weep not so bitterly about the child.
An offering let us make of her to God.
God grant she may be found by loving hearts
Who'll care for her and raise her in their home."
As soon as they had quite determined there
To leave the infant princess, their great grief
No limit knew. But ere they went away
The King took up the infant in his arms
And rocked her on his knees until she slept.
" Sleep on, heart's love, my soul, my little one,
Weep not for thy dear mother's lot. She fain
Would take thee with her, but the way is hard.
Sleep on, dear child, the apple of my eye,
The image of thy sire. Stay here, fea. not.
For unto God we trust thee, Lord of all.
Sleep on, my child, chief jewel of my crown,
And let thy father go. To look at thee
Doth pierce my heart as by a poniard's blow.
Ah, sweet my child, dear, tender little one,
Thy father loves yet leaves thee. Happy be,
And may no harm come nigh thee. Fare thee well."
The little princess slept, lulled by his voice.
He put her from his knees and placed her on
A finely woven cloth of Ind, and covered her
With satin webbed with gold. With flowing tears
The mother wrapped her in a tissue fine
Adorned with jewels like to sculptured flowers.

She seized the child and weeping murmured low:
"O dearest child, my pretty little girl!
I leave thee to the Master of the world.
Live happily, although thy mother goes
And leaves thee here. Ah, sad thy mother's lot!
Thy father forces her to quit thee now.
She would prefer with thee to stay, but, no!
Thy father bids her go. And that is why
Thy mother's fond heart breaks, she loves thee so,
And yet must leave thee. Oh, how can I live?"
The mother fainted, and the grieving King
Was fain to kill himself, so was he moved.
He took the Queen's head on his knees. And soon
By God's decree and ever-sheltering grace
She to her senses came and stood erect.
Again she wept on looking at the child.
"If I should never see thee more, sweet soul,
Oh, may thy mother share thy fate! Her life
Is bound to thine. The light is gone from out
Thy mother's eyes. Hope dies within her heart
Because she fears to see thee nevermore.
Oh, may some charitable heart, my child,
Discover thee!" The prince essayed to dry
Her tears. "Now come away, my dearest love.
Soon day will dawn." The prince in grief set out,
But ever turned and wanted to go back.
They walked along together, man and wife
All solitary, with no friends at hand,
Care-worn and troubled, and the moon shone bright.

SONG II

I SING in this song of a merchant great
And of his wealth. His goods and treasures were
Beyond all count, his happiness without
Alloy. In Indrapura town there was
No equal to his fortune. He possessed
A thousand slaves, both old and young, who came
From Java and from other lands. His rank
Was higher than Panggawa's. Wives he had
In goodly numbers. But he lacked one thing
That weighed upon his heart—he had no child.
Now, by the will of God, the merchant great
Came very early from the palace gates,
And sought the river-bank, attended by
His favorite wife. Lila Djouhara was
The merchant's name. He heard a feeble voice
As of an infant crying, like the shrill
Tones of a flute, and from a boat it seemed
To come. Then toward the wondrous boat he went
And saw an infant with a pretty face.
His heart was overjoyed as if he had
A mine of diamonds found. The spouses said:
"Whose child is this? It surely must belong
To one of highest rank. Some cause he had
To leave her here." The merchant's heart was glad
To see the bright eyes of the little one.
He raised her in his arms and took her home.
Four waiting-maids and nurses two he gave
The pretty child. The palace rooms were all
Adorned anew, with rugs and curtains soft,
And tapestries of orange hue were hung.
The princess rested on a couch inlaid with gold,
A splendid couch, with lanterns softly bright
And tapers burning with a gentle ray.

The merchant and his wife with all their hearts
Adored the child, as if it were their own.
She looked like Mindoudari, and received
The name of Bidasari. Then they took
A little fish and changing vital spirits
They put it in a golden box, then placed
The box within a casket rich and rare.
The merchant made a garden, with all sorts
Of vases filled with flowers, and bowers of green
And trellised vines. A little pond made glad
The eyes, with the precious stones and topaz set
Alternately, in fashion of the land
Of Pellanggam, a charm for all. The sand
Was purest gold, with alabaster fine
All mixed with red pearls and with sapphires blue.
And in the water deep and clear they kept
The casket. Since they had the infant found,
Sweet Bidasari, all the house was filled
With joy. The merchant and his wife did naught
But feast and clap their hands and dance. They watched
The infant night and day. They gave to her
Garments of gold, with necklaces and gems,
With rings and girdles, and quaint boxes, too,
Of perfume rare, and crescent pins and flowers
Of gold to nestle in the hair, and shoes
Embroidered in the fashion of Sourat.
By day and night the merchant guarded her.
So while sweet Bidasari grew, her lovely face
Increased in beauty. Her soft skin was white
And yellow, and she was most beautiful.
Her ear-rings and her bracelets made her look
Like some rare gem imprisoned in a glass.
Her beauty had no equal, and her face
Was like a nymph's celestial. She had gowns
As many as she wished, as many as
A princess fair of Java. There was not
A second Bidasari in the land.

I'll tell about Djouhan Mengindra now,
Sultan of Indrapura. Very wide

His kingdom was, with ministers of state
And officers, and regiments of picked
Young warriors, the bulwark of the throne.
This most illustrious prince had only been
Two years the husband of fair Lila Sari,
A princess lovable and kind. The King
Was deemed most handsome. And there was within
All Indrapura none to equal him.
His education was what it should be,
His conversation very affable.
He loved the princess Lila Sari well.
He gave her everything, and she in turn
Was good to him, but yet she was so vain.
"There is no one so beautiful as I,"
She said. They were united like unto
The soul and body. And the good King thought
There could not be another like his wife.
One day they were together, and the Queen
Began to sing: "Oh, come, my well-beloved,
And listen to my words. Thou tellst me oft
Thou lovest me. But I know not thy heart.
If some misfortune were to overwhelm
Wouldst thou be true to me?" He smiled and said:
"No harm can touch thee, dear. But should it come,
Whenever thou art 'whelmed I'll perish too."
With joy the princess said: "My noble prince,
If there were found a woman whose flower face
Were fairer than all others in the world,
Say, wouldst thou wed her?" And the King replied:
"My friend, my fairest, who is like to thee?
My soul, my princess, of a noble race,
Thou'rt sweet and wise and good and beautiful.
Thou'rt welded to my heart. No thought of mine
Is separate from thee."
The princess smiled;
Her face was all transfigured with her joy.
But suddenly the thought came to her mind,
"Who knows there is none more fair than I?"
And then she cried: "Now hear me, O my love!
Were there a woman with an angel-face,

Wouldst thou make her thy wife? If she appeared
Unto thine eyes more beautiful than I,
Then would thy heart not burn for her?"
The prince
But smiled, and answered not. She also smiled,
But said, "Since thou dost hesitate, I know
That thou wouldst surely wed her." Then the prince
Made answer: "O my heart, gold of my soul,
If she in form and birth were like to thee
I'd join her with thy destiny." Now when
The princess heard these words she paled and shook.
With eyes cast down, she left her royal spouse.
But quick he seized her. With a smile he said:
"Gold, ruby, dearest friend, I pray thee now,
Oh, be not vexed with me. Light of my eyes,
Keep not within thy heart a bitterness
Because I answered thus unto thy words."
He took her in his arms and kissed her lips
And wooed her. And her face again grew sweet
The while she heard. And yet her woman's heart
Was grieved and saddened. And she sat apart,
And swift these thoughts came to her anxious mind:
"I'll seek to-morrow through this kingdom wide,
Lest there should be within the land a maid
More fair than I. To death I shall condemn
Her straight, lest rival she may be to me.
For if my lord should marry her, he'd love
Her more than me. He'd love the younger one,
And constantly my tortured heart would bleed."
They angered her, these thoughts, as if her heart
Were filled with gall. "Now may I be accursed
If I go not unto the end in love."
Her heart was not assuaged; she sighed alone.
Upon the morrow morn the King went out,
And with him many officers and men.
Meanwhile the Princess Lila Sari sent
A summons to a jeweller of skill,
And at the same time called her four *dyangs*,
Who came and sat. Dang Wilapat bowed low
And said, "Our greetings to thee, princess great."

The Queen replied: "Go forth, *dyangs*, at once
And find me gold and dust of gold, and take
It all unto a goldsmith. Let him make
For me a fan, all decked with beauteous gems,
With rubies red and pearls; and after that
A girdle virginal. Count not the price.
I want it all as quickly as may be."
And so they hastened, took the gold, and went
Outside the city, through the whole *campong*
Of goldsmiths, seeking there the best to make
The fan and girdle. And the hammered gold
Soon shone with many amethysts and gems.
It was a marvel to behold those rare
And quaintly fashioned ornaments, to deck
A sultaness. Of priceless worth they were.
Four days, and all was ready for the Queen.
But she had never eaten all this time
Because of grief. She thought the fan more fine
Than Java princess ever yet possessed.
She called the four *dyangs* and said to them:
"A secret mission have I now for ye.
Go up and down among the officers
And show this fan for sale, but never name
The price. Seek ever if there be a face
More beautiful than mine; and should ye find
A face more fair, come tell it straight to me.
If ye obey my will I'll make ye all
Inspectresses within the royal home."
Then forth the women went upon the quest.
And first among their friends they went with words
Of mystery and hints of wondrous things
They had for sale. And so these servants bore
The story to their masters, "The *dyangs*
Have something wonderful to sell." And soon
The daughters of the houses rich began
To clamor for a sight of this great prize.
Then the *dyangs* went to the houses all.
The young girls said, "Oh, tell us now the price."
Dyang Wiravan quickly answered, then
Dyang Podagah: "'Tis a princely thing;

I'll go and ask the price and tell it thee."
And so they spoke, and so they looked about
To find a face more beautiful and rare
Than their own Queen's, and wearied in the search.
"Where can we further look?" they said, and then
Bethought them of the strangers and the priests.
But in that quarter no one dared to touch
The precious things, but thought it passing strange
The Queen should wish to sell. To the *campong*
Of merchants next they went. A double line
Of ramparts guarded it. "Here is more stir
And gayety," they said, "with sport and song,
Than elsewhere have we found." And so they sought
The richest merchants. "We have something rare,"
They said, "made by an artist Javanese."
When Bidasari's servants saw these folk
They said: "Bring these things to our house and we
Will show them to our master. He will buy."
Then the *dyangs* with smiles replied: "They are
Not ours, but our good Queen's. And only we
May show them, lest a stone be lost, perchance,
And we be punished." Bidasari's maids
Were glad and said, "Wait but a moment here
Until we find what Bidasari wills."
They found her with her maids, and told the tale.
Then Bidasari bade them bring to her
The stranger folk, and said, "If I be pleased
I'll buy." Dang Ratna Watie went and told
The women that young Bidasari wished
To see their wares. The four *dyangs* came in
Together. Joy their faces all suffused,
But they seemed timid, modest, full of fear.
Then Bidasari's women said to them:
"Come, O young women, all are loyal here.
Enter, our sisters and our friends."

Now when
The Queen's *dyangs* had looked about them there
They all were dazzled, Bidasari's face
So beautiful appeared. How beat their hearts!
As they upon her lovely features gazed,

Each murmured to herself, "She is more fair
Than our great Queen."
Then Bidasari wished
To buy the fan, and sent a maid to ask
Her parents for the gold. The merchant said,
"Go see what thing it is, and weigh the gold
For her." The mother feared a trap or trick.
"Oh, do not buy the fan, my child," she said;
"I'll buy a finer one for thee. Send this
Away." But when her father saw her tears
Of disappointment, "It is thine," he said.
"What is the price? I'd buy it though it cost
Thy weight in gold, my darling. Tell me now,
Dyangs." Tjendra Melinee answered him,
"Are two timbangs too much?" "I'm very poor,"
He said; "but I will buy it for the child."
The gold was weighed. The four *dyangs* straightway
Departed, hurried to the Queen and said:
"At last we have discovered, O our Queen,
What thou hast sought. 'Tis in a near *campong*
Of merchants very rich and great. Oh, there
We found a princess fairer than the day;
More like an angel than a mortal maid.
No woman in this land compares with her.
Her name is Bidasari. And the King
Would surely marry her if once they met,
For soon she will be ready for a spouse;
Her innocence is charming. Like a cloud
The merchant and his wife keep watchful guard.
Her hair is curly, like a flower full blown.
Her brow is like the moon but one day old.
She's like a ring in Peylou made. She would
Outshine thy beauty, shouldst thou bring her here."
The princess heard and quickly said: "I feel
My hatred rise. Oh, may I never see
Her face! To hear ye speak of her inflames
My heart with anger. Say, why do ye think
That she's more fair than I?" Then made reply
The women: "Bidasari's eyes are soft.
Her smile is sweet, her skin is tinted like

The green *tjempakka,* and her graceful form
Resembles some famed statue nobly made.
Her cheeks are like the bill of flying bird.
We loved to look upon her neck. Her nose
Is like a jasmine bud. Her pretty face
Is like the yellow of an egg. Her thoughts
Are pure as crystal. And she wears her hair
In such a charming way. Her lips are like
A little polished box. The flowers she wears
But make her look the prettier. Her teeth
Are like a bright pomegranate. Ah, the heart
Doth open when one looketh on her face.
She's like a princess of the Mount Lidang.
Her features are like those of Nilagendi.
Her heels are like the eggs of hens, and make
Her seem a princess of Siam. Her fingers
More tapering are than quills of porcupine.
And solid is the nail of her left hand.
No noble's girl is Bidasari's peer."
Now when the princess heard them sing her praise
Her soul was wounded as if by a thorn.
Her dark eyes flashed. "Ah, speak no more of her,"
She said, "nor speak abroad what ye have seen.
But bring me Bidasari. I would see
If what ye say be true."
"Then we must take
Her presents first, and strive to gain by them
Her friendship, and attain our end at last."
They went to see her every day, and bore
Rich gifts.
The merchant and his wife remarked
The visits of the Queen's *dyangs,* and how
They loved their daughter. That is why they gave
Them all that they desired. But the *dyangs*
Among themselves kept saying: "How can we
Take her away? We love her so, and deep
Within our hearts we pity her. And now
Her parents have such trust in us, and load
Us down with gifts. But when, alas, at home
The princess questions us, what shall we say?

For she's a powerful Queen. Yet if we make
Unhappy this dear girl of these good folk,
Shall we not sin? And still the princess is
So violent and harsh! Her jealousy
Would know no limit should the King but hear
Of this affair."
Dang Djoudah answering spoke:
" We all can go to her and quiet her.
A word suffices oft. She is our Queen,
But to the King belongeth power supreme.
If Bidasari should disdain the throne
We shall renounce our functions at the court,
For what the Queen desires is most unjust.
And if we prove unfaithful we shall be
O'erwhelmed with maledictions." Thus they spoke
And went back to the busy-lived *campong*
Of merchants. Here they thought to go and find
Djouhara, and obtain what they desired.
A messenger went after them and said:
" To Dang Bidouri: Come at once; my friend
The princess summons you." Then the *dyangs*
Went to the Queen and found her with the King
At dinner. With malicious wink of eye
She made them understand they must not talk
Before the prince. When he had dined he took
Some *siri* from the betel-box, himself
Anointed with a perfume sweet, and went
To teach the young folk how to ride and shoot
The arrow straight, and played at many games.
Meanwhile the princess Lila Sari called
Before her the *dyangs* and questioned them:
" Why have ye come so late?" Bidouri bowed
And said: " 'Twas very hard to bring her here
To thee. The merchant and his wife do not
A moment leave her, for they love her so.
Her tiring-women ever are about.
Thou shouldst demand her of her parents, if
Thou dost desire to see her. Treat her like
Thy child, for she is still so very young!
From Bidasari's father thou wilt gain

All that thou canst desire, he is so rich,
If thou wilt only love his daughter dear.
And dost thou give command to bring her here?
Let us go all alone and summon her
For Bidasari'll freely follow us."
They tried to calm the anger of the Queen.
She bowed her head in silence, but her soul
Was very heavy, and hypocrisy
With hate and envy vied within her heart.
"They love the child, these *dyangs*," to herself
She said, "and I shall have no easy task.
I shall attract her here by trickery,
But she shall never my companion be.
With Bidasari once within my power
My heart will be no longer on the rack.
Go now, *dyangs*," she said, "and seek for me
The merchant and his wife and hither bring
Young Bidasari, whom I'll elevate
Unto the rank of princess, for I have
No child. Mazendra take with ye. And when
Young Bidasari shall arrive, conceal
Her for a day or two. And gently speak
Unto the merchant and his wife, and say
Concessions will be granted to the priests
And strangers in their quarter, should she come.
Console Lila Djouhara thus, and pledge
That he may come to see his child whene'er
His heart impelleth him." An escort went
With them, and the *dyangs* bowed low before
The merchant and his wife, and greeted, too,
Fair Bidasari. But the merchant said:
"Why come ye here in so great numbers?" Then
They straight replied: "Our most belovèd Queen
Hath sent us here with greetings unto thee,
The master of the house. If thou'lt permit,
We've come to seek fair Bidasari here."
They beat their breasts, the merchant and his wife.
"Our darling, only child! It will be hard
For her to be the servant of a prince;
For she hath had her way so long! Her traits

Are not yet formed. Go back, *dyangs*, and pray
The Queen to pardon us. Say how we grieve."
But the *dyangs* repeated all the words
Said by the Queen, and so their fears were calmed.
They hoped Queen Lila Sari would love well
Fair Bidasari. Then the merchant said:
"I will obey, and let my darling go,
So that she may become unto the Queen
A servant, and perchance a daughter loved.
Now shall she go with ye. Only I beg
The Queen to let her come back home to us
At three days' end. She is not used to stay
With strangers. Never hath she left us for
A single day." Then Dang Bidouri said:
"We'll do our best before the Queen; and why
Should she not grant to Bidasari this?"
They bathed fair Bidasari with sweet scents,
And then arranged her in rich raiment new.
A fine *sijrash* she wore with broidered flowers
Of Pekan, and a satin robe all fringed
With gold. She bore a plaque of beaten gold
Bound to a necklace, chiselled, gem-bedecked;
Her over-tunic was of yellow silk
With tiny serpents on the buttons 'graved.
Three bracelets wore the maid, and rarest rings,
And ear-rings like a wheel in motion wrought.
Chaste links of gold set forth her beauty rare,
A fair flow'r in a vase, whose perfume sweet
Wafts scented breaths as far as one may see.
They kissed her then with tears and held her close
Upon their breasts. "Be humble to the Queen,"
They said, "remember that thou art before
The King, and near the throne. Ask leave to come
To see us when thou dost desire. Speak sweetly
With low and gentle voice."

Thus they enjoined.

And then the merchant said, "*Dyangs*, if ye
Love Bidasari, see ye vex her not."
They dried their tears and said: "Be without fear.
Intrust thy daughter to our mistress dear."

"My child," he said, "I'll come to see thee oft.
Thou wilt be better there, my love, than here."
But Bidasari wept and cried: "Oh, come,
Dear mother, with me! Wilt thou not, alas?"
But the fond parents were astounded then
To learn the mother was not asked to come.
She stayed with tears, the while the father went.
As far as to the city's gates. With tears
He said: "Farewell, O apple of my eye
I leave thee here. Fear not, my dearest child."
Then Bidasari wept. Her heart was wrung.
She went. The merchant followed with his eyes.
She entered by a hidden door. *Dyangs*
And *mandars* flocked to see her, but she hung
Her head and kept her eyes downcast.
The sun
Announced the evening, and the King was still
Surrounded by his officers. 'Twas then
Fair Bidasari to the palace came,
And stood before the Queen. All the *dyangs*
Sat on the floor, with servants of the house.
Like the *pengawas* Bidasari bowed,
'Mid the *dyangs*, in presence of the Queen.
They gave her all the merchant's gifts, as sign
Of homage. All astonished was the Queen
At Bidasari's beauty. She appeared
Almost divine. Bidouri spoke and said,
"Thou seest Bidasari, O our Queen,
Lila Djouhari's daughter." At these words
The Queen was stupefied, and thought: "In truth
'Tis as they said. She is more lovely than
The fairest work of art." Bidouri told
All that the merchant and his wife had said.
The Queen inclined her head and silence kept,
But wicked thoughts were surging in her brain.
A combat raged within her heart. She feared
The King might see the maiden. "Send away,"
She said, "the nurses and the women all."
Fair Bidasari wept when they retired.
The princess called her to her side and said:

"Thou must not weep so, Bidasari. They
Will all return. When thou dost wish to go,
They will go with thee. Now depart, *dyangs*.
Ye need not care for Bidasari more.
I will procure her dames of company
And servants. You may come from time to time."
So they arose, and, with prostrations, went.
The Queen conducted Bidasari then
Into a room and left her all alone,
And all afraid.
When evening shadows fell,
The great King bade the Queen to sup with him.
He sat beside her, smiled and gayly talked,
As he had been young Bedouwandas, on
His horse, with sword at belt. "My royal spouse,
How thou dost love me! for thou wouldst not sup
Without me, though thou needest food and drink."
Now when the King had eaten, he retired
Unto his sleeping-chamber.
Still alone
And weeping much, fair Bidasari stayed,
In darkness with no one to speak to her.
She thought on her dear parents. "O my God!
Why dost Thou leave me here?" The solitude
Filled her with terror, and she wept until
The middle of the night, and thought of home.
Out spake the King: "Now what is that I hear?
What voice is that so sorrowful and sweet?"
"It is an infant crying," said the Queen.
"In all the darkness it has lost its way."
Her heart was burning, and she sent a word
To Bidasari that she must not weep,
And held her peace and waited till the dawn.
But Bidasari wept the whole night long
And cried for home. When the *dyangs* all ran
To comfort her, they found the door was locked,
And none could enter. Bidasari thought,
"What wrong have I committed, that the Queen
Should be so vexed with me?" When day appeared,
To the pavilion went the King. The Queen

Threw wide the door of Bidasari's room
And entered all alone.
                                        Then Bidasari
The Queen's hand kissed, and begged that she would let
Her homeward fare. "O gracious Queen," she said,
"Take pity on me; let me go away.
I'll come to thee again."
                                        The wicked Queen
Struck her, and said, "Thou ne'er shalt see again
Thy home." The gentle Bidasari drooped
Her head and wept afresh, shaking with fear.
"Forgive the evil I have done, my Queen,
For I am but a child, and do not know
How I have sinned against thee," falling at
Her feet she said. The Queen in anger struck
Her once again. "I know full well," she said,
"All thy designs and projects. What! Am I
To rest in peace and see thy beauty grow,
And thee become my rival with the King?"
Then Bidasari knew 'twas jealousy
That caused the fury of the Queen. Her fear
Increased, she trembled and bewailed her fate.
The livelong day she was insulted, struck,
And of her food deprived.
                                        Before the King
Returned, the Queen departed from the room
Of Bidasari. The poor child had lost
Her former color. Black her face had grown
From blows, as if she had been burnt. Her eyes
She could not open. Such her sufferings were
She could not walk. Then unto God she cried:
"O Lord, creator of the land and sea,
I do not know my fault, and yet the Queen
Treats me as guilty of a heinous crime.
I suffer hell on earth. Why must I live?
Oh, let me die now, in the faith, dear Lord.
My soul is troubled and my face is black
With sorrow. Let me die before the dawn.
My parents do not help me. They have left
Me here alone to suffer. In the false

Dyangs I trusted, as to sisters dear.
Their lips are smiling, but their hearts are base.
Their mouths are sweet as honey, but their hearts
Are full of evil. Oh, what can I say?
It is the will of God."
Such was the grief
Of Bidasari, and her tears fell fast.
Now when the King went forth again, the Queen
Began anew her persecutions harsh.
With many blows and angry words, she said:
" Why dost thou groan so loudly? Dost thou seek
By crying to attract the King, to see
Thy beauty? 'Tis thy hope, I know full well,
His younger wife to be. And thou art proud
Of all thy beauty." Bidasari was
Astounded, and replied with many tears:
" May I accurséd be if ever I
Such plottings knew. Thou art a mighty Queen.
If I have sinned against thee, let me die
At once. For life is useless to the hearts
That suffer. Hast thou brought me here to beat?
How thou hast made me weep! O Queen, art thou
Without compassion?"
All possessed with rage
The Queen replied: " I do not pity thee.
I hate thee, when I see thee. Open not
Thy mouth again." The wicked Queen then seized
The lovely tresses of the beauteous maid,
And took a piece of wood with which to strike;
But Bidasari wept and swooned away.
The King's voice sounded through the corridor,
As he returned. The Queen then hastened forth
And left a *mandar* there to close and guard
Fair Bidasari's room, that nothing should
Be seen. Then asked the King of her, " Whom hast
Thou beaten now?" The hypocrite replied,
" It was a child that disobeyed my will."
" Are there not others for that discipline?
Is it for thee to strike?" His *siri* then
He took, and kissed the Queen with fondest love.

All the *dyangs* fair Bidasari's plight
Observed, and kindly pity filled their breasts.
"How cruel is the conduct of the Queen!"
They said. "She made us bring her to her side
But to maltreat the child the livelong day.
It seems as if she wished to slay her quite."
Then secretly they went, with some to watch,
And sprinkled Bidasari's brow. To life
She came, and opened those dear wistful eyes.
"My friends," she said, "I pray ye, let me go
Back home again unto my father's house."
"Oh, trust in God, my child," said one in tears.
"My lot is written from eternity.
Oh, pray the princess great to take my life,"
The poor child cried; "I can no longer stand;
My bones are feeble. Oh, she has no heart!"
But the *dyangs*, for fear the Queen might see,
All fled.
Meanwhile the merchant and his wife
Wept all the day, and sighed for their dear child,
Sweet Bidasari. Nor did gentle sleep
Caress their eyes at night. Each day they sent
Rich presents of all kinds, and half of them
Were for the child. But naught the wicked Queen
To Bidasari gave. So five days passed
And then Dyang Menzara forth they sent.
The merchant said: "Oh, tell the mighty Queen
That I must Bidasari see. I'll bring
Her back in three days' time." The good
Dyang went to the queen and bowing low:
"The merchant fain would see his child," she said.
At this the features of the Queen grew hard.
"Did they not give their child to me? Now scarce
A day has passed, and they must see her face.
Is it thine own wish or the merchant's? I
Have said the girl could go where'er she would.
Can I not have her taken back myself?"
Then the *dyang* bowed, beat her breast, and went,
Sad that she could not Bidasari see,
And quaking at the anger of the Queen.

Of the *dyang*, fair Bidasari heard
The voice, and felt her heart break that she could
Not speak to her and send a message home.

Upon the morrow, when the King had gone
Among his ministers and men of state,
The Queen again to Bidasari's room
Repaired, to beat her more. As soon as she
Beheld the Queen, poor Bidasari prayed
To her, " O sovereign lady great, permit
That I may go unto my father's house."
The princess shook with rage, her face on fire.
" If thou but sayest a word, I'll slay thee here."
To whom could Bidasari turn? She bent
Before the will of God, and in a sweet
Voice said: " O Lord, my God, have pity now
Upon me, for the cruel world has none.
Grant now the Queen's desire and let me die,
For she reproacheth me, though naught I've done.
My parents have forgotten me, nor send
A word." The angry princess struck again
Her piteous face, and as she swooned away
A napkin took to twist into a cord
And strangle her. She summoned to her aid
Dang Ratna Wali. " Help me pluck this weed;
I wish to kill her." But the woman fled,
As base as cruel. Bidasari's ghost
Arose before her. Yet the child came back
To consciousness, and thought amid her tears:
"I'll tell the story of the golden fish
Unto the Queen, that she may know it all;
For I can but a little while endure
These pains." She spoke then to the Queen and said:
" O Queen, thou dost desire that I shall die.
Seek out a little casket that doth lie
All hidden in the fish-pond at our house.
Within it is a fish. Have it brought here
And I will tell thee what it signifies."
The princess called Dyang Sendari: " Go
And bring here the *dyangs*, with no delay,

From out the merchant's house." When they arrived:
"Go, now, *dyangs,* for Bidasari saith
There is a little casket in the pond
Where she is wont to bathe. Go bring it me,
In silence, letting no one see ye come."
Then the *dyangs* replied: "Oh, hear our prayer.
For Bidasari. How her parents grieve!
Oh, pardon, princess, let her go with us."
The Queen with smiles responded: "The young girl
Is very happy here, and full of joy.
Her parents must not grieve, for in two days
If Bidasari doth desire to go
I'll send her freely. She is vexed that ye
Come here so often." The *dyangs* bowed low,
And smiled, and called enticingly: "Come forth,
O charming child, pure soul; it is not right
To treat us so, for we have come to see
Thy lovely face, and in its beauty bask."
Sweet Bidasari heard, and could not speak,
But answered with her tears. The cruel Queen
Said to them: "Speak no more. But if ye bring
The little casket, ye will fill the heart
Of Bidasari with great joy." Forth fared
Then the *dyangs,* and found the casket small,
And brought it to the palace of the Queen.
Again to Bidasari called the good
Dyangs: "Oh, come, dear heart, and take it from
Our hands yourself." "She sleeps," the princess said.
"Come back to-morrow." So they bowed and went.
The princess hastened with the casket rich
To Bidasari's room, and opened it
Before her eyes. Within it was a box
Of agate, beautiful to see, and filled
With water wherein swam a little fish
Of form most ravishing. The princess stood
Amazed to see with eyes of fire a fish
That swam. Then was she glad, and spoke with joy
To Bidasari: "Say what signifies
The fish to thee? What shall I do with it?"
Then Bidasari bowed and said: "My soul

Is in that fish. At dawn must thou remove
It from the water, and at night replace.
"Leave it not here and there, but hang it from
Thy neck. If this thou dost, I soon shall die.
My words are true. Neglect no single day
To do as I have said, and in three days
Thou'lt see me dead."
The Queen felt in her heart
A joy unspeakable. She took the fish
And wore it on a ribbon round her neck.
Unto the Queen then Bidasari spoke,
"Oh, give my body to my parents dear
When I am dead." Again the young maid swooned.
The Queen believed her dead, and ceased to beat
Her more. But she yet lived, though seeming dead.
The joyful Queen a white cloth over her
Then spread, and called aloud to the *dyangs*,
"Take Bidasari to her father's house."
They groaned and trembled when they saw that she
Was dead, and said with many tears: "Alas!
O dearest one, O gold all virginal!
What shall we say when we thy parents see?
They'll beat their breasts and die of grief. They gave
Thee to the King because they trusted us."
But the proud Queen, her face all red with hate:
"Why stay ye? Take the wretched girl away."
They saw the Queen's great rage, and bore the maid
Upon their shoulders forth, and carried her
Unto her father's house at dead of night.
Fear seized the merchant. "Say what bring ye here?
Tell me, *dyangs*." They placed her on the ground.
The merchant and his wife, beside themselves,
With tears embraced her form. "I trusted in
The Queen, and so I sent my child to her.
O daughter dear, so young, so pure, so sweet,
What hast thou done that could the Queen displease,
That she should send thee home like this to me?
How could the Queen treat Bidasari so?
For seven days she imprisoned her and sent
Her home in death. Ah, noble child! alas!

Thy father's heart will break, no more to hear
Thy voice. Speak to thy father, O my child,
My pearl, my gem of women, purest gold,
Branch of my heart; canst thou not quiet me?
O Bidasari, why art thou so still?
Arise, my pretty child, arise and play
With all thy maids. Here is thy mother, come
To greet thee. Bid her welcome. Why art thou
So motionless? Hast thou no pity, dear,
To see thy father overwhelmed with woe?
My heart is bursting with despair because
Thou'rt lost to me."
Long time the merchant thus
Lamented. "What have I to live for now?
Since thou art dead, thy father too shall die.
It is his lot both night and day to sigh
For thee. My God, I cannot understand
Why this dear child should thus a victim be!
'Tis the *dyangs* who have this evil wrought."
Then, through the whole *campong*, the merchants all
Made lamentations, rolling on the ground,
With noise of thunder, and their hearts on fire.
They sought to speak and could not. Then began
Again the merchant, and unto his friends
Told his misfortune, asking back his child.

The Queen's *dyangs* shed tears, and gently said:
"Speak not so loudly. Thou dost know that we
Are but poor servants, and we tremble lest
The Queen should hear. If any one of us
Had done this wrong, we'd tell it to the King.
Fate only is at fault. Oh, be not wroth
With us. Our will was good. We had no end
Except to see thy lovely daughter great
And powerful. Naught the King hath known of this.
It was the Queen's mad jealousy and hate."

The merchant and his wife accepted these,
The *dyangs'* words. "It is as they declare.

The Queen was jealous and embittered thus
Against our Bidasari. To your home
Return, *dyangs*. I fear me that the Queen
May learn of your delay and punish ye."
They bowed and went, with hearts of burning grief.

The merchant and his wife then lifted up
Poor Bidasari. They were all but dead
With sorrow. On his knees the father took
The body wrapped in crimson silk. He felt
A warmth. Then he remembered that within
The water was her vital spirit still,
And, placing her upon a mat, sent Dang
Poulam, the casket from the pond to bring.
But 'twas not there. Then all the household searched,
But found it not. The merchant beat his breast.
" Branch of my heart," he said, " we all had thought
Thou wouldst become a princess. I have lost
My reason. I hoped now to summon back
Thy spirit vital, but the casket's lost.
My hope is gone. It may be the *dyangs*
Have stolen it. They're faithful to the Queen.
We may not trust in them. They're filled with hate
And trickery." Unconscious all the time
Lay Bidasari; but at midnight's hour
She for the first time moved. They torches brought
And there behind Egyptian curtains, right
And left, ignited them, with many lamps'
Soft flames. The servants watched and waited there.
The father, always at his daughter's side,
With fixed glance looked for life to come once more
Back to his darling one. She moved again.
With opening eyes she saw and recognized
Her own soft couch, her parents, and her maids.
She tried but could not speak. Her hot tears fell,
She slowly turned and looked with fondest love
Upon her parents.
When the merchant saw
That Bidasari's spirit had returned,

He took her on his knees and gave her rice.
She could not walk because such pain she felt.
She thought upon the Queen and wept afresh.
They dried her tears, and placed within her mouth
What food she liked. The merchant tenderly
Said, "Bidasari, dear, what has thou wrought
To cause the Queen against thee thus to act?"
Young Bidasari, with a flood of tears, replied:
"No wrong at all I wrought the cruel Queen.
All suddenly her insults she began,
And beatings." They were stupefied to hear
Such tales. "Light of my eyes," the father said,
"We do not doubt thine innocence. Her deeds
Were those of madness. For her haughty birth
I care no whit. Wisdom and virtue bind
True hearts alone. As friends we ne'er must name
Those false *dyangs*. Not plants medicinal,
But poison foul, are they. These days are bad.
Injustice reigns. Believe me, friends, it is
A sign the last great day shall soon appear.
Those false *dyangs* are but a race of slaves,
Insensible to all that's good. The hour
The princess knoweth Bidasari lives,
We all shall die, the princess is so wroth.
Illustrious Queen they call her—but her words
Are hard and cruel. May the curse of God
O'erwhelm her and annihilate! From thee,
O God, she shall receive the punishment
Deserved. She who pursueth thus a soul
Shall know remorse and pain. So God hath willed.
So God hath willed. Who doth another harm
Shall suffer in his turn. It shall be done
To him as he hath done to others. So,
My child, my crown, have no more fear at all.
Intrust thyself to God. The cruel Queen
Shall yet be treated as she treated thee."
The merchant thus lamented till the night
Was half departed, shedding sapphire tears.
The innocent young girl, like marble there,

Slept till the evening twilight came. Toward dawn
She swooned anew.
The merchant and his wife
Were much disturbed to see at night she came
To life, but when the daylight shone again
They lost her, and her spirit fled away.
This so distressed the merchant's heart, a lone
Retreat he sought to find. The parents cried:
"O dearest child, there's treason in the air.
Hatred and anger the companions are
Of lamentations and of curses dire.
Foul lies for gold are uttered. Men disdain
The promises of God, the faith they owe.
Oh, pardon, God! I ne'er thought the *dyangs*
Would thus conspire. But since they are so bad
And treated Bidasari thus, we'll go
And in the desert find a resting-place.
And may it be a refuge for us all,
Hidden and unapproachable.
His goods
He gathered then, and all his servants paid,
And built a home far in the desert land,
A spot agreeable. A cabin there
He raised, with ramparts hemmed about, and strong
Sasaks, and seven rows of palisades.
They placed there many vases full of flowers,
And every sort of tree for fruit and shade,
And cool pavilions. This plaisance so fair
They called Pengtipourlara. It was like
The garden of Batara Indra. All
About, the merchant set pomegranate-trees
And vines of grape. No other garden was
So beautiful. 'Twas like the garden fair
Of great Batara Brahma, filled with fruits.
When all was ready, forth they went, toward night,
And took young Bidasari, and much food.
They fared two days and came unto the spot,
A garden in the desert. Softest rugs
From China there were spread and of bright hue

The decorations were, in every tint.
The house was hung with tapestries, and ceiled
To represent the heavens flecked with clouds.
And all about were lanterns hung and lamps.
Soft curtains and a couch completed this
Enchanted resting-place. Always the light
Was uniform, and brilliant as the day.
'Twas like a palace of a mighty king,
Magnificent and grand beyond compare.
There was a table on a damp rug set,
With drinks for Bidasari, and with bowls
Of gold, and vases of *souasa*, filled
With water. All of this beside the couch
Was placed, with yellow *siri*, and with pure
Pinang, all odorous, to please the child.
And all was covered with a silken web.
Young Bidasari bracelets wore, and rings,
And ear-rings diamond studded. Garments four
All gem-bedecked upon a cushion lay,
For Bidasari's wear. When night had come
Young Bidasari waked. Her parents dear
Then bathed her, and her tender body rubbed
With musk and aloes. Then she straight was clad
In garments of her choosing. Her dear face
Was beautiful, almost divine. She had
Regained the loveliness she erst possessed.
The merchant was astonished, seeing her.
He told her then that they would leave her there,
"Branch of my heart and apple of my eye,
My dearest child, be not disturbed at this.
I do not mean to work thee any harm,
Nor to disown thee, but to rescue thee
From death." But as she listened to these words
Young Bidasari wept. She thought upon
Her fate. Into her father's arms she threw
Herself, and cried: "Why wilt thou leave me here,
O father dearest, in this desert lone?
I'll have no one to call in case of need.
I fear to stay alone. No one there'll be
To talk to me. I only count those hours

As happy when I have my parents near."
The merchant heard fair Bidasari's words
And wept with his dear wife. With bitter grief
Their hearts were shattered. Counsels wise they gave
To Bidasari. "Dearest daughter mine,"
The father said, "gem of my head, my crown,
Branch of my heart, light of my eyes, oh, hear
Thy father's words, and be thou not afraid.
We brought thee hither, to this fair retreat,
Far from the town, for, if the Queen should know
Thou liv'st at night, the false *dyangs* would come,
And who against the princess can contend?
They'd take thee back, and thus exonerate
Themselves. I'd let myself be chopped in bits
Before thou shouldst unto the Queen return.
Thy father cannot leave companions here,
But after three days he will come to thee.
Thy parents both will soon come back again."
Then Bidasari thought: "My parent's words
Are truth, and if the Queen should find I live
She would abuse me as before. Give me
One maid-companion here to be with me,"
She asked. "My child, trust not," he said, "in slaves,
Nor servants, for they only follow pay."
Then Bidasari silence kept, and they,
The father all distraught and mother fond,
Wept bitterly at thought of leaving her.
Fair Bidasari bade them eat, before
They started. But because of heavy hearts
They but a morsel tasted. At the dawn
Young Bidasari swooned again. They made
All ready to return to town. With tears
The father said: "O apple of my eye,
Pearl of all women, branch of my own heart,
Pure gold, thy parents leave thee with distress.
No more they'll have a daughter in the house.
But, dear, take courage, we shall soon come back."
They left here with a talking bird to cheer
Her loneliness, close shutting all the gates
Of all the seven ramparts. Through a wood

Bushy and thick they took a narrow path,
In sorrow, but with confidence in God.
"O sovereign God, protect our child," they said.
When they had fared unto their house, they prayed
And gave much alms.
. When evening shadows came
Young Bidasari waked, and found herself
Alone, and was afraid. With bitter tears
Her eyes were filled. What could she say? She gave
Herself to God. Alas, our destiny
Is like a rock. 'Twas hers to be alone.
It is in no man's power to turn aside
Or change whatever is by fate decreed.
All desolate sat Bidasari. Sleep
Wooed not her eyes. Now when he heard the cry
Of "Peladou," the owl lamented loud.
Upon her parents coming, loaded down
With dainties for the child, she for a while
Her woe forgot, and ate and drank with joy.
The little bird with which she talked upheld
Her courage with its soothing voice. So ran
The days away. Upon pretext he gave
Of hunting deer, the merchant daily came.

SONG III

HEAR now a song about the King Djouhan.
The wise and powerful prince e'er followed free
His fancy, and the Princess Lila Sari
Was very happy in her vanity.
Since she had killed (for so she thought) the maid,
Young Bidasari, tainted was her joy.
"The King will never take a second wife,"
She mused, "since Bidasari is now dead."
The King loved Princess Lila Sari well.
He gratified her every wish, and gave
Her all she asked, so fond was he of her.
Whene'er the princess was annoyed, the King,
With kisses and soft words would quiet her,
And sing to her sweet songs till she became
Herself again. "Poor, little, pretty wife,"
He'd say, and laugh her fretful mood away.
One night as he lay sleeping on his bed,
A dream tormented him. "What may it mean?"
He thought. "Ah, well, to-morrow morn I'll seek
An explanation." At the dawn he sat
Upon a rug Egyptian, breaking fast,
And with him was the princess. When she had
The dainties tasted, the *dyangs* arrived
With leaves of perfume. Then the King went forth
Into the garden. All the officers
Were there assembled. When they saw the King
They all were silent. To a *mantri* spoke
The King: "My uncle, come and sit thee here.
I fain would question thee." The King had scarce
These words pronounced, when, bowing very low,
The *mantri* in respectful tones replied,
"My greetings to thee, O most merciful
Of kings." He sat him near the throne. "I dreamed

Last night," the King continued, " that the moon
In her full glory fell to earth. What means
This vision?" Then the *mantri* with a smile
Replied: " It means that thou shalt find a mate,
A dear companion, like in birth to thee,
Wise and accomplished, well brought up and good,
The one most lovable in all the land."
The King's eyes took new fire at this. He said
With smiles: " I gave the Queen my promise true
That never I would take a second wife
Until a fairer I could find than she.
And still she is so lovely in my eyes,
Her equal cannot anywhere be found.
You'd take her for a flow'r. Yet when arise
Her storms of anger, long it takes to calm
Her mind, so waspish is her character.
The thought of this doth sadden me. Should one
Not satisfy her heart's desire, she flies
Into a passion and attempts to kill
Herself. But 'tis my destiny—'tis writ.
The Queen is like a gem with glint as bright
As lightning's flash. No one can ever be,
I tell thee now, so beautiful to me."
The *mantri* smiled. " What thou dost say is just,
O King, but still if thou shouldst someone find
More beautiful, thou yet couldst keep thy word.
The beauty of the Queen may fade away.
The princess thou shalt wed, O King, hath four
High qualities. She must, to be thy queen,
Be nobly born, and rich, and fair, and good."
The prince replied: " O uncle mine, thy words
Are true. Full many princesses there live,
But hard it is to find these qualities.
The Queen is good and wise and lovable.
I do not wish another wife to wed,
And wound the Queen with whom three years I've lived
In love and harmony. Yet if I saw
A quite celestial maid, perhaps I might
Forget, and marry her, and give the Queen
A gay companion." " O accomplished prince,

Thou sayest truly. Stay long years with her
Thy Queen, thy first beloved, for she hath all—
Great beauty and intelligence." They bowed
As forth from them the King went palaceward.
He sat beside the Queen, and kissed her cheeks,
And said: "Thy features shine with loveliness,
Like to a jewel in a glass. When I
Must leave thy side, I have no other wish
But to return. Like Mount Maha Mirou
Thou art." The princess said: "Wherefore art thou
So spirited to-day? Thou'rt like a boy."
"Branch of my heart, my dearest love," he said,
"Vex not thyself. Thou know'st the adage old:
First one is taken with a pretty face,
Then wisdom comes and prudence, and, with these,
One loves his wife until the day of death.
If thus thou dost deport thyself, my dear,
My heart between two wives shall never be
Divided; thou alone shalt own it all."
The Queen was charmed to hear his loving words.
At night the Queen slept, but King remained
Awake, and watched the moon, and called to mind
His dream. As dawn approached he slept, and seemed
To hear an owl's shrill voice, like Pedalou's.
When it was fully day, the royal pair
Together broke their fast. The King went forth
And orders gave, in two days to prepare
A mighty hunt, to chase the dappled deer,
With men and dogs and all apparel fit.
Then back into the palace went the King,
And told the Queen, who straightway gave commands
For food to be made ready. At midnight
Behind Egyptian curtains went to rest
The King and Queen, but slept not. Still the dream
Was ever in his thoughts and worried him.
At dawn he said farewell unto the Queen.
She was all radiant, and smiling, said:
"Bring me a fawn. I'll tell the servants all
To take good care of it, so it may grow
Quite tame." "What we can do, my dear, we shall,

So all of thy desires may come to pass."
And so the King took leave, with kisses fond,
And, mounted on a hunter brown, set forth,
With velvet saddle decked with fringe of pearls.
Lances and shields and arrows and blow-guns
They bore. The wood they entered, and the beasts
All fled before their steps at dawn's first ray.
And when the sun was up, they loosed the hounds
With savage cries. Toward noon an animal
In flight they saw, and would have followed it,
But then up spake the King and said, "We are
So hot and weary, let us linger here
For rest." One-half the company astray
Had gone, each striving to be first of all.
The King, attended by a faithful three,
Reclined upon the ground, and sent them forth
For water. So the *mantris* went to find
A river or a pond, and faring far
To Bidasari's plaisance came at last.
They stopped astounded, then approached the place.
When they were near the lovely garden close,
They said: "There was no garden here before.
To whom does this belong? Perchance it is
A spirit's bower. No human voice is heard
But just the cry of 'minahs' and 'bajans.'
Whom shall we call, lest spectres should appear?"
They wandered round the ramparts, and a gate
Discovered, shut with heavy iron bar,
And vainly tried to open it. Then one
Of them went back, and found the King, and said:
"Hail, sovereign lord, we have no water found,
But a *campong* here in the desert lone,
As splendid as a sultan's, with all sorts
Of trees and flow'rs, and not a mortal there.
'Tis girt about with double ramparts strong.
No name is seen, and all the gates are shut,
So that we could not enter."
Scarce the King
Had heard the *mantri's* word when off he rushed
To see the fair domain. Before the gate

He stood astonished. " Truly, *mantris* mine,
It is as you have said. I once was here
And then the wood was filled with thorns and briers."
'Tis not a nobleman's *campong*. It must
Have recently been made. Now summon all
The *mantris* here and see what they will say."
They called aloud, " Oh, hasten, friends, and bring
The water here." Seven times they called, but none
Responded. Said the King, " It is enough.
'Tis like as if one called unto the dead."
" We'd best not enter," said the *mantris* then,
" It may be the abode of demons fell.
We are afraid. Why should we linger here?
Return, O King, for should the spirits come
It might to us bring evil. Thou shouldst not
Expose thyself to danger." But the King
Upon the *mantris* smiled. " Ye are afraid
Of demons, spectres, spirits? I've no fear.
Break down the barriers. I'll go alone
Within the precincts." When the gates were forced,
He entered all alone. The *mantris* all
Were terrified lest harm should come to him.
They sought with him to go. He lightly said:
" No, *mantris* mine, whatever God hath willed,
Must happen. If in flames I were to burn,
In God I still should trust. 'Tis only He
That evil can avert. We mortal men
No power possess. With my own eyes I wish
To see this apparition. Should it be
The will of God, I'll come forth safe and sound.
Be not disturbed. In case of urgent need
I'll call upon ye. All await me here."
The *mantris* made obeisance and replied,
" Go, then, alone, since thou hast willed it so."
Into the plaisance strode the King. He saw
That all was like a temple richly decked,
With rugs of silk and colored tapestries
Of pictured clouds and wheels all radiant,
And lamps and candelabra hung about,
And lanterns bright. 'Twas like a palace rich.

The eyes were dazzled with magnificence.
And seats there were, and dainty tables rare.
As through the palace went the King, the more
Astonished he became at all he saw,
But nowhere found a trace of human soul.
Then spake the little bird: "Illustrious King,
What seek'st thou here? This mansion is the house
Of ghosts and demons who will injure thee."
The King was filled with wonder thus to hear
A bird address him. But it flew away,
And hid behind a couch. "The bird I'll find,"
He said, and ope'd the curtains soft. He saw
Full stretched, upon a bed in dragon's shape,
A human form, in heavy-lidded sleep
That seemed like death, and covered with a cloth
Of blue, whose face betokened deepest grief.
"Is it a child celestial?" thought the King,
"Or doth she feign to sleep? Awake, my sweet,
And let us be good friends and lovers true."
So spake the King, but still no motion saw.
He sat upon the couch, and to himself
He said: "If it a phantom be, why are
The eyes so firmly shut? Perhaps she's dead."
She truly is of origin divine,
Though born a princess." Then he lifted high
The covering delicate that hid the form
Of Bidasari sweet, and stood amazed
At all the magic beauty of her face.
Beside himself, he cried, "Awake, my love."
He lifted her and said, with kisses warm,
"Oh, have no fear of me, dear heart. Thy voice
Oh, let me hear, my gold, my ruby pure,
My jewel virginal. Thy soul is mine.
Again he pressed her in his arms, and gave
Her many kisses, chanting love-songs low.
"Thou dost not wake, O dearest one, but thou
Art yet alive, because I see thee breathe.
Sleep not too long, my love. Awake to me,
For thou hast conquered with thy loveliness
My heart and soul." So fell the King in love

With Bidasari. "Ah, my sweet," he said,
"In all the world of love thou'rt worthiest."
The *mantris* grew uneasy at his stay.
They rose and said: "What doth the King so long?
If harm befell him, what would be our fate?
Oh, let us call him back at once, my lords."
So one approached the palace, and cried out:
"Return, O prince accomplished, to us now.
Already night is near. Back thou may'st come
To-morrow ere the dawn. We are afraid
Lest spirits harm thee. Come, O King, for we
A-hungered are, and wait for thy return."
But the illustrious prince was mad with love
Of Bidasari. Pensively he cried:
"Branch of my heart, light of mine eyes, my love,
Pure gold, thou'rt like angel. Now must I
Depart. To-morrow I will come again."
With no more words he left her, but returned.
"My heart would tell me, wert thou really dead.
Some trouble hast thou, dearest one?" he cried.
"What bitter grief hath caused thee thus to sleep?"
He found the nobles murmuring and vexed.
"O King," they said, "our hearts were filled with fear
Lest evil had befallen thee. What sight
So strange hath kept thee all these hours?" The King
Replied with laughter, "There was naught to see."
But they remarked his brow o'ercast with thought,
And said, "O King, thy heart is sorely vexed."
"Nay, nay," the King replied, "I fell asleep.
Naught did I hear except the *mantri's* voice.
It surely is the home of demons dread
And spirits. Let us go, lest they surprise
Us here." He seemed much moved. "We naught have gained
But weariness. So let us all go home
To-night, and hither come again at dawn.
For I a promise gave the Queen to bring
A fawn and a *kidjang*." The *mantris* said:
"None have we taken yet. But game we'll find
To-morrow, and will save a pretty fawn."

The King, when they returned, went straight within
The palace. There he saw the Queen, but thought
Of Bidasari. "O my love," he said,
"To-morrow I'm resolved to hunt again,
And bring thee back a fawn, and win thy thanks.
I'm never happy when away from thee,
My dearest love. Thine image is engraved
Upon my heart." Then he caressed the Queen
And fondled her, but still his heart went out
To Bidasari. All night long his eyes
He did not close in sleep, but thought of her,
In all her beauty rare. Before the dawn
The royal couple rose. The King then gave
Command that those who wished should hunt again
With him. At sunrise forth they fared.

On Bidasari let us look again.
When night had gone, in loneliness she rose,
And ate and drank. Then to the bath perfumed
She went, and coming to her chamber, took
Some *siri* from the betel-box. She saw
A *sepah* recently in use and cast
It forth. She thought within herself:
"Who could have used it? Someone hath been here."
She ran through all the rooms, but nothing found
Except the *sepah* in the betel-box.
"Had it my father been, he would have left
Some food for me. Oh, he is very rash
To leave me here alone." Upon the couch
She sat and wept, and could not tell her grief
To anyone. "When we no longer may
Live happily," she said, "'tis best to die.
My parents never can forgiven be,
To leave me here like any infidel.
And if I suffer, they will sorrow, too."
The *minahs*, the *bajans*, and talking birds
Began to sing. She took a 'broidered cloth,
And 'neath its folds she sweetly fell asleep.

The King's horse flew apace to the *campong*
Of Bidasari. All the *mantris* said:

"Thou takest not the path for hunting, sire;
This is but the *campong* of demons dread
And spectres. They may do us deadly harm."
The great prince only laughed, and made as if
He heard not, still directing his fleet course
To Bidasari's garden, though they sought
His wishes to oppose. When they arrived
Before the palisades, the *mantris* cried:
"Avaunt, ye cursed demons, and begone
Into the thorns and briers." Then to the King:
"If thou wilt prove the courage of thy men,
Lead us behind the barriers, among
The evil spirits. We will go with thee."
"Nay. Let me go alone," the prince replied,
"And very shortly I'll come forth again."
They said: "O prince, to us thy will is law.
To God most high do we commend thy soul."
Alone the prince in Bidasari's home
Set foot. He was astonished, for he saw the bath
Had recently been used, and all the lamps
Were trimmed and full of oil. Then opening
The chests, he saw the traces of a meal,
And glasses freshly drained. The chambers all
He searched, and came to Bidasari's couch,
And, lifting up the curtains, saw her there,
Asleep beneath the 'broidered covering.
"'Tis certain that she lives," he said. "Perchance
It is her lot to live at night, and die
At dawn." Then came he nearer yet, and gazed
Upon her beauty. Ling'ring tears he saw
Bedewed her lashes long, and all his heart
Was sad. Her face was beautiful. Her locks
Framed it with curls most gracefully. He took
Her in his arms and cried, with kisses warm:
"Why hast thou suffered, apple of my eye?"
He wept abundantly, and said: "My gold,
My ruby, my carbuncle bright, thy face
Is like Lila Seprara's, and thy birth
Is pure and spotless. How could I not love
A being fair as thou dost seem to me?

Thy beauty is unspeakable; thou art
Above all crowns, the glory of all lands.
My soul adores thee. Lord am I no more
Of my own heart. Without thee, love, I could
No longer live; thou art my very soul.
Hast thou no pity to bestow on me?"
The more he looked the more he loved. He kissed
Her ruby lips, and sang this low *pantoum:*

Song

Within a vase there stands a china rose;
  Go buy a box of betel, dearest one.
I love the beauty that thine eyes disclose;
  Of my existence, dear, thou art the sun.

Go buy a box of betel, dearest one.
  Adorned with *sountings* brave of sweet *campak*,
Of my existence, dear, thou art the sun;
  Without thee, everything my life would lack.

Adorned with *sountings* fair of sweet *campak*,
  A carafe tall will hold the sherbet rare;
Without thee, everything my heart would lack;
  Thou'rt like an angel come from heaven so fair.

A carafe tall will hold the sherbet rare,
  Most excellent for woman's feeble frame.
Thou'rt like an angel come from heaven so fair,
  Love's consolation, guardian of its flame.

At the approach of night the *mantris* said,
"What doth the King so long away from us?"
They were disturbed, the prince seemed so unlike
Himself and filled with such unrestfulness.
"I fear me much," then said a *mantri* there,
"That some mishap hath overwhelmed the King.
Perhaps by some bad spirit he's possessed,
That he to this weird spot should fain return."
One went and cried: "Come hither, O our King!
The day declines; we've waited here since dawn."

The King responded to the call, and came
With smiling face, though pale, unto the gate:
"Come here, my uncle; come and talk with me,
Thy King. No evil thing hath come to pass."
"O lord supreme, most worthy prince, return.
If harm should come to thee, we all should die."
"Be calm, my uncle, I will not this night
Return, but he may stay with me who wills."
"O King, with spirits what hast thou to do?
Thy face is pale and worn, and tells of care."
The King but sighed, and said: "My heart is full
Of trouble, but the will of God is good. .
Here yesterday a fair celestial form
With angel face I saw. 'Twas here alone."
And so the King told all that had occurred.
"Go back," he added. "Leave me here with her.
Say to the Queen I've lingered still a day
For my amusement, with my retinue."
Then half the escort stayed, and half repaired
Back to the palace to acquaint the Queen
The King would stay another day and hunt.
When all was dark, sweet Bidasari waked
And saw the King, and tried to flee away.
He seized and kissed her. "Ruby, gold," he said,
"My soul, my life, oh, say, where wouldst thou go?
I've been alone with thee for two whole days,
And all the day thou wrapped in sleep didst lie.
Where wouldst thou go, my dove?" The gentle girl
Was much afraid and trembled, and she thought:
"Is it a spirit come to find me here?
Avaunt thee and begone, O spectre dread,"
She said, amid her tears. "No phantom I,"
Replied the King; "be not afraid. I wish
To marry thee." Then Bidasari strove
Again to flee. Then sang the King a song
That told of love and happiness. Its words
Astonished Bidasari, and she cried:
"Art thou a pirate? Why dost thou come here?
Speak not such things to me. If thou shouldst be
Discovered by my father, he would cut

Thee into pieces. Thou shouldst go alone
To death, and find no pardon in his heart.
Take all my gems and hasten forth at once."
The King replied: "'Tis not thy gems I want,
But thee. I am a pirate, but thy heart
Is all I want to steal. Should spectres come
In thousands, I would fear them not at all.
No tears, my love, bright glory of my crown.
Where wouldst thou go? Hast thou no pity, sweet,
For me? I am a powerful prince. Who dares
Oppose my will? Pure gold, all virginal,
Where wouldst thou go?" So spake the King, and fair
Young Bidasari trembled more and more.
"Approach me not," she cried, "but let me bathe
My face." "I'll bathe it for thee, dear," he said.
But Bidasari threw the water pure
Into his face. "Not that way, child," he laughed;
"My vesture thou hast wet. But I shall stay
And meet thy parents here. Oh, hearken, love.
I followed far the chase, and wandered here.
I sought a pretty fawn to take the Queen;
But now thy face I've seen, no more I wish
To go away. Oh, have no fear, my child;
I would not harm thee. When thy parents come,
I'll ask them for thy hand. I trust they'll grant
My prayer. I'll lead thee forth from this fair spot
Unto my palace. Thou shalt sit beside
The Queen, and live in happiness complete."
Sweet Bidasari bowed her head and wept,
All red with modesty. Unto herself she said:
"I never thought it was a king. How rude
I was! I hope the King will not be vexed."
He calmed her fears with tender words of love.
"Branch of my heart," he said, "light of my eyes,
Have no more fear. Soon as thy parents fond
Have given their consent, I'll lead thee forth.
My palace is not far. A single day
Will take us there. It is not difficult
To go and come." Then Bidasari knew
It was the King of that same land. With fright

She nearly swooned at thought of all the woe
The Queen had caused her. " O my lord," she said,
" I'm but a subject humble. Give me not
The throne. I have my parents, and with them
Must stay." The King was overjoyed. " My dear,"
He said, " by what names are thy parents known ? "
With low, sweet voice the tender girl replied:
" Lila Djouhara is my father's name.
He dwelleth in Pesara." " Dearest one,
Tell me the truth. Why have they treated thee
In such a fashion—why abandoned thee
In solitude? Thy father is not poor.
A merchant rich is he, of birth, who hath
A host of slaves and servants. For what cause
Hath he his daughter left in this far spot?
He is renowned among the merchants all,
Both good and honest. What hath forced him here
Within this lonely wood to hide thee, dear?
Oh, tell me all; let nothing be concealed."
She thought: " It was the fault of his own Queen.
But if I tell him all—he never saw
Me there, within the palace—should he not
Believe, I'll be a liar in his eyes."
She feared to speak and tell him of the Queen.
She thought, " So cruel was the Queen to me
When she but feared a rival, what would come
If I should sit beside her on the throne? "
Then in her sweet voice Bidasari said:
" My glorious King, I am afraid to speak.
I am not suited to a royal throne.
But since thou lovest me, how dare I lie?
If thou dost favor me, the Queen will vex
Her heart. My parents fear her. 'Tis the cause
Why hither they have brought me. Three long months
Ago I came, for terror of the Queen."
She thought on all the horror of those days,
And choked with sobs, and could no longer talk.
Then tenderly the King spake to the girl:
" Ah, well, my darling love, confide in me
The secret thy dear heart conceals. Fear naught;

The Queen is good and wise, and knoweth how
To win all hearts. Why should she render thee
Unhappy? Speak not thus, my pretty one;
The Queen could never do an evil deed.
When thou art near her, thou shalt see, my dear,
Whether she loves or hates thee."
At these words
Young Bidasari knew the King esteemed
The Queen, and felt her heart sink in her breast.
"My words are true," she said, "but still perchance
My prince cannot believe. But was I not
Within thy palace six or seven nights?
The sweat of pain became my couch, so great
Was my desire to see my parents dear.
They sent me dainties, but all the *dyangs*
Were kept as prisoners by the princess there.
She said she'd take me back herself. One day
I was, indeed, sent home, but scarce alive."
She told him everything that came to pass.
He listened stupefied, and said: "How could
It be that thou wert in the palace hid,
And I not see thee there? Why was it thou
Wert not beside the Queen? I've never left
The palace for a single day. Where wert
Thou hid? Thy strange words I believe, my dear.
Speak without fear and let me know the whole."
Urged by the King, young Bidasari told
Him all. And when the conduct of the Queen
He learned, the King was wonder-struck. A rage
Most terrible possessed him. But his love
For Bidasari mounted higher still
And his compassion. "So the Queen thus wrought!
I never thought hypocrisy could be
So great! I never in the princess saw
Such bent for evil. But be not, my dear,
Disconsolate. It is a lucky thing
Thou didst not quite succumb. No longer speak
Of that bad woman's ways. Thank God we've met!
So weep no more, my love. I'll give to thee
A throne more beautiful than hers, and be

Thy dear companion until death." "O King,"
She said: "I have no beauty fit to grace
A throne. Oh, let me stay a simple maid,
And think of me no more." The King replied:
"I will not give thee up. But I must still
Return, and meditate how I may win
Thee back to life complete." With kisses warm
He covered her fair face. She bowed her head,
And silence kept; and when the morning dawned
She swooned anew. It was a proof to him
That she had told the truth. A mortal hate
Then filled the prince's heart against the Queen.
Touched with deep pity for the maiden young,
He kissed her once again, and left her there,
So white and still, as if she lay in death.
What of the *mantris?* They awaited long
The King, in silence. Then the oldest said:
"O sovereign lord, O caliph great, wilt thou
Not now return?" "I'll come again, dear heart,"
He said, and sought the city. Straight he went
Into the palace, to the Queen, who asked:
"What bringest thou from hunting?" He replied
In murmurs: "I have taken naught at all.
For my own pleasure I remained all night."
"'Tis nothing, lord, provided no harm came
To thee. But say what thou didst seek, to stay
So long? I always have prepared for thee
The food for thy great hunts, but never yet
Have I received a recompense?" The King
To this replied with smiles: "Prepare afresh,
For I to-morrow shall depart again.
If I take nothing, I'll return at once."
As he caressed the Queen, upon her breast
He felt the little magic fish of gold
All safe. Then gave he quick commands to all.
"I'll hunt to-morrow, and shall surely bring
Some wondrous game." Now when the princess fell
Asleep he found upon her heart no more
The little fish. "'Tis as the maiden said,"
He thought. "The princess hath a wicked soul.

With such a heart I cannot go with her
Through life." Through all the night he could not sleep,
But thought upon the girl. He was as sad
As though he heard a touching song. At dawn
The royal couple rose and went to bathe.
The King into the palace came again
And sat upon the throne adorned with gems.
He donned the royal robe to wear before
The dear young girl. A vestment 'twas of silk,
All gold embroidered, with a tunic bright,
Of orange hue. His mien was most superb,
As doth become a mighty king. He bore
A quiver of Ceylon, most deftly wrought.
When all the *mantris* had assembled there,
The King within the palace once more went
And met the Queen. Caressing her he took
The little fish that lay upon her breast.
The princess wept, and at the door she cried:
"Why takest thou my little ornament?"
The great King gave no heed, and went away,
At dawn's glad hour, when birds begin to sing.
Swords gleamed and lances shone, and through the wood
They hastened on, with quivers and blow-guns,
And seemed a walking city.
Now again
To Bidasari let us turn. When dawn
Appeared, she rose and sat in loneliness,
Her face grew still more beautiful. Her state
Astonished her. "Perhaps it is the King
Who hath this wonder wrought. How happy I
To be no longer dead!" She washed her face
And felt still sad, but with her pensiveness
A certain joy was mingled, for her pain
Was passed. Her grief the "talking bird" allayed
With songs about the mighty King and love.

Song

There's *siri* in a golden vase,
Good Dang Melini plants a rose;
The King admires a pretty face,
To-day he'll come to this fair close.

Good Dang Melini plants a rose,
  Here in the garden they will meet;
To-day he'll come to this fair close,
  To man and maiden love is sweet.

Here in the garden they will meet,
  Go seek the fairest fruit and flower;
To man and maiden love is sweet,
  The King is coming to the bower.

Lo! At this very instant they approached.
Dear Bidasari hid behind the couch.
The King searched everywhere, and found at last
The maiden hiding, bathed in bitter tears.
Then kissing her, the King inquired: "My love,
Bright glory of my crown; pray tell to me
Why thou art sad." He dried her tears. But she
Still hung her head in silence. Then the King
For elephants and horses to be sent
Gave orders. "Go with *mantris* two at once,
And bring the merchant and his wife, and bid
Forty *dyangs* to hasten here forthwith."
Then went the *mantris* forth in haste, and found
The merchant and his wife and said, "The King
Inviteth ye to come." Then through the wood
The parents hurried to the plaisance fair
Of Bidasari, there to meet the King.
Before his Majesty they bowed with fear.
The great King smiled. "Be not afraid," he said,
"My uncle and my mother. Let us go
Within, to see thy lovely child. I make
Ye now my parents. We have friendly been,
And still shall be." Beside the King they saw
Fair Bidasari seated, as with steps
Still hesitating they the palace sought.
The father fond was glad within his heart,
His daughter was so beautiful. She seemed
A princess lovely of the Mount Lidang.

"Dear Bidasari, sweetest child," they said,
"Behind the King, dear daughter, thou should stand."
She made as if to go, but still the King
Restrained her. "No, my pretty one," he said,
"Thy place is at my side. So God hath willed."
The oldest *mantri*, called for counsel, spoke:
"Lila Djouhara good, what sayest thou?
Art thou not glad to see thy daughter made
A queen? What happiness hath come to thee!"
The merchant bowed before the King, and said:
"Make her thy servant, not thy wife, my lord.
Thy glorious Queen we fear. She e'er hath shown
For Bidasari hatred dire, because
A child so lovely might attract the King."
The monarch hearing him thus speak, still more
Toward him was borne. "My uncle," then he cried,
"Have no more fear. But never shall I make
A servant of thy daughter."

Then he gave
Command to build a castle in the wood.
And all the workers came, and built it there,
With ramparts three. As if by magic then
A golden palace rose. The outer gate
Was iron, loaded down with arms, and held
By demons and by Ethiopians.
These were the keepers of the gates, with steeds
Untamed. With swords unsheathed they stood alert
And waited for the King's commands. Of brass
All chiselled was the second gate, supplied
With cannons and with powder, guarded safe
By beings supernatural. The third
Was silver, such as may be seen in far
Eirak. The beauty of the castle was
Beyond compare! From far it seemed to be
As double, like an elephant with two
White ivory tusks. Where may its like be found?
Three diamonds pure reflected all the light,
Big as a melon. Now the castle built,
The King a plaisance beautiful desired

With gay pavilions, and all kinds of plants.
The middle booth nine spacious rooms displayed,
One for the royal audiences, adorned
And pleasant as a bed of flowers.
The King
A festival maintained for forty days,
With games and sports and dances to divert.
And never was such animation seen!
All ate and drank to sound of music sweet.
They passed the loving-cup and drank to each
In turn.
For forty days resounded there
The gongs and *gendarangs*, and joyous tones
Of gay *serouni* and *nefiri* glad.
"How beautiful is Bidasari!" all
Exclaimed; "a thousand times more lovely than
The Queen." Thrice happy are the merchant now
And his good wife; by marriage they're allied
To our great King, though strangers to the land.
We count it strange that Bidasari's face
In naught is like the merchant nor his wife.
Who knoweth but that she, in mortal shape,
An angel fair may be? Full many slaves
The merchant hath, but never children own."
"He found her when a babe, upon the shore,"
Another said, "and brought her up."
The King
Heard all their words. He thought: "It is the truth
And this I take as proof of her high birth.
She certainly is noble or come down
From heaven."

When four days had fled, the wives
Of *mantris* dressed the beauteous girl. They clad
Her form in satins soft of Egypt, shot
With gold, adorned with precious stones inset
And many gems. Her beauty was enhanced
The more, till she a radiant angel seemed.
She wore a tunic, crimson and pomegranate,
With buttons shaped like butterflies. She was

Adorned with *padaka* of five quaint clasps,
And belt called *naga souma.* Ear-rings rich
She had, of diamonds set in gold, and wrought
Most wondrously, as bright as daylight's gleam;
A ring most marvellous and rare she wore
Called *astakouna,* and another named
Gland kana, and a third from far Ceylon,
Studded with precious stones. Her eyes were like
The stars of orient skies. Her teeth were black,
Her face like water shone. Her chiselled nose
Was prominent and like a flower fresh culled.
When she was dressed, upon a couch of pearls
Her mother put her. Supple was her form,
And white, as she reclined, by many maids
Surrounded. In his royal garb the prince
Was clad, and dazzling to the eyes of all
Who saw. He wore a kingly crown which shone
With diamonds bright and lucent amethysts
And many stones, and all majestic seemed.
Then rice was brought. The King with pleasure ate,
And what was left he gave the *mantris'* wives.
When all had finished he perfumed himself
And gazed upon his lovely wife. Her face
And form were charming. Her soft tresses curled
In grace. Her eyes still kept the trace of tears,
Which made her lovelier. The silken folds
Of soft Egyptian curtains fell. They were alone.
"Awake, my darling," said the prince at dawn,
"Crown of my life, awake, my pretty one."
Then Bidasari waked and said, with tears:
"My friend, I had all sorts of wondrous dreams.
I saw a palm-tree tall with tufted limbs,
And fruits all ripe." When three days more had fled
And all the people saw and loud acclaimed,
Then Bidasari took the rank of Queen.
The King o'erloaded her with gifts and loved
Her tenderly. "Oh, let us live and die
Together, dear, and, as the days go by,
Think more of one another, and our love
Preserve, as in the hollow of the hand

Oil is upheld, nor falls a single drop."
So spake the King.
                                        The merchant and his wife
Were soon established in the neighborhood,
Near to Queen Bidasari's palace grand.
A hundred servants had they to fulfil
Their orders. They sent gifts to all their friends,
And food to last a month.
                                        A certain day
It chanced that Bidasari said: "O King,
Why goest thou no more within the gates
Of that thine other palace? Of a truth
Queen Lila Sari will be vexed, because
Thou hast abandoned her so long a time.
She'll think that I have kept thee from her side
Unwilling thou shouldst go." So, with all sorts
Of words, fair Bidasari strove to urge
The King to visit Lila Sari. "I
Will go to-morrow," finally he said.
He went, when morning came, and met the Queen.
She turned him back, and with sharp, bitter words
Reproached him. "Wretched one, I will not see
Thy face. I love thee not. I hate thee. Go!
Lila Djouhara's son-in-law, thou'rt not
To me an equal. Thy new wife's an ape,
Who liveth in the woods."
                                        But when the King
Heard these vociferations of the Queen,
He said: "Branch of my heart, light of my eyes,
Oh, be not vexed, my dear. It was not I
Who wrong began, but thou didst cause it all.
For thou didst hide thy deed from me, and drive
Me on to this extremity. Oh, why
Art thou now angry with me? If thou wilt
But love her, and attach thy heart to hers,
She'll pardon thee, and take thee as a friend."
As more and more enraged the Queen became,
Her wrath with strong reproaches overflowed.
"Depart from here, accursed of God! Thou art
No longer husband mine. Go live with her

Whom God hath struck, but whom thou dost delight
To honor. Formerly of noble blood
Thou wert, but now no more than broken straw.
Thou needst not further try to flatter me.
Though thou shouldst purify thyself seven times, false one,
I'd not permit thee to approach my side."
The King grew angry and replied: " 'Tis thou
Who art despicable. Thy cunning tricks
Are worthless now. Thy jealousy insane
Was without cause, and common were thy acts.
Thy wit is much below thy beauty. Ill
Will follow thee, should I protection cease."
" Have I forgot my noble birth?" she asked.
" But thou hast erred, to lower thine high estate
To people of such base extraction. Here
And everywhere thy shame is known, that thou
Art wedded to a gadabout. Is it
For princes thus to wed a merchant's child?
She ought far in the woods to dwell, and know
Most evil destiny." The King but smiled
And said: " If this event is noised abroad,
'Tis thou who wilt receive an evil name.
For who in all the land would dare prevent
The King from marrying? I ought to take
From thee all I have given. But before
The people I've no wish to humble thee.
Is it because I met thy every wish
That thou art grown so bad? Most evil hath
Thy conduct been, and I with thee am wroth,"
And in hot anger rushed the King away,
And straight repaired to Bidasari's side.

SONG IV

THIS song will tell again about the prince
Of Kembajat, most powerful. He was chased
By fell *garouda,* horrid bird of prey,
And sought another land. His way he took
Toward Indrapura. At the break of dawn
A daughter fair was born, a princess true,
Within a boat that lay upon a shore.
The Queen and he abandoned her, and went
Back to the royal palace and for days
Bemoaned her fate. Of her they nothing heard.
"Alas my child!" the father cried, "my dear,
In whose care art thou now? We do not know
If thou art dead or living. Thus thy sire
Hath no repose. Light of mine eyes, my love,
My purest gold, our hearts are torn with grief.
An evil fate was ours to hide thee there.
We do repent the deed. To think that thou
Perchance hath fallen among the poorest folk!
A slave perhaps thou art!" The prince's son
Remarked the sorrow of his parents dear,
And was profoundly moved. "Have I," he asked,
"A sister? Tell me why have ye concealed
Her far away? Did ye not care for her?
Was she a burden that ye must forsake
Her thus? Doth shame not fill your parents' hearts?"
But when he heard the tale in full, he said:
"O father, let me go to seek for her,
My sister dear. If I succeed I'll bring
Her back to thee." "Oh, leave us not, my son,"
The father said. "Thou art our only heir.
Like a tamed bird upon our shoulders fain
We've carried thee, and watched thee, day and night.
Why shouldst thou leave us now? Oh, go not forth.

Vex not thyself about thy sister dear.
From travellers we shall get news of her,
And her abode discover."
Then the prince
Bowed low and said: "My father, lord, and King,
I am but strengthened in my wish to go
And find my sister. Let me now depart,
And seek for news of her." The King replied:
"Well, go, my dearest son; thy heart is good.
Though but a child thou still dost bear a brain."
Then summoned the young prince the merchants all,
And bought much goods and questioned them in turn
About all neighboring villages and camps.
They told whate'er they knew most willingly,
For much the young prince was beloved by them.
Among them was a youth of handsome face,
Fair Bidasari's foster-brother tall.
Amid the strangers sat he near the throne;
His name was Sinapati. He was brave
And wise. Now as he watched the prince he thought,
"How strangely like dear Bidasari's face
Is his, as when a reed is split in twain
There is no difference between the halves."
His home he left when Bidasari fair
Became the Queen. He thought of her and wept.
The prince observed him there, and said, with smiles:
"Young man, my friend, from what far town art thou?
Why dost thou weep so bitterly? What thoughts
Arise in thee and make thy visage dark?"
Young Sinapati bowed and said: "My lord,
I came from Indrapura, in a ship,
My wares to sell. For that I do not weep.
But sorrow cometh to my heart whene'er
I think upon my home, and brothers dear,
And sisters."
At these words the prince rejoiced.
He thought, "From him some news I'll surely learn."
Sherbets and dainties then to all the folk
He offered, and the cup went 'round from dawn
Till noon, and then the merchants went away;

But the young prince kept Sinapati there.
Now he already strong affection felt
For him and said: " My friend, toward thee I'm moved
And look upon thee as a brother dear.
Thou dost at Indrapura live, but who
May be thy patron there?" Then with a smile
Young Sinapati said: " My patron's called
Lila Djouhara, merchant great. He owns
Some six or seven swift ships, and toileth more
Than ever since he Bidasari took
As child." In two days' time the young prince went
With Sinapati to his father's house.
" I bring thee news," he said, "but nothing yet
Is sure. Behold from Indrapura far
A youth, from whom I've things of import great.
A merchant of Pesara, very rich,
My sister must have found. All well agrees
With what to me thou saidst. Now must we seek
For confirmation of the glad report."
To Sinapati gold and gems they gave.
Then spake the King: " If this be so I'll send
An envoy bearing richest gifts, and thanks
Within a letter writ."

The youthful prince
Bowed low and said: " Oh, send me on this quest!
Lila Djouhara I would like to see.
Perhaps he's virtuous and just. If I
Am made full sure it is my sister dear,
I'll send a messenger. And if it be
I'll bring her back."

The King was moved
To hear his son thus speak. " O dearest child,"
He said: " I'm very loath to let thee go.
But thou must many horsemen take with thee,
Lest thou shouldst long be absent."

" Why should I
Be long away?" the prince replied, with bows;
" For if Lila Djouhara will not let
Her come, I shall forthwith return to thee."
The King could now no more object. He gave

Commands to make an expedition great.
With richest gifts, and food, and princely things,
And sent him forth with blessings on his head.
" Stay not too long; thou art my only hope,"
The King exclaimed; " I'm getting old, my son,
And thou my heir upon the throne must be."
They started early on the fourteenth day
Of that same month. And Sinapati rode
Beside the Prince.
Some went on foot and some
On horses. When they far had gone, the prince
Said to the youth: " Now listen, friend. When we
Arrive thou must not name my family
And rank. I'm someone from another town.
It doth not please me to declare my rank
To strangers. Should the girl my sister prove,
Thou mayst tell all, for I shall soon return."
Thus speaking, the young prince his way maintained,
And soon arrived near to the city sought.
He Sinapati left, and went within
The gates, with four companions, true as steel,
And six attendants. They at once repaired
To the *campong* of good Lila Djouhara.
They found it closed, with a forsaken look.
" There's no one here. The King hath taken all
Away, both old and young," said the *mandar*.
Then Sinapati beat his breast and said:
" What hath become of my dear patron, then?"
" Be not disturbed. No harm hath come to him.
The merchant with the King hath gone, because
The King hath married Bidasari fair,
And made of her a queen, and built a fine
New palace in the country wild. There all
Is joy and happiness." Beyond all count
Was Sinapati glad to hear these words.
Then to the prince he said: " My gracious lord,
Lila Djouhara's near at hand. He is
In highest favor with the King, and bears
A title new." They hurried forth to find
His residence. " It is the left *campong*,"

Remarked a country-man. "Thy lord is grand
And powerful now, and master of us here.
The King hath now become his son-in-law."
Then Sinapati went within the gates
And saw his mother there. Her heart was touched.
She kissed him and inquired, "Whom hast thou brought?"
"It is a friend," he answered. "Come, my lord,"
She to the young prince said, "enter and rest."
"He's so like Bidasari," to herself
She said. "What is thy name, my brave young man,
Thou seemest nobly born. In very truth
Thou'rt handsome and well mannered." Then the prince
Said: "Poutra Bangsawan I'm called. Thy son
I've followed here." But Sinapati paid
Him homage, and they knew him for a prince.
Before his door young Sinapati slept
At night to guard him safe. Next day there came
An invitation from Lila Mengindra
(Before, Djouhara). So they started forth.
Lila Mengindra was astonished quite
To see the prince's face so beautiful.
"Who is this most distinguished stranger here?"
He asked himself. "My master, speak a word
To Poutra Bangsawan, a friend of mine,"
Said Sinapati. So the old man turned
And spoke unto the prince, "Come here, my son,
And sit thee near thy father." He felt drawn
To him, he looked so much like Bidasari.
The young prince smiled and on the dais sat.
"What is thy visit's purpose?" then inquired
The good old man. The prince with bows polite
Replied: "I'm but a humble stranger, come
To find my sister. I bespeak thine aid."
"Be not afraid, my son, but trust in me,
Nor fear to give thy sister's name. If thou
Wilt have it so I'll take thee for a son;
I love thee for thou hast a face so like
My daughter's." Then the brave young prince began
And told his sister's story, how she was
In time of stress abandoned on the shore.

"And if I only knew," he said, "where now
She is, I'd be her master's willing slave."
Now when Lila Mengindra heard his tale
His joy was quite unspeakable. His love
For Bidasari's brother greater grew.
With smiles he asked: "Now, Poutra Bangsawan,
Say of what family thou art, that I
May aid thee in thy quest, and help thee find
Thy sister." Then the young prince bowed his head
And pondered, "Shall I lie?" For he knew not
If 'twere his sister. Lila saw his mood
And said: "Be not disturbed. It is most sure
That thy dear sister's here. So speak the truth,
That my old heart may be surcharged with joy.
Thy sister's seated on a throne, and like
A brilliant jewel is her family.
Be no more sorry. As for me, my heart
Is full of joy."
The prince looked in his face
And said: "Can I confide in him? I am
A stranger here and fear to be deceived."
Said Sinapati: "Speak not thus, I pray,
For everybody knows this man can tell
Ten-carat gold from dross. Now list, my lord.
Although he bids me silent be, a prince
He is, son of a powerful king, and comes
To seek his sister." Then within his heart
The former merchant much rejoiced, as if
He'd found a mountain of pure gems. He paid
His homage to the prince in proper form,
And took him into his abode, to meet
His wife and all within. The spouses two
To him exclaimed: "Dear prince, in our old age
We're very happy. When thy sister sweet
We found, o'erjoyed were we. And now the King
Hath married her, and raised her to the throne.
He hath our family to noble rank
Upraised, and covered us with benefits."
Then smiling said the prince: "I learn with joy
My sister sweet is here. When may I go

Before the King and see her? For I've come
To take her home. And yet I fear the King
Will never let her go away from him.
When I have seen her I'll return again."
In three days' time the King gave audience.
The former merchant with him took the prince,
Who sent the richest presents on before.
The princeling was most gorgeously attired
And bore himself with haughty dignity.
His robe was rich, his tunic violet
And fire. His many-colored turban bore
Bright agates. At his girdle hung his *kriss.*
He was entirely clad as prince should be,
And bracelets wore with little bells and rings.
His leggings were embroidered with bright flowers
Called *pouspa angatan.* He seemed divine—
His beauty was extraordinary. Pearls
In numbers countless covered all his garb;
An amulet he had with sacred verse
From the Koran, a diamond pure. He rode
A steed most richly housed, with *shabraque* decked
With gleaming jewels casting rays of light.
'Twas thus the prince set out to meet the King.
Lila Mengindra with him went. The prince
Approached the King's pavilion, and at once
The King remarked his beauty and his mien
Of noble grace. "Who can he be?" he thought.
Meanwhile the prince dismounted and appeared
Before the King. Full seven times he bowed
And said, "O may your happiness increase,
Illustrious sovereign!"
Then the King with smiles
Lila Mengindra questioned, "Who is this
Thou hither bringest, of such noble mien
And amiable face?"
With humble bow
The former merchant said: "This slave of thine
Has come from lands remote, from Kembajat,
Upon the seashore, since thy Majesty
He wished to see. His presents few he sent

Before him, which he hopes thou wilt accept."
The former merchant thought: "I would his rank
Divulge. But some might think I lied because
The King hath Bidasari wed, and if
She knew she was a princess born she might
Be very vain and haughty."
To the prince
The King was very friendly. "Come and sit
Here by my side," he said, "for thee I deem
A brother." "Let me here remain, my lord,
I am a poor unworthy servitor.
I hope that thou wilt pardon me. I would
I might become a subject of thy crown."
The King thought: "This may be some royal heir
Who here hath wandered. He resembles much
Our Bidasari. Pity 'tis that he
Unto another nation doth belong."
Then pleasantly he said: "Pray, truly tell
What is thine origin? Keep nothing back.
What is thy name? The whole truth let me know."
The young prince bowed him low and said: "My name
Is Poutra Bangsawan, of family
Most humble. I am searching everywhere
To find a sister lost. When she is found
I shall return at once." Then said the King:
"Where is thy sister? I will help thy search.
Stay here with me a month or two, that we
May learn to know each other and become
Fast friends." The young prince then obeisance made
And said: "I bear thine orders on my head.
Thou art a king illustrious, and I
A humble servitor. I am the son
Of good Lila Mengindra, but for long
I've absent been. My sister dear I seek.
Thine aid I do bespeak. From Kembajat
I come, a subject of thy father there, the King.
Forgive me, lord, for now thou knowest all."
The King rejoiced to hear a voice that seemed
So much like Bidasari's, and inquired
Of Sinapati, "Tell me now his race."

Then Sinapati bowed and said: " My lord,
Of princes and of caliphs is his race.
His kingdom, not so far, is most superb;
His palace is most beautiful and grand.
Swift ships within the harbor lie, all well
Equipped." At this the King enchanted was,
To find a prince was brother to his wife.
Still more he asked and Sinapati said:
" Because his realm was ravaged by the foe
He hath misfortunes suffered manifold."
Then knew the King he was of royal blood
And had adversity experienced.
The King came from his throne and said, " My friend,
My palace enter." So the King and prince
Went in. They met fair Bidasari there.
She sat beside a Chinese window quaint,
All choicely carved. She saw the King and thought,
" What fine young man is this he bringeth here? "
When they were seated all, the young prince looked
At Bidasari: " Beautiful is she,"
He thought, " my sister dear, and very like
My father." Then the King with smiling face
Said: " Bidasari, darling, speak to him.
He is thy younger brother, come to seek
Thee here. From Kembajat he came. And thy
Dear father mourns for thee the livelong day."
At this fair Bidasari sighed. She bowed
Her head and silence kept. She much was moved
Because she had not known her parents true,
But fancied them Djouhara and his wife.
" I'm but a merchant's daughter," finally
She said. " Things all uncertain this young prince
Hath told. If I'm the daughter of a King,
Why hath he left me here, and never sought
For me through all these years? 'Tis not so far
From here to Kembajat." The young prince bowed.
" Thy words I bear upon my head," he said,
" O sister dear. Pray banish from thy heart
All hatred. If thou'rt lowly born, I am
Likewise. Our realm was ravaged at thy birth.

But shortly afterward fair peace returned,
And to his own my father came again.
I've seen how much he suffers in his heart.
Thy name he never utters without tears—
He never hath forgotten thee. Forgive
Him, then, in what he was remiss. Except
For stern necessity he never would
Have thee abandoned."
Then the King with smiles
Said: "Speak to him, my dear. He tells the truth.
Thy parents wandered through a desert land
Beneath a cruel sun. Impossible
It was to carry thee through brier and brush."
Down at his sister's feet the young prince knelt.
Then Bidasari clasped him in her arms.
The brave young prince to them recounted all
The sorrows of his parents. Much he wept,
And they wept, too, as he the story told.
Then sat they down to dine. And afterward
They *siri* took and perfumes of all kinds.
Then the young prince took leave. "Where goest thou,
My brother?" asked the King. "I fain would go
Straight home to my dear parents," said the prince.
But, with a voice affectionate, the King
Replied: "Seek not Lila Mengindra. Here
Thou shouldst remain, for thou hast met within
This palace thy dear sister. There is room
Enough for thee. Stay here with all thy folk
And retinue." The prince bowed low, and forth
Unto the merchant went, and to him said:
"Within the palace now I shall remain
With all my retinue, for thus the King
Commands." The merchant said: "'Tis very well,
For where can one lodge better than within
The palace?" So the prince returned, with all
His people, to the palace of the King.
Then all the *mantris* came, and festivals
And feasts were held. As long as he remained
At Indrapura, the young prince received
All courtesies. And Bidasari fair

Was known as daughter of a mighty king.
The news was carried far and wide, and all
Repeated how her brother brave had come
To seek for her.
Queen Lila Sari heard
And was surprised. She sighed in solitude,
And felt a woe unspeakable. She said
To a *mandar:* "I was in too much haste.
On the *dyangs* I counted, but they come
No more. All four have gone and homage paid
To Bidasari. All my tricks are foiled.
In no one can I trust." Dang Lila then
Approached and said: "Acts of unfaithfulness
Bring never happiness. God's on the side
Of loyalty. Now those *dyangs* are sad
And languish after thee, but fear the King,
Dost thou not think, O Queen, thou ill hast wrought?
For while the King is absent none will come
Thy heart to cheer." The Queen replied with ire:
"Seek not to consolation give. The King
Esteems me not. I'll not humiliate
Myself before him. Who is that young prince,
So called, who hither came? A pirate's son
He well may prove, and calls himself a prince.
Go ye, *dyangs*, pay service to the King,
And he may favor ye as he did her."
She seemed most wroth. But she repented sore
In truth, and pined away in sorrow deep.
In other days she had no wish nor whim
Unsatisfied. Now all were for the King.
The Queen's heart angrier grew from day to day
As if a scorpion's sting had wounded her.
And her distress grew greater when she thought
Upon the love of other days. Her heart
Was inconsolable because so bitterly
She missed the pomp and glory of her court.
But Bidasari to the King one day
Said: "Send back these *mendars;* for if they all
Stay here, Queen Lila Sari all alone
Will be." The King with smiles replied: "Oh, no!

I will not let them go. She is so fell
And barbarous, she no one loves. She is
Much better all alone." Then to the King
Fair Bidasari said: "Thine anger was
Too prompt. She spoke in wrath because she was
Accustomed to a court. In what to thee
Hath she been wanting, that thou shouldst repel
Her thus? Thou gav'st her love, and now thou dost
Abandon her in sorrow. Be not thus
Incensed with her, for should she come to want
The shame would be reflected on thy head."
The King's face lighted, and he said: "My dear,
I went to see her, but she drove me forth
With bitter words. Her conduct was beyond
All bearing. And she heaped on me abuse."
But Princess Bidasari said: "Dwell not
On that, my friend. She was disturbed by wrath
And jealousy. In other days thou didst
Embrace and kiss her. Now she is alone.
And thou perchance didst somehow hurt
Or bruise her body." All his anger left
The King at this. He said: "O purest soul,
Thou speakest well and wisely. How could I
Not love thee, dear, and cling to thee for life?
Oh, never may we separated be!
Branch of my heart, light of my eyes, thou dost
But good desire. Thou'rt all the world to me.
I'll go to her, since thou doth ask. Perchance
A reconciliation may be made.
But she must first admit her faults. If she
Repentance shows, to see her I will go."
The merchant's wife had come and heard these words.
Her warm tears fell. She thought within herself,
"My daughter hath no vengeance in her heart."
Then Dang Bidouri brought delicious rice
Unto the King and Queen. They ate and drank,
And stronger grew their love from hour to hour.
Then gave the King commands to call the prince.
He came with smiling face and graceful bows.
"Sit here beside us," said the King, and all

The three dined there together, royal ones,
Surrounded by deft servants and *dyangs*.
They chatted gayly, and, with laughter, ate.
When all was finished, from the betel-box
The King of *siri* took, perfumed himself,
And then the prince retired.
When two short months
Had fled, the prince bethought him of his home
And parents. To himself he said, " I'll go."
He gave commands to preparation make
For his departure. " I am loath to leave
My sister," he to Sinapati said.
" My life is joyous here. But there at home
I've left my parents in solicitude."
Then Sinapati bowed and said, " With thee
I'll go."

SONG V

A CERTAIN day the *mantris* came
Before the King, in the pavilion grand.
And with them came the youthful prince, and cast
Himself before the throne. The King with smiles
Said: "Sit thou at my side, my brother dear,
I have not seen thee for a day entire."
The princeling bowed and said: "My gracious lord
If thou wilt pardon me, I would return
And give my parents dear the joyful news.
My father bade me seek my sister lost,
And still he nothing knows of her good fate."
The King replied with sorrow: "Brother mine,
Why wilt thou go so soon? We scarcely are
Acquainted, and I have not had enough
Of thy dear company." The prince replied:
"Oh, be not sorrowful, my gracious lord.
As soon as I have my dear father seen
I'll tell him what good things have come to pass.
'Twill soothe his heart to hear my sister's joy.
My parents will be glad in learning all
Thy goodness great. And pray consider me
Thy subject leal. Soon I'll return again."
The King's emotion grew. With pleasant voice
He said: "Take counsel of thy sister. Heed
What she may say." They found the Queen within,
Fair Bidasari, and attending her
Dyang Agous Djouhari. All sat down
And took some *siri* from the betel-box.
The Queen to the young prince then spoke: "Come here.
My brother, why have I thy face not seen
For two long days?" With bows the prince replied:
"I've had a multitude of things to do.
Thus came I not; for my companions all

Seek homeward to return. So I must take
My leave of thee upon the morrow morn,
When pales the silver moon before the dawn."
The Queen was grieved to hear these words, and shed
A flood of tears. Her tender heart was touched.
Beside herself with sorrow she exclaimed:
"O prince illustrious! How canst thou go,
Since we have met? I've loved thee from the time
I knew thou wert my brother. I am grieved
To hear thee say thou wilt so soon depart.
Of low extraction must I be! 'Twas wrong
For thee to call thyself my brother. I
A poor and feeble orphan am, and how
Should I the love deserve of a great prince?"
When this he heard the prince bowed low his head
And was much troubled. "Sister sweet," he said,
"Grieve not like this. I only do return
Because our parents must so anxious be.
I love thee so, my darling, that my heart
Is nearly breaking. If thou speakest thus
To me, my dear, my grief will still increase.
I could not leave thee, but I must respect
Our parents' wishes. They commanded me
All haste to make. So—sweet—I pray thee have
Compassion on me."
Much disturbed, the King
Observed the sorrow of the princess fair.
He kissed her lips, to her a *sepah* gave,
And said with tender voice: "My darling wife,
What dost thou wish? Let now thy brother go.
We'll see thy parents here ere many days."
The Queen wept bitterly, and said to him:
"His wishes I do not oppose. Let him
Do whatsoe'er it pleaseth him to do.
For I am but a stranger, a lost child,
And who should think of me or love me true?"
Then bowed the prince and said: "In very truth,
I know thou art my sister. Speak not thus.
God knows how much I love thee, sister mine.
If thou dost not permit me to depart

I'll not resist. I'm happy here with thee,
But our dear parents are in cruel doubt,
And look for news of thee. Now that I know
Thy husband is a king, our parents dear
Would be so overjoyed to learn it too!"
Then spoke the King with face all radiant,
"Return not, brother mine," he said. "I'll send
Swift messengers to bear the gladsome news
That Bidasari's found. Then, if he wills,
Thy royal father here we'll hope to see.
I'll go myself to meet him when he comes."
The young prince bowed and said: "Nay, rather send
Thy messengers, a great king cannot go
So far away." Queen Bidasari heard
These words and much rejoiced, and gayly gave
Her brother then her betel-box.
The King
Caressed his wife and said, "My dearest soul,
Love not thy brother more than me." He called
Lila Mengindra. Soon the merchant came
Before the King and prince. The King exclaimed:
"Come here, my uncle. Tell me, wilt thou take
A letter to the King of Kembajat—
To prove to him we live?"
So spake the King
And called his counsellor of state, who came
And kissed his hands. The King then bade him write
A letter, all in characters of gold.
"Well," cried the King, "let's hear the letter now."
"Now glory be to God," it thus began,
And all fair Bidasari's history
Recited. Then the King a mighty host
Assembled and with elephants and steeds
Ten *mantris* took the letter of the prince
Unto his parents. With the cavalcade
There went a *laksimana* great, who bore,
As king's ambassador, bejewelled flags
And standards rich, and presents of much worth.
Then Sinapati by the King was called
A *laksimana mantri*, and received

A fine equipment, with a hundred men
To follow him. 'Twas thus the King preserved
His reputation as a mighty king.

When he had sent the embassy, the King
Went to his wife, and they were very gay.
His love for her grew greater every day.
The former merchant also was beloved.
He gave the King good counsel, and obeyed
His orders willingly. He often dined
Together with the King and Queen. His wealth
Grew vast. No one at all could with him vie,
In Indrapura. He was much attached
To the chief *mantri.* They were equals both
In prudence, wisdom, and fidelity,
With power unquestioned over all the folk.
Beneath their sway prosperity increased,
And many merchants came from far and wide.
The kingdom was at peace. The King rejoiced,
And everyone was happy in the land.

SONG VI

THE *laksimana mantri* now I'll sing,
Who went upon the embassy. As soon
As the great King of Kembajat had news
Of his arrival, he was much rejoiced.
He told the Queen, and in the audience-hall
Awaited. Then went forth the officers
With elephants and *payongs*. A countless throng
Attended them, with music and with flags.
They met the embassy, and, with rich gifts,
They gave the King's commands. Into the town
Then entered all. The King was very glad,
As if his only daughter had returned.
All bowed before the King, who took the gifts,
While servants took the letter to the chief
Of *mantris*. And he gave it to the King.
The monarch read, and was possessed with joy.
He could not thank enough the merchant good,
Who raised his daughter to a royal throne.
He wished forthwith to go and see his child.
The letter cordial invitation gave.
But one thing troubled him: "He straight inquired,
'Hath not the prince, my son, the liberty
To come back home?'" The *laksimana* bowed
And said: "The King wished not to let him come
And begged with tears that he would stay. The Queen
Feared if her brother went she'd never see
Her father. From your children both I bring
Warm greetings. Kind indulgence from your heart
They ask, and press their invitation. I
Crave pardon for myself, O King, and hope
Thy children dear may see their father's face,
And that the kingdoms may become one realm."
At these words smiled the King. "Ah, well!" he said,

"I'll wait for seven days still." Then questions flew,
And the great king learned all about his child.

The Indrapura *mantris* went apart
When evening came. A separate palace grand
The King assigned them, with the best of food.
He orders gave for preparations great.
Unto the Queen he said: "In seven days' time,
My dear, I look to start, for I shall have
No peace until I've seen our darling child."
Then he assembled there his *mantris* all,
Both young and old, with elephants and steeds.
And all was ready to set forth, as he had wished.
The while the morning stars were twinkling still,
The royal gong resounded many times.
The guards leaped forth with joy. The officers
Came out and took their shining helms of war.
Their naked swords all glistened. It was thus
They made the glittering royal cavalcade.
Their flags and banners flaunted in the air,
All those who stayed behind were sad, as if
A knife had cut them. All together marched,
The lancers and the horsemen, and they seemed
A moving city. Soon all darkened was
The moon, as someone sorrowful. The swords
And lances glistened like an island in
The middle of the sea. Thus is described
The royal escort marching through the land.
The King was mounted on an elephant,
His *siri*-bearer seated close behind.
A rich *payong* of royalty, all tricked
With bells, was stretched above his head,
And drums and other instruments without
Cessation sounded. Thus went forth the King,
And soon to Indrapura came.
When near
He halted and forthwith an envoy sent
His coming to announce, together with
The *laksimana mantri*. "Mighty King,"
They said, "thy royal father hath arrived."

The King his heralds ordered then to call
Lila Mengindra. With a smile he said
To him: "Assemble in the square the folk
And army. Straight to my pavilion let
Them come, and all in holiday attire,
For I my father am to meet to-day."
Lila Mengindra bowed and hied him forth
To execute the orders of the King.
The King within his palace went, and sat
Upon a jewelled seat. The Queen was there,
And good Lila Mengindra at her side.
The King said smilingly: "Light of my eyes,
Let all the palace decorated be.
Assemble all the palace folk and all
The younger girls. For now without the gates
Our parents wait. To-morrow I shall go
To meet them." Then Queen Bidasari cried,
With smiles: "My brother they have come to see.
I cannot go before them and declare
Myself their daughter." But the young prince said:
"Oh, speak not thus, my sister, but give heed
To what I say to thee, and be not wroth.
If I'm the only one they love, alone
I'll go with them away." Then to the King
He said: "With my dear sister I but jest,
To quiet her alarms." He bowed before the King
And asked permission forth to go at once
To meet his father. "Nay," replied the King,
"We'll go together." A repast was served
With every kind of food. The royal three
Together ate. Then from the betel-box
They *siri* took, and perfumes sweet they used.
The prince then from the palace forth did go.
Next day the King invited him to start
With him upon the royal progress. All
The banners waved, and everyone was glad.
Then to the Queen he said: "Stay here, my love,
And I will hither bring thy father dear."
These words rejoiced the Queen. She said: "Go forth,
My dear, and I will follow with my eyes."

The King then took his leave with the young prince,
With many *mantris* following. The strains
Of gladsome music sounded. All the bells
Were rung, and those without the cavalcade
Were sad.
Ere long they came to the frontier,
And King met King. The folk of Kembajat
Were all astonished at the young King's face,
As beautiful as painter's masterpiece.
The old King looked with smiles on all. His joy
Was great. The King of Indrapura bowed
Respectfully, and made them bring to him
The elephant that bore 'neath gay *payong*
His consort's father. "Son, where goest thou?"
"I've come to seek thee." Then the old King said:
"Why didst thou come in person? 'Twould have been
Enough if thou hadst *mantris* sent instead."
His joy o'erflowed his heart. His son-in-law
He greatly loved. Upon his elephant
He said: "Approach, my son, thou art a king
Renowned. Thy body and thy soul are both
Alike, and both of royal stock!" He pressed
Him in his arms and said: "Light of my eyes,
Almighty God hath heard my many prayers,
And granted me a perfect son-in-law."
The King of Indrapura bowed and smiled
Most graciously. Then to the young prince said
His father: "Mount, my son, beside me, here."
The young prince mounted at his father's side.
He was as beautiful as chiselled gold.

Within the town the kings made entry then
Amid a joyous throng. When they had come,
The former merchant bowed before them both,
The *mangkouboumi* now. The mighty King
Of Indrapura bowed and said: "My sire,
Speak to my uncle here; for he brought up
Thy daughter." Scarcely had the old King heard
These words than he exclaimed with joy: "Come here,
My brother, let us now acquaintance make."

The old King, seated on his elephant,
Shed all about him rays of happiness,
And all the people there were greatly moved.
"This is my brother well beloved," he said,
And kissed his brow. "How great hath been his love,
His faithfulness has proved beyond compare."
The former merchant bowed, and to the King
Replied: "I am thy slave, O King, and bear
Thine orders on my head. Thou dost o'erwhelm
Thy servant with thy favor." Then upon
The royal throne, which was all gem-bedecked,
The old King sat, the young prince at his side,
With all the *mantris* near. Then came the Queen
Consort. The prince and Bidasari fair
Came from their seats, their mother to receive.
All entered then the palace. The young Queen,
Fair Bidasari, bowed and was embraced
By both her parents. With a flood of tears
Her father said: "Alas, my darling child,
Fruit of my heart, light of my eyes, keep not
A hatred in thy soul against us now.
The will of God is now made manifest.
We long have separated been. At last
We see each other with our very eyes.
Great wrong we did thus to abandon thee,
But still let not thy heart a stranger be
To us. Peace later came to our dear land—
Such was our destiny. What could we do?
We were in flight. We thought, 'May God decree
Some honorable man shall find her here!'
How can we now be glad enough 'twas thus
Ordained! What recompense can we present?"
Sweet Bidasari wept as she recalled
The past. The King her husband was much moved,
And felt great pity when her tears he saw.
And all were sad with sorrow mixed with joy,
Because they knew she was of royal birth.
Food now was served, and quickly the *dyangs*
Brought salvers for the princes. The two kings
Ate of the rice till they were surfeited,

Then to their children offered it. All took
The *siri* placed before them, and straightway
Themselves anointed with rare perfumes sweet.
When all had eaten, the five royal ones
Lila Mengindra called, and gave to him
The remnants of the feast. The kings then spoke
To him and to his wife. They both bowed low
And kissed the royal hands. Then said the King
Of Kembajat: "My children, I had planned—
In case we ever met on earth and ere
The prey of death became—a feast to give,
To last a month, and to it ye invite.
In triumph I my daughter fain would bear,
With all of ye. I would at once repair
Unto the isle of Nousa Antara,
And there I'd hold a royal festival
With all the members of our family,
And all the *bitis, mandars,* and *dyangs.*
Such was my plan—if ever I should find
My daughter dear. Now while this moon doth last
Let me the project see fulfilled before
Your parents come to die."
The gracious King
Of Indrapura at these words bowed low
And said: "I bear thy words upon my head.
It shall be done as thou hast wished, my King."
And when the evening came all was prepared.
Soft mattresses were spread, and the two queens
Betook them to their chambers, and the rich
Egyptian curtains fell. They vainly sought to sleep.
They talked together of their sorrows past
And evil days. And neither kings nor queens
That night could slumber.
At the break of day
The talking bird began to sing and prate.
A little later the *bajangs* began
Their song. Then all arose, and bathed, and broke
Their fast, and chattered and amused themselves.
The King of Indrapura then gave word
Unto the *mangkouboumi:* "All prepare

That's necessary, ere the moon be full.
Get ready all the various kinds of ships,
And load them down with every sort of arms.
Prepare all sorts of games to pass the time,
And get in order all the cannons great
And fire-arms. Thus the King commands."
Straightway
The *mangkouboumi* bowed before the King,
And went his orders to obey. He made
The ships all ready, with new paint and gold.
When three were well equipped, on board he took
The people of the city. All the old
Were left behind, but of the young none stayed.
Then to the King the *mangkouboumi* said,
"All is prepared." At this the King rejoiced,
And to the King of Kembajat sent word,
Who told his wife, and she was all aglow.
They started from the palace, kings and queen
And prince, and lovely Bidasari, too,
Attended by the courtiers all. The strains
Of music sounded and the bells were rung.
All those whose lot it was to stay at home
Were pained, as if a knife had stricken them.
The cannons roared; the royal banners waved.

In three days' sail they reached the island fair,
Of Nousa Antara, and the ships made fast.
The two queens sat and watched the deft *dyangs*
Take up the coral white and pink, and toyed
With pretty shells. The King set foot upon
The isle of Nousa Antara. The King
And his dear wife upon the shore came forth,
With their sweet daughter Bidasari pure.
The King of Indrapura with them went,
The prince walked near them on the left.
The King
Of Indrapura ordered that a tent
Be raised, and one was made. It was as large
As any palace, set with royal throne.
The two queens entered it and sought repose.

The prince before his father bowed and said,
" My royal father, let me go and hunt."
To this the King of Kembajat replied,
" Do what thou dost desire, light of my eyes."
The King of Indrapura said with smiles,
" I'll go with thee to hunt, my brother dear."
The prince replied, " I shall in truth be charmed,
My brother." " Forth we'll fare to-morrow morn,"
Returned the King of Indrapura. " Call
The folk together."
When the dawn appeared,
The King and prince together started forth,
Escorted by a band of hunters tried,
And beat the woods for game. The King and prince
And all their following made rapid work.
The game took flight. The King then drew his bow
And many animals were killed. A deer
Came running by. His arrow struck him full
Upon the shoulder, and the huntsmen seized
And quickly killed him. In the pathless woods
Of Nousa Antara there was much game.
A tiger roared, the King and prince pursued.
The tiger swiftly fled. The prince sat down
Within the forest deep. To overtake
The beast he was unable. To return
He sought, but could not find the way. Alone
He was, and in perplexity, because
His huntsmen he no longer could descry.
Then, wandering to and fro, he found at last
A pleasure garden of the days gone by,
Belonging to King Lila, beautiful
And without flaw. He was astonished quite
When he perceived a palace. All alone
He found himself, when he had entered there.
He walked about, but found no living soul.
Unto himself he said: " Can this domain
A habitation be of demons dread
And spirits? Can this be the cause of all
The solitude which reigns? " On all sides then
He looked. All suddenly a voice he heard,

But still no one could see. Amazed he stood.
The mystic voice exclaimed, "Have pity, lord,
And free me from this room." As in a dream
The prince these accents heard. He answered then:
"Who art thou? Whose strange voice is this I hear,
The while I no one see? Dost thou belong
Unto the race of demons and of spectres?
Where is the key, that I may ope the door?"
Then the *dyang* of Mendoudari said
Unto the prince: "Look toward the left, for there
The key thou'lt find that opes the palace tower."
He took the key and opened wide the door.
All those who were within, when they beheld
The prince's face, fell prostrate at his feet.
To them the prince cried out: "Say to what race
Ye do belong. This quickly tell. And whose
This palace beautiful?" Then answered him
Dang Tjindra Melini: "O Royal prince,
We are God's creatures, like to thee. And this
Fair palace of the King Lila is now
By Ifrid occupied, a spirit-king,
With whom now lives the prince illustrious,
Lila. His daughter, Princess Mendoudari,
Is shut alone within a chamber here,
And Ifrid, king of spirits, cometh oft.
On every third day cometh he. His eyes
Are brilliant as the sun." When this he heard
The prince was glad. The room he entered then.
The Princess Mendoudari sought to flee.
"Where wouldst thou go, my friend," he said. "I've sought
And found thee. Do not flee away from me."
The Princess Mendoudari said with tears:
"And art thou mad enough hither to come?
The spirits will destroy thee without doubt."
These words rejoiced the prince, and to her then
He sang a low sweet song of love and wooing.
The princess answered with a dreamy chant.
And when the young prince heard her gentle lay
He felt a yearning pity for her fate.
"Be not afraid, my dear," he said, "for I

Will triumph over all thine enemies."
Then Dang Sendari served them dainty food;
And what was left, to her the princess gave.
The prince too *siri* from the betel-box
And rare sweet perfumes used. When evening came,
A soft couch for the prince was spread. And then
The princess sought her room, and curtains drew
Of rich Egyptian stuff. The prince had asked,
"When comes the spirit-king?" And she had said,
"At early dawn." The young prince could not sleep,
But through the long night hours sang soft *pantoums*.
When daylight came the prince arose. He heard
A spirit coming to the palace. Then with fear
Was seized the princess fair. "Behold," she cried,
"He cometh." Then the young prince took his arms.
"Fear not," he said; "have confidence in God.
What he decrees must always come to pass.
If I'm destroyed, then follow me in death.
I only ask one thing of thee, my love.
When I am dead, I pray thee weep for me,
And let thy mantle be my winding-sheet.
Now let thy glances follow as I go."

I'll tell of Ifrid now—the spirit-king.
He lurked beneath the palace. When he heard
The princess talking with the prince his ire
Arose like burning flame. His cry was like
A thunder-burst. The very palace shook.
"Depart from here," unto the prince he roared,
"And feel my mighty power." Then sweet love-songs
Exchanging with the princess went he forth.
His mien was like Sang Samba's, and his face
Was nobly firm, as if he went to meet
A roaring tiger. At his side he wore
A rare carbuncled sword, and arrows bore
With points in deadly poison dipped. Ifrid,
The creature with two heads, like spectre came
With laughter horrid. He took up a stone
And hurled it at the prince, who dodged its flight.
Then full of wrath Ifrid upon him rushed.

But swift the prince let fly an arrow sharp,
And pierced his heart. One groan, and then he fell,
And died beside the river. Then the prince
Made haste to join the princess.
When she saw
The spirit Ifrid dead she much rejoiced
And bowed before the prince. Great gladness shone
In her fair face, because her woe had ceased,
And she was happy that 'twas to the prince
She owed her rescue. 'Twas as if she'd found
A mountain great of jewels. Then she said:
"Caliph a high divinity once was
And called himself King Lila. God will bless
Thee for thy deeds, O mighty prince."
The prince
With kisses said: "Thou hast a charming mouth.
Thy form is supple. Prithee tell me why
I should not love thee? Thou art beautiful
As a statue of pure gold, and thou shalt be
A princess in my palace. Well I know
Thine origin is noble, and thy race
Is high." They gayly chatted while some food
Was served. The prince, with pleasure, at the side
Of the fair princess ate. When all was done
He took some *siri* from the betel-box
And perfumes used. "Thou art a jasmine sweet,"
He said, "an antidote to every ill,
And thou shalt be my wife."
Next day the prince
Took her behind him on his horse, and they
Departed. The *dyangs* accompanied them.

Now will I tell about the *mantris* all.
Until the fall of evening, with the King
Of Indrapura, they in waiting stayed,
To welcome back the prince. And much disturbed
They were that he delayed so long to come.
The King then bade them seek the prince, and see
Why he remained so long apart from them.
Then *mantris* four set out, and hunted far

And wide, but found him not. They brought the news
That he could not be found. The King was sad
And ordered them to go and tell the King,
His wife's dear father, that the prince was lost.
The old King fainted when he heard the tale.
With oil of rose they sprinkled him, and back
Unto his senses came he. "O my child,"
He said, "my heart hath lost all hope. Where now
Art thou? I'll go, myself, to seek."
The King
Wept much, and his dear wife. And as for her—
Sweet Bidasari—she appeared to wish
To kill herself, for never on the earth
Did brother love his sister like the prince
And Bidasari. At the fall of day
Back came the King of Indrapura, sad
And weeping. Then the King of Kembajat
Said: "O my son, be silent. Do not weep,
For thou dost but increase the pain I feel."
But Indrapura's King replied: "Alas!
He was my brother true, so brave and good!"
But while they were lamenting thus the prince
Stood there before them with his consort fair.
He bowed to all. The King, his father, saw
And could not speak. He thought, "It is the voice
Of my dear son." Then recognition came
And he was wild with joy. The prince then told
How he had chased the tiger, and had lost
His way within a wood: how he had killed
A spirit there, Ifrid, the dread.
The King
Heard all he said and much rejoiced. Then came
The servants serving tasteful food to all.
The King ate with his wife and children dear.
Together they were six. All sorts of rare
And dainty food were served them, and the King
Took *siri* from the betel-box, and used
Sweet perfumes. The great King of Kembajat
Then gave a festival which lasted quite
Seven days, with music and diversions gay.

Glad joy was at its height, of pleasure born
And of the dance. The kings amused themselves.
All kinds of games they had. Intji Bibi,
A singer of Malacca, sang with grace.
The seven days passed, the Princess Mendoudari
Was all in finery arrayed. The wives
Of the two kings took her in hand. The prince
Was by the *mangkouboumi* ta'en in charge.
The princess sweetest perfumes did exhale.
Her manners were most gracious and polite
As of a well-born person. Every sort
Of gem and jewel sparkled from her robes.
She wore a ring—'twas *astokouna* called—
And yet another one, *glangkano* named,
And still another, with bright stones all carved
In fashion of Ceylon. Her tresses curled
Like to a full-blown flower, and on them shone
Full many precious stones. The *tourie* buds
Became her well. Her features were as bright
As those of some celestial being pure.
Fair Mendoudari thus was clad, and led
To the bride's seat, and at her either hand
Stood *mantris'* daughters seven with waving fans.
Meanwhile the *mangkouboumi* patiently
Achieved the tiring of the prince. He wore
A royal crown, made in the island fair
Called Nousa Antara, and a rich coat
Which opened at the sides, made in the West.
A chiselled necklace hung about his neck.
His tunic flamed with orange, like the robe
Of great Schahid Schah Pri. His girdle bright
Was cloth of *tjindi,* fringed with agates rare.
An amulet he wore with diamond pure,
With sacred words engraved of the Koran.
He wore a jewel like a butterfly,
Most beautiful, and many rings and gems.
His features of the rarest beauty were,
Like those of some divinity of heaven.
When thus arrayed, the youthful prince came forth
And made obeisance to his parents both.

He went to the appointed place, and all
The children of the court assembled there
Before him, while two sons of heralds stood
Beside him, waving fans like floating clouds.
All kept the strictest silence. Then a band
Of soldiers came, with blades all glittering.
The royal sword, all diamond decked, flashed rays
Of light. Three times around the island went
They all, with sound of music and the noise
Of bells. And all who heard in vain essayed
To estimate the number. Everyone
Ran forth to see the progress—men and women.
Some tore their garments, some their children lost,
Distracted by the pleasure and the noise.
When ended the procession, the young prince
At Princess Mendoudari's right was placed,
Within the palace. Then to them was brought
Rice called *adapadap*, and they became
A wedded pair. And all the folk dispersed.
In three days' time was Mendoudari dressed
Anew by Bidasari. She was robed
With vesture of embroidered silk. The prince
Was likewise gayly clad, to suit the glad
Occasion. Now again they made, in state,
A royal progress round about the isle.
The King and Bidasari rode in one
Grand chariot, and, within another, went
The prince and Mendoudari, his fair bride.
Then back they came for rest, upon the soft
Rich palace cushions. Then the mighty King
Of Kembajat inquired of his dear wife:
"What think'st thou, love? Shall we to-morrow morn
Return?" With smiles the Queen replied, "I bear
Thine orders on my head." Next day the hearts
Of all the royal company were filled
With joy. The officers assembled then
To take the King's commands, and he was pleased
To see them dutiful. The following morn
The song of the *bajans* awaked the King.
At early dawn each princess with her lord,

And all the officers, embarked upon
The ship. They sailed far from the island fair,
Nousa Antara, and in three days came
To Indrapura and the river's mouth.
When at the palace they arrived again,
The *mantris* came in joy and kissed their hands.
The King of Kembajat said that he wished
To go. Scarce had fair Indrapura's King
Heard that his parents to their home desired
At once to go, when he the *mantris* called
And orders gave. The King of Kembajat
Set out with his dear wife next day at dawn.
Within the palace of their daughter sweet
They met fair Indrapura's King. The King
Of Kembajat sat at his side, and said
In softest tones: "Well, Bidasari, child,
Thy parents now will homeward fare. Obey
The King, thy gracious husband, in all things.
The former merchant brought thee up. He will
A father be to thee. Strive hard to win
Thy husband's heart, and never disregard
His wishes." Scarcely had she heard these words
Than at her father's knees she fell, and shed
A flood of tears. The King embraced his child
And, weeping, said: "My daughter dear, pure gold,
My crown's chief gem, light of my very eyes,
Branch of my heart, be not disturbed, my soul,
Nor let thy heart be sad." The royal four
All wept together. Then the father said:
"My son, accomplished prince, we trust to thee
Our Bidasari. Show her the right path
If she aside should step, for hither she
As prisoner came. Correction should she need,
For us it will not be a shame." At this
Fair Indrapura's King was greatly moved.
He bowed and said: "My father, speak not thus.
I have the best opinion of the girl.
Our hearts are one, as body with the soul.
This kingdom all is hers, the guardian I
Of her possessions, and I'll satisfy

Her every wish." The King with joy replied:
" Well, daughter, jewel of my crown, thou art
No more beneath my sway, but wholly now
Under the orders of thy husband dear."
He much was moved, and to the *mangkouboumi*
Said, " Brother, take my treasures all, for we
Can never all thy goodness recompense."
The former merchant and his wife bowed low:
" Your gratitude, O prince, is great, but all
Thy treasures are thy royal daughter's meed.
For her we'll guard them." But the King replied:
" Nay, speak not thus, my brother. Should I give
All Indrapura's weight in purest gold
It would not pay thee for thy care and love.
We are to thee devoted from our hearts."
At dawn they breakfasted, but all were sad,
Because from Bidasari now must part
Her parents dear and brother. Much she wept
Because she felt her heart go out to him
Her brother. Then she said: " I've one to take
The place of parents, but where shall I find
A brother?" Princess Mendoudari bowed
To Bidasari, and they kissed with tears.
Fair Bidasari said: " My sister dear,
Sweet Mendoudari, when wilt thou return?
Stay not too long at Kembajat, for I
Could not thine absence bear. Farewell, my love."
The King embraced his daughter. Bitterly
Both wept. The royal father said, " Stay here,
My son-in-law, with thy dear wife." The King
Before his parents bowed. The youthful prince
Before the King his brother bowed, and went
To Bidasari's side, his sister dear,
With heavy heart. Then, weeping much, he said:
" O sister mine, gem of my crown, be not
So sorrowful. I go, but if thou dost
Desire, I'll come each year to visit thee."
Sweet Bidasari kissed him. But her grief
Was inexpressible. " O brother dear,
Illustrious prince," she said, " thine absence would

E'en then be much too long." The prince replied,
With bows: "Assuage thy grief, my sister dear.
For if the King permits, perhaps I may
Come sooner back to thee."
The mighty King
Of Indrapura said, in friendly tones:
"Although he be thy brother, still, my dear,
I love him much. We ne'er have had the least
Misunderstanding. Why art thou not gay?
And why art thou not willing he should go?
If 'twere not for thy father I would keep
Him here."
The King departed, followed by
His son, who took his father just beyond
The gates. The *mangkouboumi* bowed his head
Before the King, who with much ardor said,
"O father of dear Bidasari, give
Aid and protection to thy lovely child."
The *mangkouboumi* bowed again, and said:
"Whate'er is fit, I'll do. Upon my head
I bear thine orders. I thy servant am."
The prince embraced the former merchant too,
And said, "O uncle dear, my sister guide,
And counsel her if any fault she doth."
Then said the King of Kembajat, "My son,
Come, let us start at once."
So forth he fared.
The prince and all the escort with him went.
A few days passed and they were home again.
New garments to the escort all were given,
And many presents to the officers.
By *mantris* four the King rich treasures sent
Unto his children loved, with many steeds
And elephants. When safely they arrived
At Indrapura, they appeared before
The *mangkouboumi*. He presented them
Unto the King, and said: "O sire, these gifts
Are from thy son." The King replied: "Why dost
Thou bring them here, my uncle? Keep them all
In thine own treasury." Then he retired

Within and said to Bidasari sweet:
"Thy father, dear, hath sent us presents rare,
And four young *mantris*, and a thousand men
With elephants and horses. All is thine."
The fair young Queen with smiles to him replied:
"All that with me to share thou dost desire.
Whatever be thy wish, I wish it too."
The King adored his wife, and was to her
Devoted. His great happiness increased
And his domains extended every year.
When Bidasari's royal birth was known,
The news spread far and wide, and everywhere
Was told. The realm of Indrapura grew
More populous and powerful year by year.

The wicked Princess Lila Sari lived
Alone and desolate, in sadness deep
And full repentance for her evil deeds.

This song is weak because my skill is small.
My heart was deeply stirred. And that is why
I made, poor fakir I, this poem here.
I have not made it long, because too sad
I was, and troubled. Now at last 'tis done.
For this, at least, your blessings I deserve.

THE END.

SEDJARET MALAYOU

LEGENDS OF THE MALAY ARCHIPELAGO

—

[*Translated by M. Devic and Chauncey C. Starkweather*]

SEDJARET MALAYOU

ONCE upon a time lived King Iskender, son of King Darab. He traced his origin to Roum; Macedonia was his native country, and Dhoul-Garnein his surname. Now it happened that this prince set out upon his travels to find the place where the sun rose; and he arrived at the frontier of India. There reigned in this country a very powerful king, to whom half of India was in subjection; and his name was King Kida Hindi. As soon as King Kida Hindi heard of King Iskender's approach, he gave orders to his prime minister, who gathered together the armies and princes who were subject to him. When all were met together, he marched forth to meet King Iskender. The two armies engaged and the conflict was carried on with extreme activity on both sides, as is related in the history of King Iskender. Kida Hindi was defeated and taken alive. Iskender ordered him to embrace the true faith, and Kida Hindi embraced the faith and became enrolled in the religion of the prophet Abraham, the friend of God, to whom be the glory! Then King Iskender caused him to be clothed in a garment like his own, and bade him return to his own country.

King Kida Hindi was the father of a very beautiful girl, whose equal was not to be found in her day. Her face had the dazzling lustre of the sun or the moon; she was modest and discreet. Her name was Chehr-el-Beria. King Kida Hindi took his prime minister aside and said to him:

"I have summoned you to ask your advice on the subject of my daughter, whose equal in these days cannot be found. I have formed the project of presenting her to King Iskender."

The minister answered: "Your Majesty has made a wise decision."

"Very well," replied the King, "to-morrow, God willing, you shall go and find the prophet Khidar and relate to him the whole matter."

Next day accordingly the minister set out to find the prophet Khidar. After his departure King Kida Hindi commanded that the name of King Iskender should be inscribed on the coins and standards of his realm. When the minister approached the prophet Khidar he made a salaam to him, which the prophet returned and asked him to be seated. Then the minister spoke as follows:

"You must know, O prophet of God, that my King entertains for King Iskender an affection so fervent that I cannot describe it. He is the father of a girl who has no equal among the children of this world's monarchs from the rising to the setting sun. She is without a rival in face, wit, and goodness of disposition. Now the desire of the King is to present the princess before King Iskender, with the view of ultimately giving her to him for his wife."

Now the soldiers of King Souran laid siege against the walled town of Gangga-Chah Djouhan; but those on guard repulsed them, so that they could not get near. Seeing this, King Souran advanced, mounted on an untamed elephant. Taking no heed to the arrows that were launched against him by the defenders of the wall, he reached the gate and struck it with his mace. The gate gave way and King Souran entered, followed by his warriors.

When King Gangga-Chah Djouhan saw King Souran approaching, he seized his bow and shot an arrow with haste. The arrow struck the forehead of King Souran's elephant. The elephant fell on his knees. King Souran quickly leaped to the ground, drawing his sword as he did so; at a single stroke he struck through the neck of King Gangga-Chah, and the severed head rolled to the ground. The forces of Gangga-Nagara, as soon as they saw their prince fall, demanded the *aman* (*i.e.*, truce).

King Gangga-Chah Djouhan had a sister, named Princess Zaras Gangga. She was exceedingly beautiful. The victorious prince took her for his wife. Then he resumed his march.

Some time afterward he reached the city of Ganggayon. It was formerly a great city, the black stones of whose fortress survive even to this day. This fortress is at the extremity of the river Djoher. The name Ganggayon in the Siamese tongue means "treasury of emeralds." The King of the city was

Rajah Tchoulin; he was a powerful prince, to whom all the kings of the land did obeisance.

On the news of King Souran's approach, King Tchoulin called together all his troops and sent word to the kings who were his tributaries. When all were assembled he set out to repel the invaders. The multitude of his soldiers was like the waves of the sea; his elephants and horses stood up among them like islands; his flags and standards presented the appearance of a forest, and the cows' tails fluttering at the pike-heads presented the appearance of *lalang* ploughers.

The army came in four bodies and reached the banks of a river. There they saw the soldiers of King Souran, ranged like forest-trees. The Siamese exclaimed, "Pangkal," a word which means "river," and hence that river became known as the river Pangkal.

The soldiers of Siam at once joined battle with the soldiers of Kling, who were Hindoos; and the battle raged with indescribable confusion. The soldiers mounted on elephants pressed forward these great beasts; the men on horseback made their horses champ with fury; the lancers pressed home their lances; those who carried pikes plied them furiously; and those who bore sabres dealt many a doughty stroke. Blood flowed like rain. The crash of thunder would have been drowned by the shouts of the warriors and the clash of arms. The dust that rose from the plain obscured the brightness of the day like an eclipse of the sun. So complete was the confusion with which the contestants mingled that it was not possible to distinguish the combatants of either side: each assailant was at the same time the assailed, and he who struck with his weapon himself at the same moment was stricken with a blow. Sometimes the soldiers attacked a comrade by mistake. Every moment crowds of people on either side were killed and wounded, many horses and elephants had their throats cut, and the blood shed covered the ground. The dust had disappeared; the combatants were seen struggling in masses so compact that neither party was able to retire from the battle.

King Tchoulin managed to force a way by means of the elephant he rode through the innumerable horde of King Souran's soldiers; the corpses were piled up beneath his feet. A crowd of Hindoo warriors lost their lives. The rest of them began to give way. King Souran, on perceiving this, dashed forward to meet King Tchoulin in single combat. He mounted an untamed elephant eight cubits high that had no driver. But the elephant of King Tchoulin was also very brave. The two animals met; they attacked each other; the clash of their encounter was like the thunder that rends the earth; their tusks clashing and intertwining made a sound like that of a storm that never ceases. Neither could triumph over the other.

Then King Tchoulin raised himself upon the beast he rode and brandished a javelin. He hurled it against King Souran; the javelin struck the elephant on his flank and pierced deep. At the same time King Souran shot an arrow which smote King Tchoulin in the breast and came out at his back. That prince fell to the earth and expired. The soldiers seeing their king dead, broke ranks and took flight in utter disorder, pursued by the Hindoos, who put to the sword all they overtook. Penetrating the ramparts of Ganggayon the Hindoo soldiers pillaged the town; the booty was immense.

King Tchoulin had a daughter, extremely beautiful. Her name was the princess Ouangkion; she was presented to King Souran, who took her for his wife.

The King then resumed his march and arrived at Temasik. The rumor of his approach soon reached China. People said, "Lo! King Souran comes with a countless army to conquer China. He has already reached Temasik." This news was heard with dire alarm by the King of China. He said to his ministers and to his officers:

"What must be done to repel this invading multitude? If the King of Kling arrives here, he will doubtless ruin our country."

The prime minister said: "O King of the world; I have a device for repelling him."

"Very good," said the King; "do not fail to try it."

The prime minister therefore caused a *pilo*, or ship, to be fitted out with rusty needles. They took also two kinds of trees, kamses and jujube trees, laden with fruit; these were placed on board ship with the soil in which they grew. Old men who had lost their teeth were chosen for passengers and crew. To these the minister gave his instructions and they started for Temasik.

When they had reached this place King Souran was informed that a ship had arrived from China. " Go and ask these strangers," he said to his attendants, "at what distance does this country lie from us." The attendant put this question to the crew of the *pilo* and received the following reply:

" When we left China we were all still young, being scarcely twelve years old; and these trees were seeds which we had sown. But you see how old we are now, and how our teeth are fallen out; the grains of seed have become trees in fruit, and all this has happened during the time it has taken us to reach here."

At the same time they took the needles of which they had a large quantity and said as they showed them to the Hindoos:

" When we started from China, these were as thick as a man's arm, and now see how they are worn out by the rust. This will give you an idea of the length of the voyage: we could not keep count of the years and the months."

On hearing this answer of the Chinese, the Hindoos ran to report it to King Souran, to whom they repeated all they had heard.

" If the thing is as they say," replied the prince, " the land of China is still a very long way off. When shall we arrive there? We had better return home."

" His Majesty is undoubtedly right," said the officers.

King Souran meditated thus: " Behold, the contents of the land is known to me, but how can I learn the contents of the sea? I must needs enter the sea, in order to know it."

Then he summoned his engineers and skilful men, and ordered them to fashion a box of glass with lock and fastenings within, in order that he might shut himself in it. The engineers made the box of glass just as the King desired it; they furnished it with a chain of the purest gold; then they presented it to King Souran, who was exceedingly well pleased with it, and rewarded them all with rich presents.

The prince entered into the box, disappeared from the eyes of all present, and shut the door upon himself. They took the box to the sea, and let it descend even to the bottom. What treasures, what wealth, works of the Almighty, were seen by King Souran! The box fell until it reached a land called Dika. There King Souran came out of the box, and went forward, seeing most wonderful things. He arrived at a great and strongly fortified town, which he entered and saw a vast population, whose number God alone knows. This people, who call themselves the Badsam people, were composed of believers and unbelievers.

The inhabitants of the town were astonished to see the face of King Souran, and his garments they looked upon with astonishment. They conducted him to the presence of their King, whom they call Agtab-al-Ard (*i.e.,* Bowels of the Earth). This prince asked, "What man is this?"

"My lord," was the reply, "it is a stranger, who arrived a moment ago."

"Whence does he come?"

"We do not know."

Then the King addressed King Souran himself and said, "Who are you, and whence do you come?"

King Souran replied: "I come from the world; I am the king of men; my name is King Souran."

King Agtab-al-Ard was very much astonished on hearing these words. "There is, then," he said, "another world beside ours?"

"The world," replied King Souran, "contains many races."

"Glory to God almighty," said the King, full of surprise. Then he made King Souran ascend and sit with him on the royal throne.

Agtab-al-Ard had a daughter, of great beauty, named Princess Mah-tab-al-Bahri ("Moon of the Sea"). He gave her in marriage to King Souran. That prince dwelt three years with her and had three male children by her. When he thought about these three children King Souran felt much troubled. He said to himself: "What will become of them, here, under the earth? Or how shall I withdraw them hence?"

He went to see Agtab-al-Ard, and said to him: "If my sons grow up, will your Majesty allow me to see that they are brought into the upper world, in order that the royal line of Sultan Iskender Dhoul-Quameen may not be broken to the end of time?"

The King answered, "I shall not hinder you."

Then King Souran took leave of the King and prepared for his return. The King and his daughter shed many tears at parting. Then the King gave orders to bring the horse Sembrani, named Paras-al-Bahri ("Sea-horse"), which he gave to King Souran. The prince mounted the horse, which bore him from the sea, and carried him in the air above the billows.

The troops of King Souran caught sight of the horse Sembrani, and recognized in its rider their King. The prime minister at once took a beautiful mare and led it to the shore. The sea-horse saw the mare and came to land to meet her, and King Souran descended. Then the horse Sembrani went back into the sea.

King Souran said to his wise men and engineers: "Raise a monument which shall witness to my journey in the sea; for I wish the memory of it to be preserved even to the Resurrection day. Write out the story, so that it may be told to all my descendants."

In obedience to the words of the King the wise men and engineers set up a stone on which they traced an inscription in the tongue of Hindostan. This done, King Souran gathered a quantity of gold, silver, jewels, gems, and precious treasures, which he laid up under the stone.

"At the end of the centuries," he said, "there will come a king among my descendants who will find these riches. And this king will subdue every country over which the wind blows."

After this, King Souran returned to the land of Kling. There he built a mighty city, protected by a wall of black stone having seven rows of masonry thick and nine fathoms high; the engineers made it with such skill that the joints of the stones were invisible, and the wall seemed cast of a single substance. The gate was of steel, enriched with gold and precious stones.

This rampart enclosed seven hills. In the centre of the city extended a pool vast as the sea; from one bank it was impossible to discern an elephant standing up on the other. It contained very many kinds of fishes. In the midst of it rose a very lofty island, always covered with a mantle of mist. The King caused to be planted there every sort of flowering and fruit-bearing tree to be found in the world. None was lacking, and to this island the King would repair when he wished for recreation.

He caused also to be planted on the banks of the pool a vast forest wherein wild animals were at large. And when the King wished to hunt, or catch elephants in the snare, he went to this forest. When the town was completed the King called it after himself, Souran-Bidgi-Nagara, and this town still exists in the province of Kling.

In short, if one wished to relate all the rest of King Souran's history he would find it as long as that of Sidi Hanza.

The Adventures of Badang

It is related that there once lived at Salouang a husbandman who owned a slave named Badang, whom he employed in clearing forest-land. It happened one day that Badang spread his nets in the river; but on the following morning he found his net quite empty, and by its side some fish-scales and fish-bones. The same thing took place for some days following. Badang flung the fish-scales (*sisik*) into the river; from which circumstance was derived the river's name, Besisik.

Meanwhile the slave said to himself: "Who is it who eats the fish caught in my net? I must watch and find out."

With this intention he hid one day behind some trees and saw a *hantou,* or evil genius, or monster, who was eating the fish taken in his net. This *hantou* had eyes red as fire, his hair was like woven osiers, and his beard fell down to his waist. Badang drew his knife, and, screwing up his courage, rushed up to the *hantou* and seized him.

"Every day," he said, "you eat up my fish. But this time you shall die at my hands."

On hearing these words, the *hantou* was afraid, and slipped aside, wishing to avoid the hands of his adversary; but failing to do so, he said to him: "Do not kill me; I will give you what you wish, on condition that you spare my life."

Badang thought: "If I ask for riches, my master will claim them. If I ask the power to become invisible, they will put me to death as a sorcerer. Therefore it is best for me to ask for the gift of physical strength, in order that I may do the work of my master."

In accordance with this resolution, Badang said to the *hantou,* "Give me the gift of physical strength; let me be strong enough to tear down and to uproot the trees; that is, that I may tear down, with one hand, great trees, a fathom or two in girth."

The *hantou* answered: "Your prayer is granted. You wish for strength; I will give it to you; but first it is necessary that you eat up what I vomit."

"Very well," said Badang; "vomit, and I will eat it up." The *hantou* vomited, and Badang set to work to eat it. He held the *hantou* by the beard, and would not let him go. Then he attempted the uprooting of great trees; and, seeing that he tore them up with ease, he let go the beard of the *hantou*.

Afterward, coming and going through the forest, he tore down enormous trees; he carried off, roots and all, those of a fathom or two in girth. As for the small ones, he tore them up by handfuls and flung them on all sides. In a moment the forest which had been a wilderness became level as a great plain.

When his master saw this work he said: "Who has cleared our land? For I see that it is suddenly freed entirely from trees and brushwood."

"It is I," said Badang, "who have effected this clearance."

Then answered the master: "How have you been able to do this, single-handed, so quickly and in one job?"

Then Badang related all the details of his adventure, and his master gave him his liberty.

The report of these occurrences reached Singapore. King Krama immediately ordered that Badang be brought before him, and he called him Raden (*i.e.*, Royal Prince).

Once upon a time the King of Singapore ordered Badang to fetch for his repast the fruit of *kouras*, at the river Sayang. Badang went there alone in his *pilang*, or boat, which was eight fathoms long, and he punted it with a pole cut from the trunk of a kampas-tree a fathom in girth.

When he arrived at the river Sayang, he clasped the *kouras*-tree. The branches broke, the tree fell, and his head struck against a huge rock. His head was not injured, but the rock was split in two. This stone is still seen to-day on the river Sayang, and it bears the name of Balou-blah, which means the "Riven Rock." His pole and boat have also been preserved to the present day. The day following his exploit Badang started back for Singapore, with his *pilang* completely laden with sugar-cane, bananas, and *keladion*, or edible lily, root. He had eaten the whole cargo before he arrived at Djohor-the-Old.

On another occasion the King of Singapore had caused a large ship to be built, fifteen fathoms long, in front of the palace. The vessel being finished, between forty and fifty men were ordered to push it into the water. They were unable to launch it. As many as 2,000 or 3,000 persons were equally unsuccessful. Then the King ordered Badang to undertake the operation. Badang undertook the task unaided, and pushed with such force that the vessel went right across the strait to the other shore. For this feat the King appointed him *houloubalong*, or officer of military rank.

A report reached the province of Kling that among the officers of the King was a man of extraordinary strength, named Badang. Now there was a powerful athlete at the court of the King of Kling, who had no rival in the country. His name was Madia-Bibjaya-Pelkrama. The King ordered him to go to Singapore with seven vessels; "Go," said he, "and wrestle with this officer. If he defeat you, give him as a prize the cargo of the seven vessels; if you are victorious, demand of him an equal forfeit."

"I obey, your Majesty," said the athlete, and started off with the seven vessels.

When he arrived at Singapore they brought news to the King of the city, saying: "An athlete has arrived from the land of Kling to compete with Badang in many kinds of sports. If he is defeated, he will leave the cargo of his seven vessels as forfeit."

The King came out of his palace to give audience. The Hindoo athlete presented himself. The prince told him to try a bout with Badang. Badang beat him in every round.

Now facing the *balerong*, or court of audience, was an enormous rock. The athlete said to Badang: "Come, let us match our strength by lifting this stone. Whoever cannot lift it will be conquered."

"Do you try first," said Badang.

The athlete commenced, and made many attempts without succeeding in lifting it. At last, mustering all his strength, he raised it to the height of his knee and let it fall again.

"Now it is your turn, my master," he said.

"Very good," answered Badang, and lifting the stone he swung it in the air, then hurled it toward the river, at the entrance to the town, where it is still seen at the extremity of the point of Singapore.

The athlete of Kling, thus vanquished, handed to Badang the seven vessels and their cargoes; then he returned, very much saddened and mortified by his defeat.

Now the report came to the country of Perlak that there was at Singapore an officer of the King named Badang without a rival in extraordinary strength. The King of Perlak, so runs the story, had an athlete named Bandarang, also very strong and of a great reputation. This athlete was before the King when they spoke of Badang.

"My lord," he asked, "is Badang stronger than I am? If you will permit me, I will go to Singapore to try an assault with him."

"Very well; go to Singapore," said the King. Turning to the prime minister, Toun Parapatih, he said:

"Get ready a *praho*, for I am going to send Bandarang to Singapore." When all was ready, a royal litter was prepared and the minister embarked with the athlete, and after a while reached Singapore. Prince Sri Rana Ouira Krama received the King's litter in the audience-chamber, among the radjas, ministers, body-guards, heralds, and other grand officers upon his command.

Then the prince, addressing the ambassador, asked: "With what commission is our brother charged?"

The ambassador replied: "Behold, I have received the command of your illustrious younger brother to bring here this subject Bandarang, to try his strength with Badang. If Bandarang is vanquished, your brother will place at your Majesty's feet the contents of a storehouse; and if Badang succumbs, you shall offer us the equivalent."

"Very well," said the King; "to-morrow everything shall be arranged for the struggle." The King retired to the palace, summoned Badang, and said to him:

"You know, Badang, that to-morrow you will have to contend with Bandarang."

"My lord," answered Badang, "know that this man is a powerful athlete, of extraordinary strength, famous in all countries. If your slave is vanquished will it not cast some discredit on the sovereign? If your Majesty thinks it wise, let us both be called into your presence together, so that I may test him; and if I feel myself capable of competing with him, we will have the contest; but if he is too strong for me, then your Majesty can oppose the struggle."

"You are right," said the King. That is why, when night came, the prince invited Toun Parapatih Pendek, Bandarang, and their companions. When they arrived they were served with a collation. Bandarang was seated beside Badang, who began to test him. They tried each other's strength without attracting attention.

At the end of an hour, when the guests were in wine, the King asked Badang if he were strong enough to struggle with Bandarang, who declared that he was equal to him. On the other hand, when Toun Parapatih Pendek had returned to the ship, Bandarang said to him:

"Lord, if you will permit me to advise, there will be no contest between Badang and me. I might not conquer, for I have learned how powerful he is."

"Very well," said the minister; "it is very easy to arrange that."

So the minister said to the King: "It is my opinion that we should prevent this struggle; for if one of the contestants should be vanquished in some bad way, a quarrel might arise out of it between your Majesty and the sovereign your brother."

The King agreed, and the ambassador asked leave to return home. The prince had a letter written for the King of Perlak. It was carried in state on board the ship and the envoy, after receiving vestments of honor, set sail to his own country. Arriving, he told the King all that had taken place. Later Badang died and was buried at Bourou. When the news of his death arrived at that country, the King of Kling sent a carved stone, which is now seen at Bourou.

And now as to the kings of Pasey. The authors of this story declare that there were two brothers named Marah who lived near Pasangan. They were originally from the mountain of Sanggong. The elder was named Mara-Tchaga, and the younger Marah-Silou. Marah-Silou was engaged in casting nets. Having taken some *kalang-kalang*, he rejected them and cast his net anew. The *kalang-kalang* were caught again. After several attempts with the same result, Marah-Silou had these *kalang-kalang* boiled. And behold, the wretched things became gold and their froth became silver. Marah-Silou caught more *kalang-kalang*, boiled them, and again saw them become gold and silver. He had thus acquired much store of gold and silver, when one day the news came to Marah-Tchaga that his younger brother was catching *kalang-kalang*, and he was so irritated that he wished to kill him. When Marah-Silou learned of this design, he took refuge in the forest of Djawn. The place where he fished is still called the Plain of Kalang-Kalang.

Marah-Silou, established in the forest of Djawn, gave gold to those who dwelt there, and they all obeyed his commands. One day when he was hunting, his dog, named Si Pasey, began to bark on a slight hill which one would have believed made by the hand of man. Climbing the small hill he saw an ant as big as a cat. He took it and ate it up. The place was afterward called Samodra; that is to say, "The Big Ant." Now it is said that the prophet of God—blessings be upon him!—once told his companions:

"There will be a country some day, toward the south, called Samoudra. When you hear it spoken of, hasten thither to convert the inhabitants to Islam, for in that country many will become the friends of God. But there will also be the king of a country called Mataba, whom you must take with you."

A long time after this decree of the prophet, the fakir Mahomet went to Samoudra. Reaching the shore, he met Marah-Silou, who was gathering shells. The fakir asked him:

"What is the name of this country?"

"Its name is Samoudra," answered Marah-Silou.

"And what is the sovereign's name?"

"I am the sovereign of all who dwell here," said Marah-Silou.

The fakir Mahomet converted Marah-Silou to Islam and taught him the words of the creed. Now Marah-Silou being asleep dreamed that he was in the presence of the prophet of God, and the prophet said to him, "Marah-Silou, open your mouth." He opened it and the prophet spat in it, and Marah-

Silou, awaking, perceived throughout his whole body a perfume like that of spikenard. When day broke he told his dream.

"This is truly the country of Samoudra of which the prophet of God has spoken," said the fakir Mahomet. Bringing from the ship all the royal ensigns aboard, he proclaimed Marah-Silou king with the title of Sultan Melik-es-Salih.

Sultan Melik-es-Salih sent Sidi Ali Ghaiath-ed-Din to the country of Perlak. This prince had three daughters, two of blood-royal on their mother's side, and one born of a concubine. The latter was called the princess Ganggang. When Sidi Ali Ghaiath arrived at Perlak they showed him the three daughters. The two sisters of the blood-royal were seated lower than the princess Ganggang, who occupied a high seat. The latter, by order of her father, was cleaning arec nuts for her two sisters, like one doing the honors of the household. She wore rose-colored garments and a violet cloak. Her ears were adorned with *soubangs* made with the young leaves of the *lontar*. She was very beautiful.

Sidi Ali Ghaiath-ed-Din said to the King of Perlak, "That one of your daughters who is seated above is the one I ask in marriage for my master, your son." The envoy knew not that Princess Ganggang was the daughter of a concubine.

The King burst out laughing. "Very well," he said, "let the will of my son be accomplished." Then he gave orders to equip 100 *prahos*, and Toun Parapatih received the command to accompany the princess to the country of Samoudra.

Sultan Melik-es-Salih went to meet the princess as far as Djambou Ayer. He introduced her into Samoudra with a thousand honors and splendors, and married her. The marriage accomplished, the prince gave presents to the ministers and to the officers, and showed himself lavish in gold and silver to the poor of the country. As for Toun Parapatih Pendek, he took leave to return to Perlak. Sultan Melik-es-Salih and the princess Ganggang had two sons who received from the prince the names of Sultan Melik-ed-Dhahir and Sultan Melik-el-Mansour. The elder was confided to Sidi Ali Ghaiath-ed-Din and the other to Sidi Ali Asmai-ed-Din. Years passed and the two young princes had grown up. Perlak had been conquered by an enemy come from the opposite coast, and the inhabitants of the country had migrated to Samoudra. Sultan Melik-es-Salih conceived the plan of founding a city to establish his sons there. He said to the great ones, "To-morrow I shall go hunting." The next morning he set out, mounted on an elephant called Perma Diouana. He passed to the other side of the water. When he came to land his dog Si Pasey began to bark. The prince ran up and saw that he was barking before a hillock, sufficiently extended for the erection of a palace and its dependencies, level on top and well disposed. Sultan Melik had the ground cleared and built a palace and a city there. After the name of his dog he called the palace Pasey, and established as king his son Sultan Melik-ed-Dhahir, with Sidi Ali Ghaiath as minister. He divided his men, his elephants, and his royal standards into two parts, one for each of his sons.

Some time after this, the prince, having fallen ill, commanded the grandees to assemble and called his two sons and spoke as follows: "Oh, my two sons, and you all, my companions, my last hour is approaching. You men be good to those whom I leave behind. And you, my sons, beware of being envious of another's good, and of the wives and daughters of your subjects. Maintain between you the union of two brothers, abstain from all injustice, and avoid between you every cause of quarrel." He said also to Sidi Ali Gaiath-ed-Din and to Sidi Asmai-ed-Din:

"Oh, my brothers, take care of these two sons. Stir not up trouble between them. Be faithful to them and never give your allegiance to another king." The two young princes bowed their heads and wept.

As for the two ministers, "Lord," they said, "light of our eyes, we swear by the sovereign Master who created the worlds that we will never break our promises, that we will never lack in our fidelity or render homage to another king than your two well-beloved sons."

Then Sultan Melik-es-Salih named his son Melik-el-Mansour, King of Samoudra. Three days later he died and was buried in the interior of the palace. Their father dead, the two young princes, his sons, commanded the royal herald to assemble the officers and soldiers, elephants and horses, as well as the royal insignia of the country of Pasey. And the two cities grew and flourished more and more. God knows best the truth. He is our aid and our refuge.

Now this is the story of the King Chehr-en-Naoui. His power was great, his officers and soldiers innumerable. They told this prince that the country of Samoudra had a large population, many merchants, and a powerful king. Chehr-en-Naoui said to his officers:

"Which of you would be able to take the King of Samoudra?"

One of his officers very strong and brave, Aoui Ditchou, bowed and said: "Lord, if your Majesty will give me 4,000 chosen warriors, I will take the King of Samoudra alive and bring him to the foot of your Majesty's throne."

The King gave him the 4,000 warriors and 100 ships. When they were ready Aoui Ditchou sailed toward Samoudra, feigning that the ships were bent on commerce up to the very moment when they reached the end of the voyage. Then he caused it to be said that he was an ambassador of the King Chehr-en-Naoui, and the King of Samoudra sent some officers to receive him.

Landing, Aoui Ditchou put into four chests four lusty *houlou-balongs*, to whom he said: "Presently, when you are in the presence of the King of Samoudra, open the chests, leap out, and seize the King." The chests were fastened from within. They took them ashore in state as presents from the King Chehr-en-Naoui. When they were in the presence of the prince, a message couched in flattering terms was read, and the chests were brought in. Immediately the *houlou-balongs* opened the chests, sprang out, and seized the sovereign. The soldiers uttered fierce cries and unsheathed their arms to attack the band of Chehr-en-Naoui's men. But the latter cried:

"If you fall upon us, we will kill your King."

So the soldiers paused in their attack. Aoui Ditchou and his people returned, bringing with them the King of Samoudra. They crossed the sea and regained their own country. There the prisoner-King was conducted by Aoui Ditchou before King Chehr-en-Naoui, who was very joyful and loaded the head of the expedition and all his companions with honors. As for the King of Samoudra, they made him a poultry-keeper.

Now let us talk of Sidi Ali Gaiath-ed-Din. Having consulted with the principal ministers in the country of Samoudra, he equipped a ship and purchased a cargo of Arabic merchandise, for the inhabitants of Pasey at that time all knew the Arabic language. Sidi Ali and the soldiers whom he embarked on the ship with him took all the ways and manners of the Arabs. The minister being on board and all being made ready, they set sail for the country of Chehr-en-Naoui, where they arrived after a short voyage. Sidi Ali landed and went to present himself to the King, bearing as a gift a tree of gold, of which the fruits were all sorts of precious stones, and which was worth an almost inconceivable sum. When the prince saw this present he asked:

"What do you want of me?"

Sidi Ali replied, "We want nothing."

The King was highly pleased, although surprised by such a magnificent present. And he said to himself, "Now, what can be the aim of these people giving me all this?" The pretended Arabs returned to their ships. A few days after, the master of the ship returned to visit the King. This time he brought as a present a chess-board of gold of which the chessmen were of precious stones, which was worth an enormous sum.

"What do you want of me?" again asked the prince. "Speak, that I may satisfy you."

And they replied, "We ask for nothing."

Then they returned to the ship. Some time later, when the favorable monsoon blew for their return homeward, Sidi Ali Ghaiath thought upon his departure. He went to see the King, laden with a present which consisted of two golden ducks, male and female, enriched with precious stones, and in a big golden basin. He filled this golden basin with water, put in the ducks. They began to swim, dive, and pursue each other, a sight at which the King marvelled much.

"I beg of you to tell me," he said, "what you desire of me. By the God whom I worship, I swear to fulfil your wishes."

Then Sidi Ali answered: "Lord, if it is the accomplishment of your favor, we beg that you will give us your poultry-keeper."

"It is the King of Pasey that you ask of me. But, very well, I grant him to you."

"It is because he is a Mussulman," said the strangers, "that we ask him of your Majesty."

The King Chehr-en-Naoui delivered therefore the Sultan Melik-ed-Dhahir to Sidi Ali Gaiath-ed-Din, who took him on board the ship, gave him a bath, and then clothed him in royal raiment. The wind blew, they weighed anchor, set sail, and after a certain time arrived at the country of Samoudra. And God knows the truth. He is our aid and our refuge.

Now we are going to speak of the King Melik-el-Mansour at Samoudra. This prince said one day to Sidi Ali Asmai-ed-Din:

"I would like to go and see how my brother is getting along."

The minister answered, "Do not go, my lord, for fear of misfortune." And, indeed, he tried to restrain his master. The prince would listen to nothing, and finally the minister was silent. He ordered the drums to beat, in order to make the announcement, "Sultan Melik-el-Mansour is going to see the country of his brother."

Sidi Ali Asmai-ed-Din was not satisfied. He was an old minister who knew that out of every affair causes of trouble may arise. But it was his duty to obey. The prince started. He made the tour of the city of Pasey, and then entered the palace of the Sultan Melik-ed-Dhahir. There he fell in love with one of the ladies-of-honor of his brother's court, and a quarrel arose between the two brothers on her account. Sultan Melik-ed-Dhahir felt in the bottom of his heart a violent irritation toward his brother.

Now he had a son named Radja Ahmed, very young when his father was captured, but grown up when the prince was restored from the hands of Chehr-en-Naoui. Sidi Ali Ghaiath-ed-Din having withdrawn from affairs, a minister named Parapatih Toulous Toukang Sikari had replaced him in his ministerial functions. One day the King said to the minister:

"What is your opinion concerning the act of Sultan Melik-el-Mansour?"

The minister answered: "We have a means——"

"But," answered the King, "it might involve his death."

"If he dies," replied the minister, "my name shall be no longer Toukang."

"Give a family fête for your son Sultan Ahmed. We will invite Sultan Melik-el-Mansour to the festival."

Sultan Melik-ed-Dhahir gave orders then to decorate the city and made preparations for the fête, and sent to find Sultan Melik-el-Mansour. This prince was with Sidi Ali Asmai-ed-Din and his officers. They introduced the prince and his minister, but left the officers outside. When they had entered, Sultan Melik-ed-Dhahir caused them both to be seized and ordered one of his officers to conduct his brother to Mandjang. "As for you," he said to Sidi Ali, "stay here. Do not try to go with your master or I'll cut off your head."

Sidi Ali answered: "Rather let my head be separated from my body than that the servant should be separated from his master."

So the King had his head cut off. The head was thrown into the sea and the body impaled at the entrance to the Bay of Pasey. While they were taking the Sultan Melik-el-Mansour toward the east in a *prabo*, at the moment when they arrived near Djambou Ayer, the pilot saw a human head floating in the water near the rudder. He recognized the head of Sidi Ali. Informed of this event, Sultan Melik-el-Mansour caused the head to be taken from the water. It was indeed that of his minister. Casting his glances toward the land: "Behold," he said, "the Plain of Illusions." And it bears that name, "Padang-Maya," to this day. The prince sent to his brother and demanded the body of Sidi Ali; joined the head with the body, and buried both in the Plain of Illusion. Then he went back to Mandjang.

After the departure of the Sultan Melik-el-Mansour, King Melik-ed-Dhahir had the family festival. The Sultan Melik-el-Mansour had been at Mandjang three years when the Sultan Melik-ed-Dhahir bethought him of his brother.

"Alas," he said, "I was truly too unwise. For a woman my brother dethroned, and his minister is dead."

And the prince repented. He ordered some of his officers to go and find his brother at Mandjang. They therefore brought back Sultan Melik-el-Mansour with the regard due to a king. When they arrived near the Plain of Maya, the prince landed to visit the tomb of Sidi Ali Asmai-ed-Din. "I salute you, my father," he said. "Stay here, my father. As for me I go away, called by my brother."

From the interior of the tomb Sidi Ali answered: "Where would the prince go? It is better to remain here."

When the prince heard these words, he made his ablutions, said a couple of prayers, then stretched himself upon the tomb and expired. They bore to Sultan Melik-ed-Dhahir the news that his brother was dead, in the Plain of Maya, in the tomb of Sidi Ali Asmai-ed-Din. He started at once, went to the place, and had his brother, Sultan Melik-el-Mansour, buried with the ceremonies of great kings. Then, after returning to Pasey, a prey to grief, he abdicated the throne in favor of his son, Sultan Ahmed.

Some time after this, Sultan Melik-ed-Dhahir fell ill. He gave Sultan Ahmed his last instructions. "O my son," said he, "light of my eyes, treasure of my heart, never neglect the advice of your old servitors. In every affair take counsel with your ministers. Neglect not the duties of piety to God, the sovereign Master. Beware of injustice to men."

Sultan Ahmed heard in tears the last words of his father. The prince died, and they buried him near the mosque.

Sultan Ahmed was for many years on the throne and governed with much justice. Now, the author of this story says: "There was at Pasey a servant of God named Toun Djana Khatite. This man made the voyage to Singapore with two companions. Crossing the square of Singapore he passed by the palace of the King and saw the Queen. Near the palace was an areca tree, and while Toun Djana was looking at the Queen the tree split in two. At sight of this, King Sri Maharadja was extremely irritated. 'You see,' he cried, 'the conduct of Toun Djana Khatite. To call the attention of the Queen, he has acted thus. And he ordered him to be killed. So Toun Djana was led to the place of punishment, near a cake-shop, where Toun Djana Khatite received the blow of the poniard; his blood ran on the earth, but his body disappeared and no one could ever tell what became of it. The cake-shop-keeper covered the blood with the cake-cover, and the cake-cover was changed into stone, which is still seen at Singapore. According to a tradition, the body of Toun Djana Khatite was transported to Langkaoui and there buried."

Some time later came the sea-monsters called *toudaks* and attacked Singapore. They leaped upon the shore, and people who were there died in great numbers, overtaken by these *toudaks*. If they struck a man on the breast, they pierced to his back. If they struck the neck or the loins, they pierced clear through from one side to the other. There were many killed. People ran about crying:

"The *toudaks* are attacking us!"

"What shall we do?"

"How many dead? We shall all perish!"

Padouka Sri Maharadja in great haste mounts the elephant and goes forth, followed by his ministers, his body-guards, and all his officers. Arriving at the seashore he sees with horror the work of these monsters, the *toudaks*. Whoever was wounded by them inevitably perished. The number of the victims became larger and larger. The prince ordered the men to make a rampart of their legs, but in their boundings the *toudaks* succeeded in passing this barrier. They came like the rain, and the slaughter was terrible. While this was happening a young boy said:

"Why make thus a rampart of our legs? That is an artifice very much to our hurt. If we should make a rampart of the trunks of banana-trees, would not that be better?"

When Padouka Sri Maharadja heard the words of the child, "He is right," he said. And on his orders they hastened to construct a barrier of banana-tree trunks. When the *toudaks* came bounding along their snouts were buried in the tree-trunks, and the men ran up and killed them. There perished thus of these *toudaks* a number beyond computation. Their bodies formed heaps on the shore, and all the population of Singapore did not suffice to eat them. And the *toudaks* ceased their leapings. They say, by the force of their boundings the *toudaks* reached the elephant of the prince and tore the sleeve of his cloak. About this they made a song:

"The boundings of the *toudaks* tore
The mantle which the Sultan wore,
But here they ceased their onset wild,
Thanks to the wisdom of a child."

While Padouka Sri Maharadja was returning, the grandees said to him: "Lord, this child, though so young, has much wit. What will it be when he has grown up? You had better get rid of him." That is why they found it just that the King should give the order for him to be killed.

After they had caused this young boy to perish, it seems that the city of Singapore felt the weight of his blood.

Padouka Sri Maharadja reigned some time still and then died. He had as successor his son Padja Is Keuder Chah, who married the daughter of Toun Parapatih Toulous, and by her had a son named Radja Ahmed Timang-timanganga Radja Besar Mouda. This young prince was handsome and well formed, without equal in those days. When he was of age his father married him to the daughter of the King Salamiam, King of Kota-Mahlikie, who was named Kamar-al-Adjaaib, a princess of unrivalled beauty. King Is Keuder Chad had a *bendahari*, or major-domo, named Lang Radjouna Tapa, of the race of ancient inhabitants of Singapore, father of a very beautiful girl in the court of the King. The other court ladies calumniated this young woman, and the King in a rage ordered her to be impaled in the corner of the market-place.

Lang Radjouna Tapa was extremely wounded by the treatment of his daughter. "If in truth my daughter had offended," said he, "you might have simply had her killed. But why dishonor us thus?" On this he wrote a letter to Java saying, "If the Batara of Madjapahit wishes to attack Singapore let him come at once, for I will give him entrance into the fortifications."

When the Batara of Madjapahit had read this letter he caused to be equipped 300 junks and a great quantity of other boats. A hundred thousand Javanese embarked, crossed the sea, and attacked Singapore. At the end of several days King Is Keuder commanded his major-domo to carry rice for the rations of the troops. Lang Radjouna Tapa answered, "There is no more, my Lord." For he wished to betray him. At daybreak he opened the gates of the fortifications and the Javanese entered. Inside the town there was a frantic combat. So many people were killed on each side that blood flowed like water. From this came the marks of blood which are seen to this day in the Plain of Singapore. The natives ceased their struggle and King Is Keuder escaped, descending from Salitar to the Moara coast. By the will of God, the house of

Lang Radjouna Tapa was overturned, the storehouse for rice fell to pieces, and the rice was changed to earth. The *bendahari* himself and his wife were changed to stone, and these stones are still found in the ditch at Singapore. After this victory the Javanese returned to Madjapahit.

On arriving at Moara, King Is Keuder halted at nightfall. Now there came a multitude of iguanas, and, when day dawned they saw them gathered in a crowd near the halting-place. They killed them and threw their bodies into the river. But at night, iguanas again came in mass. The next morning the Singaporeans killed them, but that night as many more arrived. So that the place became putrid from the multitude of their bodies. The quarter is still called Biaoak Bousok, or "Putrid Iguanas."

King Is Keuder Chah set out and came to another place, where he built a fort. But all they constructed by day was overturned by night. And the place still bears the name of Kota-Bourok, or "Ruined Fort."

Starting from there the King advanced into the interior during many days and came to the Saning Oudjong. He found this place agreeable and left a minister there. Hence comes it that to this day Saning Oudjong is the residence of a minister. Then the King returned toward the coast near a river at the shore of the sea. The river was called Bartain. Is Keuder Chah halted at the foot of a very bushy tree. Then he began hunting. His dog, chasing some game, was struck by the foot of a little white gazelle and fell into the water. On this the prince cried:

"Here is a good place to build a city, for even the little gazelles are valiant here."

And all the grandees said, "His Majesty is right." The King therefore gave orders for the construction of a city at this place. He asked, "What is the name of this tree against which I have been leaning?"

Someone answered, "It is a malaka-tree." "Very well," said he, "let Malaka be the name of the city."

The prince established himself at Malaka. He had lived thirty-two years at Singapore, up to the capture of that town by the Javanese. He lived for three years more at Malaka, and then died, by the vicissitudes of this world, and had as successor his son Radja Besar Mouda.

This prince governed with justice. He regulated the etiquette of the court. He first established a ministry of ceremonies to direct people who came to Balerong, and forty heralds who stood below the throne ready to take the orders of the King and carry to him the words of the public. He instituted among the sons of the grandees a body of pages serving as royal messengers and bearing everywhere the royal equipage.

This prince had three sons, Radeu Bagousa, Radeu Tengah, and Radeu Anoumah, who all married daughters of Bauhara Toun Parapatih Toulous. At his death, Radeu Bagousa took his functions with the title of Toun Parapatih Permouka Berdjadjar.

When, by the vicissitudes of the world, King Besar Mouda died, his son Radeu Tengah succeeded him. The latter had a son called Radja Kitchil Bessar, who at his death was his successor. He was just and guarded the interests of his subjects. No one in his time among the kings of the world equalled him in liberality. And the city of Malaka became large, well peopled, and the meeting-place of merchants. This King married a daughter of Toun Parapatih Permouka Berdjadjar, and by her had two sons, Radja Kitchil Mainbang and Radja Makat. He reigned for a certain time, when one night he dreamed that he was in the presence of the glorious prophet of God, on whom be blessings! And the prophet said to him, "Recite the words of the creed." And Radja Kitchil Bessar did as the prophet commanded.

"Your name shall be Sultan Mahomet," said the prophet. "To-morrow at the moment of the Asr (in the afternoon) there will arrive a ship from Djedda, from which the men will descend to pray on the shore of Malaka. Follow all their orders."

"Yes, Lord," replied the prince, "I shall obey your word."

And the prophet disappeared. When day came the King awaked. He perceived upon his body the odor of spikenard and saw that he bore certain marks. "It is clear," he thought, "that my dream does not come from Satan." And he began to recite without relaxation the words of the creed.

The ladies-of-honor who were in the palace were very much surprised to hear the King speak thus. "Has the King been touched by Satan, or has he lost his wits? Let us hasten to inform the *bendahari*." They ran to tell the *bendahari*, who came at once, entered the palace, and saw the King repeating without cessation the words of the creed.

"What is this language in which the King is speaking?" said the minister.

"Last night," said the King, "I dreamed that I was in the presence of the glorious prophet." And he told his dream to the *bendahari*.

"If your dream is not an illusion," said the latter, "what is the sign?"

"Here is the sign that proves that I have really seen in a dream the prophet of God. Furthermore, the prophet told me: 'To-day, at Asr, there will arrive a ship from Djedda, from which the people will descend to say their prayers on the shore of Malaka. Follow their directions.'"

The *bendahari* was surprised at seeing the marks on the King.

"Truly," he said, "if a ship arrives at the hour stated, then your dream is a reality. If it does not arrive, we shall judge that Satan must have troubled your spirit."

The King replied, "My father is right." And the *bendahari* returned to his house.

Now at the hour of Asr there arrived a ship from Djedda which cast anchor. The master came on shore. He was called Sidi Abd-el-Aziz. He said his prayers on the shore of Malaka. The inhabitants, astonished at the sight, said:

"Why does he stoop so and prostrate himself so?"

And to see him better, the people pressed around, leaving no spot vacant, and making a great tumult.

The noise reached the palace, and the King mounted an elephant and came in haste, accompanied by his grandees. He saw the master making all the ceremonies of his prayer, and all was in evident accord with the dream.

"It is exactly as in my dream," he exclaimed to the *bendahari* and the grandees.

When the master had finished praying, the King made his elephant stoop, and took up the master with him and carried him to the palace. The *bendahari* and the grandees all became Mussulmans, and by command of the King so did all the population, men and women, great and small, young and old.

The master taught the King the ceremonies of prayer, and gave him the name of Sultan Mahomet Chah. The *bendahari* received the title of Sri Ouak Radja; that is to say, "Paternal Uncle of the King," which he was in fact. And that is the first title of the *bendahari*.

Sultan Mahomet regulated the ceremonial customs of the court. He was the first to prohibit yellow for the clothes of the person strange to the court, for handkerchiefs, borders of curtains, pillow-cases, mattresses, coverings of all kinds, ornaments of every nature, as well as for the decoration of houses.

Furthermore the use of only three kinds of garments was permitted—the *kain*, the *badjoa*, and the *destar*. It was also forbidden to construct houses with projections sustained upon pillars not touching the ground, or with pillars extending beyond the roof or with observatories. The *prahos* could have no windows in front. It was forbidden to carry clasps or ornaments of gold on the *kris*. No one strange to the court could have gold rings nor pins nor jingling bangles of gold and silver. Nobody without the royal consent had the right to wear on his clothes gilding of any sort; but the authorization once granted, one might wear it indefinitely. When a man presented himself at the palace, if he had a vesture falling beneath the girdle, if his *kris* was not attached in front, if he was not clad in a *sabec*, he was not admitted, whatever might be his distinction. If anyone entered with his *kris* attached behind, the officer took it away from him.

Such were formerly the prohibitions of the Malay kings. Whoever transgressed was guilty of *lese-majesté* and was condemned to pay a fine of one to five katis. White parasols were held in higher esteem than yellow ones, because they could be seen at a greater distance. That is why they were ranked higher; the first were for the King and the second for the princes. The objects of the king's private use, such as the spittoon, the ewer for his ablutions, the fan, and other like objects, had no fixed place, except the betel-tray and the sword, which they kept at the right and left of the sovereign. At the arrival and departure of an ambassador, the servitors of the King brought from the palace dishes and basins which were received by the head of the *bataras* and deposited near the *bendahari*. They gave a dish and a scarf to the bearer of the letter. If the missive came from Pasey or from Harau, it was received with all the royal pomp—drum, flute, trumpet, kettle-drum, and two white parasols together; but the bugle did not figure at this reception. The ministers preceded the elephant bearing the message, the *bataras* followed it with the *sida-sida*. The letter was borne by the chief of the *bedaouenda*, and they placed the elephant at the extremity of the *balei*. For the kings of these two countries were equal in greatness to the King of Malaka. Younger or older, all gave the salaam.

Having reached the audience-chamber, the letter was received by the chief of heralds of the right, the one of the left being charged with transmitting the words of the King to the ambassador, and the herald of the right transmitted the answer. If the message came from another country than Pasey and Harau, they suppressed part of the men. The *cortège* included only the drum, the flute, and a yellow parasol. They took, as was suitable, now an elephant, now a horse, and they halted outside the first exterior gate. When the message came from a more considerable sovereign, they employed the flute and two parasols, one white and one yellow. The elephant passed through the exterior gate, for formerly the royal entrance included seven fortifications. At his departure, the ambassador received a complete investiture, even were he only a simple ambassador of Rakan. The same gift was offered to our own ambassadors at the moment of their departure.

When the King conferred a title, he gave audience in the *falerong*, with the following procedure: According to the rank, the person to be honored was brought on an elephant, on horseback, or simply on foot, with parasol, drum, and flute. There were green, blue, and red parasols. The noblest were the yellow and the white, which with the kettle-drums represented the height of distinction. The yellow with the trumpet was also very distinguished; they were the parasols of the princes and greatest personages. The violet, red, and green parasols were those of the *sida-sida*, of the *bataras*, and of the *houlou balongs*. The blue and black ones served for any other person summoned to receive a title. When the personage arrived at the palace, he was detained without. Then they read before the King a very fine piece. It was a descendant of Batl that held this office. The piece read, they took it out.

He who received it was of the family of the candidate for honors. With this piece they brought a *tetampan* scarf with which the reader invested the candidate, whom he then introduced into the audience-chamber. There a mat was stretched for him to sit upon in whatever place the King designated.

Then arrived the vestments. For a personage promoted to the ranks of the *bendahari* there were five trays. The sons of radjas and the grand officers had four trays only, and so on down through the various ranks. The servitors of the King charged with this duty approached the beneficiary and placed the vestments upon his shoulders. He crossed his arms, to hold the vestments in place, and they took him outside. The etiquette in that was the same for ambassadors awarded an investiture, each according to the rights of his rank. The beneficiary dressed himself outside and then re-entered. They decorated him with a frontlet and with bracelets, for every man who received a title wore bracelets, each according to his dignity. Some had bracelets in the form of a dragon with amulets, others had bracelets of precious stones, others of blue enamel, others of silver. These wore them on both wrists, those on only one. The beneficiary thus decorated went and bowed before the King. Then he returned accompanied according to his rank, or by the person who introduced him. The *cortège* included now a drum and a flute alone, now trumpets or kettle-drums, sometimes a white parasol; but the white parasol was a rare honor, as well as the kettle-drums, for the yellow parasol and the trumpet were very hard to obtain in those times.

On festival days, when the King went forth in a palanquin, he was surrounded by high officers of state. At the head, before the sovereign, marched the *bataras* and the *houlou balongs,* each following their charge. Footmen, also before the King, bore the royal insignia. The royal pikes were at the right and left; the *bataras* had sword at shoulder. Before them marched the lancers. When the King gives a festival it is the *panghoulou bendahari* who arranges everything inside the palace, stretches mats, decorates the *balerong,* and places the *bangings* on the ceilings. It is he who looks after the repasts and sends the invitations; for the servitors of the King, his *bendahari,* his tax-gatherers, and the receiver of the port all depend on the administration of the *panghoulou bendahari.*

He invites the guests and the *temonggoreg* seats them. In the hall the guests eat four at a dish, to the end of the platform. If any one of the various fours are lacking the others eat without him, by threes or by twos or even one alone. For it is not permitted for those below to ascend to make up the number. The *bendahari* eats alone or from the same dish as the princes.

Such was in former days the etiquette of Malaka. There were many other regulations, but to relate them all would weary the attentions of my readers. At the month of Ramadhau, at the twenty-seventh night, while it was still light, they went in state to make adorations to the mosque. The *Temonggoreg* was at the head of the elephant. They first took in state to the mosque the betel-tray, the royal insignia, and the drum. When night came, the King started for the mosque, following the ceremonial of festival days, made the prayer of perfumes, and returned.

The next day the *laksamana* carried in state the turban, for the Malay kings were accustomed to go to the mosque in a turban, a *badjon,* and a *sarong.* These vestments were forbidden at weddings except by express permission. It was also forbidden to dress in the Hindoo fashion. Only those persons who had worn this costume for a long time were allowed to wear it at prayers and at weddings. Festival days, great or small, the *bendahari* and the grandees assembled at the palace, and the *panghoulou bendahari* brought in pomp the palanquin. As soon as they saw it appear, the persons seated in the *balei* descended and stood about. Seven times they beat upon the drum, and each time the trumpet sounded. After the seventh, the King set out on an elephant and came to the platform erected for that purpose, which he mounted. At sight of him, all those present bowed to the earth, except the *bendahari,* who mounted the platform to receive him. The palanquin having approached, the King placed himself in it, and they started for the mosque according to the ceremonial above mentioned.

Such was formerly the etiquette of the Malay kings. Such I learned it, such I tell it. If I commit any error, I desire to be convicted by anyone who has given attention to this story, and implore the indulgence of the reader.

CHOICE EXAMPLES OF FRENCH SCULPTURE.

GRACE.

Photo-engraving from the original statue in the foyer of the Grand Opera House at Paris.

Just as to French literature belongs the honor of having given to the world of letters some of the most profound classics of modern times, so to French art belongs the genius of idealization in its supremest manifestation. In its conceptions poetry is never lacking, and M. Loison, in this symbolizing of the Spirit of Grace, has given fresh evidence of the spiritual altitude of the French in art.

THE PRINCESS DJOUHER-MANIKAM

[*Translated by Aristide Marre and Chauncey C. Starkweather*]

THE PRINCESS DJOUHER-MANIKAM

THIS is the history of the Princess Djouher-Manikam, whose renown is celebrated in all lands, windward and leeward.

There was in the city of Bagdad a king named Haroun-er-Raschid, sovereign of a vast empire. He was a prince who feared God the almighty, and worthy of all praise, for he was a king descended from the prophet. After having lived for some time in his kingdom, he desired to start on a pilgrimage. So he addressed his ministers and his military chiefs and spoke to them as follows:

"O you all, my subjects, my officers, what is your opinion? I would fain make a pilgrimage to the house of God."

The cadi, prostrating himself, answered: "Sire, King of the world, the will of your sublime Majesty is very just, but in my opinion your departure would cause the ruin of the inhabitants of the fields, and those of your subjects who accompany you will have much to suffer."

The prince, having heard these words, said: "The opinion of the cadi is loyal, and you, my officers, tell what is your advice."

The officers arose, then they prostrated themselves and spoke as follows: "Sire, King of the world, we, your servants, beg you a thousand and a thousand times to cause your forgiveness to descend upon our heads, but how will your Majesty accomplish the pilgrimage? In whom can you trust to protect the country and watch over the palace?"

The prince having heard these words of his officers, none of whom approved of the pilgrimage, kept silence and restrained his anger, and then departed and returned to the palace. Some days after this, by the will of the most high God, the heart of the prince felt more keenly still the desire to make the pilgrimage. He gave orders to gather together the interpreters of the law, the wise men, and the *muftis*, as well as the officers. When they were all assembled, the prince went to the audience-chamber, and there before the officers of the court he questioned one of the doctors. It was the *mufti* of the city of Bagdad. He, prostrating himself, said: "The pilgrimage of his Majesty would be an excellent work, but is it of absolute necessity? For the voyage will be very long, and there is no one, my lord, who would be capable of ruling in the place of your sublime Majesty."

The prince answered: "He in whom we first of all place our trust is God. We shall hope then in the blessing of his envoy. We shall leave the cadi here, and if it pleases God the most high, we shall return promptly as soon as we have accomplished the pilgrimage."

The King therefore caused to be equipped and provided with all sorts of provisions, those of his subjects who were going to accompany him, and when the favorable moment had arrived he started with the Queen, some of the maids-of-honor, and his son named Minbah Chahaz. He took his son, but he left behind, guarded in the palace, his daughter called the Princess Djouher-Manikam. In those times there was no one in the country of Bagdad who surpassed in beauty the Princess Djouher-Manikam. Furthermore, she had in her heart the fear of God the most high and worthy of all praise, and would not cease her prayers.

After travelling for some time, the prince her father arrived at Mecca, and fulfilled his duties as a pilgrim. He recited the appropriate prayers. But observing that there was still a great quantity of provisions, the prince said to his officers:

"It is good for us to wait a year or so, for our provisions are yet considerable."

The officers replied: "It is well, lord of the world! Whatever may be your Majesty's commands, we place them above our heads." "Since it is thus," answered the prince, "it is fitting that we should send a letter thus conceived: 'Peace and blessing upon the cadi: I place my trust in God first of all, and in the cadi, to guard my kingdom, palace, and my child the Princess Djouher-Manikam. Be a faithful guardian, neglect nothing in the cares to be given to my kingdom, for I am going to remain another year for the great pilgrimage.'"

The prince's letter reached the cadi. The latter gave all his efforts to the good administration of the country, and, according to the words of the prince, he avoided every negligence.

But one night while he was on watch near the fortifications of the King's palace, Satan came to him and slid into his heart a temptation. The cadi thought in his heart: "The King's daughter is of a marvellous beauty; her name, Djouher-Manikam, is charming; and her face is lovely. Since it is thus, I must marry this daughter of the King." The cadi called the man who was guarding the gate, exclaiming:

"Ho! Guardian of the gate! Open unto me."

The guardian of the gate demanded, "Who is there?"

The cadi replied, "It is I, the cadi."

So the guardian promptly opened the gate, and the cadi entered within the fortification, then went up into the palace and found the princess there saying her evening prayers. He hid behind the lamp in a corner which was dark. When her prayer was finished, the Princess Djouher-Manikam cast her eyes in that direction and saw there was someone standing there in the shadow, so three times again she said the "verse of the Throne"; but she saw that the vision had not yet vanished from her eyes.

Then the princess said in her heart: "What in the world is that? Is it a ghost? Is it a demon? Is it a djinn? If it were, it would have necessarily disappeared when I recited the 'verse of the Throne.'"

The cadi heard these words and said: "O Princess Djouher-Manikam, it is I, the cadi."

"What are you doing here?" asked the princess. He answered, "I wish to marry you."

The Princess Djouher-Manikam said: "O cadi! Why do you act so to me? Have you then no fear of God the most high and worthy of all praise? Do you not blush before the face of my ancestor the prophet Mahomet, the envoy of God? May the peace and blessings of God be upon him! As for me, I am the servant of the Lord and I belong to the religion of the envoy of God. I fear to marry now. And you, cadi, why do you act so? My father gave you a charge. He sent you a letter which commanded you to protect the country and all who dwelt in his palace. Why do you conduct yourself in this fashion toward me?"

The cadi, hearing these words of the Princess Djouher-Manikam, felt a great confusion in his heart. He went out of the palace and returned home full of trouble and emotion. When it was day, the cadi sent a letter to the King Haroun-er-Raschid at Mecca. It was thus conceived: "Your Majesty left me to be guardian of his kingdom, his palace, and his daughter. Now, the Princess Djouher-Manikam desires to marry me. This is the reason why I send this letter to your Majesty." Thus spake the cadi in his letter.

When it reached the prince and he had read it, he immediately summoned his son Minbah-Chahaz. He came in haste, and the King gave him a cutlass and said, "Return to Bagdad and slay your sister, because she will bring shame upon the family by marrying now."

Minbah-Chahaz bowed before his father. Then he set out to return to his own country.

Arriving at the end of his journey, he entered the city, and went up to the palace of the Princess Djouher-Manikam. She was filled with joy and said, "Welcome, O my brother!"

Minbah-Chahaz answered, "O my little sister, our parents will remain for the great pilgrimage."

The brother and sister thus chatting together, the Princess Djouher-Manikam said, "O my brother, I wish to sleep."

"It is well, my sister," answered Minbah-Chahaz; "sleep while your brother combs his little sister's hair." And the princess Djouher-Manikam slept.

Her brother then took a cushion, which he slipped under the head of the young virgin his sister; then he thought in his heart: "If I do not execute the commands of my father, I shall be a traitor to him. But, alas, if I kill my sister, I shall not have a sister any more. If I do not kill her, I shall certainly commit a crime against the most high, because I shall not have obeyed the order of my father. I will fulfil then my father's will. It is a duty obligatory on all children. What good are these subterfuges?" His resolution thus confirmed, he bound his handkerchief over his eyes and directed his cutlass against his sister's neck. But at that instant, by the will of God the most high, a little gazelle came up and, by the power of God the most high, placed its neck upon the neck of the princess Djouher-Manikam, saying, "I will take the place of the princess Djouher-Manikam." And the little gazelle was killed by Minbah-Chahaz. That done he unbound his eyes and saw a little gazelle lying dead with its throat cut, by the side of his young sister the princess Djouher-Manikam.

At this sight, Minbah-Chahaz was stricken with astonishment. He thought in his heart: "Since it is so with my sister, she must be entirely innocent, and cannot have commited the least fault. Nevertheless, although I am confident that she was calumniated by the cadi I must tell my father that I have killed her."

Minbah-Chahaz set out then for Mecca, to find the prince his father. When he had arrived at Mecca he presented to his father the cutlass still stained with blood. The King Harouner-Raschid cried, "Praise be to God, the Lord of the worlds. Our shame is now effaced, since you have poniarded your sister and she is dead." Such were the deeds of this first story.

The princess Djouher-Manikam, having awakened after the departure of Minbah-Chahaz, saw that her brother was no longer there; but that at her side there was a little gazelle with its throat cut. She thought in her heart: "The cadi has slandered me to my father, and that is why my brother came here with orders to kill me." The princess Djouher-Manikam felt a great shame and thought in her heart, "Since it is so, I must retire to a hidden place." Now in the King's park there was a solitary place in the midst of a vast deserted plain. There was a pond of very agreeable appearance there, many kinds of fruit-trees and flowers, and an oratory beautifully built. The princess Djouher-Manikam set out and retired to this place to pray to God the most high and worthy of all praise. She was established there for some time when, by the will of God the most high, a certain thing happened.

Second Story

There was in the country of Damas a king who was named Radja Chah Djouhou. This King wished to go hunting in the deserted forests. His first minister said to him, bowing low: "O my lord, King of the world, why does your Majesty wish to go hunting in foreign countries?"

King Chah Djouhou replied: "I insist upon my plan of going to hunt in foreign lands, in forests far removed from ours. I wish to go from place to place, from plain to plain. Such is my will." The prince set out therefore accompanied by his ministers, his chiefs, and his servants.

They had all been hunting for some time and had not yet found a single bit of game. The prince had directed his march toward the forests of the country of Bagdad. These forests were of immense extent. The heat was excessive, and the prince, being very thirsty, wanted a drink of water. The people who generally carried water for the King said to him: "O lord, sovereign of the world, your Majesty's provision of water is entirely exhausted."

The prince then asked of his officers and servants: "Which of you can get me water? I will reward him with riches and with slaves."

These words were heard by one of his officers named Asraf-el-Kaum. He said: "O my lord, sovereign of the world, give me the vase which will serve for water, and I will go and seek water for your Majesty."

Then the prince said to the people who had brought water for his use, "Give my emerald pitcher into the hands of Asraf-el-Kaum."

The latter bowed low and started to seek water. Seeing from afar a very large fig-tree, he advanced in that direction. Arriving near the tree he saw at its base an oratory and a pond. At the oratory there was a woman of very great beauty. The splendor of her countenance shone like that of the full moon at its fourteenth day. Asraf-el-Kaum, astonished and moved with admiration, thought in his heart: "Is this a human creature, or is it a peri?" and Asraf-el-Kaum saluted the princess Djouher-Manikam, who returned the salutation.

Then the princess asked him, "What is your desire in coming here to my dwelling?"

Asraf-el-Kaum answered, "I have come here to ask you for water, for I have lost my way."

The princess said, "Take water, lord."

Asraf-el-Kaum plunged the emerald pitcher into the pond, and filled it with water. Then he asked permission to return.

Arriving near the King Chah Djouhou he presented the pitcher to the prince, who seized it quickly and drank.

"Asraf-el-Kaum," said the prince, "where did you find such fresh and delicious water? In all my life I have never drunk the like."

Asraf-el-Kaum answered: "O my lord, sovereign of the world, there is a garden in the middle of the plain, and in this garden there is a very large and bushy fig-tree, and at the foot of this tree there is a pond, and near this pond there is an oratory. At this oratory there was a woman who was reading the Koran. This charmingly beautiful woman has no equal in this world. I saluted her and then returned to the presence of the sovereign of the world. That is what I saw, my lord."

"Conduct me to this place," said the King.

"O sovereign of the world, if your Majesty wishes to go thither, let it be with me alone. Let not my lord take his people with him, for it is a woman, and naturally she would be ashamed."

The prince set out then on horseback with Asraf-el-Kaum. The princess Djouher-Manikam, seeing two cavaliers approach, thought in her heart: "I must hide myself, so that I may not be seen." So she left the oratory and went toward the fig-tree. She addressed a prayer to God the most high and worthy of all praise, in these terms:

"O God, I beseech thee, give me a refuge in this tree, for thy servant, O Lord, is ashamed to look upon the faces of these infidels."

Then by the will of God the most high, the tree opened in two and the princess Djouher-Manikam entered by the split, and the tree closed and became as it was before. The King Chah Djouhou and Asraf-el-Kaum arrived at the oratory, but the prince saw nothing of the princess Djouher-Manikam. He was astonished and said:

"O Asraf-el-Kaum, the woman has gone. But just a moment ago I saw her from afar, seated at the oratory, and now she has suddenly disappeared." The prince added: "O Asraf-el-Kaum, perhaps, as with the prophet Zachariah (upon whom be blessings!), her prayer has been answered and she has entered this tree."

Then he offered this prayer to God the most high and worthy of all praise: "O God, if thou wilt permit that this woman be united to thy servant, then grant her to him."

The prayer of the King Chah Djouhou was heard, and a woman of dazzling beauty appeared before his eyes. He desired to seize her, but the princess Djouher-Manikam pronounced these words: "Beware of touching me, for I am a true believer." Hearing these words the King Chah Djouhou drew back, a little ashamed. Then he said:

"Woman, what is your country? Whose child are you, and what is your name?"

The princess answered: "For a long time I have dwelt here, and I have no father nor mother. My name is Djouher-Manikam."

The King, hearing these words of the princess Djouher-Manikam, took off his cloak and gave it to the princess, who covered all her body with it. Then she got up and descended to the ground. Then King Chah Djouhou, dismounting from his horse, received her, put her on his horse, and took her to the country of Damas.

Asraf-el-Kaum then said to the King: "O my lord, sovereign of the world, you made a promise to your servant. Be not careless nor forgetful, my lord."

"Asraf-el-Kaum, be not disturbed. I will fulfil my promise to you. If it pleases God, when I have arrived in our own country, I shall certainly give you all that I promised you." King Chah Djouhou set out for the country of Damas.

After a certain time on the way, the prince came to the city of Damas and entered his palace. He commanded one of his pages to summon the cadi, and a page went promptly to call him. The latter, in all haste, entered the presence of the King. Chah Djouhou said: "O cadi, marry me to the princess

Djouher-Manikam." And the cadi married them. After the celebration of the marriage the prince Chah Djouhou gave to Asraf-el-Kaum 1,000 dinars and some of his slaves, both men and women. King Djouhou and Princess Djouher-Manikam were happy and full of tenderness for each other. Within a few years the princess had two sons, both very beautiful. The prince loved these children very fondly. But above all he loved his wife. He was full of tender solicitude for her, and bore himself with regard to her with the same careful atention that a man uses who carries oil in the hollow of his hand. Some time later Princess Djouher-Manikam had another son of great beauty. The prince loved this third child tenderly. He gave him a great number of nurses and governesses, as is the custom for the children of the greatest kings. And he never ceased to bestow upon him the most watchful care.

It happened one day that the ministers, the chiefs, and the courtiers of the King, all gathered in his presence, were enjoying all sorts of sport and amusements. The prince showed himself very joyous, and the princess herself played and amused herself with the three children. Her countenance shone with the brightness of rubies; but happening to think of her father, her mother, and her brother, she began to weep and said: "Alas, how unhappy I am! If my father, mother, and brother could see my three children, necessarily their affection for me would be greater." And the princess Djouher-Manikam burst into sobs. The prince, who was not far from there, heard her, and as the princess did not stop weeping he asked her: "O princess, why do you weep thus? What do I lack in your eyes? Is it riches or physical beauty or noble birth? Or is it the spirit of justice? Tell me what is the cause of your tears?"

Princess Djouher-Manikam answered: Sovereign of the world, your Majesty has not a single fault. Your riches equal those of Haroun. Your beauty equals that of the prophet Joseph (peace be upon him!). Your extraction equals that of the envoy of God (Mahomet). May the benediction of God and blessings rest upon him! Your justice equals that of King Rouchirouan. I don't see a single fault in you, my lord."

King Chah Djouhou said: "If it is thus, why then does my princess shed tears?"

Princess Djouher-Manikam answered: "If I wept thus while playing with my three children, it is because I thought that if my father, my mother, and my brother should see my three children, necessarily their affection for me would be greater. And that is why I shed tears."

King Chah Djouhou said to her: "O my young wife, dear princess, are your father and mother still living? What is your father's name?"

Princess Djouher-Manikam answered, "O my lord, my father is named Haroun-er-Raschid, King of Bagdad."

Clasping her in his arms and kissing her, the prince asked her: "Why, until this day have you not told the truth to your husband?"

And the princess answered: "I wished to avow the truth, but perhaps my lord would not have had faith. It is on account of the children that I tell the truth."

King Chah Djouhou answered: "Since it is so, it is fitting that we should start, and make a visit upon King Haroun-er-Raschid."

He called his ministers, ordered them to make all the preparations, and commanded them to place in order ingots of gold and ingots of silver on which were graven the name of King Haroun-er-Raschid; and his ministers' vestments woven of goats' hair and fine wool, stuffs of price, many kinds of superb precious stones of various colors, formed the burden of forty camels, which bore these presents to the King, his father-in-law, in the city of Bagdad.

During the night Princess Djouher thought in her heart: "If the two kings meet, there will necessarily be discord, and at the end separation." Having thus thought she said to her husband: "O sovereign of the world, do not set out at the same time with me, for in my opinion the meeting of the two kings would have as a final result a disagreement. Permit me therefore to start first with the three children, that I may present them to my father and mother. Give the command to conduct me to the country of Bagdad, near my father, to whomsoever you shall judge worthy of your confidence for this mission."

When the prince heard these words of the princess whom he loved so tenderly and whose wishes he granted, he ordered his ministers and chiefs to arrange the transport of the princess and her children. Addressing the ministers he said as follows: "O you my ministers, whom among you can I charge to conduct safely my wife and three children to Bagdad, near their ancestor King Haroun-er-Raschid?"

No one among them dared approach and speak. All held silence. Then the prince, addressing the oldest minister of all, said:

"O my minister, it is you to whom, following the dictates of my heart, I can trust to accompany my wife and three children. For I have always found you loyal and faithful to me. Beside, you are older than the other ministers. And you have the fear of God the most high and worthy of all praise as well as respect for your King."

The minister said: "O my lord, it is in all sincerity that your servant puts above his head the commands of your Majesty. I shall do my whole duty in conducting the princess and her children to the King Haroun-er-Raschid."

So the King Chah Djouhou trusted his wife and his three children to this perfidious minister, reposing upon the promise he had made. Forty camels were laden with presents, forty nurses for the children, one hundred ladies in the suite of the princess, a thousand cavaliers, well armed and well equipped, formed the escort. The princess took leave of her husband. He held her clasped in his arms, and, weeping, covered her and his three children with kisses. He bade her to present his homage to her father the Sultan Haroun-er-Raschid, his salutations to her elder brother Minbah-Chahaz, and to place at the feet of their majesties a thousand and a thousand apologies, and to make his excuses to her brother Minbah-Chahaz. Then the prince said to the wicked minister:

"O my minister, you must go now, and lead the camel of my wife, for I have perfect confidence in you. Above all, guard her well."

But the King did not lean upon God the most high and worthy of all praise, and that is why God punished him.

When the prince had finished speaking to the minister the latter said: "O my lord, King of the world, your servant bears your command on his head." So the cavalcade started on the march. Princess Djouher-Manikam mounted her camel with her three children. A body-guard held the van. She proceeded accompanied by the wretched minister and all the escort, wending from day to day toward the city of Bagdad. They had reached one of the halting-places when day was turning into night. The minister then erected a tent so that the princess might repose in it. The people put up their tents all about. Princess Djouher-Manikam dismounted from her camel and entered the tent, with her three children. The tents of the nurses and ladies-in-waiting surrounded the tent of the princess in a circle. In the middle of the night a violent rain began to fall. Then the wretched minister, stirred by Satan, was stirred in his heart. He thought: "The King's wife is most beautiful; beautiful, indeed, as her name, Djouher-Manikam. I must marry her."

So the rebel minister started, and entered the tent of the princess, and asked her to marry him. He found her seated by her three children, occupied in chasing away the mosquitoes. When the princess saw him enter her tent she asked him: "O my minister, what brings you to my tent at this hour in the middle of the night?"

The minister answered, "I have come to beg you to marry me."

The princess then said: "Is that what brings you here? And it was to you that the King intrusted me on account of your great age, and as if you were my father. It was in you that he put all his confidence that you would take us safely, me and my children, to my venerable father, King Haroun-er-Raschid. What must be your nature, that you should so betray his trust?"

The wretched minister replied: "If you refuse to marry me, I will kill your children."

"Never," said the princess, "never shall I consent to marry you. And if you kill my children, what can I do against the decree of God, save to invoke his name?"

The minister killed one of the children. When it was dead, he made the same demand on the princess for the second time, and she answered: "Never shall I consent to marry you."

The minister said: "If you refuse, I shall kill another of your children."

The Princess Djouher-Manikam answered: "If you slay my child, it is by the decree of God, and I submit to his will."

The minister killed the second child.

"No," repeated the princess. "Never shall I consent to wed you."

The wretched minister said: "Then I will kill your third child."

"If you kill him, what can I do but to submit to the will of God, and invoke his name?" The third son of the King was killed.

Questioned anew, the princess said again, "Never shall I marry you."

And the wicked minister said: "If you will not marry me, I will kill you, too."

Then the princess thought in her heart: "If I do not appear to yield, he will kill me, too, without a doubt. I must employ a trick." Then she said: "Await me here, until I wash from my clothes and my body the stains of my children's blood."

The minister accursed of God replied: "Very well. I await you here."

Then the princess Djouher went out of her tent. The rain was falling in torrents. The princess, fleeing precipitately, walked during the whole night, not knowing where she was going. She had walked many hours when day broke. The princess arrived thus near a tree in the midst of the plain, and, having measured its height with her eyes, she climbed into it. At this moment there passed along the road a merchant who had made his sales and was returning to the city of Bassrah. His name was Biyapri. Passing beneath the tree he raised his eyes and beheld a woman seated in the tree.

"Who are you?" he said; "are you woman or djinn?"

"I am neither demon nor djinn, but a descendant of the prophet of God (may blessings rest upon him), a disciple of the prophet Mahomet, envoy of God."

Biyapri climbed up the tree, put her on his camel, and taking up his journey conducted her to the country of Bassrah. Arriving at his house he desired to marry her. But she put him off saying: "Wait, for I have made a solemn vow before God not to look upon the face of a man for forty days. When the time expires, that will be possible. But if these forty days have not yet run I should surely die." So Biyapri installed her on his latticed roof and lavished attention and care upon her.

Immediately after the flight of the princess Djouher-Manikam the minister commanded the whole escort to return and present itself to the King Chah Djouhou. He said to his people: "O all your servants of the Queen, see what has been her conduct. Her three children are dead, and it is she who killed them. After that she disappeared. Where has she taken refuge? Nobody in the world knows that. As for you, depart, bear the bodies of his three children to King Chah Djouhou, and tell him all the circumstances."

Arriving in the presence of the King, they reported all the circumstances of the minister's treachery toward the princess, and the murder of his three children. They added that the minister had departed, leaving word that he had gone to find the princess, and had taken with him his own three sons, forty soldiers, and the treasure.

When the prince had heard these words he was struck with a stupor. But his sorrow at having let the princess go without him was useless. He caused the three young princes to be buried. The King shed tears, and all the people of the household filled the air with cries and sobs, so that the noise seemed like the bursts of thunder, while the funeral ceremonies were proceeding according to the customs of the greatest kings. After that the King descended from his royal throne and became a dervish, the better to seek in all lands his well-beloved spouse. He had with him three slaves only. One of them was named Hestri.

"Go," he said to him, "go seek your mistress in all countries." And he gave him a horse and some provisions.

Hestri said: "May your Majesty be happy! O lord, King of the world, whatever be your commands, your servant places them upon his head." Hestri bowed low, then mounted his horse and rode away toward the city of Bassrah.

After proceeding some time he reached Bassrah, and passed by the house of Biyapri. At this very moment the princess Djouher-Manikam was sitting on the roof of Biyapri's house. She looked attentively at the face of Hestri as he was passing by the house and called to him saying: "Hestri, what brings you here?"

Hestri, casting his glance toward the roof, saw the princess Djouher-Manikam and said to her: "I was sent by your husband to seek you, princess."

She replied: "Go away, for the present. Come back when it is night. As it is broad daylight now I fear lest Biyapri should discover our departure."

Hestri, bowing low, replied, "Very well, princess." He walked here and there, waiting till night should come. When it was dark he returned to the house of Biyapri and waited a few minutes. Then he called the princess.

"Wait," she said, "for Biyapri is still watching." Hestri stooped down, and fell asleep near Biyapri's house, having first of all tied the bridle of the horse to his girdle.

The princess Djouher-Manikam descended from the roof, and mounted the horse while Hestri was yet sleeping. She sat on the horse waiting till Hestri should awake. But an Æthiopian robber, who had come to rob the storehouse of Biyapri, saw the horse whose bridle was attached to the belt of Hestri. He unfastened the bridle and led the horse to the middle of the plain. In the mind of the princess it was Hestri who was thus leading the horse. But the moon having risen, the Æthiopian saw seated upon the horse a woman of a striking and marvellous beauty. The heart of the Æthiopian was filled with joy. He said in his heart:

"For a very long time have I been stealing riches. Truly, I have acquired no small store of jewels, pearls, precious stones, gold and silver, and magnificent vestments of all sorts. But all that is nothing in comparison with the marvel I have just now found and who will become my wife, the light of my eyes, and the fruit of my heart. Now shall I enjoy in peace the happiness of having such a wife."

The house of the Æthiopian robber was seated on the top of a hill. He conducted the princess thither, showed her all it contained, and gave it to her, saying: "O my future bride, it is to you that all which this house contains belongs. Make use of it according to your good pleasure." The princess said, "First of all, be tranquil." And she thought in her heart: "This is my destiny. First I was with Biyapri, and now I have fallen into the hands of an Æthiopian robber. It is by the will of God that this has happened to his servant." The Æthiopian robber was bent on having the marriage celebrated at once, but the princess said: "I cannot be married now, for I have made a vow to God the most high not to see the face of a man for three days."

The Æthiopian robber desired to drink, and said: "Come, let us drink together."

"In my opinion," observed the princess, "if we begin to drink both together you will become heavy with wine, and I, too. Then they will take me far from you and kill you. Come, I will fill your cup and you shall drink first. When you have drunk enough, then I will drink in my turn, and you shall fill my cup."

The Æthiopian robber was very joyful at these words of the princess. "What you say is true," said he. He received with great pleasure the cup from the hands of the princess and drank. After emptying the cup many times he fell down in the stupor of intoxication, losing his senses and becoming like a dead man. The princess Djouher-Manikam put on a magnificent costume of a man, and adding a weapon something like a *kandjar*, went out of the house. Then mounting her horse she rode forward quickly and came to the foot of the hill. She directed her course toward the country of Roum, and continuing her journey from forest to forest, and from plain to plain, she reached the gate of the fortifications of the city of Roum at the moment when the King of that country had just died.

When the princess Djouher-Manikam had arrived outside the fortifications of Roum, she sat down in the *baley*, near the fort. She was marvellously beautiful, and her vestments, all sparkling with gold, were adorned with precious stones, pearls, and rubies. A man happening to pass by saw her, and was seized with astonishment and admiration. For in the country of Roum there was nobody who could compare with this young man, so handsome and so magnificently attired. He asked:

"Whence come you and why did you come here?"

The princess answered: "I know not the place where I am at this moment. I came from the city of Damas."

This citizen of Roum took leave and went away to present himself to the vezir and tell what he had seen. The vezir, having heard him, went out promptly to find the young man. As soon as he had approached him and had seen his remarkable beauty and his splendid vestments decorated with precious stones, pearls, and rubies, the vezir seated himself by him and said:

"Young man, whence do you come, and why did you come to this land?"

The princess answered: "I wish to travel through the world for my pleasure. That is my will."

The vezir replied: "Would you like to have us make you King of this country?" The princess replied: "For what reason should I wish to be king in this country? And by what means could it be achieved?"

The vezir replied: "Our King is dead."

"Is there no child?" asked the princess.

"The King has left a child," answered the vezir, "but he is still very little, and incapable of governing his subjects. That is why we will make you King of this country."

The princess Djouher-Manikam answered: "Why not? What prevents? If you all will follow my counsel I will accept the throne of this country."

The ministers said, "And why should we not follow the commands of my lord?".

The vezir conducted her to the palace. All the ministers of state and the high officers assembled to proclaim as their king the princess Djouher-Manikam. That done, the princess took the name of Radja Chah Djouhou.

After reigning some time her spirit of justice and her perfect equity in the government of her subjects rendered her name celebrated in all the foreign countries. Radja Chah Djouhou said to her minister:

"O minister, have built for me a *baley* outside the fort." And the ministers and the officers commanded them in haste to construct the *baley*. As soon as it was built they came to announce it to the King. The latter said:

"O my vezir, is there in my kingdom a man who knows how to paint?"

"Yes, my lord, king of the world, there is a very skilful painter here."

" Let him come to me."

" Immediately, my lord," said the vezir, and he ordered a slave to go and summon the painter. The painter came in all haste and entered the presence of Radja Chah Djouhou, bowing his head to the floor. The prince said to him:

" O painter, have you a daughter who knows how to paint?"

The painter answered: " Yes, my lord, king of the world, I have a daughter very skilful in the art of painting."

" Tell your child to come here."

The painter bowed again and went to find his daughter. " O my child," he said, " the fruit of my heart, come, the King calls you."

Then the painter's daughter quickly set out, accompanied by her father. They together entered the presence of the King, who was still surrounded by his ministers and his officers. The painter and his daughter bowed their heads to the floor. The prince said:

" Painter, is this your daughter?"

" O my lord, king of the world, yes, this is my daughter."

" Come with me into the interior of the palace." And at the same time the prince started and entered his apartments, followed by the daughter of the painter. He led the way to a retired place, and said: " My daughter, make my portrait, I pray you, and try to have the resemblance good." Then the princess Djouher-Manikam clothed herself in woman's raiment, and in this costume she was ravishingly beautiful. That done, she commanded the artist to paint her thus. She succeeded perfectly and the portrait was a remarkable likeness, for the daughter of the painter was very skilful. When her work was finished she received a large sum in gold. The prince said to her:

" Come, sister, let this remain a secret. Reveal it not to anyone in the world. If you tell it I will slay you, with your father and your mother."

The daughter of the painter said: " O my lord, king of the world, how could your servant disobey your Majesty's commands?" She bowed low, and asked permission to go home.

Radja Chah Djouhou, in the presence of his ministers and his subjects, said to the vizier: " O vizier, place this portrait in the *baley* outside the fort, and have it guarded by forty men. If anyone coming to this portrait begins to weep or kiss it, seize him and bring him before me." The portrait hung in the *baley*, and the vezir ordered an officer to guard it with forty soldiers.

When the Æthiopian robber came out of his drunken slumber he saw that the princess Djouher-Manikam was no longer in his house. So he went out-of-doors weeping, and took up his journey, going from country to country until he arrived at the city of Roum. There he saw a *baley*, and hanging there a portrait which bore a perfect resemblance to the princess Djouher-Manikam. Quickly he climbed to the *baley*, and, holding the portrait in his arms, he wept and covered it with kisses.

"O unhappy man that I am! Here is the portrait of my well-beloved for whom I was seeking. Where can she be?"

The guards of the *baley*, seeing the act of the Æthiopian, seized him and bore him before the King. They told the deed.

The prince said: "Æthiopian robber, why did you act thus in reference to this picture?"

The Æthiopian answered: "O my lord, king of the world, I ask you a thousand and a thousand pardons. Your servant will tell the truth. If they kill me I shall die; if they hang me I shall be lifted very high; if they sell me I shall be carried very far away. O king of the world, hear the words of your humble slave. A certain night I had started out to rob. I found a horse, and on its back there was a woman of the most marvellous beauty. I took her to my house. I fell asleep in my cups. My beloved one disappeared. I became mad, and so it is, O king of the world, that your slave came to the fort and saw the portrait hanging at the *baley*. This portrait is the faithful picture of my well-beloved. That is why I weep."

The prince said: "O my vezir, let this man be carefully guarded. Treat him well and give him plenty to eat." On the other hand, Biyapri, after forty days, mounting the roof, saw that the princess Djouher was no longer there. He became mad, abandoned his house and all his wealth, and, becoming a dervish, went from country to country seeking the princess Djouher-Manikam, without ever finding her. Coming to the country of Roum he saw the *baley* situated outside the fort, and stopped there. Then he saw the portrait, and, observing it with the closest attention, he began to weep. Then he took it in his arms and covered it with kisses.

"Alas, my well-beloved!" he cried, "here indeed is your picture, but where can I find you?" He was immediately seized by the guard and led before the King of Roum.

"Biyapri," said the prince, "whence do you come, and why did you act thus?" Biyapri answered: "O my lord, king of the world, your slave asks pardon a thousand and a thousand times. I will tell the whole truth. If they kill me, I shall die; if they hang me, I shall be lifted very high; if they sell me, I shall be taken very far away. When I was engaged in commerce I passed under a tree, and saw that in this tree there was a woman of the most marvellous beauty. I took her and carried her to the city of Bassrah and installed her on the roof of my storehouse. A certain night she disappeared without my knowing where she had gone. Then, O king of the world, I became as one mad and left my native land. Arriving at the country of Roum I saw a *baley* outside the fort and came to sit down there. Then, my lord, I saw the portrait hanging at the *baley*. It exactly resembles my beloved, whom I lost. I pressed it in my arms and covered it with kisses. Such is the truth, O king of the world."

The prince then said to his minister: "O minister, let this man be carefully guarded and give him food and clothes."

The King of Damas, after abdicating the throne, had left his kingdom, and in the costume of a dervish had started to travel through the different countries. Arriving at Roum, the King Chah Djouhou saw a *baley* situated outside of the fort, and went to sit down near it. The prince looking closely at the portrait, which was exactly like the princess Djouher-Manikam, burst into a flood of tears and exclaimed:

"Alas! Fruit of my heart, my well-beloved, light of my eyes! It is, indeed, your picture. But you, whom I seek, oh, where are you?"

Speaking thus, the prince took the portrait in his arms and covered it with kisses. Seeing this, the guards of the *baley* seized him and carried him before the King.

The King said to him: "My lord, whence do you come?

How have you wandered into this country? And why did you behave thus about my portrait?"

The King Chah Djouhou answered: "Know that my wife, who is named the princess Djouher-Manikam, has disappeared far from me. It is for that reason that I have left my kingdom, and that I, dressed as a dervish, have walked from country to country, from plain to plain, from village to village, seeking her whom I have never been able to find. But arriving in your Majesty's country I saw hanging at the *baley* that portrait, which is of a striking resemblance to my wife. It is for this reason that I wept in contemplating this picture."

The princess smiled, and at the same time her heart was softened at seeing the conduct of her husband. She said to her prime minister: "O my minister, I confide this person to your care. Treat him worthily, give him the best of food and a suite of attendants. He is the King of Damas."

The minister therefore, by command of the princess, departed and conducted the King of Damas to a fine house, furnished and equipped according to the needs of kings.

The minister took all the riches which had been intended as presents for the King Haroun-er-Raschid. The ingots of gold and of silver, the rich garments in fine stuffs of the country of Rouzoungga, as well as the vestments of the princess Djouher-Manikam and of her three children, were transported and sold in the city of Bagdad. But the King Haroun-er-Raschid, seeing that his name and that of his daughter, the princess Djouher-Manikam, were graven on these ingots of gold and silver, seized all these riches.

The minister of the country of Damas said, "These riches are mine."

On his side the King Haroun-er-Raschid said: "These riches are mine, for my name and that of my child are engraved on these ingots of gold and silver."

The minister said, "Since your Majesty declares that these treasures are yours, we must try this case in a court of justice."

The King of Bagdad answered: "It is well. We will go wherever you wish."

"Very well," said the minister; "let us go then before the

King of the country of Roum. That prince has the reputation of being extremely just. Each of us shall plead his cause."

The prince answered: "It is well." The minister replied: "O king of the world, let us start without delay."

So the King Haroun-er-Raschid set out with his son Minbah-Chahaz, his chief warrior, and his soldiers. The cadi accompanied the prince. On his side, the minister of the country of Damas started, accompanied by his three sons and forty soldiers of the country of Damas. After proceeding some time, they arrived at the city of Roum and entered the fortifications. Each one of them presented himself before the King and pleaded his cause.

The King Haroun-er-Raschid expressed himself as follows: "O king of the world! I present myself before your Majesty to ask your impartial judgment. The minister of the country of Damas brought to Bagdad, among other precious objects, ingots of gold and ingots of silver, on which are engraved my name and that of my daughter, the princess Djouher-Manikam. I seized these, and come to your Majesty to decide my claim to them."

The King of Roum said: "If it pleases God the most high, this affair shall be judged with the best of my powers." The King of Roum continued: "My officers and you, my ministers and chiefs, seek all the divine inspiration to decide the difference existing between the King of Bagdad and the minister of Damas."

The officers bowed low and said: "O my lord, king of the world, whatever they may be, we shall put the commands of your Majesty above our heads and shall carry them out to the letter." And they deliberated on the character of the dispute.

The King of Bagdad declared: "These objects are precious to me, for they bear engraven upon them the names of myself and my child."

On the other hand, and at the same time, the minister Damas declared, "These precious objects are mine."

The ministers and chiefs were very much embarrassed, and said to the King: "O king of the world, we, all of us, are unable to judge this dispute. It is too difficult for us. Only the impartial judgment of your Majesty can decide it."

The prince said: "It is well. I will pronounce sentence, if it please God the most high, provided that you consent to accept it."

The King of Bagdad answered: "O king of the world, judge between us according to your impartial justice."

The King of Roum then said: "O minister of Damas, and you, King of Bagdad, is it the wish of both of you that I should give judgment according to the judgment of God the most high?"

And they both answered: "That is what we ask, the judgment of God."

The prince replied: "If you consent on both sides, it is well."

"I consent to it," said the minister of Damas.

"And I, too," said the King of Bagdad.

The King of Roum then spoke in these terms: "In conformity with the law of the most high God, I ask this question of the King of Bagdad: Have you a daughter?"

The King of Bagdad replied: "Yes, king of the world, I have a daughter and a son."

"And have you at present these two children?"

The King of Bagdad answered: "I have my son, but my daughter—I lost her."

The King of Roum, continuing, said: "What is the cause of the loss of your daughter?" The King of Bagdad answered: "O king of the world, hear my story. While I was gone on a pilgrimage with my wife and my son, whose name is Minbah-Chahaz, I left my daughter to watch over my palace. Arriving at the end of my pilgrimage, I sent home a letter to the cadi, conceived as follows: 'May peace be with the cadi: I shall wait still for the grand pilgrimage about a year longer. As for all that concerns my kingdom, my palace, and my daughter, the princess Djouher-Manikam, watch with greatest care, and beware of any negligence in the protection of my kingdom and my child.' Some time later the cadi sent me a letter at Mecca, couched in these words: 'O king of the world, your servant has received the command to watch over the palace and the princess. But the princess now desires to marry me.' After I had read the letter from the cadi I called my son Minbah-Chahaz, and said to him: 'Start at once for

Bagdad, and slay your sister.' My son Minbah-Chahaz started immediately for Bagdad, and killed his sister. Then he returned and found me at Mecca. His cutlass was still blood-stained. Then I cried: 'Praise be to God the Lord of the universe, our shame is effaced.' Such is my story, O king of the world."

The King of Roum said: "It is well. Now I shall pronounce judgment." And addressing the minister of Damas he said to him: "O minister of Damas, tell me the truth if you wish that at the day of judgment the prophet should intercede for you (may the peace and blessings of God be upon him!). Speak and tell the truth. Say whence come these riches, in order that I may pronounce my judgment between you."

The minister of the King of Damas said: "O my lord, king of the world, I will lay at the foot of your Majesty's throne the completed story from the beginning. I received a mission from the King Chah Djouhou: 'O my minister,' he said, 'start, I send you to the city of Bagdad, taking my three children to their grandfather, and my wife, the princess Djouher-Manikam, to her mother and her father, the King Harouner-Raschid.' I set out, therefore, with the escort which accompanied the princess Djouher-Manikam, and we arrived at our first halting-place. When it was night I erected a tent, and the people of the escort all put up tents around that of the princess. But Satan breathed into my heart a temptation. This thought came to me: 'The wife of the King is wonderfully beautiful, and she has such a pretty name! I will go and ask her to marry me.' So I entered her tent. At that moment she was seated by her sleeping children, occupied in keeping away the mosquitoes. The princess demanded, 'O my minister, why do you come here?' And I answered, 'I have come to ask you to marry me.' The princess said: 'Have you no fear of God the most high? No, I cannot marry you. What would become of me if I should do such a thing?' Then I said, 'If you will not agree to marry me, I will kill one of your children.' The princess answered: 'If you kill my child it will be by the judgment of God, and what can I do but to invoke his name?' Then I killed one of the children. When he was dead I asked again if she would marry me, and I killed another of the children. When this one was dead I asked the same question. The princess answered, 'I cannot marry when I am already married.' I said to her, 'If you will not, then I will kill the third of your children.' The princess Djouher-Manikam answered, 'If you kill my third child, it will be by the judgment of God, and what can I do but invoke his name, for I am only a woman?' So I killed the third child. After the death of this last child of the King, I put again my question to the princess. She would not corsent to marry me. I said to her, 'If you don't, I will kill you.' She answered: 'If you kill me, it is the decree of God. But wait awhile, for I wish to wash my garments and cleanse the traces of my children's blood from my body.' I said, 'It is well. We will have the wedding-feast to-morrow.' She left the tent. It was raining in torrents. I could not discover where she went. Such is my story, O king of the world."

The King said, "Minister of the country of Damas, have you any sons?"

He answered, "Yes, my lord, king of the world, I have three sons."

The prince said: "Let your three sons come here, in order that I may give judgment quickly, according to the law instituted by the prophet (may the peace and blessings of God be upon him!). Behold what his law prescribes: The minister killed the children of the princess Djouher-Manikam. It is not, therefore, the minister who should be punished with death, but his children should be slain. The execution of this judgment will be the just application of the law of retaliation between the minister and the princess."

The minister summoned his three sons. As soon as they had come, he pointed them to the King of Roum.

The latter said to his minister, "O minister, where is the Æthiopian whom they brought here?" The Æthiopian robber was brought out, and prostrated himself before the King of Roum.

The King of Roum said to him: "Æthiopian, return to your own country and change your mode of life. You will never see again the woman for whom you are seeking." And the prince gave him a *keti* of gold.

Then the prince said: "O my minister, where is Biyapri?

Let them bring him here." So they brought Biyapri. When he arrived he bowed low before the prince.

The prince said: "Biyapri, go back to your own country and change your conduct. The woman whom you seek you will never see again." And the prince made him a gift of two *keti* of gold.

The King of Roum then said: "Let all assemble. I am about to pronounce judgment between the King of Bagdad and the minister of Damas." The minister and the officers assembled therefore in the presence of the King, together with many of his subjects.

The King of Roum said: "O my executioner, let the three children of the minister of Damas be all killed; such is the divine command." So the children of the minister of Damas were all three killed.

After they were dead the prince said: "Minister, return to the country of Damas, with a rag for your girdle, and during your last days change your conduct. If you do not know it, I am the princess Djouher-Manikam, daughter of the Sultan of Bagdad, wife of Chah Djouhou, my lord, and the sister of Minbah-Chahaz. God has stricken your eyes with blindness on account of your crimes toward me. It is the same with the cadi of the city of Bagdad."

The minister of Damas, seized with fear, trembled in all his limbs. He cast himself at the feet of the princess Manikam, and thus prostrated he implored pardon a thousand and a thousand times. Then he returned to Damas all in tears, and overwhelmed with grief at the death of his three sons. The cadi, covered with shame on account of his treachery to the Sultan of Bagdad, fled and expatriated himself.

The King of Roum commanded them to bring the King Chah Djouhou and give him a garment all sparkling with gold, and he sent him to dwell in the company of his father-in-law, the Sultan of Bagdad, and his brother-in-law, the prince Minbah-Chahaz.

Then the princess Djouher-Manikam retired. She entered the palace and returned clad in the garments of a woman. She then went out, accompanied by ladies of the court, and went to present herself to her father, the Sultan of Bagdad. She bowed before her father, her brother the prince Minbah-Chahaz, and her husband, the King Chah Djouhou. The princess said: "O all of you, lords and warriors of the country of Roum, know that I am a woman, and not a man. Behold my father, the Sultan Haroun-er-Raschid, King of Bagdad. Behold my brother, whose name is Minbah-Chahaz; and behold my husband, the King Chah Djouhou, who reigns over the country of Damas. From the time when you placed me upon the throne of Roum, if I have committed any fault by error or by ignorance, you must excuse me, for constantly the servants of God commit faults by error or ignorance. It is only God alone who forgets not, nor neglects, and is free from error or ignorance."

The grandees of the country of Roum said: "Never has your Majesty committed the least fault, either by ignorance or by error, during the time you have reigned over the country of Roum. Nevertheless, among the judgments just now rendered there was a fault committed by your glorious Majesty. The minister killed, the princess killed, both did it voluntarily. It was a fault of judgment for the princess Djouher-Manikam to have killed the children of the minister, just as the minister committed a fault in killing the children of the princess. There was a likeness there. Still, if it pleases her Majesty to remain upon the throne of Roum, we should all be very glad of it."

The princess Djouher said: "I shall take leave of you, my lords. It is good that we should make the young prince king, and that he should replace me on the throne."

The ministers and the officers of Roum responded, "Whatever be the commands of your Majesty, we place them above our heads."

Then the princess made the royal prince her successor, and the ministers and officers and subjects all bowed low, placed their hands above their heads, and proclaimed him King.

The princess Djouher-Manikam said: "O my child, here are the last instructions your mother gives you: You must practise justice so that God will make strong your realm. To you, my ministers and officers, I confide my child. If he commits some faults by negligence or by ignorance, I pray you take them not too much to heart, for my child is young, and he has not yet attained all the maturity of his judgment."

The ministers and officers answered: "O your Majesty, may your prosperity grow forever! How could it be possible for us to disobey your commands?"

The princess replied: "O my child, above all must you observe justice and be patient and liberal toward your ministers and officers and all your subjects, so that the favors of God may increase upon your person and that your kingdom may be protected by God the most high by the grace of the intercession of the prophet Mahomet, the envoy of God (may the peace and blessings of God be with him!). O my child, you must govern all your subjects with a spirit of justice, for in this world, until death, we ought to seek the truth. O my child, above all forget not my last instructions." Then, taking in her arms the royal child, she kissed him.

The Sultan Haroun-er-Raschid having told the Sultan of Roum that he wished to return to the country of Bagdad, the Sultan gave orders to his ministers to assemble the grandees, the officers, and the soldiers, with elephants, horses, and instruments of music. All came with presents, for the Sultan of Roum wished to accompany the Sultan Haroun-er-Raschid as far as Bagdad and carry him the presents. The favorable moment having arrived, the Sultan Haroun-er-Raschid departed from Roum, directing his way to the country of Bagdad, from plain to plain, and from halting-place to halting-place. After journeying some time, they rejoicing all the way, they arrived at the country of Bagdad.

The ministers, the chiefs, and the soldiers came out to meet the Sultan Haroun-er-Raschid, and they entered the palace. Then the Queen hastened to find the Sultan and her daughter, the princess Djouher-Manikam. Meeting her daughter, she pressed her in her arms and covered her with kisses. She said in tears: "Alas, my child! the fruit of my heart! I, your mother thought that she would never see you again." And she covered her body with tears and kisses, while she kept repeating, "Alas, my child! I thought you lost forever." Then the Queen bowed before the Sultan Haroun-er-Raschid. Her son, Minbah-Chahaz, then came to bow before his mother, but the latter pressed him in her arms and kissed him. Then her son-in-law, King Chah Djouhou, advanced and bowed before the Queen in his turn. And she pressed him in her arms and kissed him. All were in tears.

The Sultan Haroun-er-Raschid started for the hall of audience, and gave orders to one of his heralds to assemble his ministers, his warriors, and his subjects. When they were all gathered together the Sultan said: "Now I wish to entertain the ministers, the chiefs, and the officers who escorted us here." When the Sultan had finished entertaining them they desired to take leave and return to the country of Roum. The Sultan Haroun-er-Raschid made them gifts of vestments of honor, to each according to his rank. They prostrated themselves at his feet, and then returned in peace to the country of Roum.

Afterward, the Sultan Haroun-er-Raschid ordered one of his heralds to assemble his ministers, his officers, and his subjects. Once gathered together, the prince said: "O all of you, my ministers and my officers, you must build me a house of baths seven stories high, on the public square of Bagdad."

All responded, "O my lord, king of the world, whatever your commands may be, your servants place them above their heads." And all, ministers, officers, and subjects, gave themselves to the work, each of them doing what was directed by the architect. After some time, the palace of baths was finished. It was sumptuously adorned with curtains of silk, canopies, tapestries woven with gold and fringed with pearls. Rugs embroidered with gold were stretched on the different floors, and there was a quantity of torches and lanterns.

Then the builders came before the King and said: "O my lord, king of the world, your slaves have finished their work according to the commands of your Majesty."

The King Haroun-er-Raschid gave thanks unto God the most high, worthy of all praise, the true Lord who accords to his servants all their needs.

Then the festivals began. For forty days and forty nights the bands never stopped playing. There were sports, banquets, amusements of all sorts. They gave themselves noisily to pleasure, because the Sultan was going to proceed to the ceremony of the bath of the two spouses, his children. When the watches were finished and the favorable moment had come, the Sultan was arrayed in a magnificent garment embroidered with gold, while the princess Djouher-Manikam was adorned by her mother with superb veils and vestments trimmed with jewels, with pearls and precious stones of an incomparable richness. The spouses thus adorned, the Sultan made them mount a palanquin. His son, Minbah-Chahaz, was clad in a splendid costume.

The Sultan mounted his horse Sembaran, and his saddle was of carved gold. Surrounded by young princes and lords, by officers of his court and the standards, Haroun-er-Raschid marched at the head. He advanced, followed by princes, ministers, and officers. The wives of the grandees accompanied the Queen with her maids-of-honor, and all the musical instruments gave forth their harmonious sounds. Seven times they made the circuit of the city. When the two spouses had arrived at the foot of the Palace of Baths the Sultan made them ascend. Then came the spouses of the grandees with the Queen, who showered them with rice-powder mixed with amber and musk, and poured on their heads spikenard and *curcuma* (turmeric). They were both plunged into a bath of rose-water and extracts of all sorts of aromatic flowers, together with water from the sacred fountain of Zemzem.

The ceremonies of the bath finished, the two spouses went out of the Palace of Baths and went into the King's palace. On their arrival, they served a repast to the princes, the *orilemas,* the doctors of the law, the priests, the ministers, the officers, the common people, men and women. All without exception took part in the feast. When it was ended one of the doctors of the law recited the prayer asking God for perfect happiness, sheltered from all danger in this life and the next. Then he sprinkled showers of the most charming perfumes.

After that the Chah Djouhou went to find the Sultan, and said to him: "O my lord, king of the world, I have to ask your Majesty a favor and pardon. I wish to take leave of your Majesty and return to the country of Damas, for the country of Damas is forsaken, O my lord."

The Sultan said, "It is well, my lord. Your country, truly, is separated from its King. If it were not for your kingdom I would wish never to be separated from you, now that I have my daughter back again. But if I am inclined to commit a fault, do not comply with it."

Radja Chah Djouhou answered: "Your daughter is like a

soul which has entered my body. That is how I feel. But the countless favors of your Majesty to me, I place them above my head."

The Sultan Haroun-er-Raschid then said to his prime minister: "O my minister, get ready to start 3,000 soldiers and 300 horsemen. And have elephants or horses well equipped to transport my two children, husband and wife." When the escort was ready, then the Sultan commanded them to open the place where his treasures were stored, and forty-four camels were laden with riches, with vestments of woven gold and precious objects such as are found only in the palaces of kings.

All these preparations being finished, Radja Chah Djouhou took leave of his father-in-law, his mother-in-law, and his brother-in-law, Minbah-Chahaz. The latter all held in their arms and covered with kisses the princess Djouher-Manikam, as well as Radja Chah Djouhou. He and his brother-in-law Minbah-Chahaz wept as they embraced, and the people of the palace burst into sobs with a noise like that of the waves breaking on the seashore. Finally the princess Djouher and the King Chah Djouhou, after bowing before their father, mother, and brother, set out for the country of Damas, to the imposing sound of all the instruments of music. The Sultan Haroun-er-Raschid and his son, Minbah-Chahaz, conducted them outside of the fortifications. When they were far off, the Sultan went back to his palace, walking sadly with his son, Minbah-Chahaz, and praying God to bless his children.

After some time on the journey, the King Chah Djouhou arrived at the country of Damas. The officers and the soldiers sallied from the fortifications of Damas and went to meet the prince. The ministers and the officers bowed low at his feet, all rejoicing over the happy return and perfect health of the King and Queen. The prince entered his palace, and the two spouses lived full of tenderness for each other.

I will not prolong this story of the princess Djouher-Manikam, which has become celebrated in all countries to windward and to leeward. I close it here, giving my best wishes to those who shall read or hear it, and particularly to those who shall copy it!

MAKOTA RADJA-RADJA;

OR,

THE CROWN OF KINGS

—

[*Translated by Aristide Marre and C. C. Starkweather*]

MAKOTA RADJA-RADJA*

KINGS who are of the true faith, who have wisdom and follow justice, cause men worthy of their confidence to travel through their kingdom, to serve as their eyes and ears, and to make reports on the state and condition of their subjects, so that, knowing the cause, they may examine for themselves the conduct of the servants of God. But there are kings who do not rest contented with the report of their servants, and go themselves by night to see the condition and hear the complaints of subjects. Then they make by day a thorough examination of the matters thus come to their knowledge, in order to regulate them with justice and equity.

A story will illustrate this. Zeyd Ibries Selam tells what follows: The prince of the believers, the Caliph Omar (may God be satisfied with him!), judged the servants of God with equity during the day, and after pronouncing his judgments he went out of the city on the side toward the cemetery called Bakia-el-Gharkada. There he cut stone to gain money enough for the maintenance of his house, and when night had come he went through the city to know the good and evil of the servants of God. One night, says Zeyd Ibries Selam, "I accompanied the prince of the believers, Omar. When he was outside of Medina, he perceived a fire in an out-of-the-way place, and turned his steps thither. Scarcely had he arrived when he heard a woman with three children, and the latter were crying. The woman said: 'O God the most high, I beseech thee, make Omar suffer what I am suffering now. He sleeps satiated with food, while I and my children are starving.' The prince of the believers, Omar, hearing these

* Or, "The Crown of Kings."

words, went to the woman, and with a salutation said, 'May I approach?'

"The woman answered, 'If it be by way of goodness, come.'

"He approached her and questioned her about her situation.

"The woman said: 'I come from a far place; and as it was dark when I arrived here, I could not enter the city. So I stopped at this place. My children and I are suffering from hunger and we cannot sleep.'

"The Caliph inquired, 'What is there in this kettle?'

"The woman answered: 'Nothing but water. I put it in the kettle so that the children should imagine that I was cooking rice—perhaps, then, they would go to sleep and stop crying so loudly.'

"As soon as Omar had heard these words he returned promptly to the city of Medina. Arriving at a shop where they sold flour, be bought some and put it into a sack. In another shop he bought some meat. Then lifting the sack to his shoulders he carried it out of the city. I said to him:

"'O prince of the believers, give me this sack, that I may carry it for you.'

"'If you bear the weight of this sack,' said his glorious Majesty to me, 'who will bear the weight of my fault, and who will clear me from the prayer of this woman in the affliction of her heart when she complained to the Lord of my negligence?'

"Omar, having said these words, continued to walk in tears until he had come near the woman and her children. Then he gave her the flour and the meat, and they ate till their hunger was appeased. The woman with a satisfied heart cried:

"'May God the most high hear my prayer and render you benefits, since you are so full of compassion for the servants of God and are so much better than Omar.'

"The Caliph said to her, 'O woman, blame not Omar, for he knew not how you fared.'"

There was once a king in the country of Syria named Malik-es-Saleh, very pious and just, and continually preoccupied with the state of his subjects. They say that every night he went to the mosque, cemeteries, and other solitary places, in search of strangers, fakirs, and poor people who had neither home nor family. One night, arriving near a mosque, he heard the voice of a man inside the edifice. He entered and saw a fakir there. He could not see him distinctly, because he was covered with a mat. But he heard him, and this is what he said: "O Lord, if on the judgment-day thou shalt give a place in heaven to kings who are forgetful of the fakirs and the poor, then, O Lord, grant that I may not enter there."

Malik-es-Saleh, hearing these words, shed tears. He placed a piece of stuff before the fakir with 100 tahil of silver, and said to him:

"O fakir, I have learned from the glorious prophet (may peace be with him!) that fakirs become kings in heaven, after a life of self-sacrifice on earth. Since I am King in this perishable world, I come to you with the weakness of my nature and baseness of my being. I ask you to be at peace with me, and to show yourself compassionate to me when the moment of your glory in heaven shall have arrived."

When the Sultan Zayad sat upon the royal throne of Ikak, the country was infested with malefactors, brigands, robbers, assassins, and the like. The compounds were destroyed, the houses pillaged, and the people killed. The inhabitants could not sleep a single night in quiet, nor pass a single day in safety at home. A crowd of people came with their complaints to the Sultan Zayad, saying:

"The compounds are destroyed, the houses are pillaged, and the men are killed." All throughout Irak one heard nothing but reports of this kind.

One Friday the Sultan went to the mosque to pray. He then shut all the doors and said to the people in the mosque: "O servants of God now present in this mosque, know that a duty is imposed upon me. I must protect my subjects, for I shall have to give an account of my actions on the day of judgment. There are now in this country large numbers of malefactors, and many of my people have been ruined by them. It is my duty to repress these disorders. So, then, listen to what I have to say, and repeat it to those who are not present. I swear to you that all who shall, three days from now, leave his house after the hour of evening prayer, shall be put to death."

When the three days had passed and the fourth night arrived, Sultan Zayad mounted his horse and traversed the city with an escort of cavaliers. Outside of the city he came to a place and saw a man standing under a tree in the middle of a flock of sheep and goats. He said to him, "Who are you?"

The man said: "I come from a far-off village, and I am bringing sheep and goats to the city to sell them, and with their price to buy what I can for my wife and children. When arrived at this place I was so tired that I could not enter the city, and was obliged to stay here, with the intention of entering at daybreak and selling my sheep and goats."

Sultan Zayad, having heard this response, said: "Your words are true, but what can I do? If I do not put you to death to-morrow, when the news spreads, they will say Sultan Zayad is not faithful to his word. They will regard me with disdain, and no one will obey my orders. And the wicked ones will commit violent acts upon the good ones, and my country will be ruined. Heaven is better for you than this world." So he had him put to death and ordered that they should take his head.

During that same night all that he met were killed and beheaded. They say that in the course of that first day 500 persons were put to death. At dawn he had all these heads exposed on the highways, and published this proclamation:

"Whosoever shall not obey the commands of Sultan Zayad shall suffer the same fate."

When the people of the country saw these heads exposed at all sides on the earth, they were frightened, and a respectful fear of Sultan Zayad filled all hearts.

The second night Sultan Zayad went out again from the city, and that night 500 persons were killed.

The third night he remained out of the city till morning, but he did not meet a soul.

The following Friday Sultan Zayad went to the mosque, said his prayers, and declared: "O servants of God, let no one after to-day shut the door of his house nor his shop. I take upon myself the charge of replacing those of your goods which shall be destroyed or stolen."

They all obeyed his orders, for they feared him greatly. Their doors remained opened for several nights, and they never suffered the slightest loss. But after a while a man complained to the Sultan, saying, " Last night someone stole from me 400 tahil."

The Sultan said: " Can you swear to it? "

The man swore to the facts, and the Sultan had 400 tahil counted out to him in place of those he had lost. The following Friday, after prayers, forbidding anyone to leave the mosque, the Sultan said: " O servants of the Lord, know that 400 tahil have been stolen from the shop of a certain man. Unless you denounce the robber, not one of you shall escape, but to-day shall all of you be put to death."

Now, as he had rigorously commanded attendance at Friday's prayer service, the whole town had come to the mosque. They were seized with fright, for they knew that the Sultan kept his word, and they denounced the robber. The latter gave back the 400 tahil and received his punishment.

A long time afterward the Sultan Zayad asked, " At what place in my kingdom do they fear robbers most of all? "

" In the Valley of the Beni Ardou, in the country of Bassrah, for there they are numerous."

Sultan Zayad one day had the highways and paths of the valley strewn with gold and silver, precious stones, and stuffs of great price. All these things lay there a long time and not one was taken. Then the Sultan ordered them to take up these riches and give them to the fakirs and the poor. Then he rendered thanks unto God that he had thus securely established his law among his subjects.

Now it was in the times when Nouchirvan governed with justice and equity, protecting his subjects and causing his kingdom to prosper. One day he asked the grandees of his court, " Are there in my kingdom any places deserted and without inhabitants? "

The grandees who were there answered, " O king of the world, we know not in all your Majesty's realm a place which is not inhabited."

Nouchirvan kept silence, and for many days did not leave the palace. He summoned to his private chamber a learned doctor named Bouzor Djambour, and said to him:

" I desire to know with certainty if all parts of my realm are peopled, or if there is any which is not. How can I be sure of this? "

"To have your Majesty's desire fully satisfied you have only to abstain from leaving the palace."

Saying this, Bouzor Djambour took leave of the King and went to the audience-chamber of the King. He spoke to those assembled there as follows: "O ministers, generals, and all present, know that his Majesty is ill. Now, in order to cure him you must find for me a little bit of earth from a place in ruins and uninhabited. Those who are faithful servants of the King will not hesitate to accomplish immediately this act of devotion in his service, and to start at once in search of the remedy I have named."

These words were scarcely uttered when men were sent out to search the towns and villages and find some earth from a place in ruins and uninhabited. They found only one house in ruins, and the governor of the town said as follows about it: "A merchant once established in this dwelling. He died and left much wealth. As none of his heirs came forward, we closed the doors with stones and mortar, waiting for them to arrive. So the house has fallen to ruin."

Then the people took a little earth from beneath the house and took it to the King, telling him what had happened. Then the King called an assembly and said:

"Know all that my illness proceeded only from my fear that there might be in my kingdom a house in ruins. Now that it has been shown to me that there exists in my whole realm not a single place in ruins, but that the country is well populated, my malady is cured, seeing that my kingdom is in a perfect condition."

In the time of Nouchirvau a man sold his compound to another man. The buyer of this property, while engaged in making repairs, found in the earth many jars filled with gold which someone had buried there. He went immediately to the one who sold him the premises and told him the news. The seller said:

"That gold is not mine, for I did not put it in the ground. I sold you the compound; the discovery that you have made is yours."

The buyer replied: "I bought the premises alone: I did not buy gold; so it is yours." As each refused to take the treasure, they went to the King Nouchirvau and recounted the affair to him, saying, "This gold should be the property of the King." But King Nouchirvau would not take the gold. He asked the two men if they had children. They replied, "Yes, my lord, we have each a child, a boy and a girl."

"Well," said the King, "marry the girl to the boy, and give them the gold you found."

In ancient times a King of China fell ill and as a result of his malady he lost his hearing. He wept in sorrow over this affliction and grew very thin and pale. His ministers came one day and asked him to tell them in writing his condition. He answered: "I am not ill, but so weakened by my inquietude and distress that I can no longer hear the words of my subjects when they come to make their complaints. I know not how to act not to be guilty of negligence in the government of my kingdom."

The ministers then said: "If the ears of your Majesty do not hear, our ears shall replace those of the King, and we can carry to his Majesty the complaints and regrets of his subjects. Why, then, should his Majesty be so much disturbed over the weakening of his physical forces?"

The King of China answered: "At the day of judgment it is I, and not my ministers, who will have to render account of the affairs of my subjects. I must therefore myself examine into their complaints and troubles. I am sure that the burden of ruling would be lighter for me if I could have tranquillity of spirit. But my eyes can see, although my ears are deaf."

And he commanded them to publish this edict: "All who are victims of injustice must reduce their complaints to writing, and bring them to the King so that he may look into their troubles."

They tell also the following story: There was formerly in the city of Ispahan, a king whose power and glory had filled him with pride. He commanded his ministers to build him a palace in a certain place. The ministers, with the architects, ordered the slaves to level the ground so as to form a vast esplanade and cause to disappear all the houses of the neighborhood. Among these houses, they say, there was one belonging to an old woman who was very poor and without a family to help her. In spite of her great age, she went to work as well as she could, in different places, but could scarcely exist on her earnings. Her house near the site selected for the new palace was old and in a tumble-down condition. They tell that one day having gone a long distance to find work she fell ill and remained a long time without being able to return to her house. Then the architects who were building the palace said, "We must not let this hovel remain standing so near the King's palace." So they razed the hut and levelled the earth, and finished the palace with all sorts of embellishments. The King, taking possession, gave a grand house-warming festival.

Now on this very day it so happened that the old woman returned home. Arriving she could find no traces of her house, and was stupefied. In one hand she held a stick, in the other some dry wood for her fire. On her back she bore a package of rice and herbs for cooking. She was fatigued with a long journey and faint with hunger. When she saw that her house had disappeared she knew not what to do nor where to go. She burst into tears. The servants of the King drove her away, and as she went, she fell and spilled her rice and herbs and fell down in the mud. In this state of indescribable desolation she exclaimed, "O Lord, avenge me on these tyrants!"

The old woman had hardly ceased speaking when the voice of some unseen being was heard above her saying, "O woman, fly quickly from this spot, for the anger of God is advancing upon the King." In horror she got up and fled in all haste. Again she heard the voice saying, "O woman, look behind you at the palace." She looked behind her and saw the palace, the King, and all his ministers and servants engulfed in the bowels of the earth by the will of God. And to this day that place vomits fire and smoke as a mark and a warning.

In the Kitab Tarykh it is told that in ancient times under the kings of Persia named Moah, who followed the rules of justice, men were happy. But after these kings, Izdegherd-ibn-Chahryar reigned over Persia. By his harsh tyranny he destroyed the high reputation of the kings of Persia and wretchedly closed a series of reigns lasting 4,000 years and noted all over the world for justice and equity. Under the rule of this miserable tyrant countless numbers of men perished and a great many prosperous and famous cities were devastated. All the better classes of citizens were plunged into the most frightful distress and the most lamentable desolation, and it would be impossible to tell how great and wide-spread was the mourning. Now while all were groaning in affliction the King made merry.

One day in his presumptuous pride he assembled his ministers and his generals to show his royal power and his domination over the people. He was seated on his throne, surrounded by a crowd of courtiers, when suddenly a beautiful horse crossing the city at a gallop went straight into the palace of the King, among the ministers and the grandees. They all admired the beautiful horse, the like of which none had ever seen. Nobody dared to seize him as he pranced from right to left. Suddenly the horse approached the throne and laid down at the feet of the King. The King patted and stroked him, and the horse never moved. Then the wicked King began to laugh and said: "O my ministers, you see how far my greatness goes. It is only at my throne that this wonderful horse has stopped. I will mount and ride him on the esplanade." The King ordered a saddle brought, and was placing it on the horse with his own hands, when he received such a kick over the heart that he was immediately killed. Then the wonderful horse vanished, and no one saw where it went. The people all rejoiced and said, "Of a truth, this mysterious horse was one of the angels of God sent to exterminate a tyrant."

It was in the time of this King, and by his tyranny, that the kingdom of the sovereign of Persia was ruled and fell into the hands of another people. King Khochtacab, the most celebrated of all the kings of his time, by his power, greatness, and magnificence, had raised in rank a man named Rassat Rouchin, a name which in Persia signifies "sincere and brilliant." Influenced by this fine name, the King forgot all prudence, and without any proof of his capacity he raised this man to power and made him minister, turning over to him the care of the most important affairs in his kingdom and giving him all his confidence. His ostensible conduct was irreproachable, and his acts had for everybody the appearance of honesty and truth. One day the minister Rassat Rouchin said to the King: "The people, on account of our leniency and goodness, are forgetting their duty, and are showing no more deference nor respect. We must inspire them with fear, or affairs will not prosper."

The King in his blind confidence responded, "Do whatever you think is right." As soon as the minister had come from the palace of the King he addressed a proclamation to the towns and villages in which he said: "His Majesty is irritated with his subjects. You must all come with presents to appease his anger." From all sides arrived princes and ministers and grandees of the realm, with precious and magnificent objects. Seized with fear they sought counsel of the minister Rassat Rouchin.

"How," said they, "dare we present ourselves before his Majesty in his present state of anger against us?"

Then the minister responded: "If the instant of death is not yet come for you, I will try to save you. I tremble to admit you to the King. But what can I do? On account of the critical situation I will go alone before the King and present your case." So every day he conducted them only as far as the door of the King. There they were told of the fines to which they had been condemned. He took in this way what they had, and sent them home.

This sort of thing continued for a long while until the means of the people were exhausted and the treasury became absolutely empty. The King, always full of confidence in the uprightness of the minister, was in complete ignorance of all this. But at that time there was a king who was an enemy of King Khochtacab. When he learned that the subjects of the latter were suffering cruelly from the oppression of his minister and that his generals were weakened by hunger, he took heart and invaded the kingdom. Then King Khochtacab commanded that his treasury should be opened, and that they should take out all the wealth to gratify the army, gain the hearts of the generals, and defray the expenses of the war. But he found that there was nothing left in the treasury. The army, weakened, was incapable of resisting. The King, shut up in his fort, found it impossible to attack the enemy, and they ravaged and despoiled the kingdom.

The King, having been considered so great, was cruelly wounded by shame at his defeat. He knew not which way to turn his steps. His soul was profoundly troubled. One day, when he had gone forth from the city, wandering at random through plain and forest, he saw a shepherd's hut in the distance, at the door of which were two dogs hanging by the neck. Seeing the King, the shepherd approached and led him to his hovel and served him with the best food he could afford. But the King said:

"I shall not eat until you have told me why you have hanged these two dogs at your cabin-door."

The shepherd responded: "O king of the world, I hanged these two dogs because they betrayed my flock. As my flock was wasting away, I hid one day to see what took place. The wolf came and the dogs played with him and let him carry off sheep and goats. So I hanged the two dogs as faithless traitors."

The King returned to the city and thought over this singular story. "It is a lesson for me," he said, "a revelation. It is impossible not to see that my subjects are the flock and I am the shepherd, while my minister has acted like the shepherd's dogs, and the enemy who has my kingdom is the wolf. I must examine into the conduct of my minister and see with what fidelity he has served me."

When he had returned to the palace he called his secretaries and bade them bring the registers in which the accounts of the kingdom were kept. When these registers were opened he saw that they mentioned only the name of the minister Rassat Rouchin, and included such statements as: "Intercession of Rassat Rouchin in favor of princes so and so, ministers such and such, and grandees this and that, who ask pardon for their faults. Rassat Rouchin took their treasures and granted them grace." There was nothing else in the registers. When the King saw this he said:

"Who rests his faith upon a name goes often without bread,
While he who faithless proves for bread shall lose his soul instead."

These words the King had engraved in letters of gold and fastened to the gate. And at this gate he had the false minister hanged as the dogs were hanged at the cabin-door.

A King of Persia, in a fit of anger against his wife for a certain fault which she had committed, commanded his prime minister to put her to death, together with her nursing infant. The minister, on account of the furious anger of the King, did not dare to plead the Queen's cause, but took her to his mother's house. The minister found another woman who had been condemned to death and had her executed, telling the King that it was the Queen who was beheaded. The King's child grew and flourished until he had become a handsome young man. But the King grew more and more morose and melancholy, and shut himself up in the palace. The minister, noticing this continual sadness of the King, said:

"O king of the world, what has come over the heart of your Majesty? Pray tell me the cause of your sorrow."

And the King said: "O minister, how should I not be sad and disturbed? Here I am getting old and I have no son to cause my name to live and protect my kingdom. That is the cause of my sorrow and unhappiness."

When the minister heard these words he said, "O king of the world, your sorrow shall not long endure, for you have a son, capable of preserving and protecting your kingdom. This son of yours has intelligence, education, natural gifts, and great personal beauty, and is of most excellent character."

The King said, "Where is this son of whose existence I have been unaware?"

The minister answered, "Your Majesty is not aware of his existence, but I know that he is very much alive." The minister then related how he had spared the lives of the Queen and her child. The King was transported with joy, and cried, "Happy the king who has such a minister!"

The minister bowed low and said, "When shall your son, the prince, present himself?"

The King answered: "Go seek forty young men of his age, build, figure, and complexion. Have them all dressed alike. Bring these forty young men with my son to a certain place in the plain. Await me there, but tell not this secret to a soul. When I have arrived at the spot then cause these forty young men to present themselves before me. If my son is among them I shall most certainly recognize him."

The minister took leave of the King, and with a heart filled with joy set about doing what the King had ordered. When the King had arrived at the spot chosen his minister advanced, followed by forty-one youths, all dressed alike. As soon as the King had seen them he recognized his son and called him to his side. Then he went back to the city with him and all the grandees. The next day he invited the latter to a great festival, and gave to each of them a splendid present. He turned over his kingdom to his son, taking care to place him and his government under the tutelage of the good minister who had saved his wife and brought him up. Then the King went into a religious retreat, and as long as he lived occupied himself in the service of God.

The Sultan Alexander, called the Two-Horned, at the beginning of his reign sent an ambassador to King Darius, who was then at the zenith of his greatness. On his return, this ambassador made his report to King Alexander. The latter read it, but had doubts over a certain word therein contained. He questioned his ambassador about the word, saying, "Did you hear that exact word from the mouth of King Darius?"

The ambassador replied, "I heard it with my own ears."

King Alexander, not being able to believe it, wrote a second letter, mentioning this word, and despatched to King Darius another ambassador, charged to deliver it. When King Darius, reading the letter of King Alexander, came to this special word, he took a knife and cut it out, then wrote a letter to King Alexander, in which he said: "The sincerity of the soul of the King is the foundation of his realm and his greatness. His words, therefore, should be faithfully transmitted and reproduced by his ambassador. I have cut out of your letter a certain word, because it was never pronounced by me. And if your former ambassador were only here I would cut out his lying tongue even as I have cut out the word from your letter."

When this answer of King Darius's was borne to King Alexander he read it and summoned before him the faithless ambassador. "Why," said he, "were you willing, with a word, to cause the loss of many men and countries?"

"Because they showed me little deference and did not treat me well."

King Alexander said: "Foolish man! And you thought that we sent you to look after your own personal interests, and neglect those of the nation?" He commanded that his tongue should be torn out, and made a proclamation, saying, "This is the fate of traitors who falsely report the words of kings."

In the Kitab Tarykh the following is recounted: The Sultan Homayoun sent an ambassador to the King of Khorassan. When this ambassador, on his arrival in the country, had delivered the letter of the Sultan to the King, the latter asked:

"How does your King conduct himself regarding his subjects? How does he govern them?"

"The rule of conduct and the mode of government used by my King," answered the ambassador, "are to make himself loved by all his subjects."

The King asked, "Of what nature is the affection of your King for his subjects?"

"That of a mother and father for their children and grandchildren."

"In hard and calamitous times, how does your King conduct himself?"

"He shows that he cares not for riches, for the door of his treasury is always open."

"In the daily receptions how does your King behave?"

"The receptions of my King resemble the gardens of Paradise refreshed by sweet breezes and scented with the balmy breath of sweetly smelling plants or like a sea filled with pearls and corals."

The King asked again, "And in council how speaks your King?"

The ambassador answered, "All those who hear my King in council become wise if they lack wisdom, and brave if they lack courage."

The King of Khorassan was enchanted with the answers of the ambassador, loaded him with presents, and said to him: "The spirit and judgment of your King are reflected in the person of his ambassador. They should all be like you." And he addressed in answer to the Sultan a letter filled with compliments and felicitations.

In the Kitab Tarykh it is related that the Sultan Mahmoud was fond of his servant Ayaz on account of the excellence of his wit and judgment. The other servants of the Sultan were jealous of Ayaz, and murmured against him. One day the ministers and grandees were in the presence of the Sultan Mahmoud, and Ayaz was standing respectfully before him. Someone brought a cucumber as a present to the Sultan. The Sultan sliced it and ate a morsel. He found it very bitter, but gave no sign of this. He handed a piece of it to Ayaz, saying, "Eat some of this cucumber and tell me how it tastes, so that the others present may eat some of it also, and tell us if they ever ate anything like it." Ayaz saluted, and ate of the cucumber with an appearance of pleasure.

"It is very good."

The King made the others eat of it. They found that it was bitter, and were angry with Ayaz, and asked how he dare to lie in such a manner.

"It is true," said the Sultan; "how could you say it was good?"

Ayaz answered with respect: "May the Lord bless the king of the world! How many favors have you given me! How many sweet and savory dainties! How, then, could I make a wry face over one bitter morsel? I ought, on the contrary, to declare that the bitterness of this mouthful is completely annulled by the delicious sweetness of the others, so that your Majesty shall continue to bestow dainties upon me as before."

A certain king, vain of his royal power, had a servant who was very pious and a true believer, very punctilious in the practice of his religious duties. The King distinguished him above all the others as one in whom he could trust on account of the integrity of his heart. He had given him this order: "Go not far away from here, day or night. Keep close watch, and neglect not my service." The servant, after finishing his religious duties, took his post, where the King from time to time sent for him. But the King had need of him, and he was not to be found. They sent to look for him, but in vain, and the King grew very angry with him. Finally the servant arrived and prostrated himself before the King. The latter, full of wrath, demanded:

"Why are you late? Why don't you pay attention to my orders?" And he commanded that the man be punished, to make him more attentive to the King's service.

But the servant replied, "If I am late, it is only on account of the great embarrassment in which I find myself placed."

"What embarrassment? Tell me."

The servant, bowing low, spoke as follows: "My embarrassment comes from the fact that I have two masters to serve. The first is the true Master, he who created the universe and the children of Adam, whose punishments are very severe. The second is only the servant of the former, and not the true master. I am obliged to attend to the service of the true Master before the service of the second. That is the embarrassment in which I find myself."

When the King heard these words he shed abundant tears, and said: "From this day forth you are free. Follow the service of the Lord, and do not forget to pray for me."

The servants of the King should love their King more than they love their own life, their mother, their father, their children, their grandchildren, their family, their riches, and all that belongs to them. In a word, for them the person of their King should be above all, so that one may call them true servants of the King, and that in all truth they may be termed his favorites. They tell the story that one day the Sultan Mahmoud Ghazi (may grace be upon him!) was seated on his throne, surrounded by his ministers and his officers, among whom was Ayaz. The Sultan said to his treasurer:

"Go to the treasure-chamber. Take to a certain place gold, silver, precious stones, and other objects of great value. For we are going there to amuse ourselves, and present these treasures to those who shall accompany us."

One day the Sultan started to go and amuse himself at that place, and as soon as the news spread abroad, a great number of people followed him there. When he arrived he halted at a spot level, clean, and well lighted, and said to his treasurer:

"Expose my treasures here, in this place, so that all those who are happy shall obtain a present according to their degree of happiness, and that one may know who are those who have the most luck and those who have the least."

All hearing these words quickly approached, pressing forward, with their eyes wide open and their looks fixed on the treasurer, praying him to exhibit the presents at the designated place. At this very moment the Sultan spurred his horse to a gallop and rode from their presence. When he was far away and out of their sight, he stopped and looked behind him. There he saw Ayaz, the only one who had followed him. The others, preoccupied with getting their share of the treasures, never suspected that the Sultan had gone and was already far away from them. The Sultan, halting a moment, returned to the city.

On their side, the ministers and the grandees, having taken possession of the most precious objects, returned joyfully to their homes. On the way they compared notes with each other about their shares of the treasure. One said, "I had the best luck"; and another, "No, I had the best." And all, whoever they were, said the same thing, for all except Ayaz had their share of the King's presents. So they said among themselves, "It is clear that the one who has no luck is Ayaz."

Some jealous ones added: "In truth, Master Ayaz has no luck at all. By his lack of intelligence and good judgment he has had none of the Sultan's presents."

Ayaz heard all these remarks, but kept silence. Some days later, the Sultan came out of his palace and sat upon the throne. All the grandees came into his presence. Ayaz was standing before him. The Sultan asked:

"Who among you had no luck?"

The ministers answered: "It is Ayaz! He did not get a single one of your Majesty's many presents. It is clear that he has no luck, for he left all those precious objects and came back with empty hands."

The Sultan said: "O Ayaz, are our presents without value in your eyes, that you disdain them? I don't know why you took nothing that was within your grasp. You would have prevented them from saying that you have no luck. What was your motive in doing a thing that has the approbation of nobody?"

Ayaz responded: "May the days and prosperity of the King increase! May the presents never tarnish that he has given to his servants. As for me, I have more luck than those who received the presents of your Majesty."

The Sultan said, "O Ayaz, prove to me the truth of your words."

Ayaz responded: "If they found some part in the largesses which were given them, I found the author himself of those great gifts. If they found gold, I found the master of the gold. If others found silver, I found the master of silver. If others found precious stones, I found the master of precious stones. If others yet found some pearls, I found the ocean of pearls. Who, therefore, O king of the world, among all those who vaunt themselves as having luck, has more than I have?"

The Sultan replied: "O Ayaz, tell me what is the meaning of your words. Where is all that which you say you found?"

Ayaz responded: "May the most high protect the person of the king of the world, more precious to me than all those objects of price! In whatever place may be his august person, there I am, and I thus obtain all that my heart desires. When I am with your Majesty, and your Majesty is with me, what do I lack? Who, then, has more luck than I have?"

One day the Sultan Alexander was plunged in sadness, and kept himself shut up in his palace. The wise Aristotle came before him, and seeing him absorbed in sad thoughts, asked him:

"Why is the Sultan so sad and what keeps him from going out of his palace?"

The Sultan Alexander answered: "I am grieving at the thought of the smallness of this world, and of all the troubles I am giving myself and others for the sake of reigning over a world that is so little worth. It is the vanity of my works that renders me sad."

Aristotle replied: "The reflection of the Sultan is just, for what, in truth, is the world? Certainly it has not enough importance by itself that the Sultan should occupy himself with a vain kingdom. But the government of this world is a mark of the sublime and eternal kingdom of the other world, and this kingdom the Sultan can obtain by governing this present world with justice. Your Majesty must therefore give all his cares to the government of this world, to obtain finally in the other world a kingdom of which the greatness is beyond measure and the duration is eternal."

The Sultan Alexander heard with pleasure the words of his wise counsellor.

Two qualities are essential to kings, generosity and magnanimity. When a minister remarks, in his king, sentiments unworthy of his rank, he should warn him of the fact, and should turn him from unworthy actions. They tell that a king, having made a gift of 500 dirhems, his minister said to him: "I have heard from the mouth of wise men that it is not permitted to kings to make a present of less than 1,000 dirhems!"

One day Haroun-er-Raschid made a gift of 500 tahil. His minister, named Yahya, made by signs and by gestures every effort to prevent him from doing this. When all those who had been present were gone, Haroun-er-Raschid said:

"O Yahya! what were you trying to do with all your signs?"

The latter replied: "O prince of true believers! I was trying to say that kings should never let it be seen that they are capable of making presents of less than 1,000 dirhems."

One day King Mamoun-er-Raschid heard his minister, named Abbas, say to a servant, "Go to the bazaar and buy something with this half-tahil."

Mamoun-er-Raschid was angry with him and said: "You are capable of dividing a tahil in two! That is not proper in a minister; you are not worthy of the name," and he forthwith desposed him from office.

In the Kitab Sifat-el-Molouk it is related that the King Chabour, giving his last instructions to his son, said as follows: "O my son! whenever you make a present to anyone, do not bestow it with your own hands. Do not even examine or have brought into your own presence the gifts that you make. Whenever you give a present, see that it be at least the equivalent of the revenue of a town in value, so that it will enrich the recipients, and make them and their children and grandchildren free from adversity. Furthermore, my child, beware all your life of giving yourself up to operations of commerce in your kingdom. For this kind of affairs is unworthy a king who has greatness of character, prosperity, and birth."

King Harmuz received one day a letter from his minister in which he said: "Many merchants being in town with a great quantity of jewels, pearls, hyacinths, rubies, diamonds, and other precious stones, I bought all they had for your Majesty, paying 200,000 tahil. Immediately afterward there arrived some merchants from another country who wanted to buy these and offered me a profit of 200,000 tahil. If the King consents I will sell the jewels, and later buy others."

King Harmuz wrote to his minister the following response: "What are 200,000 tahil? What are 400,000 tahil, profit included? Is that worth talking about and making so much ado? If you are going into the operations of commerce who will look after the government? If you buy and sell, what will become of the merchants? It is evident that you would destroy thus our good renown, and that you are the enemy of the merchants of our kingdom, for your designs would ruin them. Your sentiments are unworthy a minister." And for this he removed him from office.

In the Kitab Sifat-el-Houkama it is said: "There is a great diversity of inclinations among men. Everyone has his own propensity. One is borne naturally toward riches, another toward patience and resignation, another toward study and good works. And in this world the humors of men are so varied that they all differ in nature. Among this infinite variety of dispositions of soul, that which best suits kings and ministers is greatness of character, for that quality is the ornament of royalty.

"One day the minister of the Sultan Haroun-er-Raschid was returning from the council of state to his house when he was approached by a beggar who said: 'O Yahya! misery brings me to you. I pray you give me something.'

"When Yahya had arrived at his house he made the beggar sit down at the door, and calling an attendant said to him: 'Every day give this man 1,000 dinars, and for his food give him his part in the provisions consumed in your house.'

"They say that for a month the beggar came every day and sat at Yahya's door, and received the sum of 1,000 dinars. When he had received them at the end of the month, 30,000 dinars, the beggar went away. When informed of his departure, Yahya said: 'By the Lord! if he had not gone away, and had come to my door for the rest of his life, I should have given him the same daily ration.'"

In the Kitab Tarykh the following is told: "There was

once upon a time a Persian king named Khrosrou, remarkable among all the kings of Persia for his power, his greatness of character, his goodness, and the purity of his morals. His wife, named Chirine, was of a rare beauty, and no one at that time could be compared to her, for she possessed all the virtues. Khrosrou passionately loved Chirine, and among the books, famous in the world, which speak of loving couples, there is one called 'Khrosrou and Chirine.' One day Khrosrou was seated in the palace with his wife Chirine, when a fisherman brought in a fine fish as a present to Khrosrou. The latter ordered them to give him a present of 4,000 dirhems.

"'You are wrong,' said Chirine.

"'And why?' asked the King.

"'If, in the future, you made one of your servants a present of 4,000 dirhems he will not fail to say forthwith, "I am considered as the equal of a fisherman." If your present is less than 4,000 dirhems, then necessarily he will say, "I am considered as being less than a fisherman," and your actions will sadden his heart.'

"Khrosrou said: 'Your observation is just. But I have spoken, and I cannot reverse what I have said, for it is shameful for a king to fail in keeping his word.'

"Chirine replied, 'Never mind, I know a way, and no one can say that you broke your promise.'

"'What is this way?' asked Khrosrou.

"Chirine answered: 'Put this question to the fisherman, "Is this a fresh-water or a salt-water fish?"

"'If he answers, "It is a fresh-water fish," say, "I want a salt-water one," and the contrary. Then he will go away and you will be released from your foolish promise.'

"Khrosrou, who by love of Chirine could not help hearing her advice and following it, put the question to the fisherman. But the latter, suspecting a trap, said, 'It is both.' King Khrosrou began to laugh, and gave him 4,000 dirhems in addition.

"The fisherman, having received his 8,000 dirhems, put them in a sack and went away. On the journey, a dirhem fell to the ground, and the fisherman, lowering his sack, began to search for the dirhem that had fallen. When he found it, he placed it with the others and took up his march again.

Khrosrou and Chirine had both been witnesses of his action. Chirine said to Khrosrou: 'Behold the baseness and the lack of judgment of the fisherman. He wearied himself to hunt for one dirhem when he had a sack full of them. Recall him and do him shame.'

"Khrosrou, who from his love for Chirine was incapable of resisting her words, and always obeyed them, recalled the fisherman and said to him: 'Of a truth, you have a low soul, and possess neither judgment nor dignity. What! One of your 8,000 dirhems was lost and you deferred your journey until you had found it? That shows the baseness of your soul and your lack of judgment.'

"The fisherman made obeisance and answered: 'May the prosperity of the king of the world increase! I sought not the dirhem on account of its money value, but only on account of the greatness and importance of the words engraved upon the coin. On one of its sides is written the name of God most high. On the other side is written the name of the King. Had I not found the dirhem, and had left it on the ground, then people passing would have trodden upon it, and the two names inscribed upon it, and which ought to be glorified by all men, would have been despised and disgraced, and I would have been the accomplice of all the passers-by who trod upon it. That is why I took the trouble to find the dirhem.'

"Khrosrou was pleased with this answer and gave him still another 4,000 dirhems. The fisherman, filled with joy, took his 12,000 dirhems and returned to his home."

A man had committed a serious offence against King Haroun-er-Raschid. Condemned to death, he succeeded in escaping. But he had a brother. The King summoned the latter and said to him: "Find your brother so that I may kill him. If you do not find him I will kill you in his place." This man not finding his brother, the King Mamoun-er-Raschid ordered one of his servants to bring him to be killed. But this servant said: "O prince of believers! if the one who received the command to put this man to death brings him for that purpose and at the same time a messenger comes from your Majesty with an order not to kill him, ought he not to release him?"

King Mamoun-er-Raschid answered, "He certainly ought to release him, on account of my orders."

"O prince of believers," answered the servant, "the Koran says, 'He who has a burden shall not bear another's.'"

Then the King said: "Set the man free, for this must cover his case, and means that the innocent should not perish for the guilty."

They tell that, a pundit appearing one day before the Sultan Ismail Samani, King of the country of Khorassan, the Sultan received him with great distinction, and at his departure saluted him most respectfully and escorted him to the door, taking seven steps behind him.

The next night he dreamed that the glorious prophet (with whom be peace!) spoke thus to him: "O Ismail, because you honored one of my pundits, I will pray God that after you seven of your children and grandchildren shall become great and glorious kings." They say that for many years the kingdom of Khorassan flourished under the paternal government of the successors of this Sultan.

The Sultan Abdallah Tlahir, as soon as he had taken possession of the throne of Khorassan, received the homage of a large number of his subjects. At the end of several days he asked, "Is there anyone of distinction in the country who has not come to present himself before me?" They told him, "There are two persons that have not come, one named Ahmed Arab, and the other named Mahomet Islam. But these two men never present themselves before kings and ministers."

The Sultan replied, "Since they will not come to find kings and ministers, I must go to them." So one day the Sultan repaired to the house of Ahmed Arab. The latter, immediately arising, remained standing a long time facing the Sultan. Then regarding him fixedly he said to him: "O Sultan, I had heard tell of your beauty, and I now see that they spoke the truth. Make not of that body the embers of hell." Saying this he returned to his prayers. The Sultan Abdallah Tlahir went away from the sheik's house weeping.

He then betook himself to the house of Mahomet Islam. At the news that the Sultan was coming to see him, the sheik shut the door of his house, saying: "I ought not to see him. I ought not to speak to him."

The Sultan departed in tears and said: "Friday, when the sheik goes to the mosque I will go to him."

When Friday came he was on horseback, surrounded by soldiers, awaiting the arrival of the sheik. As soon as he perceived him, he dismounted, approached him on foot, and saluted him. The sheik asked: "Who are you? What do you want of me?"

The Sultan answered: "It is I, Abdallah Tlahir. I have come to see the sheik."

The latter, turning away his face, said to the Sultan, "What connection is there between you and me?"

The Sultan fell at the feet of the sheik, in tears, in the middle of the highway, and, invoking God the most high, spoke as follows, "O Lord, forgive my faults, on account of the many virtues of this faithful sheik." And he was forgiven and became a good man.

The imam El-Chafei (may mercy be with him!), going from the city of Jerusalem to the country of Egypt, halted in a town called Ramla. One of the inhabitants of this town took him into his house and entertained him with many attentions. The companions of the imam El-Chafei perceived that he felt a certain inquietude, but none of them knew the reason for it. The more the master of the house showered his attentions and civilities, the more disturbed the imam seemed to be. Finally at the moment when the imam was mounting his horse to continue his journey, the master of the house arrived and put a writing into his hands. On reading this, the imam lost his worried air, and, giving orders to pay the man thirty dinars, he went on his way rejoicing. One of his companions asked him:

"Why were you so disturbed? What did the writing say? And why did you show so much joy in reading it?"

The imam El-Chafei answered: "When our host took us to his house I noticed that his face lacked the characteristic signs of honesty. But as he treated us so well I began to think perhaps I was mistaken in judging him. But when I read the writing he handed me I saw it was as follows: 'While the imam has been here I have spent on him ten dinars. He ought therefore to pay me back twenty.' So then I knew that I had made no error in reading his character, and was pleased at my skill."

The story is told that one day as the prophet Solomon was seated on his royal throne, surrounded by men, spirits, and birds, two women came before him, each claiming possession of a child. These two women kept saying, "It is my child," but neither could give proof. All their arguments amounting to nothing, the prophet Solomon commanded that the child should be cut in two, and that each woman should take half. When the executioner advanced, drawing his sword, one of the women bursting into sobs cried out in anguish: "O Prophet Solomon, don't kill the child. Give it to this woman, it is all I ask!"

As the murder of the child never drew a tear nor a movement of anxiety from the other woman, Solomon commanded them to give it to the woman who had wept, because her tears proved her to be the true mother, and that the child belonged to her, and not to the other woman. Thus did King Solomon show his wisdom in judging character.

O you who are magnificent! listen, I pray you, and hear to what degree of sublimity generosity is lifted. In the Kitab Adab-is-Selathin it is said that two qualities were given by God in all their perfection to two men—justice to Sultan Nouchirvan, King of Persia, and generosity to a subject of an Arab sultan named Hatim-Thai. The author of that work says that in the time of Hatim-Thai there were three kings celebrated throughout the whole world, and rivals in showing the perfection of generosity—the King of Roum, the King of Syria, and the King of Yemen. But as none of them was as famous as Hatim-Thai, they became jealous of him and united in hostility toward him. They said: "We are the kings of vast countries, and shall we suffer a simple subject of an Arab sultan to be counted as more generous than we are?" And each of these kings thought to try Hatim-Thai and destroy him.

The first of the three who attempted the undertaking was the King of Roum. This King said to one of his ministers: "O minister, I hear tell that there is among the Arabs a man named Hatim-Thai, and that he is reputed the most generous man in the world. I am displeased that my name is not as noted for generosity as his. I want to make a proof and see if his fame is true or false. I have heard that Hatim-Thai possesses a horse which he loves as he does his own soul. Well, we will ask him to give us this beloved horse."

The minister sent an envoy, with suitable presents and a letter to give to Hatim-Thai. He arrived in a great storm of wind and rain which permitted no one to attend to his affairs abroad. It was already night, and Hatim-Thai had made no preparations to receive a guest, but he received the stranger with the marks of the highest respect and greatest cordiality.

"What need brings you here to-night?" he asked.

"Nothing but to visit you," replied the envoy, and he never mentioned that evening his mission from the King of Roum.

As there was nothing in the house to eat, Hatim-Thai killed his favorite horse and served it for his guest's supper. As soon as it was day, the envoy presented the gifts and the letter from the King of Roum. When he read the passage in the letter where the King asked for the horse which had just been killed, Hatim-Thai turned pale and could not say a word. The envoy, observing him in this state, imagined that he regretted the gift of his horse, and said:

"O Hatim-Thai, if it is not with pleasure that you give your horse to my master, think no more about it, and let me return to my country."

Hatim-Thai answered: "O envoy of the King of Roum! if I had a thousand horses like that one I should give them all without a moment's hesitation. But last night I asked you the motive which brought you hither, and you said it was merely to visit me. So I killed the horse for your food, and that is why I am afflicted with sorrow at my lack of foresight." He sent the envoy back home with many other horses as a gift.

The envoy told the whole story and the King of Roum said: "The renown of Hatim-Thai is deserved; he is the most generous of men." He made an alliance of friendship with him, and the fame of Hatim-Thai grew apace.

The second one who tested Hatim-Thai's generosity was the King of Syria. He said: "How can Hatim-Thai, who lives in the woods and the plains, occupied in pasturing goats, camels, and horses, be more generous than so great a King as I? I will put him to the proof. I will ask rich presents that he cannot give, and he will be shamed and humiliated before kings and peoples."

So the King of Syria sent an envoy to Hatim-Thai to ask for 100 red camels with long manes, black eyes, and very tall. Camels of this sort are hard to find, only kings having four or five. When the envoy had arrived he told Hatim-Thai what the King of Syria asked of him. Hatim-Thai was full of joy hearing the words of the envoy, and hastened to regale him bountifully with food and drink. Then he searched among his camels, but found none such as the King of Syria desired. He ordered search to be made among the peoples of his nation, Arabs and Bedouins, offering a large price. By the will of God a Bedouin succeeded in finding 100, and Hatim-Thai asked only the delay of one month in payment. The envoy returned home with the red camels and many other presents. Seeing them, the King of Syria was struck with astonishment and cried: "Behold, we wished only to test Hatim-Thai, and now he has gone into debt to satisfy our desire. Yes, truly he is the most generous man in the world."

He commanded them to send back to Hatim-Thai the 100 red camels loaded with magnificent presents. As soon as they arrived, Hatim-Thai summoned the owner and gave him the camels with all their burden of riches, without keeping anything for himself. When the envoy, returning home again, recounted all these things, the King of Syria marvelled and exclaimed: "No one can equal Hatim-Thai. He is generosity itself, in all its perfection."

The third king, that is, the King of Yemen, was very generous, and wanted no one to rival him in this particular. So when he heard of the fame of Hatim-Thai for generosity, he was vexed and full of sorrow. He said: "How can that poor Hatim equal in generosity a great king like me? I give alms to the poor, I feed them, and every day I give them clothing. How is it possible that anyone can dare to mention the name of Hatim-Thai in my presence as the most generous of men?"

Now, at that time an ambassador of the King of Maghreb arrived at the Court of the King of Yemen, who spoke of the wonderful generosity of Hatim-Thai. He felt as if his heart was burning, but did not let his grief appear, and said to himself:

"Everybody repeats the praises of Hatim, one after another, without knowing exactly who he is, of what birth, and what are the means which permit him thus to give hospitality. I shall cause him to perish."

The King of Yemen summoned a Bedouin, a bandit celebrated for his ferocity, without pity for the life of a man. The Bedouin arrived, and the King gave him gold, silver, and clothing. "O Bedouin," he said to him, "if you will perform an affair for us, we will give you whatever you ask."

The Bedouin answered: "O my lord, king of the world, what is your Majesty's will?"

The King of Yemen replied: "There is a man named Hatim-Thai, of the tribe of Thai, on the confines of Syria. Go to this country, and employ all the tricks you can to kill him. When you have killed him bring me his head. If you succeed in doing as I wish, whatever you ask, it shall be given you."

These words of the King filled with joy the Bedouin's heart. He said to himself: "Here is a good piece of work. For an old tattered cloak I will kill a man. Why then should I hesitate a moment for a superb cloak of scarlet?"

Taking leave of the King, the Bedouin set out promptly and went toward Syria in search of Hatim-Thai. After a while he arrived at a village near to Syria, and there he met a young man of a rare beauty. His face bore the marks of virtue, his language was full of sweetness and affability, his soul was righteous, and his heart compassionate. He asked the Bedouin where he was going. The latter answered, "I am from the country of Yemen, and am going to Syria."

The young man replied: "O my brother! I wish you would do me the favor to rest for a day and a night in my house, and I will do the best to entertain you. After that you shall go on your journey when you wish."

The Bedouin heard these words with pleasure, and went into the young man's house. There he was treated magnificently and regaled so lavishly that he thought he had never seen and eaten so much. He slept peacefully all night. At dawn he said farewell, eager to gain the end of his journey. The young man said to him: "O my brother, if it is possible, stay two or three days longer, I beg you, so that by my hospitality I may show all the sincere affection that my heart feels for you."

The Bedouin replied: "O my brother, truly would I remain some time longer here, had I not a most important and delicate mission to fulfil. It is impossible for me to stay and enjoy myself here, while I have not yet accomplished my errand."

The young man answered: "O my brother, what is this difficult and delicate affair which prevents you from staying here? If you will tell me, doubtless I shall find some means of coming to your aid, and lightening the burden which weighs so heavily upon your heart. But, now, what can I do since you tell me nothing?"

Hearing these words, the Bedouin kept silence. He said to himself: "This affair is not easy to execute. It might be of use for me to have a prudent and discreet companion to confer with him about it. Perhaps I should do well to talk of it to this young man and ask his advice."

And nevertheless he dared not yet trust his secret, and his perplexity was written on his countenance. He could not utter a single word, and remained very anxious.

The young man observing the state of the Bedouin said to him: "O servant of God, your embarrassment is evident; you fear to open your heart to me. God alone, in truth, knows the secrets of his servants. But, in your present situation, it may be that I can be of some benefit to you."

The Bedouin, hearing these words of the young man, said to him: "O my loyal friend, know then that I am an Arab-Bedouin of the country of Yemen; that of all the Bedouins of Arabia there is not one so wicked nor so great a thief as I, and that my fame as a bandit is celebrated throughout all Yemen. The King, having resolved upon a wicked deed, ordered his minister to find a man capable of performing it. As I had the reputation of being the greatest bandit of the country of Yemen, I was summoned to the presence of the King. As soon as his Majesty saw me he loaded me with presents and said: 'If you do as I wish I will give you many more presents of gold and silver and other magnificent things.' I replied, 'O my lord, king of the world, what is this affair?' 'You must go and kill a man named Hatim-Thai, who lives on the confines of Syria.' To this I replied: 'O my lord, king of the world, I am only a Bedouin, a poor robber, wandering in the forests and the plains. For drink I have but the brackish water of the marshes. For food I have only rats and locusts.' On account of my wretchedness, I obeyed the wishes of the King, and promised to execute this affair. But here I am, in a very embarrassing situation, for I do not know this Hatim-Thai, and I don't even know where his tribe is, the Ben-Thai."

The young man, hearing these words, began to laugh, and said: "O my brother, be not disturbed. I know this Hatim-Thai, and I will show him to you." These words rejoiced the Bedouin. The young man continued: "O my brother, know that the tribe of Ben-Thai inhabit this village, and that the man named Hatim-Thai is himself in this tribe. If you will follow exactly what I indicate to you, you will certainly accomplish your mission."

The Bedouin answered: "O my brother, I place my life in your hands. What must be done?"

The young man answered: "O my brother, there is a place where Hatim-Thai goes for recreation. It is an extremely deserted place, which no one ever visits. When he gets there he eats, drinks, and then he sleeps, his head covered with a cloth, and his horse tied near by. You will arrive at that moment, you will promptly execute the wish of the King, you will jump upon the horse and dash away from this place and go wherever you like."

The young man went then to show the place to the Bedouin, and giving him a poniard with two edges well sharpened, he said: "O my brother, to-morrow Hatim-Thai will come to this spot. Forget nothing that you have to do."

All the instruction of the young man were followed by the Bedouin. Early in the morning Hatim-Thai repaired to the designated place. He ate, he drank, and when he had finished his repast he tied his horse near by. Then, covering his head with a cloth, he fell fast asleep. At this very moment the wicked Bedouin arrived. By the will of God, just as he was about to assassinate the young man, a thought came into his heart. "Hatim-Thai is celebrated throughout the whole world for his generosity and his benevolence. Before I kill him, while he is still alive, I want to see his face." And he raised the cloth that covered his head. At the sight of the countenance of the sleeping young man he fell at his feet and covered them with kisses, saying: "O my friend! What have you done? You ought not to act thus!"

Hearing these words of the Bedouin, the young man said: "What could I do? For the one called Hatim-Thai is I. The head that the King of Yemen wants is mine. What other means could I employ?" He conducted the Bedouin to his house, regaled him again, and gave him all he needed.

Then the Bedouin took leave and returned to his country. As soon as he arrived in Yemen, he went before the King and recounted all the circumstances relative to Hatim-Thai.

Having heard the story the King shed tears, and said: "Of a truth, Hatim-Thai is liberal, benevolent, and noble, brave and generous." Afterward the King of Yemen made a friendship with Hatim-Thai that lasted as long as his life.

When the Sultan Yakoub invaded Khorassan and besieged the capital, the Sultan Mahomet, shut up in the city, made such a strong resistance that for a long time it was impossible to capture the place. But his ministers betrayed him by sending to Sultan Yakoub letters which showed how it might be taken. One only of these ministers, named Ibrahim Hadjib, abstained from sending any traitorous letters, and remained faithful to his master. After a while the city was taken and Sultan Yakoub ascended the throne. Then all the most important people of the country came to pay homage to him. The ministers who had betrayed the former Sultan were conspicuous in their demonstrations of joy. The Sultan Yakoub gave a pleasant reception to those who came, and made them suitable gifts.

After this he asked, "Who has not come to present himself before me on this day of rejoicing?"

The ministers immediately answered, "Ibrahim Hadjib is the only one who has not come to present his congratulations."

Then the Sultan asked, "Why has he not done so? Is he ill?"

"No," they answered, "he is not ill."

The Sultan summoned Ibrahim Hadjib, and the latter came into the royal presence. The Sultan, observing on his countenance evident marks of care and sorrow, spoke thus to him: "Ibrahim Hadjib, are you the minister in whom the Sultan Mahomet placed his confidence?" He replied in the affirmative.

"From what motive, Ibrahim Hadjib, did you keep silence, and send me no word of advice while the ministers of Sultan Mahomet, now here, sent many letters to show me how to capture the city? Why did you refrain from appearing before me at court to-day, at the same time with the ministers and grandees? Why, now that you are here, are you the only one to wear a sad and mournful appearance and a long face, while all the others show their joy? To all these questions you must truthfully respond. And if you speak not the truth you shall be put to death."

"If the Sultan wishes to hear the language of truth and will not be vexed by it, I will reply to each of his questions. To the first question, why I sent no letter betraying my King, I will say: Know, Sultan, that the Sultan Mahomet was the King of this country; that he gave me many presents and had full confidence in me, thinking that in the moment of danger I would be his companion and his counsellor. How could I, then, betray him? I knew you not, and had received no benefits from you. Would it have been just for me to send you letters and cause the fall of one who had been so bountiful to me?"

"Your words are just and true," said the Sultan Yakoub.

Ibrahim Hadjib continued: "As to the question why I abstained from presenting myself at court to-day, and why I wore so sorrowful a face, I answer: Know that I could not present myself before the Sultan, because he was the enemy of my master and benefactor, and brought about the ruin of my lord. That is why I wore a sad face in your presence. Beside, the children and grandchildren of my lord are plunged in grief and anxiety, and how could I be happy in your presence, like these hypocrites, who are very different elsewhere? I have told the truth."

When the Sultan Yakoub had heard these words of Ibrahim Hadjib, he cried: "God be praised! Up to this time I have heard tell of ministers, I have seen many kinds, but never have I seen nor heard of a minister like this one. Now, only for the first time have I seen a true minister and listened to the words of truth." The Sultan Yakoub loaded Ibrahim Hadjib with favors, made him prime minister, and gave him the name of father. As for the other ministers, he caused them to perish, with their whole families. Then he published this proclamation:

"Behold the fate of those who are faithless to their promises and commit treason toward their King, for they cannot be counted as men."

Published by

Facsimile Publisher
Ashok Vihar, Delhi-110052 (India)
Website: www.facsimilepublisher.com

Distributed by

GYAN

Gyan Books Pvt. Ltd.
5, Ansari Road, Daryaganj, New Delhi-110002 (India)
E-mail: books@gyanbooks.com, Website: www.gyanbooks.com

2 222000 013400